the Ivory Adventure Classics

A collection presented by
Wolfe Publishing Co., Inc.

Limited Edition of 1000

Henry M. Stanley

Dr. Emin Bey

(EMIN PASHA.)

STANLEY'S START WITH TIPPU TIB AND ESCORT ON THE EMIN PASHA RELIEF EXPEDITION.
(Drawn by Mr. Herbert Ward, Artist with the Emin Pasha Relief Expedition.)

STANLEY

AND THE

WHITE HEROES IN AFRICA

BEING

AN EDITION FROM MR. STANLEY'S LATE PERSONAL WRITINGS ON

THE EMIN PASHA RELIEF EXPEDITION

And Discoveries in the Dark Continent, with Other Matter from the Works of His Companions and Predecessors,

INCLUDING THE

EXPLORATIONS AND ADVENTURES

OF

BRUCE, MUNGO PARK, CLAPPERTON, DENHAM, LANDER, BARTH, ANDERSSON, MAGYAR, DU CHAILLU, BURTON, SPEKE, GRANT, BAKER, SCHWEINFURTH, HOLUB, GORDON, MOFFAT, CAMERON, WISSMANN, SERPA PINTO, JUNKER, PETERS, LIVINGSTONE, EMIN PASHA, AND OTHERS.

ARRANGED BY

D. M. KELSEY, AUTHOR OF "PIONEER HEROES," "DEEDS OF DARING BY BLUE AND GRAY," ETC.

---

250 ILLUSTRATIONS.

Wolfe Publishing Co., Inc.
6471 Airpark Drive
Prescott, Arizona 86301

Originally published in 1890 by H.B. Scammell

"Publisher has made every attempt to reproduce this book as original - some copy and pictures will be marginal in their appearance. The reader is asked to make exceptions for the areas where good reproduction was not possible."

Manufactured in the United States of America
Reprinted August 1988

ISBN: 0-935632-74-3

1988
Wolfe Publishing Co., Inc.
Prescott, Arizona

PREFACE.

THE arrival of Henry M. Stanley from the coast of Africa after nearly three years' absence in the interior, again arouses the enthusiastic attention of the civilized world, who look with eagerness for his accounts of the history and results of the Emin Pasha Relief Expedition which he conducted to a triumphant end. In this substantial volume this want is supplied and by following the hero's own language. But a proper introduction to and understanding of the great African problem requires that the intensely interesting work which has been done by his companions or predecessors be also related. For this end, libraries containing hundreds of volumes on the subject of discovery and explorations in Africa have been ransacked for the materials of what is here presented; and this statement of the authorities consulted does not include special biographies, works on missions, or the many periodicals from which information has been derived. In addition to the material thus accessible, volumes not always obtainable in libraries have been procured elsewhere. We feel justified in the assertion that every possible source of information has been made to contribute to the pages of this volume.

The above statements will also bear out the assertion that few subjects command more attention at the present day than this very one of the explorations of the Dark Continent. It may be urged, on the other hand, that "of making many books there is no end," and that since there are many in the libraries published upon this subject, another is unnecessary. But there is this point to be considered: Such libraries are not accessible, except in the large cities; and even there, no one has so complete a collection on this special subject as the sources to which we have had access. Shall one who wishes to know what has been done in this part of the world, purchase the volumes in which that information is contained?

It would require a small fortune; the early works of Livingstone and Stanley alone are published at $5 per volume, and several of them are in two volumes each. Again, some of the other books are rare, and would be "cheaply purchased at their weight in gold," although some portions of their pages would rather cause the average reader to value them at their weight in lead, for heavy reading.

But even in the cities, there is need for such a work as the present. Shall the reader who wishes to be well-informed upon all the issues of the day devote precious weeks and months to the perusal of hundreds of volumes, to searching through back numbers of periodicals for information which has not yet found its way into any but the most recent books, when in a single volume he may find all that he cares to know?

The authors of the earlier works have embodied in them the results of researches which the world cannot afford to lose—geographical, ethnological, botanical, zoological information at first hand. Such information the present volume does not pretend to include in anything like its original form; for the simple reason that space does not permit. If the recital of the stirring adventures of these great explorers, from the earliest to the latest and greatest, excites in you the desire to know more of them, turn to their own volumes, and listen to what they would teach you of the minutiæ of the Dark Continent, its botany, its zoology, its water supply, its vast deserts, its mineralogy, etc., etc.

No one can tell Stanley's or Emin's story as well as themselves; and the same is true of all the others. It is for that reason that the words of the explorers themselves are so faithfully adhered to. In some cases condensation has not allowed of invariable quotation; but even here, the actual wording has been followed wherever possible; little but the person of the nouns and verbs being changed.

It would be useless to make acknowledgments of indebtedness to any particular authorities. In all cases, the originals have been used; and the names of the men whose adventures are detailed will prove a sufficient clue to the works which have furnished the principal part of a chapter.

D. M. KELSEY.

CONTENTS.

CHAPTER I.

THE OUTSKIRTS OF A CONTINENT.

CHAPTER II.

EARLY EXPLORATIONS OF AFRICA.

CHAPTER III.

JAMES BRUCE.

CHAPTER IV.

THE AFRICAN SOCIETY.

CHAPTER V.

CLAPPERTON AND DENHAM.

CHAPTER X.

SIR SAMUEL W. BAKER AND HIS HEROIC LADY.

CHAPTER XI.

SCHWEINFURTH IN THE HEART OF AFRICA.

CHAPTER XII.

DR. HOLUB, THE AUSTRIAN HUNTER AND EXPLORER.

CHAPTER XIII.

CHRISTIAN MISSIONS IN AFRICA.

CHAPTER XIV.

LIVINGSTONE THE MISSIONARY.

ILLUSTRATIONS.

AN ANCIENT EGYPTIAN GARDEN.

STANLEY

AND THE

WHITE HEROES IN AFRICA.

CHAPTER I.

THE OUTSKIRTS OF A CONTINENT.

BEFORE giving any account of later African exploration as prosecuted by adventurous spirits from modern civilized nations, it will be well to glance over the past, and take, as it were, a bird's-eye view of occurrences and progress in those parts of "The Dark Continent" where history had already been made, some of it thousands of years old. From what is to follow it will be seen that Africa has been penetrated by civilization, or, rather, semi-civilization, only on its outskirts. The vast area of its central barbarism has always remained comparatively a *terra incognita*—a deep and dark mystery of tens of millions of savage tribes and teeming animal and vegetable life, occasionally penetrated a little way by some humble missionary, daring adventurer or desperate military expedition.

A brief comparison of Africa with other parts of the world shows that in point of size, it ranks next to Asia; the coast of Africa has been so thoroughly explored that its area may be definitely calculated; it is about three-fourths the size of Asia, more than three times as large as Europe, one and one-half times as large as all North America, or four-fifths as large as North and South America together.

This vast land, the Continent of Deserts, as it has been called, supports a population greater, according to the estimates of good authorities, than the population of North and South America combined. Its mountains may not tower to such a height as the Himalayas; but in comparison with its rivers, the streams of other continents, with the exception of the Mississippi and the Amazon, are scarcely worthy to be mentioned. The great Nile, beloved by the Egyptians, which receives no tributary for more than a thousand miles, and yet maintains the volume of its stream as it passes along the very edge of the desert, has been known for so long a time that we need not here compare it with the rivers of other continents; shrouded in mystery for thousands of years as its sources have been, it has ever been ranked as one of the longest, if not the longest river of the world; and the judgment has not been reversed by modern explorations. But it is the Congo which is the most notable river of this great continent; it is the Congo which is for us the most wonderful discovery made known by these many adventurers, at the cost of such fearful loss of human life.

The Amazon, the Mississippi, the Nile, the Ganges, the Volga, all discharge their waters by means of several streams, forming, by their alluvial deposits, deltas. But the mighty flood of the Congo sweeps far out to sea the deposits which might otherwise obstruct its mouth, and, by a single stream, seven miles and a half broad, and in many places twelve hundred feet deep, it pours into the Atlantic a volume of water which is, at the lowest estimate, twice as great as that of the Mississippi at the time of the March floods; and according to some authorities, nearly four times as great. According to Stanley's calculations, when the river is lowest, the volume at a point two hundred and fifty miles inland from the sea is greater by one-fourth than the greatest outflow of the Mississippi, at the season above stated. Is it wonderful that the earliest explorers sought to ascend this mighty river?

All the histories tell us that Egypt was the seat of Africa's earliest civilization; but if we may trust tradition, there was a time when Egypt had no existence: the land of the Nile was once buried beneath the waters of the Mediterranean. According to this tradition, after its emergence, it was settled by colonies from Ethiopia or Nubia. This is the Nubian tradition on the subject; but the theory seems to be unnoticed by the Egyptians. The Ethiopians of the days of Diodorus claimed that the Egyptians had learned their arts and sciences from the ancestors of the more southern race. How far this is true, is neither important nor possible to determine; but it must be remembered that there is a remarkable similarity between the monuments of antiquity existing in Egypt and those existing in Nubia. The tradition is supported by figures which are found in temples at Philæ and Elephantine; in these places are sculptures representing priests of a red color, a hue which in Egyptian representations symbolizes Egyptians, who are being consecrated by other men black in color. It will be remembered that the word Ethiopian means simply dark-skinned, and was originally applied to Arabs as well as to other races by the fair-skinned Greeks; and Ethiopia was the ancient name of Nubia. These colored sculptures, then, would seem to give evidence that far back in antiquity the Nubians claimed that they had taught the Egyptian priests, and that the claim was allowed.

It seems to be clear that the civilization of ancient Egypt was derived from Meroe; but, the question arises, whence came the civilization of Meroe? Proceeding down the river from this point, the people gradually reclaimed the land about its mouth, where there was one vast morass; and the northern part of the country soon outstripped the older portion in development.

As to the source of the laws of Meroe, and the corresponding development of the people in other respects, it is conjectured by some writers that their knowledge of arts, sciences, and government was derived from ancient India; but this is only an evasion of the difficulty; for if the civilization of Meroe was derived from India, where did the civilization of India come from, and how did it get to Africa?

The early history of Meroe, then, is the point at which we must begin; since discussion, or rather conjecture, of the times preceding are best left to the antiquarian specialist. The first great epoch of Egyptian history is called by the name of Menes. Authorities differ greatly as to the time at which this monarch lived, and this work is no place in which to discuss the chronology, there being as much variation in opinions of authorities as 5700 B. C. and 2000 B. C.—a difference of almost four thousand years.

Before the time of Menes, the nation is said to have led a strictly patriarchal life; he instituted the first laws and divine worship, built the temple of Ptah, turned the course of the Nile to the westward of its original direction, founded Memphis, and finally met the end of being devoured by a crocodile.

How much of these wonders were accomplished by Menes, and how many by his successors, it is, to say the least, doubtful; this dynasty reigned about two hundred and fifty years; and some of the older pyramids are attributed to the race of Menes.

GREAT STATUE OF THE NILE.
Personifying the River as a Father Surrounded by His Dependent Children, the Inhabitants of Egypt.

The greatest name with which we meet in this early history is perhaps that of Cheops, a king of the fourth dynasty. Every schoolboy knows that the largest of the great pyramids of Gizeh bears the name of this king, who built it by means of a forced conscription, and thus caused his name to be handed down to posterity as that of a tyrant, equally feared and hated by his people.

The arrival of a tribe of thirty-six persons of Semitic race, during the supremacy of the twelfth dynasty, is supposed to have reference to the removal of Jacob and his sons to Egypt. The Shepherd Kings made themselves masters of the country during the era of the fifteenth dynasty; but the Egyptian kings of Upper Egypt overthrew them, and restored the legitmate line in the sixteenth dynasty.

The city of Thebes was, for many years, the object of the peculiar care of the Egyptian kings, and was embellished with many of the fruits of their conquests. Syria, part of Mesopotamia, Assyria, Phœnicia and Central Asia paid tribute to them, and this tribute was converted to the use of the city and its temples. This was during the era of the seventeenth dynasty; a period when not only foreign countries were made to contribute to the glory of Egypt, but her own powers were taxed to do so. The ancient temples were restored; the quarries of Turah were opened; the copper-mines of Magarah recovered. The famous monument of this period is the great Sphinx.

The kings of the eighteenth and nineteenth dynasties ceased to use, as sepulchers, the pyramids which their predecessors had built for that purpose; and excavated long tunnels in the mountains of the Arabian chain west of Thebes. But there were few innovations in Egyptian art, as a rule. Being strictly symbolic, a change in form destroyed or changed the meaning. There is a story of an artist who had grown tired of seeing the gods represented with their feet close together, and sculptured one image, having one foot a little in advance of the other; and was nearly "lynched" by the indignant populace for his originality; since to place the gods in such a position of motion would indicate the possibility of their leaving Egypt.

Thirty dynasties of native kings ruled this ancient country, before it was made a mere province of another government. In the year 340 B. C. it became subject to Persia; and from that time its history is the history of a subjugated people.

The next important event, after this conquest, was the overthrow of the Persian rule by Alexander the Great, and the foundation of Alexandria. This city, one of eighteen which bore the name of the great conqueror, is the only one which to-day is known by its ancient appellation. When Egypt passed under the Greek rule, it became the center of learning and philosophy, and was long famous for its schools, its museum, and its library.

The battle of Actium, in 30 B. C., made Egypt a Roman province, the last of the Greek rulers being Cleopatra. Its governors from this time forth were Romans of the equestrian order, or that rank next below the Senatorial.

At the division of the empire, near the close of the fourth century of our era, Egypt fell to the Eastern Empire, and

The Nile at Old Cairo.

eventually became one of the great patriarchates of the Eastern or Greek Church, the patriarch of Alexandria being esteemed equal in dignity to him of Constantinople. But religious feuds arose, which ended in civil dissensions; and the country fell under the rule of Persia. In this condition it continued for twelve years; the Persian viceroy then endeavored to throw off the yoke of his own country, and make himself independent king of Egypt. In order to accomplish this, he called in the Arabs to help him. They did indeed assist him to throw off the supremacy of Persia, but only to establish their own; and Omar I. became ruler of Egypt in the year 640 of our era, the 19th of the hegira.

Cairo was built about forty years later, and strongly fortified by subsequent rulers. Egypt remained independent under its Mohammedan rulers until 1517, when it became a province of Turkey, administered by pashas. Constant rebellions of the Mamelukes, and the violence of contending factions, distracted the country, and rendered it incapable even of such prosperity as a Turkish province may hope to enjoy. Invaded by Bonaparte in 1798, the entire country was held by France for three years; but they were finally expelled by the united efforts of the Turks and British, and the government restored to the Ottoman Porte. From that time, the history may be briefly summed up, being too well known to require that more should be done than simply to refresh the memory as to dates. The rise of Mohammed Ali in 1806 seemed to be the beginning of a new era of prosperity; the Mamelukes were destroyed, a regular army was formed, security was increased, irrigation (here of vital importance) was improved, and European civilization introduced. Parts of Arabia and Syria were also rendered tributary, and it was probable at one time that Mohammed would become sultan. But the quadruple alliance in 1840 interfered with his plans, and reduced him to the previous condition of pasha of Egypt. M. de Lesseps' scheme of the Suez Canal did much for the material prosperity of Egypt at the time; though the wretched mismanagement of the finances, as in most Mohammedan countries, undoes the effect of much that would otherwise be beneficial.

The condition of the Egyptian finances became so hopelessly involved that in 1876 the revenue was put under the management of European commissioners; but this system proving unsuccessful, another commission of inquiry was appointed. Such was the influence which they exerted that before long it was announced that the khedive had accepted the European idea of constitutional government, and had appointed a ministry. When the pressure was removed, however, the khedive arose from this subject condition; and in 1879, summarily dismissed the ministry so formed. The affairs of Egypt were again made the subject of international discussion, and the offending khedive was finally deposed by his suzerain, the sultan of Turkey, the late ruler's eldest son being proclaimed viceroy in his stead.

The history of Nubia is so bound up with that of Egypt, that but little need be said concerning it. The term Nubia is comparatively modern, the old name of this country being Ethiopia, in allusion, as above stated, to the dark complexions of the inhabitants. These, however, are not of the negro race, but are more nearly akin to the Egyptians. The country had been independent of Egypt until 1820, when it was subdued and brought under the rule of its ancient masters. The chief attraction to travelers is in the ruins of ancient temples and other monuments of the Egyptian race.

To the south-east of Nubia lies a country which was the object of interest enhanced by mystery, even in the far back days of Solomon. From Abyssinia, very probably, came the Queen of the South to visit the wise king at Jerusalem; and it is claimed among the Abyssinians to this day that their monarch

Palace of the Khedive at Alexandria.

is descended in direct line from Solomon and the queen of Sheba. Converted to Judaism upon the return of their queen, the people of this country retained that faith, in more or less purity, until the middle of the fourth century of our era, when they were converted to Christianity by missionaries from Alexandria. There was a temporary return to Judaism in the tenth century; but on the fall of the usurping monarch who had reintroduced the older religion, the people came back to the Christian faith.

Abyssinia has always been in the midst of enemies; and frequently it has taxed her powers to the utmost to preserve her independence. During the fifteenth century, the people appealed to the Portuguese for assistance; it was promised, on condition that they rejected the Greek Catholic faith, which they had professed for more than a thousand years, and accepted that of their new allies, the Roman Catholic form of belief. To this condition the rulers agreed, and Portuguese missionaries were sent to Abyssinia.

But the people could not be persuaded to accept the new faith; and this division between monarch and subjects weakened the power of the former. There was a long struggle between them, which, like most religious wars, was conducted with very little religion visible on either side. Finally, the people triumphed; the Portuguese missionaries were banished, the old form of worship was restored, and the king became a mere puppet in the hands of his nominally subject chiefs.

The dissensions introduced by the effort to establish a new creed were followed by troubles from without: the Turks on the north, and the Gallas on the south, constantly harassed the unfortunate people. But after the Portuguese missionaries left the country, Abyssinia seems to have sunk into profound darkness, so far as the rest of the world was concerned; it was as nearly forgotten as any country on the face of the earth could be; and it was not until after the travels of Bruce had been made public that it was recalled to the minds of men.

It is not our purpose in this chapter to follow the steps of any discoverer; that must belong to a later part of the volume. We take up the narrative, then, at the point where Bruce and his immediate successors leave it.

These immediate successors of Bruce did not indeed penetrate to the heart of the country, as he had done; but although they made use of his observations, they endeavored to throw much discredit on his assertions regarding points which they had not reached; and their efforts were one of the chief agencies in causing his statements to be received with incredulity.

When the French were to all appearance engaged in a struggle for the conquest of the world, Great Britain, that no power, however insignificant, might be neglected, sent an envoy to the court of Abyssinia. This gentleman, however, went no farther than Tigre, the northern province of the kingdom; and when there was no further danger from Napoleon, even this effort at intercourse was given up.

A little later than this, there was a Protestant mission sent to this country; but some civil disorders, in which the missionaries remained faithful to the displaced chiefs, caused them to be sent from the country. Roman Catholic missions were then established; and for some time the chief missionary was regarded by the natives with almost as much respect as their own bishop, nominally of the Greek Catholic Church, if it can be called so when it had no positive connection with the head of that organization.

In 1847, a British consul was sent to Abyssinia; but, unfortunately, his headquarters were fixed at Massowah, which is just without the boundaries of the kingdom; and this was by no means pleasing to the Abyssinians. Things were in this condition with relation to the outer world when the renewal of internal broils gave new interest to the country's history.

When the power of the kings had become limited to the mere title, the real authority was vested in a number of chiefs, each of whom bore the title ras. One of these chiefs, in the early part of the present century, named Dejaj Comfu, ruled over a province of Amhara, the central part of the empire. His brother had died and left a widow and son, the latter named Kassai, who were so poor that the mother supported herself and child by selling kosso. When Kassai grew up, he joined the army of his uncle, who was engaged in a contest with the Turks, and distinguished himself by his courage. Dejaj Comfu died suddenly; his three sons quarreled about their inheritance, and a neighboring chief was called in to settle the dispute. He proposed to end the matter by assuming the authority himself, and conquered the best part of the province. But Kassai resisted him, and, collecting a band of determined soldiers, fled to the mountain fastnesses. Here for a time he was involved in continual strife; but at last the real ruler of the country, Ras Ali, the step-son of the king, recognized that it was a useless effort to try to subdue him, and consequently made terms.

Ras Ali, to cement the alliance which he concluded with the rebel, gave him his daughter in marriage; and for a while everything was lovely. But Kassai, to whom we may now give the name of Theodore, which he assumed later on, insisted on being recognized as ras of Kuara. Ali determined to crush him; an army was sent against Kassai, and he was again driven to his mountain fastnesses. Issuing thence, he gave battle, and defeated and slew the chief who had been sent against him. Ras Ali next took the field in person, although now the war was on his part rather defensive than aggressive; Kassai drove him to the old stronghold of his family, where he maintained for a time a determined resistance, but was at last obliged to yield. Ali then sought refuge in the country of the savage Gallas, where he died shortly afterward.

Having secured the person of the king, Kassai called upon the chief of Tigre and Semen, Dejaj Ouble, to pay him tribute. The demand was refused; nor was Kassai strong enough to enforce it. In the absence of power, he resorted to diplomacy, or, rather, to intrigue. The weight of the Church, he knew, would be against him in any contest with Ouble, for the bishop was in his power; he therefore decided to tamper with the Padre de Jacobis, who, as already stated, had acquired much influence over the people. He assured the missionary that if he were king of Abyssinia, the Roman Catholic religion should be restored; and Padre de Jacobis promised his help with this condition.

But in a battle fought in February, 1855, Ouble was defeated and captured; with him was taken the Coptic bishop. With a lack of good faith which was afterward recognized as a prominent characteristic, Kassai approached the bishop, and, disregarding his agreement with Padre de Jacobis, entered into an agreement by which he, Kassai, was to be crowned king of Abyssinia by the Coptic bishop. A few days after the battle, the ceremony took place; Kassai assuming the name of Theodore.

The choice was not due to caprice; there was an old tradition that a King Theodore was to reign in Abyssinia, conquer the kingdom of Solomon, and restore the ancient glory of Ethiopia. Kassai, of course, represented that he was the person alluded to in the prophecy. He had some difficulty in persuading his people that he was a descendant of Solomon and the queen of Sheba, as their traditions declared that the ruler of Abyssinia must be; and it does not appear that they were ever thoroughly convinced; but at any rate he silenced them for a time upon that subject.

It does not appear, however, that Theodore ventured to ignore the real king; he used all the ceremony toward him which was demanded by the custom of the country; but soon after the coronation of Kassai took place, the king died suddenly. Alarmed by this circumstance, the people submitted without a struggle; and Theodore was left free to extend his dominions by foreign conquest.

Various attempts at missionary work in Abyssinia were made during the period from 1856 to 1863, with the permission and approval of Theodore. For a time it seemed that friendly relations would be established between the great European pow-

KING THEODORE GIVING AUDIENCE.

ers and this far-off, half-savage country; but the suspicious jealousy of the king, and an unfortunate chain of circumstances, doomed this hope to disappointment. Infuriated by what he considered insults to his royal dignity, Theodore received coldly all attempts at explanation; English messengers were overawed by being received by the king surrounded by lions, and were robbed of their dispatches and maltreated; Englishmen were tried for the crime of disrespect to him, and sentenced to death. The missionaries and the English consul were arrested and imprisoned; the envoy who was sent to treat with him, was kept waiting for a year, and then was thrown into prison. Theodore now conducted himself like a madman, and subjected men, women and children who fell into his power to inhuman tortures. The British government demanded the release of the imprisoned subjects of the queen; he took no notice of the communication. An expedition was accordingly fitted out at Bombay for the invasion of his country; and although delayed considerably, at last reached Abyssinia and came within sight of Magdala, a small town to which the royal residence had been removed from Gondar. Here the Abyssinian and the English forces encountered each other; and Theodore sustained such a decided defeat that he gave up all the European captives in his hands. Three days later, Magdala was stormed, and taken; among the Abyssinians killed in the assault was Theodore.

The history of Theodore may be considered the point of culminating interest in Abyssinian history; and with his death we now pause, leaving things of later interest to be considered at another time.

Returning now to the northern part of Africa, since that is the portion which has been longest known to the civilized world, we find Fezzan upon our path. This country, indeed, is hardly to be included in the list of those with which ancient Europe was acquainted; and its history may be briefly summed up. The original inhabitants belonged to the Berber race, the aborigines of northern Africa; but it was invaded by the Arabs in the fifteenth century, and the original inhabitants have sunk into insignificance. It is now attached to the government of Tripoli. It remained comparatively unknown, so far as Europe and America were concerned, until attention was directed to it by these African explorers who made Mourzouk their starting-point.

The Barbary States comprise that territory which to the Romans was emphatically Africa, that portion of the con-

BERBER FAMILY CROSSING A FORD—SCENE IN ALGERIA.

tinent which has been styled the forehead of Africa. Its most famous cities in antiquity were Carthage and Utica, founded by the Phœnicians, and Cyrene, a Greek colony. But these were near the coast, and the country south of them was unknown, and peopled by tribes of Mauri and Numidians, wholly uncivilized. The Carthaginian territory became a Roman province; and the same year that saw the destruction of Carthage saw Greece and her dependencies brought wholly under the Roman rule. The African provinces were among the richest which acknowledged the authority of Augustus; and although there was a nominal sovereign, he was tributary to the great emperor. The ruins of large towns and of splendid monuments and useful works, here, as elsewhere, attest the power and the practical skill of the Romans.

As the Roman power declined in Europe, Barbary suffered; for there were wild native tribes that had not been wholly subdued, there were religious differences, there were ambitious Roman officials who saw in the weakening of the central power an opportunity to strengthen their own authority until it became independent. Any one of these causes would be sufficient to distract a state; what, then, must have been the result of all combined! Weakened by such troubles, they fell an easy prey to the Vandals, who subdued the country, and savagely misgoverned it for more than a century. After their expulsion by Belisarius, the native tribes of the Mauri and the Berbers made themselves masters of the interior, and the Romans and Greeks, or the representatives of those ancient peoples, were restricted to a few points on the coast.

In the seventh century, shortly after the hegira, began that great wave of Mohammedan conquest which swept along all the shores of the Mediterranean, sparing only Italy. Greece fell; Spain was invaded and no small portion of it held by the new-comers. They established themselves in Africa with little difficulty, and before the end of the eighth century, nearly all the inhabitants of the Barbary States had either been slain or compelled to embrace the Mohammedan religion. An Arab dynasty was established; and has been practically maintained, although the territory has been divided into different governments.

Morocco was formed into a separate monarchy about the end of the fifteenth century. It enjoyed considerable prosperity, and its limits were extended at one time, as far south as Timbuctoo. But this great empire soon fell to pieces; and in 1642 the present dynasty became the rulers of Morocco and Fez, to

MANNER OF BOERS RECEIVING A VISIT.

which their sovereignty was limited. Rebellions of the mountain tribes and other domestic disturbances have retarded the development of the country, even during the present century; and it is a sufficient commentary upon its condition less than a hundred years ago to state that in 1814 the slavery of Christians was formally abolished, and three years later the government officially condemned the system of piracy.

Tripoli was the second of the Barbary States to assume an independent history. Conquered by the Turks shortly after the middle of the sixteenth century, the sovereign authority of the sultan was more or less strong, according as the local ruler was a man of ability and popularity. It had been practically nothing for something over a century when, in 1835, an expedition was sent out from Constantinople, which overthrew and imprisoned the ruling dey, and established a new Turkish pasha, who should be more strictly dependent upon the main government.

Toward the close of the sixteenth century, Tunis appears as a distinct state from the remainder of Barbary. In 1575, it was conquered by the Turks and made a province of their empire. This suzerainty has fluctuated from time to time, and is not now felt, since the French have established themselves as the practical masters of the country.

Algeria was, from the time of the Mohammedan conquests, divided into a number of petty states. We hear of it in connection with the expulsion of the Moors from Spain, as affording an asylum to the refugees; but its medieval reputation was exceedingly bad: it was nothing more or less than a nation of corsairs. For some reason or other, the attempts made by European nations, notably Spain, to crush them, were invariably unfortunate. The native ruler had, during the sixteenth century, put himself under the protection of the sultan; at the beginning of the seventeenth century, the Turkish janissaries obtained from their ruler the right to choose for themselves a dey who should share the power of the pasha. The result of this divided authority was such dissension that the European nations took advantage of it, and made new attempts to chastise the pirates. But no decisive result followed.

At the beginning of the eighteenth century, Algeria became practically independent of Turkey; and its career of crime was unchecked, even by that extremely slight limitation. At last the depredations became unbearable. The presence of powerful fleets in the Mediterranean during the Napoleonic

LANDING OF NAPOLEON III. IN ALGIERS.

wars had to some extent kept them within bounds; but this pressure removed, the Algerines became worse than ever. The United States was the first nation which undertook to chastise them; an American fleet defeated an Algerine fleet in 1815, and obliged them to recognize the invincibility of the American flag. The English admiral had, about the same time, extorted from the other Barbary States the recognition of the international law respecting the treatment of prisoners; but Algeria refused to make such concessions to civilization. An English and Dutch fleet bombarded Algiers; and after half the town had been laid in ruins, its batteries silenced and the fleet and magazines destroyed, the soldiers forced the dey to yield. A treaty was made in 1816 by which piracy was abolished (on paper) and Christian slaves to the number of more than a thousand released without ransom.

The very next year, Algerian piracy was as bad as ever; and the dey returned only mocking and insulting answers to all remonstrances. But his death in 1818 resulted in the succession of a dey under whom the Moslem power was overthrown and Algiers conquered by France.

From this time forth, we find the history of Algeria a story of subjugation and conquest of the native tribes by the French. There is much gradual progress to record, toward civilization; but nothing more that is necessary to the understanding of the present state of Africa.

Southward from the coast of Morocco, extend the sea-limits of the Great Sahara Desert. Here, if the dreams of modern science are ever realized, there may be,some day, a great nation.

While Senegambia was settled by three nations, the Portuguese, the French, and the English, the latter have so far dominated the others that their settlements are the most noteworthy. The nucleus, Sierra Leone, was established in 1787, when four or five hundred destitute negroes of London were sent thither by a party of philanthropists; a few years later, some of the same race, to the number of almost twelve hundred, who had been colonized in Nova Scotia, were transferred to the home of their race; the climate of the American peninsula having proved too severe for these children of the tropics. Since the abolition of the slave trade by Great Britain in 1807, slaves captured by the British cruisers have been put ashore here, until the population amounts, according to the latest obtainable figures, to about forty thousand souls.

The example of the British government in establishing an African colony for negroes was soon followed by the United

States; and in the last day of 1816, an association was formed for the purpose of founding a colony of emancipated negroes. The first attempt was unsuccessful, a very unhealthy site having been chosen; but it was renewed in 1821, and since then the colony has continued to grow in numbers and wealth. There has not been the large emigration from the United States which the founders expected, but the Republic of Liberia has maintained its ground.

Native Diamond Thief Compelled to Disgorge.

Portuguese settlements, the most important of which is St. Paul de Loanda, are scattered along the east cost of southern Africa; but of Portuguese settlements in general we shall have more to say when we come to consider the eastern coast. Of the Congo Free State, this is not the place to speak, as the present pages are intended merely to show the state of Africa before the Stanley expeditions.

Dismissing thus summarily the various divisions which are marked on the map of what was once known as Lower Guinea, we come to the great settlement at the southern extremity of the continent. The first comers, here as in other parts of Africa, were the Portuguese; but the first permanent settlement was made by the Dutch in 1652. The constant intercourse between Holland and her East Indian possessions made it desirable to have some sort of a half-way station, and it was for this that the settlement at the Cape of Good Hope was intended. In the course of a hundred and fifty years, however, the dominion of the Dutch was gradually extended, until they were masters of nearly the whole of what is now known as Cape Colony.

After a contest lasting for about ten years, this territory came into the hands of the British in 1806; since that time, many of the resources of the country have been developed.

The most famous of these is the diamond-fields, which are in Griqualand, a section which has only within a comparatively short time been brought into Cape Colony. The Kimberley mine is the best known, because the most productive of large stones. The rich copper ore found in Namaqualand has added largely to the wealth of the colony.

In 1856 Natal was erected into a separate colony, free from the control of the governor of the Cape. This region had been discovered by the Portuguese in 1497, and named by them from the circumstance that they landed on Christmas day. But no effort was made at settlement which proved at all successful until 1838, when a number of Dutch Boers, emigrants from the Cape, established themselves here. There was a struggle between the Boers and the British, but five years after the settlement, Natal was formally proclaimed a British colony. The event of its history which is most readily recalled is the Zulu war of 1879, in which Cetewayo and Sir Garnet Wolseley figured as the leaders, and in which the Prince Imperial of France met his death.

The Boers, impatient of British rule, had retired to Natal from the Cape; but the action of the British government in following them up to their new home caused them to establish themselves in yet another new country, which has been given the name of the Orange River Free State. The country was described, in 1836, as a "howling wilderness," but after Natal was declared a British colony in 1843, the few settlers who had, between these two years, taken refuge there, had their numbers largely increased by dissatisfied Boers from both the Cape and

Natal. In spite of their efforts to escape the rule of the Cape authorities, this new settlement was, after much opposition, annexed to the British Empire; but it proved to be ungovernable, and in 1854, it was formally given up, and the inhabitants formed a government according to their own wishes.

Driven from Cape Colony to Natal, from Natal to Orange River territory, the Boers who feared that the annexation of the latter country to the British crown would be a permanent one, again retreated across the Vaal. Here they established settlements, which in time came to be known as the Transvaal Republic; and this was maintained until 1877. In that year the British decided to annex this, too, to their empire; but the Boers thought otherwise; and, after a struggle, the independence of the country was maintained. It should be noted that while the British authorities unite in accusing the Boers of all possible crimes toward the natives, the Boers have maintained themselves peaceably in South Africa, while the British have waged no less than seven bloody wars with the natives during the period of their dominion.

The Portuguese settlements along the eastern coast have been made with a view to trading with the natives. The principal article of traffic has been slaves. "Around these places the natives are more demoralized than in any other part of Africa, European vices being grafted on the baser passions of heathenism. The white race, which ought to be the type of a higher and purer mode of life, has become degraded and hateful in the eyes of the natives."

A notice of Madagascar will be more appropriate in connection with the subject of mission work in Africa; and other territories, which have come into prominence since African discovery received the impulse which has culminated in the expeditions of Stanley, will be briefly noticed in connection with the travelers who first made them known.

CHAPTER II.

EARLY EXPLORATIONS OF AFRICA.

ALTHOUGH the country which occupies its extreme northeastern portion was the seat of the earliest civilization known to the world, Africa has long been, above all others, the continent of mystery. Egypt had solved engineering problems which are not far within the capacity of the nineteenth century, before Greece and Rome had learned the rudiments of art or science; and Greece and Rome were the teachers of all Europe; yet every nook and corner of Europe has been thoroughly explored, while there are still vast wildernesses in Africa where the white man's foot has never trod. Less than a century ago, even the great rivers had not been followed to their sources; the Nile itself came from a region of mystery, and no man had fathomed the secret of those annual overflows which had enriched Egypt since the days of the first Pharaohs.

The interest in the exploration of Africa, however, the desire to know more of this great tract which lies so directly under the equator, is not altogether of modern growth. The Father of History himself, Herodotus, who lived in the fifth century before our era, endeavored to obtain accurate information regarding Africa. For this purpose, he visited Egypt in person; but the Egyptians could not tell him much. They knew only a portion of the northern coast, besides their own country. The region nearest to them was well known, and we find full accounts of the temple of Jupiter Ammon and the wonderful spring in its vicinity; but as we follow the account of the historian, in his description of the peoples living farther toward the West, we find them less satisfactory. For some distance beyond Carthage, indeed, the character of the soil and the nature of the inhabitants are accurately described; but soon we find fact mingled with fable, and at last we come to the long and lofty range of Atlas, which is the pillar of heaven, and beyond which the historian does not think of going.

But even before the days of Herodotus, the Carthaginians, those adventurous mariners of antiquity, who without chart or compass had come even to Cornwall, had coasted beyond the Pillars of Hercules, as the rocks on either side of the Strait of Gibraltar were called, and traded with the natives. Just how far down the western coast of Africa they went, modern authorities have not agreed among themselves. A naval expedition set out from Carthage about the year 570 B. C., under Hanno as commander, which passed far beyond the entrance to the Mediterranean. Gosselin says that they reached the point where the Sahara begins; Rennell considers that they succeeded in passing this barren coast, and finished their expedition about the point where Free Town now stands; while Bougainville believes them to have been still more adventurous, and to have gone as far as Cape Three Points, which is about the middle of the southern coast of Guinea. This last theory has not been accepted by many authorities; and the question really is, did they pass the desert coast or not? One answer supposes a run of six hundred miles; the other, a voyage five times as long. Hanno had a fleet of sixty vessels, with thirty thousand souls on board; it hardly seems credible that so vast a number could have carried with them, in the comparatively small vessels of the times, a sufficient stock of food and water to serve them during their slow and uncertain passage along the coast of Sahara; and the account which has come down to us distinctly tells us that they were forced to turn back, because of the sterile and inhospitable nature of the coast.

It is not until after the destruction of Carthage that Eudoxus, a native of the city of Cyzicus, comes upon the scene as an African explorer; and there is no other, of any note, until his day. Alexandria was then the center of naval enterprise, and her Greek rulers the most zealous patrons of all undertakings of the kind. To Ptolemy Euergetes the adventurer appealed, and the question of exploring the Nile to its sources was seriously discussed. But the arrival of a native of India, whom some Alexandrian sailors had rescued from shipwreck, turned their attention to India; and for a while the subject of African exploration was permitted to rest. Eudoxus made one voyage to India, and set out upon a second; but was driven by a storm upon the coast of Africa, shortly after emerging from the Red Sea. The coast line here extends toward the southwest; and Eudoxus was inspired with the idea that the circuit of Africa, from the entrance to the Red Sea to that of the Mediterranean, was to be made by a determined navigator. From that time forth he was possessed by one ambition, to be the circumnavigator of Africa.

Whether he succeeded or not, is not clear; in the strict sense of the words, he did not succeed, for he did not make the whole circuit. It may be that he coasted along all that portion of the seaboard which had not been previously explored; but certainly his voyage did not extend from the Straits of Bab-el-mandeb to that of Gibraltar. One observation which he records led the geographers of antiquity to believe that he was fabling; it proves to us that he told the truth: he narrates that when he had passed a certain point on his voyage, the sun shone to the northward of his vessel. The ancients, unacquainted with the southern hemisphere, could not credit this; they believed the assertion to be on a par with his accounts of peoples without tongues, and of those who having no mouth, received all their food through the nose. To us, on the other hand, this observation of a phenomenon previously unknown is proof positive that he passed the equator. From a careful examination of his assertions, it appears probable that he did not accomplish his great object, even if we take the limited meaning of the term circumnavigation above stated; but sailed as far south along the eastern coast as Cape Delgado, about ten degrees south of the equator.

The explorations of Eudoxus were made about the year 130 B. C.; and so little credence did his theory that Africa was bounded on all sides by the ocean obtain, that Ptolemy the geographer, who lived during the second century of our era, represented the Indian Ocean as an inland sea, bounded on the south by Africa, which extended easterly and then northerly until it reached the coast of China. His delineation of the northern coast of this continent was, in the main, correct; but he believed the western coast to be nearly a straight north and south line, instead of inclining nearly fifteen degrees of longitude from the Straits of Gibraltar to Cape Verde, as more modern surveys prove. He draws the eastern coast nearly correct, as far south as the equator; and for more than a thousand years, there was but very little more than this known of the Dark Continent.

We are accustomed to consider Mohammedanism as the foe of all progress; but the case was different during the middle ages. When the faith of Islam was first firmly established, the

Saracen princes became the patrons of art and science; and their schools became famous seats of learning. Their conquests had extended far to the West, and they had obtained a

Moorish Warrior.

foothold even in Europe itself, in the domains of the most Catholic King. Across the Mediterranean, they had established themselves in Morocco and other Barbary States; here they early introduced the camel, useful to their native Arabian deserts, and soon to become indispensable in Africa. By the aid of the ship of the desert, they crossed the vast wastes which had hitherto been impassable, and founded states along its southern boundary; their object being mainly commercial, since they wished to obtain gold and slaves from the natives.

Many of the names recorded by the Arabian chroniclers are retained in a spelling but slightly varied at the present day. Their Ghana has become Kano, Tocrur is Takror, and Bornou is unchanged.

Their account of western Africa is confused and vague, showing that their explorations and settlements were confined to the district about the Niger. Of the northern part of the eastern coast, they knew but little; for Nubia and Abyssinia were both Christian countries, and the races of differing faiths were jealous of each other's explorations and investigations. South of Abyssinia, they had explored the coast pretty thoroughly as far south as Madagascar, and had formed settlements at various points along the coast of Mozambique, which were in their possession when the earliest Portuguese navigators ventured around the Cape of Good Hope and reached the eastern coast from the south.

Rome, as the representative of western civilization, had, from the earliest times, made many efforts to extend her empire toward the East; but had been steadily resisted by the Semitic races. These efforts were not relaxed, even after western civilization had found other representatives. Toward the end of the fifteenth century, however, the fall of Constantinople and the expulsion of the Moors from Spain seemed to establish the boundaries of the Aryan empire and of the Semitic; and the people of the former race, no longer struggling vainly for a foothold in the East, sought new worlds to conquer in the West. Even before these events had actually come to pass, the results of the movement had begun to be felt. The same spirit which sent Columbus westward to find India, sent the Portuguese southward to explore the coast of Africa.

The local position of Portugal, and its constant wars with Morocco, were the circumstances which seem to have directed the minds of the people to the exploration and settlement of Africa. Prince Henry, the younger son of John I., seems to have been the first man of any influence to undertake the work. Rapid progress was made along the shore of the Sahara, and before long the Portuguese navigators had reached that fertile country which we now call Senegambia.

There were many material advantages to be hoped for from a constant intercourse with this part of the world; but the Portuguese were not content with looking for those things which they were sure existed. Some early travelers in eastern Asia had told of a mysterious personage whom they called Prester John; probably some Nestorian bishop, possessed of a degree of temporal power. The Portuguese had heard vague rumors of the Christian king of Abyssinia, and forthwith concluded that he was Prester John. The dominions of this ruler, it was reported, reached far inland; and the adventurous spirits who had embarked upon this series of undertakings decided that it would be comparatively easy to reach his capital by an overland journey from the Gulf of Guinea.

Their anticipations of the results of such success seem to have been as vague and uncertain as their knowledge; but whatever they expected to be the consequence of having reached the court of Prester John, they spared no pains in the effort to do so. They penetrated into the interior as far as Timbuctoo, and must have gained a fairly accurate knowledge of that portion of the continent. Unfortunately, the information so acquired was either lost, or sedulously kept from the world at large, until modern discoveries had made their jealous secrecy useless.

They continued to prosecute their discoveries along the coast, and in 1471 reached the coast of Guinea, where they built Elmina, the Mine, so called because of its position on the Gold Coast. The Pope gave them a title to all lands which should be discovered in this part of the world, and the king of Portugal assumed the title of Lord of Guinea. Hitherto, the progress of the discoverers had been marked by wooden crosses; but the king now gave orders that they were to erect stone pillars, twice the height of a man, surmounted by leaden crucifixes. In 1484, Diego Cam sailed from Lisbon, and erected such a pillar at what was then the most southerly limit of Portuguese discovery—the mouth of the Congo, a river which, from this circumstance, has frequently been called "The River of the Pillar" by the Portuguese writers.

The Congo did not long remain the boundary, however. A number of the natives had been taken to Portugal by Cam, and an expedition to reconvey these to their native country set out in 1490. Many missionaries accompanied the fleet, and strenuous efforts were made to Christianize the country. The natives, at first, willingly received the new faith; but when the missionaries discovered that they had not renounced polygamy, and had no intention of doing so, it was found that the efforts had not been so successful as they at first appeared. Other failures to renounce their former practices became apparent, and the missionaries became despondent; one of them, it is said, died from the effects of the disappointment.

How long they struggled against the persistency of paganism, we do not know; we only know what were the results of their self-sacrificing work in their voluntary exile. When Europeans again reached the mouth of the Congo, there was neither trace nor tradition of the Portuguese missionaries.

Before the date of this second expedition to the Congo, which ended so disastrously for those who remained after the vessels had returned to Portugal, Bartolommeo Diaz had sailed southward, and approaching land when in about twenty-six degrees of south latitude, had followed the coast-line closely until he had almost reached the southern extremity. Here he was buffeted about by contrary winds; but at last cast anchor in Algoa Bay, having rounded the Cape of Good Hope without knowing it. Being rejoined by his companion vessel, from which the storm had separated him, he set out on his return; and then noted his discovery. The cape was at first called "Cape of All the Storms;" but on his return, the king gave it the more auspicious name which it now bears. Diaz was greeted with much enthusiasm; but for some reason, was soon cast into the shade by Vasco de Gama, who was made his superior in the expedition of 1497.

While Diaz was the discoverer of the Cape of Good Hope, Gama was the first to make any use of the discovery. In the year above named, he sailed around the southern point of the continent, touched at various points on the eastern coast, which had hitherto been wholly unknown to Europeans, and securing the services of an intelligent Arab pilot, struck boldly across the Indian Ocean for India. A second expedition, in in 1502, saw the founding of the Portuguese colonies of Mozambique and Sefala, on the eastern cost of Africa.

The Portuguese supremacy over Guinea was ended when the mother country became involved in wars with the Dutch, which resulted favorably for Holland. Following close in the footsteps of the men of the Low Countries, came the French and English, lured by the hope of obtaining many slaves, and then by the expectation of finding in Africa another and a richer Peru.

The first English expedition, which was dispatched in 1618, was under the command of Richard Thompson. It was formed for the purpose of exploring the Gambia, and reached the mouth of that river in December of that year. The Englishmen met with fierce resistance from the Portuguese, of whom there were still many in this region; but maintained their station on the river, and sent home for re-inforcements. Most of the men upon the second expedition fell victims to disease; the commander of the third party heard, shortly before reaching his destination, that Thompson had fallen by the hands of his own men.

The fate of this first of English explorers of Africa has never been fully investigated. The history of the times is full of perilous adventures in which the spirit of the leader was more daring than that of his men; possibly Thompson, like Columbus, would have urged his followers onward on an unknown path; but, unlike Columbus, met with no favoring signs at the critical moment. In the way of positive testimony, we have only the representations of the crew, that their leader was oppressive and intolerable—interested evidence.

The leader of this third expedition, intended for the relief of the first, of which Thompson was the chief, was Richard Jobson, who has given us the first satisfactory account of the great river districts of western Africa. Jobson was the first white man who obtained any accurate information regarding the manners and customs of the interior African tribes, and recorded such knowledge in a form readily accessible.

The Portuguese professed entire ignorance of the misfortunes which had befallen Thompson's command, although the first English expedition had, on one occasion at least, suffered severely at the hands of these earlier settlers. Taking their protestations for what they were worth, Jobson pushed on in the ascent of the Gambia, and soon reached the farthest point which had been attained by his predecessor. The advent of a trading-vessel was a great event in the eyes of the natives, who eagerly pressed toward the river, to exchange the products of the country for the commodities of the strangers.

Jobson expected to reach Timbuctoo, by a comparatively short journey; for Europeans generally had no good idea of the dimensions of Africa. He succeeded in getting to Penda, where he was presented at the primitive court of the king by a merchant who had acted as guide; and then set out upon his return. His whole progress, he bitterly complains, had been much hindered by the merchants who formed a part of his company, and who were utterly indifferent to everything except their own profit. His return was further delayed by the condition of the river; the dry season was now far advanced, and it was difficult to descend such a shallow stream.

For the next forty years, the political condition of England was such as to forbid much foreign enterprise on the part of her people. But when the civil dissensions were ended and Charles II. was recognized as king, new moves were made toward exploring this country, which promised so rich a reward. In 1665, an expedition was fitted out by private enterprise, for the exploration of the Gambia, with a view to finding the sources whence the natives derived their stores of gold. All appliances for extracting gold from the mixtures in which it is found were carried with them; but their expectations were not wholly fulfilled. At one place by twenty days' labor, they succeeded in extracting twelve pounds; and the leader declared, subsequently, that he had found the mouth of the mine; but as he never made any use of the knowledge, it is probable that his assertion was unfounded.

Another expedition was sent out in 1720 by the African Company, of which the Duke of Chandos was then director. Of this expedition, Capt. Bartholomew Stibbs was the leader. It was with difficulty that he could persuade his guides to accompany him above the Falls of Barraconda, a point which they declared was the end of the world, and beyond which there were only the rudest and fiercest savages. He at length succeeded in persuading them, however, and ascended the river for some distance above the falls, though not as far as Tenda, which Jobson had reached. The expedition of Stibbs is of importance, because of its effect upon the spirits of English explorers of Africa. Hitherto the Gambia had been confounded with the Niger; it was thought that by ascending the former, the explorers might with comparative ease penetrate far into the interior, even to Timbuctoo. Stibbs declared that he had ascended the stream far enough to be able to judge of its size; he had seen no evidence of any great river; it issued from no lake, as the Niger was said to do; it was nowhere called by a name similar to Niger; the natives declared that at twelve days' journey above the falls it dwindled to a rivulet, which fowls might wade across. Despite the arguments which the English Company's factor on the Gambia drew from history, Stibbs persisted in the statement of facts of which he had personal experience. It came to be felt that the legends concerning the Niger were without foundation; and a degree of discouragement was experienced which for some time effectually put an end to the desire for exploring this portion of

Africa. It does not seem to have suggested itself to them that the Niger might really exist, a little farther from England than the stream which they had assumed was the one that they sought.

While the English were exploring the Gambia, under the impression that it was the Niger, the French were making a similar mistake as to the Senegal. Shortly after the expedition commanded by Jobson, the French made a settlement near the mouth of the Senegal, which they named after the patron saint of their country and their king, Saint Louis. Accounts of this settlement were brought home, in 1637, by Jannequin, a young man of rank whose fancy sent him on a trip thither. For some time, however, the French seem to have made no great effort toward exploring the interior for any considerable distance.

The settlement had been made under the auspices of a company to which Louis XIV. had granted a patent, giving exclusive right of territory and privileges of settlement, trading, and exploration. This was the method employed by this king in furthering enterprises of the kind; and when one company became bankrupt, through extravagance or mismanagement, nothing was easier than to grant a patent for another. In this way four successive companies were formed having for their object the settlement and exploration of this part of Africa. It was not until 1697 that they were under the management of a man who seems to have been thoroughly enthusiastic over the purpose for which the company was organized. In that year, the Sieur Brue was appointed director-general of the company's affairs.

He at once began his preparations for penetrating into the interior, intending to visit the Siratik, or king of the Foulahs, whose territory lay four hundred miles up the river. He seems to have met with no difficulty in prosecuting his journey; but was well received, first by the envoys, and then by the king himself. Presents of great value in the eyes of the natives, but costing only about sixty or seventy pounds sterling, were tendered as an evidence of the friendly feeling of the white men, and graciously accepted. Having accomplished the immediate object of his journey, the Sieur returned to St. Louis.

He set out again the next year, having a more extended object in view. His first trip had been solely for the purpose of cultivating friendly feelings with the natives; in the second, he sought to ascend the Senegal as high as possible, and open up trade with the natives. He established the fort called St.

Joseph, which was long the principal seat of French commerce on the upper Senegal; but failed to accomplish much beyond this; being compelled to return before the river fell so as to cut off his retreat. He obtained from the natives much information respecting the interior; unfortunately, their assertions were not always to be reconciled; especially was this the case in regard to the Niger, which seems for the first time to have been recognized as a stream distinct from the Gambia or the Senegal. According to the statement of some of the natives, the Niger flowed westward from the lake; according to others, it flowed eastward; the former account of it represented it as separating into the two channels of the Senegal and the Gambia; but the great French geographers of the time adopted the other opinion.

Brue wished to penetrate to the gold mines in the interior; but the tyranny of the earliest Portuguese settlers had been such that the natives of that section were resolved not to permit the white men to enter their country again. Brue indeed secured the services of an intrepid advance, who, laden with presents, endeavored to persuade the the natives to admit the party; but the project failed of accomplishment. Nor could Brue obtain from France the assistance which he required, if he made an effort to possess himself by force of the riches of the interior.

Brue appears to be the last Frenchman of this period who made any considerable effort to explore the interior; and his journey was not prompted so much by a desire for knowledge as by a desire for the products of the land. It is true that there were other directors of the company who undertook expoditions, but they were of but small extent. For many years, the chief interest which the French took in Africa was due to the prosperity of the gum trade, of which St. Louis was the headquarters.

CHAPTER III.

JAMES BRUCE.

OWING, perhaps, to the length of time by which we are separated from them, there is much less personal interest attaching to the earlier explorers than to most men who venture into an unknown country for the purpose of solving its mysteries. James Bruce may be considered the first African explorer to whom a real personal interest attaches. This may, perhaps, be due, in his case, to the elaborate care which he has taken to acquaint the world with the results of his journeyings. Five ponderous quartos were required to tell the story to his own satisfaction. Certainly in these volumes there is much that needs to be taken with a grain of allowance, for Bruce is notorious for exaggerating his own importance; but there is less that is untrue than his contemporaries imagined. As in the case of Eudoxus, they refused to believe things which have since been confirmed by a wider experience. Stripped of exaggerations, and reduced to a small compass, that it may come within the limits of the present chapter, the story will be briefly told.

Bruce was the son of a Scottish gentleman, and was born at his paternal seat of Kinnaird House in the county of Stirling, in 1730. His early tendency was toward the Church; but at the desire of his father he became a student of law. This, however, he gave up before he had progressed far enough to be entitled to admittance to the bar, and decided to go to India. While he was making ready to undertake this journey, he fell in love, and married. This, for a time, put an end to his travels, except to France, whither he took his young wife, and where she died in less than a year after their marriage. Bruce seems now to have returned to the idea of traveling, although not to that of going out to India. He traveled for some time in Spain and Portugal, as well as in France; and acquired a knowledge of the languages of these countries as well as of Arabic.

The rumor that war was about to be declared between Great Britain and Spain induced Bruce to offer his services upon an expedition of some danger. The offer was under consideration for some time, but was not accepted. It paved the way, however, for other missions, of not much less danger, and of much greater importance to the world. Lord Halifax desired him to go to Barbary, to study the ruins of architectural beauty which travelers reported to exist there, and make public the information so obtained. In the course of the interviews between them, the subject of exploring the Nile was broached; and Bruce afterward declared that at this instant of his life his heart suggested to him "that this great discovery should either be achieved by me, or remain, as it had done for the last two thousand years, a defiance to all travelers, and an opprobrium to geography."

Shortly after the conversation which prompted this resolve, Bruce was appointed British consul at Algiers. Here he remained for two years, the intervals between the duties of his troublous office being fully occupied by studies. He learned here, from a venerable Greek priest, the modern Greek language, which was afterward of great use to him in Abyssinia. He also acquired much valuable knowledge of surgery.

Finally succeeding in effecting a recall, for his life at Algiers had by no means been all that his fancy painted it before starting, Bruce began the work which the prime minister had suggested—visiting and taking views of the ruins of Barbary. With this end in view, he traveled through the greater part of northern Africa; and it was three years after he left his consulate before he sailed from Cyprus for Egypt, to seek the sources of the Nile.

Arrived at Cairo, he was fortunately mistaken for a skilled astrologer by the all-powerful Coptic secretary of Ali Bey, who was at the head of the government. This reputation, together with his skill as a physician, obtained him peremptory letters of recommendation from the bey to various potentates through whose territories he must pass. Thus equipped, he set out from Cairo in December, 1768.

His progress up the Nile was marked by no misfortune. On the contrary, the same knowledge which had served him so well at Cairo again came into play at his time of greatest danger, when he was in the power of an Arab chief. The chief was ill, and Bruce relieved his pain; the Arab could not sufficiently thank him; but pronounced a solemn curse on any of his people who should molest the traveler. This chief advised him, when he admitted that his object was to reach Abyssinia, to return to Kenek, and go thence overland to Kosseir; thence to cross the Red Sea to Jiddah, near Mecca, and from that port to sail for Abyssinia. Notwithstanding this advice, Bruce continued his journey until he reached the first cataract, near Assouan; then he returned, and followed the old chief's advice,

First Cataract of the Nile, near Assouan.

traveling across the country under the protection of a caravan of the adviser's followers.

Bruce spent considerable time in making a survey of the Red Sea; and it was not until September, 1769, that he finally anchored in the harbor of Massowa, the ancient port of Abyssinia. This country had been the goal of Portuguese travels in a previous century. We have already seen that rumors of a Christianized country in the heart of Africa led the early Portuguese explorers of Guinea to imagine that they had at last heard of the location of Prester John; in the sixteenth century, missionaries of this nation reached Abyssinia from a different direction. According to tradition, the Abyssinians had been converted to Judaism by their sovereign, the Queen of the South who visited Solomon; in the fourth century of our era they were converted to Christianity. The Portuguese missionaries made strenuous efforts to turn them from the Greek Catholic to the Roman Catholic form of faith, and for a time seemed to be successful; but they were finally compelled to abandon the attempt. For almost seventy years, there had been no communication whatever between this country and Europe. Abyssinia seemed almost to have been blotted from the map of the world. The immense distance, the climate in which it was situated, the deserts which nearly surrounded it, and the barbarous character of the tribes which surrounded it, were of themselves enough to deter most travelers; and the dangers of the route had not been softened in the accounts of the returned unsuccessful missionaries.

It was with considerable difficulty and after a delay of two months, that Bruce escaped the naybe of Massowa, who demanded handsome presents in addition to those which the traveler had voluntarily bestowed upon him. But having left Massowa, and thus escaped the importunities of the naybe, his delays and difficulties were not by any means at an end. The favor of a relative of the naybe warned him against taking the easier road, since it might be dangerous; and the rough and mountainous pathway which was thus recommended as safer was the scene of suffering. But by great address, Bruce succeeded in winning the favor of the natives with whom he came in contact; and after a journey which occupied ninety-five days, he came in sight of Gondar, the capital of Abyssinia, about four hundred miles from Massowa.

Here he had the good fortune to effect a cure of several persons who were suffering with smallpox; among them was a child of Ras Michael, the real ruler of the kingdom; for the power of the king was but nominal. Much to the dismay of Bruce, the gratitude of these persons whose friends he had cured took the form of securing for him official appointments about the person of the king; however high the honor which they intended to bestow, this proceeding would have put an end to his attempts at discovery as effectually as their most determined enmity could have done.

The country was disturbed at the time by the revolt of Fasil; and the royal army marched from the capital against the rebel. Bruce of course accompanied it, though not always with the main body of the troops; and it was while on this expedition that he obtained his first sight of the Nile, and of one of its magnificent cataracts. This was the one which is known as the sixth (in ascending the river) and is about sixty miles north of the modern Khartoom.

Massowa.

Fasil, alarmed by the strength of the army which had pursued him, gave his allegiance to the king; and does not seem to have met with any punishment for his rebellion. The royal army returned to Gondar, Bruce of course accompanying it. His desire to find the fountains of the Nile had only been whetted by the sight of the river; and he was more determined than ever to proceed upon his quest.

Fasil's embassadors had heard of the fame of the physician from the far country, and besought him for something which would cure a cancer on the lip, with which Fasil's principal general was afflicted. They declared that Fasil would be better pleased with a medicine which would restore his favorite to health, than with the magnificent appointments which the king lavished upon the repentant rebel. Hearing this assertion, Bruce requested that the king would give him the village of Geesh, and the source of the Nile; evidently supposing that the latter was not far from Gondar. Indeed he asserts distinctly that he had been within fifty miles of the head of the river when obliged to return, with the rest of the king's army, to the capital. The request was granted, and ratified by a solemn oath from the king; while Fasil's embassadors undertook that their master should act as his guide.

But the truce between the king and this powerful rebel was of short duration; the very morning after this promise was made, certain provinces which had suffered severely from the devastations of the royal army on its late march rose against the king; or rather, against his chief adviser. It was not for several months, therefore, that Bruce was enabled to set out on his journey.

October 28, 1770, he and his party began the undertaking. His instruments required six men for their transportation, relieving each other at stated intervals. His difficulties, however, were now all in his own cause; he was no longer exposed to danger through the quarrels of others; he was at last engaged in the actual work of exploration.

Proceeding on their journey from Lake Tsana, they turned southward; for it must be remembered that the traveler was in search of the source of the Blue Nile, which is sometimes considered the main river. They found many peasants flying before Fasil's army, which had been put in motion for some reason with which the explorer was not acquainted. Fasil was at Bamba, a small village of miserable huts; and thither Bruce went, knowing well that the rebel chieftain could forward him in his object. Perhaps it would be well to let Bruce tell the story of their first interview in his own words:

"After announcing myself, I waited about a quarter of an hour before I was admitted. Fasil was sitting upon a cushion, with a lion's skin upon it, and another stretched like a carpet before his feet. He had a cotton cloth, something like a dirty towel, wrapped about his head; his upper cloak or garment was drawn tight about him over his neck and shoulders, so as to cover his hands. I bowed, and went forward to kiss one of them, but it was so entangled in the cloth that I was obliged to kiss the cloth instead of the hand. This was done, either as not expecting I should pay him that compliment (as I certainly should not have done, being one of the king's servants, if the king had been at Gondar) or else it was intended for a mark of disrespect, which was very much of a piece with the rest of his behavior afterward.

"There was no carpet or cushions in the tent, and only a little straw, as if accidentally, thrown thinly about it. I sat down upon the ground, thinking him sick, not knowing what all this meant. He looked steadfastly at me, saying, half under his breath:

"'Endet nawi? bogo nawi?'

"Which in Amharic, is:

"'How do you do? Are you very well?'

"I made the usual answer:

"'Well, thank God.'

"He again stopped, as for me to speak. There was only one old man present, who was sitting on the floor mending a mule's bridle. I took him at first for an attendant; but, observing that a servant, uncovered, held a candle to him, I thought he was one of his Galla; but then I saw a blue silk thread which he had about his neck, which is a badge of Christianity all over Abyssinia, and which a Galla would not wear. What he was I could not make out; he seemed, however, to be a very bad cobbler, and took no notice of us.

"'I am come,' said I, 'by your invitation and the king's leave, to pay my respects to you in your own government, begging that you would favor my curiosity so far as to allow me to see the country of the Agows and the source of the Abay (or Nile), part of which I have seen in Egypt.'

"'The source of the Abay!' exclaimed he, with a pretended surprise; 'do you know what you are saying? Why, it is God knows where, in the country of the Galla, wild, terrible people. The source of the Abay! Are you raving?' he repeats again; 'are you to get there, do you think, in a twelvemonth or more, or when?'

"'Sir,' said I, 'the king told me it was near Sacala, and still nearer Geesh; both villages of the Agows, and both in your government.'

"'And so you know Sacala and Geesh?' says he, whistling, and half angry.

"'I can repeat the names that I hear,' said I: 'all Abyssinia knows the head of the Nile.'

"'Aye,' says he, imitating my voice and manner, 'but all Abyssinia won't carry you there, that I promise you.'

"'If you are resolved to the contrary,' said I, 'they will not. I wish you had told the king so in time, then I should not have attempted it; it was relying upon you alone that I came so far—confident, that if all the rest of Abyssinia could not protect me there, that your word singly could do it.'

"He now put on a look of more complacency.

"'Look you, Yagoube,' says he [Bruce had assumed the name of Yagoube, the Arabic form of his own Christian name]; 'it is true I can do it, and, for the king's sake, who recommended it to me, I would do it; but the chief priest, Abba Salama, has sent to me to desire me not to let you pass farther; he says it is against the law of the land to permit Franks like you to go about the country, and that he has dreamed something ill will befall me if you go into Maitsha.'

"I was as much irritated as I thought it possible for me to be.

"'So, so,' said I, 'the time of priests, prophets, and dreamers is coming on again.'

"'I understand you,' says he, laughing for the first time; 'I care as little for priests as Michael does, and for prophets too; but I would have you consider the men of this country are not like yours; a boy of these Galla would think nothing of killing a man of your country. You white people are all effeminate; you are like so many women; you are not fit for going into a province where all is war, and inhabited by men, warriors from their cradle.'

"I saw he intended to provoke me; and he had succeeded so effectually that I should have died, I believe, if I had not, as imprudent as it was, told him my mind in reply.

"'Sir,' said I, 'I have passed through many of the most barbarous nations in the world; all of them, excepting this clan of yours, have some great men among them above using a defenceless stranger ill. But the worst and lowest individual among the most uncivilized people never treated me as you have done to-day under your own roof, where I have come so far for protection.'

"'How?' he asked.

"'You have, in the first place, said I, publicly called me Frank, the most odious name in this country, and sufficient to occasion me to be stoned to death, without farther ceremony, by any set of men, wherever I may present myself. By a Frank you mean one of the Romish religion, to which my nation is as adverse as yours; and again, without having ever seen any of my countrymen but myself, you have discovered, from that specimen, that we are all cowards and effeminate people, like or inferior to your boys and women. Look you, sir: you never heard that I gave myself out as more than an ordinary man in my own country, far less to be a pattern of what is excellent in it. I am no soldier, though I know enough of war

ABYSSINIAN RAW MEAT FEAST.

to see yours are poor proficients in that trade. But there are soldiers, friends and countrymen of mine, who would not think it an action to vaunt of that, with five hundred men, they had trampled all your naked savages into dust.'

"On this, Fasil made a feigned laugh, and seemed rather to take my freedom amiss. It was, doubtless, a passionate and rash speech.

"'As to myself,' continued I, 'unskilled in war as I am, could it be now without any farther consequence, let me be but armed in my own country-fashion, on horseback as I was yesterday, I should, without thinking myself overmatched, fight the two best horsemen you shall choose from this your army of famous men, who are warriors from their cradle; and if, when the king arrives, you are not returned to your duty, and we meet again as we did at Limjour, I will pledge myself, with his permission, to put you in mind of this promise, and leave the choice of men to your option.'

"This did not make things better. He repeated the word duty after me, and would have replied, but my nose burst out in a stream of blood and that instant a servant took hold of me by the shoulder to hurry me out of the tent. Fasil seemed to be a good deal concerned, for the blood streamed out upon my clothes. I returned, then, to my tent, and the blood was soon stanched by washing my face with cold water. I sat down to recollect myself, and the more I calmed, the more I was dissatisfied at being put off my guard; but it is impossible to conceive the provocation without having proved it. I have felt but too often how much the love of our native soil increases by our absence from it; and how jealous we are of comparisons made to the disadvantage of our countrymen by people who, all proper allowances being made, are generally not their equals, when they would boast themselves their superiors. I will confess farther, in gratification to my critics, that I was from my infancy of a sanguine, passionate disposition; very sensible of injuries which I had neither provoked nor deserved; but much reflection from very early life, continued habits of suffering in long and dangerous travels, where nothing but patience would do, had, I flattered myself abundantly, subdued my natural proneness to feel offences which common sense might teach me I could only revenge upon myself.

"However, upon farther consulting my own breast, I found there was another cause that had co-operated strongly with the former in making me lose my temper at that time, which, upon much greater provocation, I had never done before. I found now, as I thought, that it was decreed decisively that my hopes of arriving at the source of the Nile were forever ended; all my trouble, all my expenses, all my time, and all my sufferings for so many years were thrown away, from no greater obstacle than the whimsies of one barbarian, whose good inclinations I thought I had long before sufficiently secured; and, what was worse, I was now got within less than forty miles of the place I wished so much to see; and my hopes were shipwrecked upon the last, as well as upon the most unexpected, difficulty, I had to encounter."

But Bruce's fears were without foundation. That night, Fasil sent him two lean sheep, and a guard of men to protect him during the night. The next morning, twelve horses, saddled and bridled, were brought to him by Fasil's servant, who asked him which he would ride. Bruce left the man to select a quiet horse for him, and forthwith mounted the one which was offered to him. The animal proved to be wholly untamed; but Bruce managed to keep his seat, and finally sent him back to Fasil as an entirely safe horse to ride. He then mounted his own horse, and showed the admiring natives something of his marksmanship.

Fasil was witness, not only of his shooting, but of his riding; although he protested that he had not sent the wild horse himself; he had none, he said, fit for the saddle, except the one which he himself rode; but any of his horses, driven before the party, would ensure their safety from the attacks of surrounding savages. He again protested that he was innocent of any desire to injure the traveler, and assured him that the groom who had taken him such a horse was in irons, and would be put to death within a few hours.

"'Sir,' replied Bruce, 'as this man has attempted my life, it is I that should name the punishment.'

"'It is very true,' replied Fasil; 'take him, Yagoube, and cut him in a thousand pieces, if you please, and give his body to the kites.'

"'Are you really sincere in what you say?' said Bruce; 'and will you have no after excuses?'"

He swore solemnly that he would not.

"'Then,' returned the traveler, 'I am a Christian; the way my religion teaches me to punish my enemies is by doing good for evil; and therefore I keep you to the oath which you have sworn, and desire you to set the man at liberty, and put him in the place he held before; for he has not been undutiful to you.'"

One of the attendants,turning to Fasil, said, while a murmur of approbation ran through the assemblage:

"Did I not tell you what my brother said about this man? He was just the same all through Tigre."

Fasil replied in a low tone, which Bruce's ears barely caught:

"A man that behaves as he does may go through any country."

In an interview which Bruce afterward had with Fasil, the latter promised a guide who was thoroughly acquainted with the country through which they were to pass, and who had the additional recommendation of being well known as an attendant of Fasil's, so that the stranger's safety would be by this means secured. He then invested Bruce with the government of Geesh, in accordance with the king's grant. He also swore seven Galla chiefs to defend Bruce to the utmost if he should be attacked, and to see that he wanted for nothing which their stores could supply.

October 31, the party set out. Bruce notes that the Galla chiefs paid but little attention to him, although they lavished every possible mark of respect upon the saddled horse which Fasil had given him, to be led in advance of the party. On the third day after they left the camp of Fasil, they came in sight of the mountain of Geesh. The long-sought fountains of the Nile were just beyond it.

But the winding stream must be followed for no little distance before they could reach this elevation. Nor would the inhabitants permit them, when it was necessary to cross the river, to ride across on their horses or mules. They insisted that Bruce and his party should take off their shoes, and even signified that they would stone those who attempted to wash the dirt from their clothes. Patiently forbearing any protest against these superstitious notions, older than the Christianity which they nominally professed, Bruce endeavored to comply with their demands, and restrained his servants, who would have returned rudeness for rudeness.

While the sight of Fasil's horse prevented any of these half-savage natives from attacking the party, it was of disadvantage to them in another way. Seeing the sign of the chief's protection, the inhabitants concluded that the party had been sent out for the purpose of collecting taxes. The human mind appears to have a natural prejudice against the collector of taxes; and in oriental countries, this feeling is not lessened by the enormity of the imposts exacted. The natives accordingly fled from their homes and hid themselves and their portable property; so that Bruce was at some trouble to obtain the necessary provisions.

Following the windings of the constantly lessening stream, they journeyed until a little after noon of the fourth day. They had then arrived at the summit of a mountain, from which they had a distinct view of all the remaining territory of Sacala, the mountain of Geesh, and immediately beneath them, the Nile itself, strangely diminished in size, and now only a brook that had scarcely water enough to turn a mill. The mighty river at this point and at this season was not four yards wide, and barely four inches deep. It ran swiftly over a bottom of small stones, with hard black rock appearing among them. A little below the point at which Bruce saw it at this time, it is full of inconsiderable falls; but at this point, it was easy enough to pass. The guide pointed out to the traveler the position of the two hillocks of green sod where the fountains of the Nile were to be found; and Bruce ran down the hill toward the point.

He had been cautioned to remove his shoes when approaching the the spot, since the people about this place were even more bigoted in their reverence for the river than those whom the party had before encountered; it was then in the guise of a reverent worshiper that he approached the spot toward which, for many years, his thoughts had been directed. But let him tell his own story of the feelings which in this hour of success possessed him:

"I came to the altar of green turf, which was in the form of an altar, apparently the work of art, and I stood in rapture over the principal fountain, which rises in the middle of it.

"It is easier to guess than to describe the situation of my mind at that moment—standing in that spot which had baffled the genius, industry, and inquiry of both ancients and moderns for the course of near three thousand years! Kings had attempted this discovery at the head of armies, and each expedition was distinguished from the last only by the difference of the numbers that had perished, and agreed alone in the disappointment which had uniformly and without exception followed them all. Fame, riches, and honor had been held out for a series of ages to every individual of these myriads these princes commanded, without having produced one man capable of gratifying the curiosity of his sovereign, or wiping off this stain upon the enterprise and abilities of mankind, or adding this desideratum for the encouragement of geography. Though a mere private Briton, I triumphed here, in my own mind, over kings and their armies; and every comparison was leading nearer and nearer to presumption, when the place itself where I stood, the object of my vainglory, suggested what depressed my short-lived triumph. I was but a few minutes arrived at the sources of the Nile, through numberless dangers and sufferings, the least of which would have overwhelmed me but for the continual goodness and protection of Providence. I was then, however, but half through my journey, and all those dangers which I had already passed awaited me again on my return; I found a despondency gaining ground fast upon me, and blasting the crown of laurels I had too rashly woven for myself."

He soon recovered from this feeling of despondency, in outward appearance at least; and drank to the health of the king (George III.) in the waters of the newly discovered fountain. He remained at Geesh four days, making various surveys and astronomical observations. The result of about forty observations made at this time places the head-waters of the Blue Nile in north latitude 10o 59' 25," and 36o 55' 30" east longitude; the barometer indicating an elevation of something more than two miles above the level of the sea.

Some slight description of the scene which he had come through such difficulties and dangers to behold may not be out of place here. The hillock of green sod, which he compares in form to an altar, even if it had not been purposely fashioned in that shape, is in the midst of a small marsh, about twelve feet in diameter, surrounded by a wall of sod, at the foot of which is a shallow trench which collects the water. In the center of this hillock there is a hole, filled with water, which appears perfectly still; there is no appearance whatever of ebullition upon its surface, such as is usual in springs; this hole the traveler found by measurement to be about three feet in diameter and six feet deep. At the distance of ten feet from this hillock, there is a second fountain, eleven inches in diameter and eight feet deep; and at twenty feet there is a third fountain, two feet in diameter and six feet deep. Both these smaller fountains are surrounded by walls of sod and trenches similar to the embankment about the first which the traveler saw. The water from all these unites in one stream which, the discoverer calculated, would fill a two-inch pipe.

In regard to the importance of Bruce's discovery, there have been many things said by those who would wish to lessen his fame. It is urged, first, that he was not the first European who had discovered the source of the Nile. It is true that the

Portuguese Jesuits who, shortly after the foundation of their order, went as missionaries to the Greek Catholics of Abyssinia, explored the surrounding country with more or less thoroughness; one of their number, Paez, had actually visited and described in writing this spot, one hundred and fifty years before it was seen by Bruce. But this description, which had been written originally in Portuguese, had been published only in a Latin translation; more than this, it contained such a number of incredible statements that the friends of Paez were not anxious that it should be read, lest it cast discredit upon his reputation for veracity. Thus the knowledge was doubly locked up; the intelligence may be said never to have reached the ear of the public; and certainly the question where the Nile has its source was regarded as one which had never been satisfactorily answered.

It is also said that the source of the Blue Nile is not the source of the Nile; that the White Nile is the larger river, the main stream; and that therefore the head-waters of this river should be regarded as the true fountains of the Nile. Bruce himself admits that this is true; more than this, that were it not for the constantly flowing stream of the White, fed by the tropic rains, the waters of the Blue Nile would be lost in the desert before they reached Egypt. But, he urges, and others have supported this opinion, the usage of the surrounding tribes shows that the Blue is regarded as the Nile, equally at least with the White. But while it cannot be denied that Bruce solved only the easier of the two problems, and left the more difficult for a later generation, it must be admitted that the fact of his being the pioneer in this portion of the continent (if we except the Portuguese, whose history had caused the natives to look with enmity upon all white men) gives him equal honor with those who have solved the more intricate and difficult question of the source of the White Nile. A recent authority, surveying the field of African discovery from the vantage-ground of modern knowledge of the Dark Continent, declares that Bruce's journey forms an epoch in the annals of discovery.

The discoverer's return through Abyssinia was considerably delayed by the disturbed state of the country, where, as during the past year, intestinal wars were raging. He was further alarmed by the fear that the old rule would be enforced, which forbade a stranger to leave the country. He could only secure the king's permission to depart by promising to return, as soon as his shattered health would permit, with as many of his family as possible, and a full supply of horses and arms. As a recognition of the soldierly service which he had rendered, the king presented him with a gold chain of one hundred and eighty links, weighing about three pounds and a quarter, a weight equivalent to that of $500 and over in gold.

Notwithstanding this apparent willingness to have him leave the country, the king threw many trifling difficulties in the way of his doing so; and these circumstances, combined with that troubled state of the country to which reference has above been made, prevented his departure for more than a year after the actual discovery of the sources of the Nile. Late in December, 1771, he left Gondar, his route lying through Sennaar. The journey thence to Assouan occupied more than eleven months; and was performed only by incredible exertions through a country heated by the nearly direct rays of the sun, and covered with heat-reflecting sand. It was more than a year after leaving Gondar that he reached Cairo, whence his route home was mere child's play to the journey which had preceded.

Bruce horrified his countrymen by his description of the barbarous customs of the Abyssinians, and got roundly scoffed at, for instance, for his stories of cutting off steaks from a live cow. Nevertheless, at the present day, raw meat feasts are none the less practiced than then. When all the guests are assembled, the animals are slaughtered, and within three minutes the choicest morsels of raw meat, of the fattest, are brought in palpitating for the chief and those of high rank. Long knives are handed round to all, and each cuts himself a large piece from the part offered him.

Bruce also described the Abyssinians as never making a new law, as with their usual superstition and obstinacy they ascribe to their ancient statutes a Divine or sacred authority. Thus, when a case is before the judges, they say: "Let us hear what the *Fitha Negust* (their law-book) says." It is opened solemnly, and the first passage which can be found bearing at all on the subject, is read and acted upon, all other considerations being disregarded. On the occasion of a lawsuit, both parties, accuser and accused, must find security or be fastened together during the continuance of the suit; and afterwards the loser must again give security on all the points for which he may be condemned. Also he must hand over a certain amount, according to the importance of the case, to the judges, who get no other pay beyond the numerous presents which they receive on all hands.

AN ABYSSINIAN LAWSUIT.

The returned traveler was received with much distinction, not only in his own country and among his own people, but in France and Italy as well. But there soon arose dissatisfaction with the reception which they accorded him. His assertions regarding the manners and customs of the people and the nature of the countries through which he had passed, were received with incredulity, which wounded and angered his proud and sensitive spirit. He retired to his paternal seat, and to some extent secluded himself from the scientific world. About twelve years after his return, he published the account of his travels in five large quarto volumes, illustrated by plates and maps. But the printed statements commanded but little more respect than those which he had uttered by word of mouth; it was seriously doubted that he had ever been in Abyssinia at all; and it was not until his observations and descriptions were confirmed by other travelers in the same region that his reputation for truthfulness emerged from this undeserved cloud. Bruce felt the unbelief of the world very keenly; but with the fortitude of a Stoic, nerved himself to bear it, trusting only that his daughter, a little child at the time of the publication of his great work, would live to see her father vindicated. This hope, however, was never fulfilled; the daughter lay upon her death-bed when the earliest movement towards confirming the father's statements was made; and although it was told to her, the demonstration of his reliability was then so incomplete that it could not satisfy one so devotedly attached to his memory as she had always been.

The explorer who had passed through so many dangers met with death at a social gathering in his own house. Hurrying forward to assist an old lady to her carriage, his foot failed him, he fell down stairs, and never spoke again. He died at the age of sixty-four.

CHAPTER IV.

THE AFRICAN SOCIETY.

INCITED, perhaps, by the knowledge of what had been accomplished by Bruce, although there were at the time grave doubts that that traveler had reached the goal which he claimed to have attained, a number of Englishmen interested in the advancement of geographical science, in 1788, formed "The African Society." It will be noticed that this was before Bruce's volumes were published, when his achievements were still a matter of hearsay; it was some years before the French expedition to Egypt stimulated interest in that country; and no other country had yet taken decided interest in the exploration of the second largest continent.

We have already noted that the Portuguese had rounded the Cape of Good Hope, and found a maritime path to India. They had also established various colonies on the coast of Africa, one of which was on the slopes of Table Rock, and was surrounded by a few fields a little inland, which afforded the grain needed for food, and also sustenance for their cattle. Of this colony and of others they had been dispossessed at a very early day by the Dutch, who had also supplanted them, to a considerable extent, in the East Indies. The Dutch found this colony, which now bears the name of Cape Town, surrounded by savages whose name is still a synonym for rude ignorance and incapability of civilization. The Hottentots were not only low in the scale of life, but they were lacking in that feeling of unity which has preserved so many a savage race against the encroachments of men superior in arts and arms. They were easily managed by the new-comers, because there was little tribal unity among them. The Portuguese and Dutch had little trouble in maintaining themselves there; and had tne former nation kept possession of the field, and retained its ancient vigor, the surrounding country might have been thoroughly explored in a comparatively short time. As it was, although Cape Town was founded in 1652, and a tolerably correct map of the coast as far north as the mouth of the Great Fish River, made shortly afterward, the easy-going, phlegmatic successors of the Lusitanians allowed matters to remain in exactly the same condition for a full century. Their dominion was bounded by the limits of the Hottentot tribes; with the fiercer Kaffirs they had nothing to do.

Ten years before the formation of the African Society, Captain Henry Hope, under the authority of the Dutch government, had penetrated some distance into the interior with a caravan of about ninety persons. His mission was for the purpose of studying the animal and vegetable forms to be found there, the singularity of which, as seen from a few specimens sent from Cape Town, had excited the wonder of naturalists. On his return, he published at Amsterdam a work containing plates of the giraffe, the zebra, the hippopotamus, the gnu, and other animals then almost wholly unknown to Europe.

Shortly after the ventures of Hope, similar missions were undertaken by Sparrmann, a Swede, and Le Vaillant, a Frenchman. Their journeys, however, were more in the interests of botany and zoology than of geography; so that an extended notice of their travels would be out of place here. Sparrmann deserves our notice chiefly for the reason that he made the most accurate map which had been made up to that time of the coast from the Cape of Good Hope to the mouth of the Great Fish River—a section which had long been known to the Dutch settlers, but the maps of which contained some errors, then first corrected.

This preliminary notice is necessary, in order that we may see what was the condition of African exploration at the time of which we write. The African Society was formed of persons possessed of much vigor and a keen desire to prosecute their object; but its finances were in such a condition that the most it could do was to pay the expenses of those who might volunteer as explorers. Under such circumstances, it was feared that few or none would be found to undertake the task which combines so much danger and hardship; but the fears were without foundation in fact.

Scarcely had the needs of the Society become known, when Ledyard volunteered for the undertaking. He had sailed around the world with Captain Cook, had spent several years among the savage tribes of America, and had made a journey, with the most scanty means, from Stockholm around the Gulf of Bothnia, and thence to the remotest portion of Asiatic Russia. On his return from this last expedition, he presented himself before one of the managers of the Society, who at once declared he was the very man they wanted.

"When can you start?" was the first question which the assembled managers put to him.

"To-morrow," was the concise and wholly satisfactory reply.

They were not indeed ready for him to start so soon; but the answer showed the man's readiness. Preparations were at once begun, and not many weeks had elapsed before he sailed for Alexandria. Here he spent some time, preparing for his journey into the interior; for it had been arranged that he was to traverse the whole length of the continent. While the expectations of the members of the African Society were raised to the highest pitch, and they congratulated each other upon having secured the services of a man so admirably adapted to their work, news arrived that Ledyard was dead. From the very threshold of the intended exploration, he had passed to that country which is in truth the Undiscovered.

But they were not discouraged by this first misfortune. Even before Ledyard had set out, the Society had been engaged in making arrangements for Lucas, an ex-vice-consul to Morocco, who was very well acquainted with the languages and customs of the northern part of Africa, to accompany the caravan which was understood to take the most direct route into the interior. But Lucas was not able to penetrate farther than Mesurata; and the most that he could do was to draw up a view of central Africa from the statements of Imhammed, an Arab who had intended to accompany him on his journey; these statements being supplemented and confirmed by those of Ben Ali, a Moorish trader who was then in London. While this view was indeed imperfect, it was a great improvement upon anything of the kind which had before been attempted.

The third agent of the Society was Major Houghton, who, like Lucas, had been for some years consul to Morocco. He undertook to reach Timbuctoo by following the course of the Gambia as nearly as was practicable or advisable on land. He was kindly received by many of the native chiefs, and once communicated with his countrymen by their means. Through this channel, also, came other news of him: some Moors had persuaded him to accompany them to Tisheet, a place in the Great Desert where salt is obtained. This was very much out of the direct path to Timbuctoo, although the facts were doubtless misrepresented to Houghton. When he saw that he was leaving the road which he intended to keep, he remonstrated, but they would not permit him to return. Their sole purpose had beeen to rob him; and having stripped him of every article in his possession, they allowed him to leave their party when they had gone far enough in the desert to prevent his being succored by whites or friendly natives. He wandered about for some time in the desert without food or shelter, till, at length, he died of exhaustion.

The Society at once determined to send a fourth explorer out, if any one could be found to undertake the task. Mungo Park, a native of Scotland, a young man of about twenty-four, volunteered. He had been educated as a physician; and after his appointment spent two years in preparing himself specially for the work. He sailed in May, 1795; and reached the mouth of the Gambia in the next month. He intended to follow much the same route as Major Houghton had marked out for himself—ascend the Gambia as far as practicable, then strike across the country until he should reach the Niger. He was attended only by a few negro servants when, early in December, he set forth on his quest for the Dark Waters, as the natives still call this long-sought river. The first native king whom he met admired his coat so much, that it was impossible to avoid offering it as a present; since the failure to do so would probably have been the forerunner of a robbery; the second, under pretense that he had paid no duties on entering the territory, stripped him of all goods which he did not contrive to hide before the arrival of the customs officials; the third, under the excuse of acting as his guide and guard through a wild country, compelled him to give, as nominal presents, half of the little that remained to him. Truly had it been said, by a yet earlier traveler, that the beggars of Europe may learn much, in point of unblushing voracity, from the higher classes of savage Africa.

For a time, the traveler did not meet with any more beggars; perhaps because he had but little left which could tempt them. He received information from a chief who appeared to be friendly, that it would be impossible for him to take the direct route to Timbuctoo, as the country was then the scene of war. His only alternative was to go by way of the Moorish kingdom of Ludamar, a perilous route, which had already proved fatal to one explorer, his predecessor, Major Houghton.

He feared much from the bigotry and barbarity of the Moors;

but after some delay, succeeded in obtaining a safe conduct to Goombo, a place on the frontier of Bambarra. After this he progressed slowly, finding the negroes kind and hospitable, the Moors insulting and thievish. Finally, having arrived at Sami, early in March, he was commanded to await the coming of a Moorish prince's favorite wife, who was anxious to see what a Christian looked like.

Dr. Mungo Park.

Transported to the capital, Benown, he was compelled to submit to many indignities; for the Moors could not be persuaded that a European was neither a locksmith nor a barber by nature. He suffered, also, from lack of food and water; for the dry season was on, and his jailers feared the supply of drink would run short if they indulged their prisoner too freely.

The favorite was not at Benown, and was apparently in no

hurry to see a Christian, who could just as well be kept until she chose to come and look at him. While awaiting her arrival, his situation every day became more dangerous, as the hatred of the Moors by whom he was surrounded increased. It was even resolved that he should be put to death. Even under such circumstances, it was worse than useless for Park to endeavor to escape; since his only path lay through the desert, which would not be passable until the beginning of the wet season if he could not stop at the oases where the Moors had settlements.

The favorite at length inspected the curiosity; and finding him less dreadful than she had expected, graciously took him under her powerful protection. His safety would now have been in a measure assured, since he accompanied the army under the command of her husband; but this army was attacked and put to flight by the enemy; the alternatives to those who were captured were, as in all African wars, death or slavery; and Park fled into the desert.

When he considered himself safe from pursuit, he climbed an immense tree to see what his future course should be. Around him was an illimitable waste; he had escaped the fury of savage man, it seemed, only to fall a victim to no less savage nature. Parched with thirst, he eagerly hailed a flash of lightning as a portent of rain; but it proved to be the forerunner of a sand storm, in which he nearly perished. At last he saw a brighter flash, and this was indeed the indication of a refreshing shower. Receiving the moisture upon his clothing, he wrung from them sufficient to quench his burning thirst for a time.

Thus refreshed, he journeyed on, mounted on the back of the horse whose fleetness had enabled him to escape from the Moors. After several repulses from the villages where he tried to obtain food, he reached a point where he considered himself safe from the Moors; and determined to rest there for two or three days.

Pushing onward, his horse soon became so completely worn out that he was obliged to lead, instead of riding it; and his own clothes were in such a miserable plight, his shoes being entirely gone, that he was the subject of jibes from all whom he met. At length, however, he saw rising before him the smoke of Sego, a town which he knew was on the Joliba or Niger River. Spurred on to new exertions by the prospect of such near success, he overtook some former fellow-travelers, who had, a little while before, distanced him.

"See the water!" said one of them, shortly afterward, pointing. "Looking forward, I saw," said he, "with infinite pleasure, the great object of my mission, the long sought for majestic Niger, glittering in the morning sun, as broad as the Thames at Westminster, and flowing slowly to the eastward. I hastened to the brink, and having drunk of the water, lifted up my fervent thanks in prayer to the Great Ruler of all things, for having thus far crowned my endeavors with success."

Having been robbed of all his possessions by the Moors, Park had no presents with which to conciliate the court of Sego, and hence met with a very cool reception. He was kindly treated, however, by an old woman from whom he asked a night's shelter; and the king finally gave him a bag of cowries, of value sufficient to maintain him and his horse for fifty days, and sent him on his way.

The traveler continued to descend the Niger, halting at Sansanding. Here the natives insisted that he should perform his evening devotions publicly, and partake of a meal of eggs. The first of these propositions he declined, but accepted the second. They brought him a number of raw eggs, which they imagined would best please him; but finding that he would not eat them in that condition, his host killed a sheep and prepared him a plentiful supper. On so slight a thread does the explorer's chance of a satisfying meal sometimes hang.

Park had proceeded but a short distance from Sansanding, when his faithful horse gave out; and he was obliged to proceed by some other means. Covered with blisters, and suffering severely from the stings of insects, he resolved to hire a boat and descend the river to Silla. Here he was received very coldly; and learned that at Jenne, the next large town, the power was really in the hands of the Moors, whose influence would increase as he journeyed eastward. He was told, by many of the negroes, that the Moors of that portion of the country were fanatical and bigoted in the extreme; one of them related that he had entered a public inn of that country, when the landlord had spread a mat on the floor, saying to him:

"If you are a Mussulman, you are my friend, sit down on this mat; if not, you are my slave, and with this rope will I lead you to market."

Alone, without influence or other means of conciliating these people, from whose milder brethren he had already suffered much, Park concluded that it would be his wisest course to return, and make known to his countrymen the measure of success which he had achieved. This was not small; for up to this time, the direction of the Niger had been a subject of dispute. It seems that every possible theory had been advanced by those who had heard that there was a great river in this part of Africa. The ancients believed that it flowed into the Nile; the people of the middle ages, as we have seen, were under the impression that it flowed into the Atlantic Ocean; and their immediate successors, the earliest Portuguese and English explorers, identified it with the Senegal or with the Gambia; later writers have confused it with the Congo. Park was the first European who followed its course for any considerable distance, and thus determined that its direction was eastward, and not westward.

Not all his misfortunes had beset him on his journey toward the Niger; some awaited him on his return. He proceeded without more than ordinary adventures until he reached the mountainous country west of Bammakou; here he was set upon by two men, and robbed of the very clothes which he wore; his worst shirt, a pair of trousers and his hat being all that was left to him. It was particularly fortunate that the robbers did not carry off the last-named article, as he carried his memoranda in the crown of it.

The articles of which he had been robbed were recovered by the exertions of a chief to whom Park appealed; but this was only after a delay of two weeks; and unfortunately, his pocket-compass was broken when it was returned to him. On the remainder of his way, he was, on the whole, hospitably treated; although the people who were on his route were suffering, to some extent, from famine. He had the good fortune to fall in with a caravan, the leader of which assured him it was impossible to traverse the country at that season; but offered to support him in the meantime, and when the proper time for the journey arrived, to conduct him in safety to the settlements. This offer was accepted, and the bargain concluded; his guide, on their arrival at Pisania, on the Gambia, receiving double the stipulated price. They reached this point in June, 1797, just two years after Park had arrived in Africa. The traveler was so hindered by various circumstances that it was not until Christmas day that he reached London, where he was received by his friends as one risen from the dead; for fairly well authenticated proofs of his death had actually reached them many months before his return, and had never been contradicted.

But the explorer was not content to rest upon his laurels. He was ready, at the first intimation that his services were required, to set out again. But it had been seen, by this time, that the enterprise of private individuals, or even of associations, was not sufficient for the success of such great undertakings; nothing could do so well as a government expedition. The second expedition of Park was, therefore, undertaken under the auspices of the British government, and was intended to have sailed in 1801. But the war with France, and the consequent agitation of the public mind, delayed the proceedings, so that it was not until the latter part of January, 1805, that the party actually set out.

Forty-three white men accompanied Park upon this expedition, which was provided with a native guide. The leader provided the whole party with asses at the Cape Verde Islands; the breed of these animals being excellent, and they being well fitted for traversing the rugged hills that form the watershed between the Niger and the rivers that empty into the Atlantic by a westward course.

When they were ready to set out from the western coast, it was evident that the rainy season could not be far distant; and at this portion of the year, travel was beset with many dangers for Europeans. It would have been prudent to have remained near the coast until the rains were over; but inaction was impossible to Park, in his enthusiastic state of mind. He insisted on proceeding on his way; and accordingly set out from Pisania early in May.

The party was so strong, that it was not dependent upon the protection of the petty kings through whose territories they must pass; but they no longer had any claim upon the hospitality of these chiefs; and were considered as fair prey for the depredations of many who had received Park well, when he was alone and friendless. With much exertion the party reached Sansanding. They had traveled by water a great part of the way since reaching the Niger, and had therefore avoided some of the fatigue which a journey overland would have occasioned. But there was a danger inseparable from the country at that season; the heat and moisture combined proved fatal to nearly all the party. Before they reached Sansanding, thirty-nine of the party had perished; Park writes that not one of these had died from any accident,nor had they had any contest with the natives. One of the five survivors was deranged by the terrible experiences through which they had passed.

But the indomitable spirit of the explorer would not yield, even when his companions fell thick around him. When his brother-in-law died, he wrote: "I then felt myself as if left a second time lonely and friendless amid the wilds of Africa." Nevertheless in the same dispatches in which he communicates the lessening of his party, he expresses his determination to press onward at all costs; and speaks of the journey down the Niger as a journey homeward. He adds: "Though all the Europeans who are with me should die, and though I myself were half-dead, I would still persevere."

Canoe Traveling on African Rivers.

The party purchased three slaves, so that, with the guide, their number was nine. It would appear that they passed rapidly down the river, which was now, in consequence of the heavy rains, in a very favorable state for their enterprise. But the king of Yaour, or Yauri, a city more than half way between Timbuctoo and the sea, became much offended because the white men passed his residence without offering suitable presents. He sent a party to pursue them. This party went by land and took possession of a pass where rocks hemmed in the river, so that there was but a narrow channel. When Park arrived at this place, he thought to force his way past the obstruction; but they assailed him with darts, stones, pikes, and arrows. He defended himself a long time; two of the slaves were killed; the crew threw everything they had into the river, and fired constantly at the savage enemy. At last, overcome by numbers and fatigue, unable to keep the canoe against the strength of the current, Park seized one of his companions, and jumped overboard. What words were uttered, if any, we know not; but one after another of the three survivors followed the example set by these two, and all were drowned. The only soul remaining, a slave, stood up in the boat and cried for mercy. They took him and the boat to the king; and savage revenge was gratified.

The story is told by the guide, who was found and induced to seek for information of those who had seen the party after his own contract had been fulfilled, and he had left them to return to the settlements. As thus told, it was confirmed by what later travelers heard; for the journeys of Mungo Park excited almost as much interest in Africa as in his own country, and long remained a favorite topic with those through whose country he traveled. The very spot where he perished has been identified.

The narrative of the second expedition of Mungo Park has been rather out of the line of our direct narrative; since we are now concerned with those explorers sent out by the African Society. But the first expedition of Park had been made under the auspices of this association; and while the second was under the patronage of the government, certainly it would never have been so assisted if the first had not been prompted by private enterprise.

The African Society made several other attempts to explore the interior of Africa; but was uniformly unfortunate. That venture which came nearest to being successful was made by Frederic Hornemann in 1797–1803. This young man, who was a student of Gottingen University, offered his services to the Society and had them accepted as soon as his character was known to them. He proceeded to Egypt, where he was detained some time by the hostility to Europeans which had been excited by Bonaparte's landing in that country. When the great French general reached Cairo, he was liberated; and he joined a caravan which was setting out for Mourzouk, the capital of Fezzan.

It was Hornemann's intention to proceed across the desert by some one of the numerous caravan routes, and explore the country surrounding the Niger from that direction. After many delays, he left Mourzouk for the south; various letters reached England, but after a little while, of course, they ceased entirely; he was in the new country, whence communications could not be expected. Time went on; and six years after his departure from Europe, a Fezzan merchant informed the British consul at Tripoli that Hornemann was alive and well at Kashna, where he was held in high veneration as a Mussulman Marabout; for he had chosen to assume the Mohammedan religion, in its outward observances at least, in order to escape the the persecutions to which every Christian was subject in Mohammedan countries. This was the last that was heard of him; until a later traveler learned that he had succumbed to the diseases of the climate at some point on the Niger, probably at some time in the year 1803. Hornemann first transmitted to Europe accurate information respecting Fezzan, and also the eastern Soudan. He corrected an error which had long had currency; namely, that the term Houssa meant a single empire or city; he discovered that it included a number of independent states.

The interest which the British government felt in the exploration of Africa was not allowed to languish because the first expedition sent out had resulted fatally to all concerned. In 1816, two parties were sent out, the one to explore the Niger from the westward, as Park had already done, the other to ascend the great river which empties into the Atlantic Ocean about six degrees south of the equator. We know this as the Congo; but although it was called by that name in 1816, it was a well understood thing that this was merely a sectional name; that the same stream which the natives inhabiting the country around its mouth called the Congo, the people living near its headwaters knew as the Joliba or Niger. In short, the British government sent out these two expeditions, that one might descend the Niger, and the other ascend the Congo, and meet each other.

Unfortunately for the progress of geographical knowledge, the reason why this plan must fail was obscured by the fact that their efforts failed long before either expedition had reached a point at which it might reasonably hope to meet the other. That to the Congo ascended the river as far as the great cataract without any especial adventure; but shortly after passing the falls, disease affected many of them; and the leaders of the expedition having all died, the subordinates sailed for home.

A similar fate overtook the other party, which consisted of

one hundred men. Their chosen route lay through the Foulah territory, or slightly to the south of that selected by Park. Six months after leaving the coast, the remnants of the party made their way back. One member of it afterward attempted to cross to the Niger by Park's old route along the Gambia, but did not penetrate as far into the interior as the previous explorer had done.

In 1821, Major Laing, who had been sent on a mission through the countries of the Timannee, Kooranko and Solima tribes, with a view to making arrangements for trading, learned from the natives that the sources of the Niger were much nearer the south than had been previously supposed. From the reports of the natives, he was inclined to fix the point a very little above the ninth degree of north latitude—an opinion which modern geographers have amended only by fixing the meaning of "very little" as twenty-five minutes of latitude.

The African Society may be considered to have accomplished its object, not indeed by securing for the world a more accurate knowledge of the geography of the great southern continent, but in having awakened the interest of the public, and particularly of the representative of public opinion, the king's government. Accordingly, we find it now attracting much less notice than at first; and finally, some forty years after its organization, it was merged in the Royal Geographical Society.

CHAPTER V.

CLAPPERTON AND DENHAM.

THE British government was thoroughly in earnest in the desire to obtain more accurate information regarding the interior of Africa. There was one circumstance which was regarded as very favorable: at the court of Tripoli this country was regarded with much respect and some friendship. This feeling was largely due to the prudence and ability of the consul, Mr. Warrington, whose advice was constantly sought by the pasha on almost all matters of importance. Great Britain then might ask protection for whom she would, and it would be given; and scarcely any more influential power, in this respect, could be invoked; for the pasha of Tripoli was a ruler whose name was dreaded in the kingdoms of interior Africa.

It was no exercise of statesmanship which had given him this pre-eminence; neither was it any hereditary submission to his authority. The simple fact was, that he was almost the only ruler of whom they had ever heard, whose followers were armed with muskets. It was the magic power of gunpowder which so exalted him in their eyes; and it is said that on more than one occasion the natives have expressed their surprise that he had not, long since, compelled all Europe to embrace the Mohammedan faith.

Under such favorable circumstances, the government resolved that there should be no further delay, after leaders for a new expedition had been secured. Notwithstanding the fact that every line upon the map of Africa which had been drawn within the past half century represented the sacrifice of more than one life, there were not wanting volunteers for the service. Major Denham, of the army, Lieutenant Clapperton, of the navy, and Dr. Oudney, a naval surgeon of considerable acquaintance with natural history, were selected for this work.

They proceeded at once to Tripoli, where they arrived November 18, 1821.

The pasha received them with much ceremony, and invited them to a hunting-party on the borders of the desert. But the rather obsequious attention which they received did not blind their eyes to the prevailing barbarism; they saw clearly, in more than one instance, that they were dealing with a man who was no more than half-civilized; and they realized that their difficulties had begun.

The party set out for Mourzouk, and presented there the letters which the pasha of Tripoli had provided them with; but the sultan of Fezzan was by no means disposed to obey the commands of his superior; perhaps because he was doubtful of that superior's sincerity in commanding him to assist these strangers. He evaded their request to provide them with an escort, and declared that he must visit the court of Tripoli in person; they could await his return, when he would attend to their request. They were not a little doubtful as to whether they ought to accept the invitation of Boo Khalloom, a great merchant who asked them to accompany an expedition which he was preparing for a journey across the desert to Bornou. While they were hesitating, both Boo Khalloom and the sultan departed for Tripoli, to watch each other in the intrigues which each intended to conduct there.

Chafing under this uncalled-for delay, Major Denham resolved that he would hasten matters. He accordingly returned to Tripoli in person. An interview with the pasha was highly unsatisfactory; for the prince who had professed such readiness to serve the English was ready to evade the obligation if he could, and would promise nothing sufficiently definite to satisfy the impatient explorer. Under such circumstances, Major Denham resolved that he would return to England and lay the case before the authorities there. He accordingly set sail; the pasha heard of his departure, and, thoroughly alarmed at the result of his temporizing policy, sent several messengers after Denham. One of these vessels finally overtook that in which the Englishman had sailed, while it was performing quarantine at Marseilles; and informed him that the pasha had actually made arrangements with Boo Khalloom to escort the party to Bornou. Major Denham accordingly returned at once, and found the great merchant awaiting him on the borders of the desert.

While Boo Khalloom is called a merchant, he was very different from the man whom that term usually suggests to our minds. Being obliged to conduct his assistants, with the stores of goods, across a country inhabited by savage, warlike, and thieving tribes, it was necessary for him to provide a guard, and to be enough of a soldier to manage this guard himself; for he could not always depend upon hired chiefs. These soldiers become veterans, and are a source of anxiety to the prince in whose territory they may chance to be; their employer is a man to be dreaded. Then, too, in most cases at least, the merchant of the desert is not above those means of obtaining goods at the expense of others which he deprecates when he is the victim. To put the matter plainly, he resorts to robbery when he can; and considers this quite as legitimate a method of replenishing his stores as that of purchasing in the market. At that time, too, it must be remembered that the slave trade had not been abolished; there were slaves, not only in the United States, but in the British colonies where the climate was such as to make their labor profitable; in addition to the trade which was surreptitiously carried on by the dealers in human flesh and blood with these two great nations, and others of similar rank, there was a constant demand for slaves from Mohammedan countries, where the traffic was not prohibited by law. The slave trade was one which offered large profits when the goods could be obtained for nothing, and sold at a high price. The Arab merchants of the desert, then, scrupled not to enter upon great slave-hunting expeditions, as we shall find later on.

Arrived at Mourzouk about the end of October, 1822, Major Denham found both his companions prostrated by disease. This was not a promising beginning; but persuading themselves that a change of air would be beneficial, the two invalids soon declared themselves ready for the journey; and went onward to Gatrone, even before the merchant was prepared to begin the journey. Major Denham was left in Mourzouk to complete the necessary arrangements, and to watch over the fidelity of Boo Khalloom.

The expedition, when finally it was ready, numbered two hundred and ten Arabs, under different chiefs, besides the merchant and his English proteges. The latter, having been received into their camp, and having eaten of their bread and salt, were protected by the inviolable law of the hospitality of the desert.

Through the wastes where not a living thing, outside of the group of beings that composed the caravan, could be discerned, where the earth was crusted with salt that glittered in the crevices like frost, where the ripple of the blowing sand murmured like a gentle stream, where every noise was rendered doubly impressive by the solemn stillness, they journeyed on the path marked out by the footsteps of a thousand caravans. Soon the lonely grandeur of the desert received a new element of horror—their way was strewn with the skeletons of those who had trodden this very path, and died, of starvation, of thirst, or at the hands of the marauding tribes that would haunt their footsteps. Sometimes they were found singly; at places they would be seen in groups of fifties and hundreds; while at the wells of El Hammar they were almost innumerable. The horses' feet would crash among the bones before the rider was aware of their presence; and the skulls would bound before them like balls.

In this approach to the territory of Soudan the travelers began to witness the exercise of mutual plunder between the caravan and the natives. However strict a guard was kept, an animal would occasionally stray off; and this was seized by the inhabitants of the region as their rightful booty. Even a dog had been killed, and every shred of his flesh eaten. A gorgeously dressed herald had been sent forward to announce their coming to the sultan of Bornou; they found him tied to a tree, literally stripped of his gay accouterments. On the other hand, no sooner did the caravan come within sight of any village than the inhabitants were seen fleeing at full speed, carrying with them all their portable goods. The Arabs, in great indignation at being thus mistrusted, pursued them, solely with a view of correcting the misapprehension under which they labored. The correction of this misunderstanding, however, as the Englishmen found, involved the most rapid process of plunder which they had ever witnessed. In a few seconds the camels were relieved of their burdens, and the owners stripped to the skin. On such occasions, Boo Khalloom insisted upon restitution being made, as soon as the matter was brought to his attention; but the white men were not a little doubtful as to whether he would have done so if they had not been of the party.

The expedition advanced rapidly until it reached the most northern province of Bornou, and arrived at its chief town, Lari. Here they beheld, glowing with the golden rays of the sun, the vast expanse of Lake Tchad. Major Denham hastened to the shores of this inland sea, which were darkened by immense bevies of water-birds of various species. Overcoming his scruples at the slaughter of fowls so tame, he fired several times among them, and soon filled a large basket with the game.

It was evident that the bed of the lake was constantly changing; for although this was not the rainy season, they saw long stalks of the grain called gussub growing in places that were entirely under water.

They found the country of Bornou under a double rule, real and nominal. Some twenty years before it had been subdued by the Fellatas; but a peasant had headed a successful revolt against their foreign masters, and was in consequence regarded with intense affection and respect. The claims of the hereditary monarch, however, were not to be lightly set aside; so that he received all honor, and was surrounded by the appearance of regal authority, while the real power was in the hands of the successful soldier. Fortunately for the travelers, the latter agreed to forward their plans, although they afterward proved to be wholly incomprehensible to his illiterate mind.

In the wilds of Africa as well as in the midst of civilization, vanity rules the human mind. This favorable decision of the chief was partly influenced by the fact that Major Denham assured him the king of England had heard of him. Much gratified, the dusky sheik turned to his lieutenant and remarked that that must be in consequence of their late success in some petty strife with their neighbors. The lieutenant demanded to know if the king had heard of him.

"Certainly," replied Denham, without a moment's hesitation.

"The king of England must be a great man," was the verdict of all.

Further propitiated by the gift of a music-box, and a little alarmed by the magical power which must be possessed by a man who could display sky-rockets, the sheik agreed to send the party forward to the sultan. Proceeding to the city where his majesty resided, they were, after due formality, admitted to his august presence. They found him surrounded by about three hundred courtiers; they deposited the presents which they had brought with them; not a word was vouchsafed them, and of course they could not speak until they were spoken to; they were conducted from the presence of the sultan, and that was all they ever saw of him.

Nevertheless, this presentation in due form enabled the real ruler to grant them the privilege of remaining in the country, and of prosecuting their journey when it should please them.

Bornou is not the only country in the world where useless forms are insisted upon, as if essential to the welfare of the world.

Having dispatched his affairs in Bornou, Boo Khalloom wished to make an expedition into the Soudan; but his followers had other aims in view. They wished to attack a village in the Mandara Mountains, to the south of Bornou, and carry off the people as slaves to the markets of Fezzan. Boo Khalloom resisted this proposal, but was overruled, even his own brother and the sheik siding with the others. He conducted the affair in person.

The sheik had forbidden the English travelers to take part in this expedition, and it seems that no such prohibition ought to have been necessary. But Major Denham was so bent upon exploring the country that he decided the end would justify the means; and succeeded in evading this command to remain in Bornou.

The party was accompanied by a body of Bornou cavalry, commanded by the principal general, Barca Gana. They chose a path which was so little used that twelve pioneers had to precede the main body, to clear out the thick undergrowth; and their provisions were of the simplest kind.

At length they reached Mora, the capital of Mandara. The sultan of this tribe was on the most friendly terms with the ruler of Bornou, and there was a close alliance between them. The fact that the Bornou party had come to make slaves of Mandara villagers does not seem to have been regarded as a breach of their treaty. On the contrary, the new-comers were received in a very friendly manner; and even their white companion was treated with courtesy until the Mandarans had asked the question: "Is he Moslem?" This being answered in the negative, Major Denham was eyed with much suspicion, and was not again allowed to enter the palace. The Mohammedan doctors belonging to the court spared no pains to induce him to become a convert to their faith; and having failed to do so, classed him in point of religious belief with the pagans. Major Denham pointed to a party of the savage neighbors of the Mandarans devouring a dead horse, and demanded of Boo Khalloom if he had ever seen the English do the same; thinking by this means to show that his countrymen were of higher rank in the scale of civilization.

"I know," replied the Arab, "that they eat the flesh of swine, and God knows that that is worse."

His appeal being thus answered, the gallant major seems to

have given up the defense of his religion, and borne their insults in silence.

The appearance of the party of Arabs and Bornouese greatly alarmed the people of the villages, savages who paid tribute to the sultan of Mandara and should have had protection from him. They sent in ambassadors with gifts and entreaties that they might be spared. The sultan was apparently moved by these appeals, and intimated to Boo Khalloom that these people might be won over to the true faith of Islam by gentler means than being sold into slavery, for their expedition of course, had a religious coloring. But Boo Khalloom did not trust his host, and privately told Major Denham so. The aim of the sultan was to persuade the Arabs of the caravan to attack some strong Fellata outposts near the boundaries of his territory; if the garrisons were defeated, that enemy was out of the way; if Boo Khalloom's men were routed, that was none the worse for the Mandarans.

For some reason, Boo Khalloom allowed himself to be persuaded to undertake this campaign; perhaps his unruly followers preferred it; perhaps he acted under absolute compulsion from the sultan, who was his master de facto, while his party was in Mandara. They set out gaily, the united bodies of cavalry presenting a warlike appearance which inspired the English soldier with high hopes of success. He did not then know what arrant cowards can be found in a body presenting such a fine martial array. They attacked a Fellata town, and the Arabs drove the garrison and inhabitants to a smaller place just beyond it. Continuing the fight, the enemy was compelled to take refuge in a third and stronger position, inclosed by high hills, and fortified in front by numerous swamps and palisades. This was likewise attacked, and its defenses forced, the Fellatas being terrified by the guns of the Arabs.

This was their last stronghold, and had the Arabs been supported by a single charge of the gorgeous cavalry, the victory would have been won. But they were "kid-glove soldiers," if the expression may be applied to savage warriors; their trappings and accouterments were part of a show which had nothing behind it. They remained at a safe distance, from danger, keeping carefully under cover from the arrows and spears of the enemy.

The condition of the Arabs was alarming; scarcely a man was left unhurt, and their horses were dying under them. Boo Khalloom and his steed were both wounded with poisoned arrows; Major Denham's horse was so wounded in the shoulder that the animal could scarcely support his weight. Seeing their condition, the Fellatas dashed in among them. Even then, a timely support from their companions might have turned the tide of battle; but the Bornouese and Mandaran cavalry, headed by the sultan of the latter people, turned and fled as fast as their gorgeously caparisoned horses would carry them from the scene of conflict.

Major Denham was in a truly alarming position; his horse staggered and fell; then, alarmed by the noises behind him, while the Major was upon the ground endeavoring to raise him, sprang up and darted off. Four Arabs who were gathered around him were stabbed by the infuriated Fellatas; and he momentarily expected the same fate. It was from no regard to the white man's nationality or services that he was spared; the strokes of the dagger would have cut his clothes, which his enemies were anxious to preserve.

He was taken prisoner, then, unhurt; and was at once stripped to the skin, while his captors proceeded to divide the spoil. While they were quarreling over the division of his clothes, he contrived to slip away, and rejoin his fleeing friends, the remnant of the Arabs.

The whole party that had set out from Fezzan had suffered most severely. Forty-five of their number, including their chief, had fallen; and they had lost all their camels and other property. To keep themselves from starvation, they were obliged to beg from Barca Gana. The sultan treated them with the utmost contumely, notwithstanding the fact that they had suffered while fighting his battle.

Returning to Bornou, after this experience of African warfare, Major Denham accepted an invitation from the sheik of that country to accompany an expedition against the Mungas, a rebellious tribe on the southwestern boundaries of the country. They set out in state, even the sultan and his harem accompanying them for some distance, in order to lend pomp to the occasion. Their route lay along the River Yeou or Gambarou, through a country which had been desolated by warfare, and actually depopulated, the inhabitants who had escaped the sword being carried into slavery.

On this journey, they did not wholly escape danger from the devices of the late inhabitants. The Tuaricks are the scourge of all this portion of Africa, and frequently make predatory inroads upon defenseless villages, carrying off men, women, children and cattle. Against them the people have but one mode of defense; they dig pits, at the bottom of which they imbed sharp stakes; the surface is then restored, so that the unwary invader supposes that he is riding along a smooth stretch of country; rider and horse fall into the trap, and are impaled upon the stakes, sometimes killed; even when but wounded, they are unable to extricate themselves without assistance. Unfortunately for other travelers, these pits are so cunningly contrived that they deceive neutrals as well as enemies, and more than once Major Denham barely escaped falling into one of them.

Arrived at the point where the conflict was expected to take place, extensive preparations were made. The sultan, who had sent his harem back and proceeded on the journey, reviewed the troops, who numbered nine thousand spearmen, besides other forces. Having done this, he turned his attention to other preparations, and spent three nights in inscribing bits from the Koran upon little scraps of paper. Major Denham consented to send up some sky-rockets, as additional aids to the prowess of the soldiers. The enemy was, by some means, kept informed of the sultan's nightly occupation; the rockets spoke for themselves; and the rebellious Mungas, who had been described as fierce and bold warriors, came in by hundreds, offering submission; and the rebel chief at last appeared, and surrendering unconditionally, found himself heaped with honors and robes by his forgiving master.

This expedition enabled Major Denham to become acquainted with the southwestern portion of Bornou, and to trace with exactitude a considerable portion of the River Yeou; although neither the head-waters nor the mouth were visited by him. His next effort was to explore the Shari, a river of which he knew only that it flowed into Lake Tchad, and that upon its banks the kingdom of Loggene was situated. In this expedition he was accompanied by Mr. Toole, a young adventurer who had set out from Europe, after his departure, to join him; and had crossed the desert from Tripoli with some one of the numerous caravans. They struck the river at the town of Showy, which is situated just at the head of the delta by which it empties into the lake; they descended it to the mouth, then retraced their steps, and ascended it as far as Loggene, the capital of the country of the same name. They found this a handsome city, with unusually wide streets. They were received very kindly by the sultan, who inquired, when they were introduced to his presence, if they were seeking female slaves; his majesty wished to be informed, as he had several hundreds of whom he was willing to dispose at low rates. Declining this offer of merchandise does not seem to have excited any anger on the part of the would-be seller; he simply solicited a poison "which would not lie," to be used against his son; and accompanied the request with a bribe of three lovely black damsels. It is needless to say that this proposal excited much horror, at which the sultan only laughed. He need not be considered an exceptionally unnatural monster, however, for making such a request; for the son himself asked the explorers for a similar poison, to be used against his father.

Notwithstanding these instances of savage disregard of human life and one of the closest ties of nature, Major Denham found these people farther advanced, in many respects, than their neighbors; they made a better quality of cloth, and had even a rude coin of iron, which passed current among them—an approach to money which was not possessed by any of their neighbors. But the people seem to have had no idea of honesty; and it was all that Major Denham and his companion could do to keep the contents of their pockets in safety.

The death of Mr. Toole, and the rumor that a considerable body of Begharmis were about to attack Bornou, determined Major Denham to return. This attempt was repulsed without much difficulty; but worse fortune attended an aggressive movement of the Bornou army. Certain islands along the south-eastern shores of Lake Tchad, are populated by a tribe of Arabs; it was designed to attack these, riding through the water, which is so shallow as to require no bridge. But the Bornou army was hurried forward by its desire for plunder, and the safe paths through the lake were unknown to them; the assailed tribe, on the contrary, were thoroughly familiar with the place, and could ride as rapidly and surely through the water as on land. The failure of this expedition, which ended in a disgraceful flight, prevented any farther attempt, at that time, at exploring the eastern shores of Lake Tchad.

We have thus far followed the adventures of Major Denham. His companions had not been inactive. Dr. Oudney and Mr. Clapperton proceeded nearly due east from Kuka, their first goal being the ancient town of Kano. Before they reached this point, however, Dr. Oudney died, and was buried near the banks of the Komadgu River.

Proceeding unaccompanied by any of his own nation, but under the protection and guidance of a caravan, Mr. Clapperton visited many different towns of Houssa, in which he was received with much distinction; for it was rumored that the

INTERIOR OF AN ORIENTAL HAREM.

white man could, at will, convert men into asses, goats, or monkeys; and that he could readily transform a handful of dust into as much gold. The traveler, showing with what difficulty he obtained an ass for his own riding, and that he was not possessed of an undue quantity of the precious metal, re-assured the frightened natives, who dreaded that such remarkable powers might be turned against them and their country.

Having remained some little time in Kano, and become familiar with the customs of the place, and particularly with the market, Mr. Clapperton succeeded in securing the escort of another caravan, which was going as far as Sakati. This appeared to the traveler to be the most populous city which he had seen in the interior of Africa; and one of the best-planned and most substantially built. He was well received by the sultan, a man of considerable intelligence, to whom his instruments afforded much interest.

The sultan boasted not a little of the extent of his empire and his power over allied tribes. Mr. Clapperton listened to such boasts with much gravity, and was perhaps impressed by them with an exaggerated idea of his host's dominions. This is scarcely to be wondered at, since that whole country was then, except for the explorations of the Portuguese and the first expedition of Park, a *terra incognita* to Europeans. It had been his aim, during this whole journey, to reach the coast by a route leading westward and southward from Bornou; and he asked from this powerful and friendly monarch a guide to the Gulf (or Bight) of Benin.

It must have been somewhat embarrassing to the sultan of Sakati when the stranger asked him to give the name of some one of his seaports at which the English might land; for such seaports are like those of Bohemia, of which Shakespeare speaks in the "Winter's Tale." In fact, his majesty's dominions did not extend to a point within several hundred miles from the sea; but this was a circumstance of which it was not worth while to inform the stranger.

In addition to this reason for refusing him the guide that he had requested, Mr. Clapperton was feared by the Arab merchants. If he opened up a communication with the coast, they argued, their profits derived from goods brought across the desert would be materially diminished. Influenced by these two considerations, the sultan begged of Mr. Clapperton that he would dismiss the idea from his mind; the country was full of rebellious tribes, against whom not even his mighty protection could always avail; and the traveler, he feared, would in this rash endeavor meet with grievous harm. There may have been some sincerity in this pretext, though; for the country was really in a very bad condition. The explorer was told that he could reach home only by retracing his steps; and finding that this was indeed the case, he returned to Kuka by a slightly different route.

Among the results of this expedition, was the obtaining of an account of Mungo Park's death; or rather, a confirmation of what had been previously told. Mr. Clapperton was extremely anxious to obtain the journal of the earlier traveler, which he had heard was still at Yauri; but the refusal of the sultan of Sakati to afford him a guide, as we have seen, prevented him from going farther south.

The two travelers met at Kuka, and proceeded thence to Tripoli by way of Mourzouk; arriving at London in June, 1825, or almost four years after the time of their departure.

Mr. Clapperton (who was promoted to the rank of captain shortly after his return) had been much impressed by the sultan of Sakati's boasts in regard to the extent of his territories; and considered that some of that potentate's expressions implied a promise to send a guard to certain coast towns, for the purpose of escorting any expedition which the English might send, into the interior. He thus represented matters to the British government, which promptly responded by placing him at the head of such an expedition, and naming Captain Pearce and Mr. Morrison as his associates. The former was an excellent draughtsman, the latter an experienced surgeon.

The whole affair was managed with such determination, that before the end of the year in which Denham and Clapperton had returned to London, this second party had reached the Gulf of Guinea, and was engaged in hunting for the towns which the sultan had named to their leader. It is needless to say that no such towns were found; nor could they hear of any guard or guide that had been sent to conduct them to Sakati.

They were not discouraged by this failure; but resolved to penetrate the country, alone and unguided. Advised by a countryman who had long been a resident of the coast, they resolved not to ascend along the banks of the river, where the marshes bred pestilence of all kinds; but to push forward by an overland route from Badagry.

The very beginning of the journey brought discouragement to the leader by the death of his followers. Setting out on the seventh of December, they imprudently slept in the open air during two nights. From the fever which all three thus contracted, Captain Clapperton alone recovered; and proceeded on his perilous journey, attended only by his faithful English servant, Richard Lander, and a not very trusty African, whom he had hired at Badagry.

After a journey of about sixty miles, the travelers entered the kingdom of Yarriba, which had long been reported on the coast as the most powerful and populous kingdom of the interior, holding even Dahomey in subjection. They found agriculture advanced to a degree beyond their expectations; the looms were more ingenious machines than Clapperton had yet seen in Africa; while the cloths which they made were dyed with the finest of indigo.

Among the Arabs far in the interior, and the negroes who had had many dealings with them, the white men had found no very flattering reception; whatever kindness was shown them was rather in spite of, than because of their color; and the fact that they were enemies of the prophet was an additional reason for their proscription. With the pagan negroes of this country there was no such religious reason for enmity; and besides this, they had heard reports from the coast of the white men's wonderful superiority in all arts and manufactures, and viewed these representatives of the favored race almost as beings of a superior order. On entering any town, therefore, they were received with the most flattering demonstrations of respect, and in some instances singing and dancing were kept up through the whole night to celebrate their arrival.

Their passage of the mountains north of Guinea was marked by welcomes extended in the same spirit; everywhere they found those who were ready to help them on their way, either by providing them with stores of food, or by furnishing them with guides over the difficult passes of the mountains. The only obstacle was the fact that in many cases they were so earnestly besought to remain for several days with their dusky hosts that they could not refuse the request.

The fame of their coming had preceded them, and scarcely had they crossed the mountains before an embassador arrived from the king, with a numerous train of attendants, mounted and on foot. The arrival of this guard of honor was in one sense unfortunate for those whom they came to escort; for, claiming free quarters among the people of the town, they devoured all the obtainable food with such avidity that the hunger of the explorers was hardly satisfied.

At Katunga, the capital, they were welcomed by the entire population, and dramatic representations, crude indeed, but representing the highest state of the art in Yarriba, were gotten up for their entertainment.

Although the king professed his desire to serve the strangers by every means in his power, he refused to further their journey to the country of the Fellatas. To have penetrated to the kingdom of Yarriba and to have visited its monarch ought to be enough to have accomplished in one journey. Finally, after much persuasion, seeing that the strangers were determined to proceed, he offered to send them into the interior by a safer route than that which they had chosen, although it was more circuitous.

The first town of importance through which they passed was Kiama: at Wawa, a little farther on, a singular adventure befell the travelers. An Arab widow of twenty, dark-brown in color, and in figure nearly like a water-cask, was extremely anxious to secure a white husband. She first selected Lander, who, Captain Clapperton says frankly, was better looking than his master; but the man repulsed her so decidedly that she turned her attentions upon the master. It was not enough that she invited him to her house; she followed him from place to place; and his negro servant having accepted a wife from among her slaves, she claimed that the customs of Africa gave her a claim upon him. Under such circumstances, Captain Clapperton at once ordered his follower to return his wife to her former owner; this was done, and the widow was compelled to cease her persecutions. It was intimated to Clapperton that her designs had not been only upon himself as a husband; she had intended to secure power as well, by dethroning the king, aided by the courageous white men; and share the throne as well as her enormous wealth with the Englishman.

The party touched the Niger at Boussa. Here they found seven boats awaiting them, with an embassy from the king of Yauri, promising that if they would visit him at his capital he would deliver up to them the books and papers of Park, which were still in his possession. He flatly refused, however, to turn these documents over upon any other condition. For some reason, which does not plainly appear, Captain Clapperton decided not to continue his course along the river, in accordance with this request; but to defer the visit to Yauri until a subsequent journey. He received from the people of Boussa, however, the fullest accounts of Park's death; and

AN ARAB TRADER'S PARTY.

they explained the attack upon him and his companions by saying that they had been supposed to be a band of Fellatas come upon a predatory expedition. As the Fellatas are given to such raids upon their neighbors, this explanation is, if not wholly true, at least probable.

Reaching Kano without adventure worthy of special notice, he found the whole surrounding country in a condition of turmoil which augured ill for the further prosecution of his journey. There was not a quarter in which the merchants dare send a caravan. Accordingly, he left nearly all his baggage at Kano, and proceeded to Sakati without any other incumbrance than the gifts which were designed for his friend the sultan.

He found a different reception awaiting him, however, from that which he had so confidently expected. The untutored minds of the African princes could not understand why the king of England should go to the trouble and expense of sending missions, with gifts to the native princes, for the mere purpose of satisfying curiosity regarding the nature of the country and the character of its people. Their suspicions were aroused that all was not right; and the sultan of Bornou had written to the ruler of Sakati that it was by means of such wiles as these that the English had trampled on India; winning their way at first with gifts, and then maintaining their foothold with the sword. The writer therefore advised that Clapperton should be put to death at once.

But since this letter had been written and received, war had broken out between the two sultans. The chief of Sakati's suspicions against Clapperton were not allayed by his adviser having become his enemy; on the contrary, he was simply jealous of that adversary, and of the gifts that Clapperton might have for him. The Englishman had left six muskets at Kano, and it was presumed that these were intended as a present for the sultan of Bornou; as the sultan of Sakati had barely forty in his army, this number would be a valuable acquisition. It was therefore demanded that Clapperton should send for them, and present them to his host at Sakati; he declined; whereupon the governor induced Lander, by false pretenses, to bring his master's baggage on from Kano, and forcible possession was taken of the six precious guns. It was in vain that Clapperton remonstrated against this outrage and denounced it in terms which were hardly prudent, considering that he was wholly in the power of those who had committed it; the reply was that he might be glad he had lost his muskets, as long as he kept his head.

Nor was this all to which he had to submit. The sultan demanded that the letter which Clapperton bore to the sultan of Bornou should be shown to him; Clapperton of course refused; when the letter was forcibly seized.

The leader of the expedition, as we have seen, had recovered from the disease which had killed his two followers at the very outset; but possibly the recovery was not so complete as he had hoped. At any rate, a subsequent exposure had again affected him; and this anxiety and chagrin concerning the result of his mission so worked upon his mind that he was completely prostrated. No longer a favorite at the court, as he had been on the occasion of his former visit, those who had made loud professions of friendship now deserted him entirely; and he was left alone with his one countryman, the faithful Lander. He sank gradually; and after expressions of fullest confidence in his tried companion, gave him instructions as to the disposition of his property, and died.

Softened by the death of the man whom he had so ill-used, and flushed with victory over his enemies, the sultan allowed Lander to bury his master with every mark of respect; and supplied him with the means of returning home. The chief advised him to return by way of the desert; but Lander appears to have had enough of the Arabs, and preferred to retrace his steps through the negro countries.

There seems to have been something more than a hatred of the Arabs at the back of this determination. Lander had evidently caught his master's spirit; and with a resolution scarcely to be expected, in this connection, from a man occupying such a station, he decided that he would settle the vexed question of the course of the Niger. It should be remembered that even as late as 1825-6, the civilized world was in doubt upon many points of African geography; the assertion, indeed, might be made of a period sixty years later; but at the time indicated, geographers had two theories regarding the Niger. Its general course, they knew, was toward the southeast as far as the town of Fandah; but whether thence it flowed south to the Gulf of Guinea or east toward the interior and thence into the Congo, they were not sure. This was the problem which Lander proposed to solve.

His journey was not marred by special adventure until he had reached Dunrora, which, he was told, was due east of Fandah. He promised himself that in ten or twelve days at the farthest he should have reached the solution of this great problem,

But while he was thus on the very brink of discovery, he was withheld from it. Four horsemen overtook him, and delivered to him the positive command of the King of Zeg-zeg that he should return with them to Zaria. He resisted their persuasions as long as he could; but they informed him that if they returned without him they should lose their heads; he accordingly yielded. The King of Zeg-zeg took great credit to himself for having saved Lander's life; for, he said, war had broken out between the sultan of Sakati and the people of Fandah, so that any one known to have visited and bestowed gifts upon the former would be in great danger from the more southern nation. Whether this were so or not, Lander was not permitted to follow the route which he had chosen; but returned along the same road by which he and his master had come.

In all the places through which he passed, anxious inquiries were made about "his father," as the people called Clapperton; and the answer was received with genuine regret. He reached Badagry November 21, 1827; and after many delays landed in England in the following April.

Were we to follow chronological order strictly, it would be necessary here to turn aside from the record of explorations made by Englishmen, and consider those made by men of other nations. But the travels of the Landers are so closely connected with those of Captain Clapperton, and their discoveries so nearly a following out of his intentions, that we have thought it best to continue the narrative of the faithful follower's adventures.

After his return to England, Richard Lander submitted to the British government his plan for the exploration of the Niger; it was approved; and he, together with his younger brother, John, was commissioned to set out from Badagry, and explore the country as thoroughly as possible between that and Lake Tchad.

With this end in view, they embarked at Portsmouth, January 9, 1830; and arrived at Cape Coast Castle February 22, "having had a quick but boisterous and unpleasant passage of forty-two days." It was nearly a month after that date before they reached Badagry, being delayed at various points along the coast.

On the twenty-second of March, they set out upon their lonely journey into the country removed from all traces of civilization. The two Landers were the only white men of the party; they were fortunate enough to secure the services of

Pascoe, the native who had accompanied Captain Clapperton and accepted a wife at the hands of the enamored widow; he was now married to another woman, whose possession did not entail any evils upon his employer. Besides this man, they had four other natives, two of whom were qualified to serve as interpreters.

They did not feel much encouraged by the reception accorded them by the king of Badagry. His whole manner was so cold and silent that they could only augur his unwillingness to assist them on their mission, until they learned that his army had recently suffered a severe defeat, and his best generals been captured and put to death. The chief himself was just recovering from a severe illness; and to add to other misfortunes, the building which had contained his stock of gunpowder had taken fire by accident, and been totally destroyed in the explosion which ensued. Thus re-assured as to the reason of the chief's seeming indifference, the travelers took heart.

They were extremely anxious to leave Badagry as soon as possible, for they foresaw that the rainy season would put a stop to their travels for several months. In addition to this reason, it soon became plain to them that if they remained long at Badagry, their stock of presents would be quite exhausted. But the king was by no means ready to see them depart. In anxious care to ensure their safety, he had sent messengers to Jenna, whither they proposed to go, to see that the road was quite safe, and to let the governor of Jenna know that he was to expect them. The messengers returned at last, but before the Englishmen were notified of the fact, they were sent back on some other errand; and the strangers must again await their return.

When they had been at Badagry for some time, the chief expressed a desire to examine the presents which they were taking to the princes in the interior. They accordingly invited him to their quarters for that purpose. His mode of examination was this: he would look on languidly while the Landers unpacked their stores and displayed the various articles; if anything particularly pleased him, he would take it in his hand for a closer examination; and would hand it, not back to the travelers, but to one of his attendants. Nor was this all. Finding that they lacked many things which he desired, he caused them to write down a list of things which the king of England was to send him, including four coats for himself, exactly like those worn by his majesty of the British empire, and forty of a plainer style for his captains; fifty muskets, twenty barrels of gunpowder, and a few other small notions. This list he said he would send to Accra by one of his head men, who would wait there until the articles should be ready for him. It was the opinion of the Landers, writing some time later, that the messenger must have waited there for some time.

Satisfied by the possession of this list, the king agreed to furnish them with one horse, and sold them another. He also agreed to have a canoe in readiness to transport them up the river for some distance. At last, they escaped from Badagry, and late at night on the last day of March, having been delayed some hours waiting for the promised canoe, they embarked.

They proceeded on foot, having hired twenty natives to carry their baggage; the horses were to follow them, in care of messengers of the king's. But on the fourth day after setting out, two men arrived from Badagry with the intelligence that the horses had proved unmanageable, in the canoes, having kicked out the bottom of one and upset another. The king had therefore, much to his regret, been unable to forward them as he had promised. History does not record how sincere was his regret that his messengers forgot to take with them the money that had been paid him for one of the horses, and the two saddles with which the travelers had taken care to provide themselves.

Their journey was not impeded by any open hostility of the natives, although in their published journal they frequently complain of the evasions of the chiefs when assistance was requested, and the wholly unnecessary delays to which they were subjected. Remembering the cordial reception which had been given Captain Clapperton, and the friendly concern of the various chiefs when he himself returned alone after his master's death, the elder Lander had reckoned upon the same feeling being showed toward himself and his brother. But unfortunately for them, no less than one hundred and sixty governors of towns and villages between the starting point on the coast and the Kong Mountains had died from natural causes or been slain in war since the former expedition. The new rulers were either but slightly acquainted with their duties, or not sure that their actions would meet with the approval of the superior, the king of Yarriba, resident at Katunga.

There arose another occasion of delay. The Landers were affected by the climate to such an extent that their health

AFRICAN SUPERSTITION—FETISHMEN AND THEIR RITES.

suffered severely. Fortunately, they were not both prostrated at once; so that neither was without careful and affectionate attendance.

Shortly before the middle of May, they arrived at Katunga; having journeyed, first, by canoe up the river a short distance from Badagry; then on foot overland; then by means of horses or canoes whenever such were obtainable; but by far the larger part of the journey had been made on foot. Well received by the monarch of Katunga, they were assigned to the same hut which had been occupied by Captain Clapperton.

The Moussa River divides the kingdom of Yarriba from that of Bornou. A day or so after the arrival of the travelers at Katunga, a messenger brought news that the Fellatas had arrived at this river, and had attacked a town upon its banks. As their route lay through this very town, it was necessary that they should delay their journey until a messenger who was to be sent to Yauri could learn if his mission would be safe. He would then proceed to Yauri by way of Kiama. It seemed a little suspicious to the travelers that this event should have taken place exactly at this time, and at such a place as to affect the safety of their progress; but they wisely kept their suspicions to themselves, since the expression of them could do no good, and would only offend the savage chief upon whose good humor they were dependent.

Their delay might have been less irksome to men so desirous of discovering important facts, if they had been permitted to make inquiries; but the Yarribans evidently do not encourage curiosity; the questions which the travelers put regarding the nature of the country, distances, the customs of the people, and all other circumstances, received replies which were either contradictory or obviously false, or else the inquirers were were told plainly to ask no questions. Added to this, they found that their interpreters had such an imperfect knowledge of both languages that their versions of what was said could not be relied upon in all cases; so that they decided that they could believe only what they saw. Annoying as these failures to obtain information must have been to them, these circumstances have vastly increased the value of the record found in their joint journal.

The travelers found that the people of Kiama, a town which they reached toward the latter part of May, were professedly Mohammedans, although, like the other inhabitants of this part of Africa, they were extremely superstitious, trusting much to fetishes. This condition of religious belief is true of many other towns, but in none had they found it more strongly marked than in Kiama.

No event of importance marked their journey until the middle of June, when they came within sight of the city of Boussa, which they found situated on the mainland, instead of on an island, as it had been described by Captain Clapperton; and descried in the distance the faint outlines of two hills, at the foot of which, their guide informed them, lay the town of Yauri. Before them rolled the Niger, the first goal of their journey.

But the appearance of the famous stream was far from fulfilling their expectations. At this point, says the elder Lander, the Niger, "in its widest part, is not more than a stone's throw across at present. The rock upon which we sat overlooks the spot where Mr. Park and his associates met their unhappy fate; we could not help meditating on that circumstance, and on the number of valuable lives that have been sacrificed in attempting to explore this river."

The travelers were a little doubtful as to the wisdom of stating their errand openly, and at first merely gave out that they were traveling to Bornou by way of Boussa. Finding that the king was well disposed toward them, however, they sent a message by their interpreter, saying that if any books or papers belonging to Mr. Park were in the king's possession, he would do the travelers a great service by delivering such into their hands, or at least permitting them to examine the documents. To this the king replied that he was a very little boy when Mr. Park and his companions had been lost in the Niger, and he knew not what had become of his effects; all traces of the white men had been lost at the death of the late king.

This was a damper upon their hopes, until their host informed them that a first application of any kind was not favorably considered; that if they expected any attention to be paid to it, they must renew it. He further assured them that he knew one book of Mr. Park's had been preserved.

The request was accordingly renewed; and after some little demur, the king undertook to find the man who had the book. The following afternoon his majesty again paid the travelers a visit, followed by a man who carried under his arm a parcel wrapped in a cotton cloth, evidently a book. Here was the volume, then, of the earlier explorer's journal; it is hard to say which had the rosier anticipations, the Europeans who expected to secure such a prize to science, or the African who looked for a great reward from the English king. Unfortunately for the hopes of both, the treasured volume proved to be only a set of logarithmic tables, from the pages of which a few loose papers, such as an English invitation to dinner and a tailor's bill, fluttered as they opened the book.

Late in June, after a somewhat dangerous passage up the Niger, they arrived at Yauri. Here they found the people somewhat more communicative than they had been at Boussa; and obtained considerable information regarding the visit of Mr. Park to this country. His gun and cutlass were still preserved, and Lander found no difficulty in exchanging his own fowling-piece for the former.

The sultan of Yauri had assured Captain Clapperton, in a letter, that he had possession of Mr. Park's papers; and the Landers now endeavored to obtain them; but after some days' delay, it became evident that he had nothing of the kind. They were therefore most anxious to proceed on their journey.

It would be useless, however, for them to ascend the Niger any farther, having no means of conciliating the chiefs in whose territories they might be obliged to travel. It will be remembered that they had allowed the rapacity of the chief of Badagry to denude them of the bulk of their stores; their only hope now was in reaching salt water, and returning home for a fresh supply. Meanwhile, the metal buttons on their clothes afforded them the means of buying the articles of which they stood in actual need.

Their stay at Yauri was prolonged by the caprice of the sultan, but it was not until they had had some communication with the king of Boussa that they suspected they were actually prisoners. By the interference of their late host, however, they were enabled to leave the town sooner than would otherwise have been the case. He provided them with a canoe in which to descend the river; for recent wars had made the overland route unsafe; and they were desirous of avoiding Badagry.

It was about the first of August when they left. The land along the river-bank was largely planted in corn, which was now almost ripe. The living scarecrows afforded much amusement to the Englishmen. Upon a platform ten or twelve feet high, a man, woman or child would be stationed to frighten away the small birds which often damage the crop very much. Sometimes a line would be attached to neighboring trees, having calabashes filled with stones strung upon it; the watcher by rattling these would be enabled more effectually to perform his duty.

It would be supposed that the Africans themselves would possess some definite idea regarding the course of this great river; but when the travelers had arrived at a point a few miles below Boussa, they were not a little concerned to find that it was here believed by some persons that the river took a turn to the eastward, and emptied into Lake Tchad.

Arrived at Boussa, they found the king by no means disposed to favor their journey thence; he told them gravely that he would have to consult the Black Water (the Niger) to see if it were safe for them to proceed further. They presented him with a silver medal and chain, and informed him that it was a token of the special friendship of the king of England; the savage chief was much delighted, and told them later that his interview with the river had been the means of securing a promise from the stream that it would conduct them in safety to its termination.

Yet the time for their departure had not yet come. They were obliged to pay a visit to a neighboring chief, whose assistance had enabled them to reach Boussa on their journey northward; and after their return to Boussa he detained them on one pretext or another until it was evident that they were very nearly destitute; then at last they were permitted to depart.

They wished to stop at as few towns as possible in their descent of the river; both because they would thus save time, and because they had not the means of conciliating the chiefs. They therefore provided themselves with as much food as their means would allow; enough, according to their calculation, to last for three weeks or a month; and on the twentieth of September embarked upon their voyage.

Their journey was without special adventure until they reached the village and market of Kirree. Here they met with a fleet of about fifty canoes, ascending the river. To the joyful astonishment of the travelers, the British Union Jack was seen floating above the heads of the new-comers, most of whom were clad in garments of European cut. But all their fond anticipations vanished as they saw that the men in the canoes were all natives. The leader, who was in the first boat, beckoned to the elder Lander to approach; to resist was hopeless; the canoes held each about forty men, all of whom appeared to be well armed; their own square-built vessel was incapable of speed. Under such circumstances, Lander determined to sell his life as dearly as possible, and encouraged his followers to do the same.

CROSSING A RIVER IN THE WILDS OF AFRICA.

The assailants were evidently bent upon robbery, and relieved the Landers' boat of her entire cargo while the crew were defending themselves. Having accomplished this, they departed, leaving the little party to lament the loss of their goods.

This was not all they did, however; large as the attacking party was, they gave chase; hoping to overtake the boat in which the booty was placed, and compel its return. In the mean time, the younger Lander, who had gone on ahead in another canoe with a part of the attendants, had discovered his brother's plight and come to his rescue.

Such was the eagerness of the robbers to share the plunder, that many of the war-canoes clashed against one another, and three or four were upset. The boat of the younger Lander was also upset, and he was unable to reach his brother's vessel; nor could the elder afford him any assistance. Theirs was now a desperate strait. They were in reality prisoners in the hands of this war-party; and were hurried on board one of the war-canoes and taken to a neighboring island.

Here, while the prisoners were kept in the canoe, a palaver or council of war was held. They were not without hope; for they were visited by a person in a Mohammedan dress, who assured them that they were not without friends; that all the Mohammedans who had come to attend the market were favorably disposed toward them; and that a large party about to arrive would take the part of the strangers.

Summoned to the market-place after some hours of suspense, they were requested to examine the booty, and say if it embraced all of their property. It was far from being complete; the most serious losses being their guns, including that which had belonged to Park, most of the journal of the elder Lander, together with their stock of buttons and needles, on which they had relied as the means of purchasing supplies. The box containing their books, including one journal, their medicine chest, and a carpet-bag containing a little clothing, comprised all that lay before them; the remainder of their property, they were told, had been sunk in the Niger.

While the palaver was thus proceeding, it was suddenly interrupted by wild cries; a number of the savages who had manned the war-canoes made a dash to recover this spoil which had been taken from them. The effort proved unsuccessful, however; the sally was repulsed, and the council proceeded with its deliberations.

These lasted all day. Late in the afternoon, the decision

was rendered. It was to this effect: the Landers were to have what things had been taken from the water restored to them; and the person who had first commenced an attack upon John Lander was to lose his head, for having acted without his chief's permission. The travelers, however, were to be considered as prisoners, and were to be conducted to Obie, king of the Eboes (the tribe which had attacked them) that he might decide what should be done with them.

The journey to the Eboe country occupied about three days; during this time our travelers might have observed the river more attentively if their captors had not decided that the heavy fog which arose at times was due to the fact that the river, which had never seen a white man before, was offended at the sight; so that the two Englishmen were obliged to lie down in the canoe, and suffer themselves to be covered with mats.

Reaching the town of the Eboes, before they were received by the king, they learned from a native who boarded their vessel, and who was a man of some consequence, being no other than Gun, the son of king Forday, who, with king Jacket, governed all the Brass country, that besides a Spanish schooner, an English vessel, named the Thomas, of Liverpool, was lying in the "first Brass River."

They were received with some distinction by the king, who took several days to make up his mind as to what should be done with them. He finally announced that according to the laws of war, their persons and property belonged to him; and that he had decided to hold them for ransom, the price of the party, consisting of the two Englishmen and their attendants, being fixed at the equivalent of twenty slaves. This determination, he said, he would communicate to the white men whose vessel lay near the mouth of the river; and the captives must possess their souls in patience as best they might. It was in vain that they remonstrated with him, trying to persuade him to send them forward, that their countrymen might be assured of their safety before paying the ransom; but his mind was made up.

After considerable argument, however, extending over a space of two or three days, King Boy, the brother of their first acquaintance, Gun, made the following offer: If they would give him an order on the captain of the vessel lying near the mouth of the river for thirty-five barv, or the value of as many slaves, and also for a cask of rum, he would undertake to transport them to the sea coast, and would pay the ransom demanded out of this sum.

It is needless to say that this offer was eagerly accepted, and that the required order was immediately written out. Embarking at once, the party of about sixty men set out on their passage to the mouth of the Niger.

They made the journey in a single canoe, hollowed from the trunk of a tree; the vessel being about fifty feet long, wide enough for three men to sit abreast, and drawing something over four feet. The canoe was adorned with a number of flags, of which the peoples near the coast have a plentiful supply.

They left the Eboe country November 11; late on the evening of the 14th, the travelers, to their great joy, observed that the river was influenced by the tide; they were surely nearing the sea. The next day, after traveling all night, they arrived at king Forday's town, where they met with the master of the Spanish vessel which has been mentioned; and where their arrival was made the occasion of ceremonies intended to be imposing, of the meaning of which they had not the least idea. They were finally told that Richard Lander was to be taken to the coast, while his brother and the attendants were detained as hostages.

Lander set out with high hopes; the only circumstance which dampened his ardor was that his brother must remain behind; but this was but for a few days at the most; and anything else was plainly impossible. They left king Forday's town on the 17th, and on the next day saw two vessels lying at anchor at the mouth of the river.

One of these was the Spaniard, whose master they had seen at Brass Town; the other was the ship of their own countrymen. They first visited the former, but found small cheer; the crew were all sick, and scarcely able to move; six had died during the six weeks that they had been there. Lander bade his new acquaintance adieu, and returned to the canoe, which now directed its course toward the English brig.

He found this in even a worse condition than the Spanish vessel; only four of the crew remained, and these were lying sick in their hammocks, while the captain seemed to be in the last stages of disease. To him Lander stated his case, and displayed his instructions, assuring him that the amount paid for the ransom of himself and his brother with their attendants would most certainly be repaid by the British government. To his surprise and dismay, the captain utterly refused to take any such risk.

Lander was now indeed in a dreadful position; his last hope

had failed him, and he knew not which way to turn. He appealed to King Boy to take him to Bonny, where there were other English ships; but the savage retorted:

"No, no; this captain won't pay, Bonny captain no pay; I won't take you any further."

A second appeal to the captain produced a response that if he could get his brother and their eight people on board, they should be taken away; further than this, the officer would not go. But the news that the attendants were, two of them seamen with more or less experience, and three others who might be of service to him, he relented somewhat, and even gave Lander a piece of beef and some rum to send to his brother by King Boy, who was very discontentedly setting out on his journey back for the remainder of the party.

The captain had no notion of giving any ransom for the captives; but expressed his determination to get the party on board and then set sail. Lander was much worried for fear that the party would not arrive in time; for Captain Lake swore that if they were not there by the twenty-third he would sail without them. Fortunately for the explorers (for the party did not arrive until late at the night on the day set) his mate had been captured and was held by the pilot as security for pilotage which Lake refused to pay; and the brig was obliged to wait a day longer, until he managed to escape.

John Lander and the attendants arrived, and were received on board. King Boy made many appeals for his money, but was answered with oaths and abuse. Finally, the arms of the vessel were made ready, and thus warned, the savage desisted from his just demand.

Owing partly to the unfavorable winds, and partly to the lack of pilotage, the vessel was four days in trying to pass the bar at the mouth of the river. Finally, November 28, 1831, she passed it, and the travelers sailed slowly away from the mouth of the Niger toward Fernando Po, whence they went to Rio Janeiro, and thence to England, landing in their native country June 10.

The Landers accomplished the exploration of the Niger from the point where Park's death had taken place to its mouth, thus determining that its course was not eastward to the Nile or Lake Tchad, or southeasterly toward the Congo. The great river between the desert and the Gulf of Guinea, it was now certain, was the same as that at the mouths of which British vessels had long been trading.

CHAPTER VI.

ADVENTURES OF DR. BARTH AND COMPANIONS.

THE discoveries made by the Landers awakened no small enthusiasm among a certain class of Englishmen; and soon after the brothers arrived in their own country an association was formed, having for its purpose the establishment of a settlement on the upper waters of the Niger. The expedition, however, proved a failure; many of those who set out died from the effects of the unhealthy climate, or from wounds receved in contests with the natives. The project was abandoned; and for fifteen years no further movement toward the exploration of Africa was made by the British government.

In 1849, it was decided to send out another expedition, under the leadership of Mr. James Richardson. A German scientist was to be invited to accompany him, providing that the German would contribute two hundred pounds toward traveling expenses. The offer was accepted by Dr. Heinrich Barth, who was then lecturing at the University of Berlin upon comparative geography. Family reasons induced him to seek a substitute in Dr. Overweg; but his offer had already been accepted by the British government; and the result was that both accompanied Mr. Richardson.

While Mr. Richardson was the leader appointed for the expedition, Dr. Barth has always been much more prominently known in connection with it; being the only one of the three who returned in safety.

There were many delays attending their departure from the regions of civilization; so that, although Barth and Overweg arrived in Africa before the close of 1849, the party did not set out from Tripoli until March 24, 1850. Their journey to Mourzouk occupied a little more than a month; and it was the thirteenth of June when they set out from the capital of Fezzan.

Acting by the advice of the British consul at Mourzouk, they had pursued a plan of which they were soon to see the evil. Mohammed Boro, a man of considerable importance in Negroland, having a house and numerous connections in Sakati, as well as in other places, had been solicited to protect the travelers. He was on his way back from a pilgrimage to Mecca, and was, of course, numerously attended.

Dr. Heinrich Barth.

This man had been recommended to them by the former governor of Fezzan, Hassan Pasha; but for some reason the consul distrusted and underrated him. The adventurers therefore engaged the services of certain representatives of the chiefs of Ghat; or rather, negotiated for these services. The knowledge that this had been done greatly enraged Mohammed Boro, who swore that the travelers should not be safe from his people while crossing the desert.

The first adventure with which any of them met, befell Dr. Barth. Riding aside from the main road to visit a mountain which loomed in the distance, the distance proved to be greater than he had anticipated. He was but scantily provided with water; and the food which he carried was simply dry biscuit and dates.

Reaching the elevation at last, he found nothing to repay him for his trouble. A dry, narrow, pinnacled crest, there was neither inscription nor sculpture to be found; nor could he, from the summit, see any traces of the caravan to which his little party belonged.

Fatigues which elsewhere would be but trifles for a strong man, are upon the desert no slight things. Lacking water and food (for the dry bread was hardly eatable without water to wash it down), he was soon completely exhausted by the heat. Anxious lest his party, thinking he was in the advance, should have pushed on, he made desperate efforts to reach the encampment. But his endeavors were vain; and it was not until after a night spent alone in the desert that he was found by an Arab of the caravan, who had tracked him by his footsteps in the sand.

This occurred in the course of their journey to Ghat; up to this point, however, they were on comparatively well known ground; if the details of the road were strange, the cities which formed the several destinations were known to them and to their countrymen; but now, they were to set out into what was indeed a strange country.

The caravan was not pervaded by that unity which is to be desired in a small party traveling through a dangerous country. In addition to the trouble which always exists between Christians and Moslem, Boro Mohammed was a companion to be dreaded; and just as they arrived at Mararraba, his anger began to show itself. Still there was no open attack; and even though the caravan was followed by a party of freebooters, there was no conflict until after the travelers had passed the northern boundary of the oasis of Air.

Before actually beginning hostilities, however, the freebooters sent embassadors to say that they would retire without molesting the caravan, if the Christians accompanying it were given up to them. This modest demand being refused, they retired for further consultation; while the people of the caravan took counsel as to the probable result of this.

They found, the next morning, that, in spite of their guards, all their camels had been stolen in the night. Hardly had this discovery been made, when an emissary of the freebooters invited the principal men of the caravan to a council.

The first demand which was made was that the "infidels" should be put to death; but this their Mohammedan companions would not assent to. Failing to secure this concession, the highwaymen invited them to return by the same way that they had come. This proposition being declined, they demanded that the Christians should become Mohammedans. The Moslem of the caravan would not mention this to their companions. Finally, the assailants suggested that the caravan should be allowed to pass unmolested, if half the goods and baggage of the travelers were given up. This was getting down to business, and a compromise was finally effected by which goods to the amount of about fifty pounds sterling were given up to them. At last the leader professed himself satisfied, and volunteered his protection for the future. Of course Boro Mohammed could have prevented this robbery if he had been inclined to do so.

Nor was this the only instance of such robbery during this part of their journey. Mr. Richardson estimated that the journey from Tajetterat to Tin-Tillust, a distance of about three hundred miles, had cost the government two hundred and fifty pounds sterling.

Arrived at this point, they received unmistakable statements regarding the intentions of the chief, Annur. If they wished to proceed with the caravan to Soudan, he would place no obstacle in their way; but if they wished his protection, they must pay liberally for it. The sum which he fixed seemed to Mr. Richardson very excessive; but Dr. Barth thought it better to pay it at once than to be plundered *ad libitum*, as they had been.

Annur stuck to his agreement, however; a rare virtue with his kind. He treated them with little consideration until Dr. Barth began to prepare for a visit to the sultan of Agades, when he became more attentive. This town, once as large as Tunis, is really of equal importance with Timbuctoo, that city so long sought by Europeans; but by some strange chance has not attracted any such attention as its neighbor.

The journey was attended by no incident of importance, although it required several days; and the traveler was graciously received by the sultan. The festivities which he attended, however, were scarcely a source of unmixed enjoyment; going to see a national dance, he was pursued to his quarters by armed natives, having a narrow escape from death.

CARAVAN APPROACHING A CITY IN THE VAST DESERT OF SAHARA.

The reigning sultan had just acceded to the throne; and Barth therefore had the advantage of witnessing the grand ceremonies of installation. The new chief proposed to signalize his accession by a warlike expedition; but before setting out upon it, furnished the traveler with letters to the governors of Kano, Katsena, and Daura. Dr. Barth remained in the town for a few days after the departure of the expedition, studying the place and its people, and putting his memoranda into shape. Leaving Agades the last of October, he found, upon returning to the village of the chief Annur, that the whole population had disappeared; what had become of the more helpless members of the community, he does not say; but the chief had led a great salt caravan to Kano, and the explorers had, of course, accompanied him.

There was nothing to be done, of course, but to press on toward Kano. "*Se fatauchi se Kano!*" ("No rest before Kano!") had been the cry raised when they found that their journey must perforce be continued, without even a night's rest; but having overtaken the caravan, they found themselves obliged to submit to a delay of more than a month before the chief announced that he was ready to proceed.

Taking up the line of march the middle of December, it was almost a month before the journey was marked by any incident which can be noticed in this brief account. At Tagalel, the three travelers separated, since traveling alone had now become possible, and the exhausted state of their finances made it necessary for them to try what each could accomplish, single-handed and without ostentation, until new supplies should arrive from home.

Mr. Richardson went on the road to Zinder, while Dr. Barth and Dr. Overweg, for the time, continued their journey with the caravan. After a few days, however, the two Germans separated from each other, Dr. Overweg proposing to proceed to Tasawa, as the starting point for an expedition to Gober and Maradi.

Reaching Katsena, and presenting to the governor of that place such a scanty present as his means would allow, Dr. Barth was somewhat surprised to learn that his companion's having gone to Maradi provoked no unkindly feeling, although the two governors were bitter enemies; but was by no means re-assured when the chief remarked that since one of his companions was in the hands of the governor of Maradi, and the other in those of the ruler of Bornou, he, the governor of Katsena, would be a fool to allow Dr. Barth to escape.

By dint of patience, however, the traveler at last conciliated this formidable enemy; and was allowed to depart from Katsena after having been detained there for a couple of weeks. A journey of three days, and at last they arrived at Kano. But here some extracts from Dr. Barth's journals will prove more graphic than any condensation can possibly be:

"Kano had been sounding in my ears now for more than a year; it had been one of the great objects of our journey as the central point of commerce, as a great storehouse of information, and as the point whence more distant regions might be most successfully attempted. At length, after nearly a year's exertions, I had reached it.

"Kano was for us a station of importance, not only from a scientific, but also from an economical point of view. Instead of being provided with ready cash, we had received in Mourzouk, on account of the British government, merchandise, which, we were assured, would not only be safer than money, but would also prove far more advantageous to us. In consequence of the heavy extortion to which we were subjected on the road to Air, and of our long delay in that country, we had been deprived of the small articles which we carried for barter, so that we were entirely thrown upon the merchandise which we had forwarded in advance from Tinteggana. * * * For all these reasons, nothing could be more disagreeable and disheartening to me, though I was not quite unprepared for it, than the information which I received the very evening of my arrival in Kano, that the price of merchandise such as I had was very low. * * Our commissioner, * * * * although he had two camel-loads of goods of mine in his hands, yet left me without a single shell, "*ko uri guda*" for a whole fortnight, so that I was glad to borrow two thousand kurdi, less than an Austrian dollar, from Mohammed e' Sfaksi, in order to defray the most necessary expenses of my household. Besides, this agent urged the absolute necessity of making a considerable present not only to the governor, which I was quite prepared to do, but another of nearly the same value to the galadima or first minister, who happened to be the governor's brother, and enjoyed quite as much authority and influence. The consequence was, that I was obliged to give away the few articles of value in my possession merely for being tolerated and protected. * * * * * Being lodged in dark, uncomfortable and cheerless quarters, which I was forbidden to leave before the governor had seen me, destitute of a single farthing in cash, while I was daily called upon and pestered by my numerous creditors, and laughed at on account of my poverty by an insolent servant, my readers may fancy that my situation in the great, far-famed entrepot of Central Africa, the name of which had excited my imagination for so long a time, was far from agreeable. Partly from anxiety, partly from want of exercise, in the course of a few days I had a very severe attack of fever, which reduced me to a state of great weakness. Fortunately, however, I mustered sufficient strength to avail myself of a summons which called me into the presence of the governor, on the 18th of February; and by sacrificing what few things remained to me, I paved the way for my further proceedings, while the degree of exertion which was necessary to undergo the fatigue of my visit carried me over my weakness, and restored me gradually to health."

Leaving Kano, Dr. Barth's course was first to the south-east, then to the north-east, to Kuka, on the shores of Lake Tchad, where a rendezvous with Mr. Richardson had been arranged. His journey was prosecuted without especial adventure until the 23rd of March, when, as he rode along, he was met and accosted by a strange-looking person of very fair complexion, richly dressed and armed, and accompanied by three men on horseback, likewise armed and with musket and pistols. The new-comer inquired if he were the Christian who was to arrive from Kano, and being answered in the affirmative, told him that Mr. Richardson had died before reaching Kuka, and that all his property had been seized. Dr. Barth was at first inclined to doubt this intelligence, but later investigations proved that it was true. The leader of the mission had died in the wilds of Africa.

The position of the two Germans was now somewhat critical. Sent out by the English government, or rather allowed to accompany Mr. Richardson, they must now be doubtful how far their demands upon that government, and their promises made in its name, would be honored. Nor could they, of course, expect instructions: shortly before learning of Mr. Richardson's death, Dr. Barth had received news from home, the first in ten months; and communication with the government would be both slow and uncertain.

Dr. Barth spent some time at Kuka, exploring the city, or, rather, the two cities which are known by this name, and the neighboring country, including somewhat of the shore of Lake Tchad. His efforts to communicate with the British governmen proved unexpectedly successful, and he was assured that he was fully authorized to carry out the expedition, and to ask for means. One chief object of the journey to Kuka was to negotiate a treaty for the protection of commerce; and this the Germans were also empowered to consider.

Dr. Overweg arrived at Kuka May 4, and the travelers left that city on the 29th of the same month. Before leaving, however, Dr. Barth addressed dispatches to the government which fully show that he was aware of the greatness of the discoveries which he was about to make; his letters display no inconsiderable knowledge of the geography of the country, gathered, not from investigations of others, but from patient questionings of the natives, and shrewd observations of his own.

His path led almost due south, from Kuka to the confluence of the Faro and the Benue. It had been supposed that the latter river, known along the lower portion of its course as the Chadda, was identical with the Shari, the principal tributary of Lake Tchad; perhaps the similarity of name between river and lake was the cause of the confusion. As above intimated, however, Barth was well assured, on setting out from Kuka, that there was no connection between the two streams.

On the morning of the 18th of June, his servant cried to him: "Look, look, that is Mount Alantika!"

Straining his eyes, he discerned far in the south the vague outlines of a large but insulated mountain mass. But here, as once before, we will let the traveler tell his own story:

"It happens but rarely that a traveler does not feel disappointed when he first actually beholds the principal features of a new country, of which his imagination has composed a picture from the description of the natives; but although I must admit that the shape and size of the Alantika, as it rose in rounded lines from the flat level, did not exactly correspond with the idea that I had formed of it, the appearance of the river far exceeded my expectations. None of my informants had promised me that I should just come upon it at that most interesting locality—the Tepe—where the mightier river is joined by another of very considerable size, and that in this place I was to cross it. As I looked from the bank over the scene before me, I was quite enchanted, although the whole country bore the character of a desolate wilderness; but there could scarcely be any traces of human industry near the river, as during its floods it inundates the whole country on both sides. This is the general character of all the great rivers in this region, except where they are encompassed by very steep banks.

"The principal river, the Benue, flowed here from east to west, in a broad and majestic course, through an entirely open country, from which only here and there detached mountains started forth. The banks on our side rose to twenty-five, and in some places to thirty feet, while just opposite to my station, behind a pointed headland of sand, the Faro rushed forth, appearing from this point not much inferior to the principal river, and coming in a fine sweep from the south-east, where it disappeared in the plain, but was traced in thought, by me, upward to the steep eastern foot of the Alantika. The river, below the junction, * * * was followed in thought * * * till it joined the great western river, the Kwara or Niger, and, conjointly with it, ran toward the great ocean."

Thus clearly had Barth mapped out in his mind's eye the course of the river which other geographers supposed to be identical with a tributary of Lake Tchad. It was his intention to verify this idea by descending the stream, but his reception at Yola was such that this became impossible. The sultan of that place commanded him to return to Kuka; and such was the determination displayed by the potentate, that the traveler had no other choice.

Meanwhile Dr. Overweg had not been inactive. He had traversed Lake Tchad in an English boat which, at immense cost of labor, they had brought across the desert; and had visited nearly all the islands which are dispersed over its surface. In order to explore the country to the northeast of Kuka, the two adventurers now joined an expedition organized by some Arabs, former inhabitants of Syrtis, the destination of which was Kanem. It seems to have been fully understood from the first that their new associates were freebooters; but the Europeans did not appear to have realized fully the lengths to which they were ready to go. On one occasion, Dr. Barth was asked to act as arbitrator in a dispute which had arisen; the persons pleading their cause before him were not given to euphemisms when the actions of the opponent were described; and the effort to arrive at a peaceable solution of the difficulty was ended when the chief of the expedition rushed angrily into the tent and swore that he would shoot any one who spoke of robbery or injustice.

Such pleasing little incidents of travel as the sight of a snake more than eighteen feet long, and nearly six inches in diameter, hanging from a tree across their path, apparently ready to seize upon the first prey that presented itself, need scarcely be noted. Whatever the white men thought about it, the natives regarded it as a God-send; for when it had been shot, they cut it open and took out the fat, which they pronounced excellent.

An African Beauty.

The rapid marches of the freebooters somewhat inconvenienced the explorers; and when it was found that nothing could really be accomplished while in their company, and that the men and camels were both worn out by the unceasing exertion, it was resolved that the discoverers should accompany a caravan back to Kuka.

The next expedition which they joined had at least an appearance of respect for law and order; being a military march to enforce the obedience of a rebellious sub-chief.

Their destination was Mandara, a small mountainous country a little east of south of Kuka; but although the ostensible reason was that above stated, the real purpose of the expedition was predatory and slave-hunting. Both Drs. Barth and Overweg felt that, as representatives of the British government, they ought not to be a party to a slave-hunting expedition; but they reasoned thus: Their absence would not affect the determination of their companions, while their presence might be the means of ameliorating some of the horrors attendant upon the "hunt;" it was their sole opportunity for visiting a part of the country which would be inaccessible to them alone; and they were therefore justified in joining the expedition.

They came within a day's journey of the capital of Mandara, when they were met by emissaries from the prince, with whom a compromise of some sort, the terms unknown to the strangers, was effected. The Bornou force then turned toward the country of the Musgu, where a full supply of slaves was likely to be obtained.

Their progress was not unopposed; and in one engagement the invaders lost nearly two hundred men. Finally, however, the prince of the country was subdued, and the army, with its booty of humanity, set out on its return march. Three thousand slaves had been captured, scarcely any full-grown men among them. The heart sickens at the record of children torn from their mothers' arms, that the booty might be divided among the soldiers.

Ten thousand head of cattle, captured from the enemy, still further attested the prowess of the army which re-entered Kuka on the first of February, 1852. Dr. Barth thus reviews the results of the expedition from his own point of view:

"Thus ended this expedition, which opened to us a slight glimpse into the richly watered zone of the equatorial regions, which had been supposed to form an insurmountable barrier of a high mountain chain, and brought us into contact with tribes whose character has been represented as almost approaching to that of wild beasts. We had certainly not entered those regions under such circumstances as were most desirable to us; but on the contrary we had been obliged to associate ourselves with an army whose only purpose was to spread devastation and misery over them. Nevertheless, situated as we were, while we could not prevent this mischief, we were glad that we had been enabled to see so much."

Dr. Barth's next expedition from Kuka was toward the south-east, to the country of the Bagirmi; but he was kept waiting more than a month on the banks of the Shari, before he was allowed to cross that stream. Even when once permitted to cross it, he was detained almost as a prisoner until the sultan should have returned from a military expedition upon which he had started just before Barth reached the Shari; a period of some three months longer.

While he was awaiting the pleasure of the sultan, after that dignitary's return to his capital, a messenger from Kuka brought him dispatches from England which fully confirmed him as leader of the expedition in Mr. Richardson's stead; formal action having been taken on the subject, and the information sent overland from Fezzan. He received many private letters at the same time, which spoke enthusiastically of the project which he had formed before setting out, of crossing the whole of the unknown region of equatorial Africa, and reaching the southeastern coast. This plan, formed while in good health, and before any considerable experience of travel among the savages of the tropics had been reached, he now saw clearly was not feasible for him; and turned with a sigh of relief to the recommendation contained in the official letters, that he should endeavor to reach Timbuctoo.

Finding it impossible to penetrate any farther toward the east than the banks of the Shari, Dr. Barth returned to Kuka. During his absence, Dr. Overweg had made a trip to the south-western part of Bornou, but had returned to the capital about two months before Barth did so. Far from showing that the considerable period of rest had benefited him physically, however he seemed to the experienced eyes of the elder physician "more weak and exhausted than I had ever seen him." From the time of Barth's return, indeed (August 20), until the same day of the following month, the descent was constant into the valley of the shadow of death; and on that day he died, on the shores of the lake which he had been the first white man to explore with any degree of thoroughness.

Thus left alone, Dr. Barth allowed himself no diminution of enthusiasm. The sultan of Bornou was finally persuaded to sign the commercial treaty which had before been proposed to him; and the explorer made his preparations to depart from Kuka. Detained a short time by the fact that the surrounding country was infested by bands of freebooters and insurgents, it was the latter part of November before, with a little party of eight servants, he set out for Timbuctoo.

It is now necessary that we should pass over the space of several months, occupied by an uneventful journey westward, through a country which he or his predecessors had before explored. It was the 19th of June when he first saw the Niger, reaching its banks at the point Say, where he remained for five days.

From this point his journey was mainly by land to Saraiyamo, a point on the Niger almost directly south of Timbuctoo. While their journey thither, as narrated by the explorer himself, is full of interest, the various incidents are in themselves so trivial, compared with those of other similar expeditions, that we have not room for more than the briefest summing up.

Finding that many of his difficulties arose from the fact that he was not a Mohammedan, he decided to assume the character of one for a time. This was not hard to do; for while the Arabs of the country were bitterly hostile to those professing other religions, they were by no means well informed regarding their own; nor would their manner of worship and their various practices have been consided at all orthodox in Mecca or Constantinople. The superstition of the pagan peoples hardly exceeded that of the followers of the Prophet; and on more than one occasion Dr. Barth was taken for a "rain-maker," and requested earnestly to exercise his powers in behalf of the parched country. Whenever possible, he evaded this request, but sometimes he was obliged to offer up a prayer. The following extract from this journal may give an idea of the character of the people with whom he had to deal:

"After a long conversation about the rainy season, the quantity of rain which falls in different countries, and the tropical regions especially, I felt myself obliged to say before them the "fat-ha," or opening prayer of the Koran; and to their great amusement and delight, concluded the Arabic prayer with a form in their own language—"*Alla hokki ndiam*"—which, although meaning originally, "God may give water," has become quite a complimentary phrase, so that the original meaning has been almost lost, few people being conscious of it. It so happened that the ensuing night a heavy thunderstorm gathered from the east, bringing a considerable quantity

HILL, CALLED "THE MONKEY PALACE," IN WESTERN SOUDAN.

of rain, which even found its way into my badly thatched hut. This apparent efficacy of my prayer induced the inhabitants to return the following day, to solicit from me a repetition of my performance; but I succeeded in evading their request by exhorting them to patience. But, on the other hand, I was obliged, in addition to a strong dose of emetic, to give the governor my blessing, as he was going to the capital, and was rather afraid of his liege lord the young prince Ahmedu, while at the same time his overbearing neighbors, the Tawarek [Tuaricks] inspired him with a good deal of fear. In the sequel, he was very well received at the capital, and therefore could not complain of the inefficacy of my inspiration; but nevertheless, not having had the slightest suspicion that I was not what I had represented myself to be, he was much shocked when he afterwards learned that I was a Christian, to the great amusement of the Sheik el Bakay, who wrote to him repeatedly to the effect that he ought to be well pleased that so wicked a person as a Christian had procured him not only rain, but even a good reception from his superior."

From Saraiyamo to Kabra there is a water-course, filled mainly by back-water from the Niger; and up this the little party journeyed in a boat which they were fortunate enough to secure for the purpose. The voyage began September 5, 1853. Of course the exact dates in this connection are only important to the reader as showing the time that had been required for the accomplishment of the purpose. It was now almost four years since the traveler had left his own country.

The following day they arrived at Kabara, and set out thence to Timbuctoo, of which Kabara is the harbor. It had been disclosed to the authorities at the river-town that the traveler was a Christian, but they looked more kindly upon him because he claimed to be traveling under the protection of the great sultan of Stamboul (Constantinople). Unfortunately, however, he had no direct letter from that sovereign's representatives; one with which he had been provided having been previously delivered, and no other having been sent in answer to his repeated solicitations. He attributes all his troubles in Timbuctoo to the lack of such protection.

Of these troubles we can scarcely give a detailed description. For a time, the hostility of the inhabitants kept him a close prisoner in his hut, and this threw him into a fever. Finally, his presence in the town aroused so much discussion among the authorities, that he decided to leave, and took advantage of an expedition led by his friend the Sheik el Bakay toward the east to reach once more the country with which he was better acquainted.

For about six weeks, beginning with the middle of March, this journey eastward was continued; but at a very slow rate, sometimes not more than three miles a day being covered; and the explorer was of course wholly dependent upon the will of his escort. Finally, rumors reached them that the French had made a successful expedition farther into the interior than they had yet penetrated; and the sheik, afraid to venture farther, decided to return. There was no choice for Barth in the matter; for whatever might be the dangers and difficulties attending a residence in Timbuctoo, it was impossible for him, alone, to continue the eastward journey. The whole country was aroused by fear of the French; and the knowledge that Barth was a European caused him to be greatly feared and hated by these ignorant barbarians, who were not able to distinguish between French, German and English, or between a scientific explorer and a military spy.

The return journey was, as may be supposed, much more expeditious than the first; and a welcome surprise awaited the traveler at the gates of Timbuctoo: letters from England had arrived during his absence, which changed the whole behavior of the people. He at once, escorted again by his friend the sheik, retraced his steps eastward, reaching home by the same route as that by which he had come, or via Kuka, Mourzouk, and Tripoli. He arrived in London exactly a year from the day that he first saw Kabara.

His own summing up of what was accomplished is of greater interest than any outside view; although it may be remarked that his explorations north of the equator have been compared, not unfavorably, with those of Dr. Livingstone south of the same line.

"Thus I closed my long and exhausting career as an African explorer, of which this narrative endeavors to incorporate the result. Having previously gained a good deal of experience of African traveling during an extensive journey through Barbary, I had embarked on this undertaking as a volunteer, under the most unfavorable circumstances for myself. The scale and the means of the mission seemed to be extremely limited, and it was only in consequence of the success which accompanied our proceedings that a wider extent was given to the range and objects of the expedition; and after its original leader had succumbed in his arduous task, instead of giving way to despair, I had continued in my career amid great embarrassment, carrying on the exploration of extensive regions almost without any means. * * * * In this enterprise [of reaching Timbuctoo] I succeeded to my utmost expectation, and not only made known the whole of that vast region, which even to the Arab merchants in general had remained more unknown than any other part of Africa, but I succeeded also in establishing friendly relations with all the most powerful chiefs along the river up to that mysterious city itself. * * * * No doubt, even in the track which I myself pursued, I have left a good deal for my successors in this career to improve upon; but I have the satisfaction to feel that I have opened to the view of the scientific public of Europe a most extensive tract of the secluded African world, and not only made it tolerably known, but rendered the opening of a regular intercourse between Europe and those regions possible."

CHAPTER VII.

EARLY EXPLORATIONS IN SOUTH AFRICA; ANDERSSON AND MAGYAR.

IT is our intention to pass by, for the present, the first journeys of Dr. Livingstone; although it is necessary to sum them up briefly, that the reader may have a conception of the condition of the world's knowledge of South Africa at the time of which we are now writing. Livingtone's earliest journeys were made from his missionary station of Kolobeng as a center; the longest and most memorable of them resulted in the discovery of Lake Ngami. His journey across the continent, which was undertaken after he left Kolobeng as a missionary field, extended from Cape Town to St. Paul de Loanda, and thence diagonally across the continent to the mouth of the Zambesi. Having fixed the extent of his previous explorations, we are ready to take up the adventures of Andersson and Magyar, who followed this part of his work by theirs, which, however, ended long before his efforts were over.

Carl Johann Andersson, a Swede, and Francis Galton, an Englishman, met in London in 1850, and agreed to explore jointly the unknown country north of Cape Colony, and to penetrate from the direct south to Lake Ngami. A glance at the map will show that Livingstone's journey to this lake had been from a point to the southeast of it.

This was their plan as originally formed; but they found when they arrived at Cape Town that the Boers had threatened to kill any person who should attempt to pass through their territories. It was therefore necessary to modify their plans; and they sailed for Walfisch Bay, on the western coast; whence they intended to reach the lake by an eastward journey overland.

Missionary stations had been established at various points, and it was toward one of these, Barmen, in the country of the Damaras, that the adventurers turned their course. But mission-work among this people had not had the effects which are usually expected; they could not comprehend the assertion that

Carl Johann Andersson.

men were willing to leave their own country and brave hardship and danger, unless from self-interest. When the missionaries first came, the natives suspected them of an attempt to plunder; and withdrew with their herds into more inaccessible regions. Finding that they were not pursued, they resolved to exterminate the new-comers; but one of their own chiefs remonstrated against this plan, and finally, the Damaras became a little more friendly, and some of the poorer members of the tribe actually settled in the neighborhood of the missions. This was the attitude of the people when Andersson and Galton came into their midst.

At Barmen, they heard from some of these hangers-on of the mission that there was a large fresh-water lake, Omanbonde, lying to the southward. Here was their opportunity for distinguishing themselves, and they set off to explore it; only to return crest-fallen from the region of a dried-up marsh and a patch of reeds. There were indications that there was a lake in that locality during the wet season; but they had looked for another Ngami.

Hearing that the Damaras carried on a flourishing trade with a people of agricultural habits living north of them, the travelers determined to penetrate into this country; since the commerce existing showed that it must be passable. The country was full of fine game, and they began to congratulate themselves upon their good fortune, when an unexpected difficulty befell them: the axle of their wagon broke, and they were unable to repair the damage. Abandoning it, they took to their pack and saddle oxen; but no guides could be found, and they lost their way. From this difficulty they were rescued by a caravan which was returning from Damara-land toward the very country whither they were now going, that of the Ovambos.

They found Ondango, the country of this tribe, such an Elysium as their dreams had pictured. "Instead of the eternal jungles, where every moment we were in danger of being dragged out of our saddles by the merciless thorns, the landscape now presented an apparently boundless field of yellow corn, dotted with numerous peaceful homesteads, and bathed in the soft light of a declining tropical sun. Here and there rose gigantic, wide-spreading, and dark-foliaged timber and fruit-trees, while innumerable fan-like palms, either singly or in groups, completed the picture."

They found no such things as towns or villages; each family had its separate homestead, surrounded by high, stout palisades, outside of which lay the fields in which the family raised its supplies of Kaffir corn, calabashes, watermelons, pumpkins, peas, beans, and tobacco. Here, too, were the pastures for their herds of cattle, sheep and goats, while their dogs and fowls found a home within the palisade.

After a journey of four days from the frontier of this country, the travelers reached the residence of the chief, Nangoro; and after a delay of three days they were permitted to behold him. Enormously fat, his state of almost perfect nudity showed him off to the best possible advantage.

Nangoro had seen muskets before, as had some of his principal men; but that he had not a very intimate acquaintance with fire-arms may be inferred from his belief that their efficacy could be destroyed by blowing into the barrel. His faith in this theory was shaken, however, by demonstration of its falsity; although his followers still fell flat on their faces every time that a gun was discharged in their hearing, and remained so for some little time.

The Ovambos form a marked contrast to some other African tribes in being strictly honest; without permission, the natives would not touch anything; and the travelers could leave their camp entirely unwatched. Nor are they idle; work begins at sunrise and ends at sunset for all. There is no pauperism among them, and the aged and helpless are carefully tended; in marked contrast to the Damaras, who have a pleasant little way of knocking their old people on the head or carrying them away into the desert to starve.

But although exempt from some of the vices of their neighbors, the Ovambos are not altogether paragons. Polygamy is practiced to a great extent, each man having as many wives as he can afford to buy. It is interesting to note the quotations in this article of merchandise: a poor man could purchase a wife for two oxen and one cow; a rich man would be required to pay three oxen and two cows. We are not told whether the difference in price was occasioned solely by the difference in the circumstances of the purchaser, or whether the rich man paid for first choice. The king alone was not required to buy his wives; and one hundred and six families had considered the honor of the alliance sufficient value received for their daughters.

The travelers were anxious to reach the Cunene River, the mouth of which had been discovered by previous exploration and which they suspected was identical with a great river, flowing westward, which the natives told them lay about eight days' journey to the northward; but Nangoro, incensed at their refusal to shoot elephants for him, declared that since they would do nothing for him, he would do nothing for them; and refused to furnish guides, or even to permit them to attempt the journey through his territory. Nothing could be done, then, but to return to Barmen; and

NATIVES CAPTURING A HIPPOPOTAMUS.

there they arrived early in August, 1851; having remained about eight months in the interior.

Once in two years, a missionary vessel brought stores to Walfisch Bay; but since this was not expected till December, they must occupy the time between as best they might. Various trips were undertaken, the longest of which was another attempt to reach lake Ngami. Setting out a week after their return from Ovambo-land, they suffered terribly from the heat and drought; and finally returned without having accomplished their object, the natives assuring them that the country beyond them was impassable.

Spring-Gun Trap for Wild Animals.

They spent some time at a missionary station and settlement called Schmelen's Hope. Here the hyenas, called wolves by the colonists, were very numerous and audacious, frequently invading the sheep kraals during the dark drizzling nights, and making sad havoc. The colonists and the travelers gave chase to several, but found their efforts eluded by the cunning beasts, which escaped unharmed. Finally, by the aid of spring-guns, several were killed; and their kindred took the hint and stayed away.

A description of the trap will not be out of place. Two

young trees were selected and divested of their lower branches; or, where these were lacking, two stout posts were set in the ground. Across these the gun was lashed in a nearly horizontal position, the muzzle pointing slightly upward. A piece of wood, six inches long, was tied to the side of the gun-stock in such a way as to permit it to move slightly backward and forward. A string connected the lower end of this lever with the trigger, while to the upper end a longer cord was fixed, which, passing through the empty ramrod tube, had a lump of flesh at the end; this flesh was further secured by being stuck on the muzzle of the gun.

A fence of thorny bushes was carefully made around the spot, with but one narrow opening left, this being directly opposite the muzzle of the gun. A "drag" of tainted flesh or other offal was then arranged, leading from various quarters; and the colonists retired from the scene. It was next to impossible for the hyena to get the meat off the muzzle of the gun without blowing its brains out; and none escaped the fate.

Galton returned to England by the missionary vessel; but Andersson was not yet ready to give it up. Early in 1853, well provided with gifts for the various chiefs, he again arrived at Walfisch Bay. It was nearly the middle of the year when he reached Tunobis; from this point numerous difficulties beset him; but finally he found a road which was not entirely destitute of water. One of his adventures at a fountain where they halted for a night deserves to be here recorded; and who can tell the story as well as Andersson himself?

"Hearing that elephants and rhinoceroses still continued to resort to Abeghan, I forthwith proceeded there on the night in question. Somewhat incautiously I took up my position—alone, as usual—on a narrow neck of land dividing two small pools, the space on either side of my skarm [a shallow pit with a barrier of stones in front] being only sufficient for a large animal to stand between me and the water. I was provided with a blanket and two or three spare guns.

"It was one of those magnificent tropical moonlight nights when an indescribable soft and enchanting light is shed over the slumbering landscape; the moon was so bright and clear that I could discern even a small animal at a considerable distance. I had just completed my arrangements, when a noise that I can liken only to the passage of a train of artillery broke the stillness of the air; it evidently came from the direction of one of the numerous stony paths, or rather tracks, leading to the water, and I imagined that it was caused by some wagons that might have crossed the Kalahari. Raising myself partially from my recumbent position, I fixed my eyes steadily on the part of the bush whence the strange sounds proceeded, but for some time I was unable to make out the cause. All at once, however, the mystery was explained by the appearance of an immense elephant, immediately followed by others, amounting to eighteen. Their towering forms told me at a glance that they were all males. It was a splendid sight to see so many huge creatures approaching with a free, sweeping, unsuspecting and stately step. The somewhat elevated ground whence they emerged, and which gradually sloped toward the water, together with the misty night air, gave an increased appearance of bulk and mightiness to their naturally giant structures.

"Crouching down as low as possible in the skarm, I waited with a beating heart and ready rifle the approach of the leading male, who, unconscious of peril, was making straight for my hiding-place. The position of his body, however, was unfavorable for a shot; and knowing from experience that I had little chance of obtaining more than a single good one, I waited for an opportunity to fire at his shoulder, which is preferable to any other part when shooting at night. But this chance, unfortunately, was not afforded till his enormous bulk towered above my head. The consequence was, that while in the act of raising the muzzle of my rifle over the skarm, my body caught his eye, and, before I could place the piece to my shoulder, he swung himself round, and, with trunk elevated and ears spread, desperately charged me. It was now too late to think of flight, much less of slaying the savage beast. My own life was in imminent jeopardy; and seeing that if I remained partially erect, he would inevitably seize me with his proboscis, I threw myself back with some violence, in which position, and without shouldering the rifle, I fired upward at random toward his chest, uttering at the same time the most piercing shouts and cries. The change of position, in all human probability, saved my life; for at the same instant the trunk of the enraged animal descended precisely on the spot where I had been previously crouched, sweeping away the stones, many of them of a large size, that formed the forepart of my skarm, like so many pebbles. In another moment his broad fore feet passed directly over my face.

I now expected nothing short of being crushed to death. But imagine my relief when, instead of renewing the charge he swerved to the left, and moved off with considerable rapid-

"HIS ENORMOUS BULK TOWERED ABOVE MY HEAD."

ity, most happily without my having received any other injuries than a few bruises, occasioned by the falling of the stones. Immediately after the elephant had left me I was on my legs, and snatching up a spare rifle lying at hand, I pointed at him as he was retreating, and pulled the trigger; but to my intense mortification the piece missed fire. It was a matter of thankfulness to me, however, that a similar mishap had not occurred when the animal charged; for had my gun not then exploded, nothing, as I conceive, could have saved me from destruction.

"While pondering over my late wonderful escape, I observed, at a little distance, a huge white rhinoceros protrude his ponderous and misshapen head through the bushes, and presently afterward he approached to within a dozen paces of my ambuscade. His broadside was then fully exposed to view, and notwithstanding I still felt a little nervous from my conflict with the elephant, I lost no time in firing. The beast did not at once fall to the ground, but from appearances I had every reason to believe that he would not live very long. Scarcely had I reloaded when a black rhinoceros of the species Keitlea (a female, as it proved), stood drinking at the water; but her position, as with the elephant in the first instance, was unfavorable for a good shot. As, however, she was very near me, I thought I was pretty sure of breaking her leg and thereby disabling her, and in this I succeeded. My fire seemed to madden her; she rushed wildly forward on three legs, when I gave a second shot, though apparently with little or no effect. I felt sorry at not being able to end her sufferings at once; but as I was too well acquainted with the habits of rhinoceroses to venture on pursuing her under the circumstances, I determined to wait patiently for daylight, and then destroy her with the aid of my dogs. But it was not to be.

"As no more elephants or other large game appeared, I thought, after a time, it might be as well to go in search of the white rhinoceros previously wounded; I was not long in finding his carcass; for my ball, as I supposed, had caused his almost immediate death.

"In heading back to my skarm, I accidentally took a turn in the direction pursued by the black rhinoceros, and by ill-luck, as the event proved, at once encountered her. She was still on her legs, but her position, as before, was unfavorable. Hoping, however, to make her change it for a better, and thus enable me to destroy her at once, I took up a stone, and hurled it at her with all my force; when, snorting horribly, erecting her tail, keeping her head close to the ground, and raising clouds of dust by her feet, she rushed at me with fearful fury. I had only just time to level my rifle and fire before she was upon me; and the next instant, while instinctively turning round for the purpose of retreating, she laid me prostrate. The shock was so violent as to send my rifle, powder-flask, and a ball-pouch, as also my cap, spinning in the air; the gun, indeed, as ascertained, to a distance of fully ten feet. On the beast charging me, it crossed my mind that, unless gored at once by her horn, her impetus would be such (after knocking me down, which I took for granted would be the

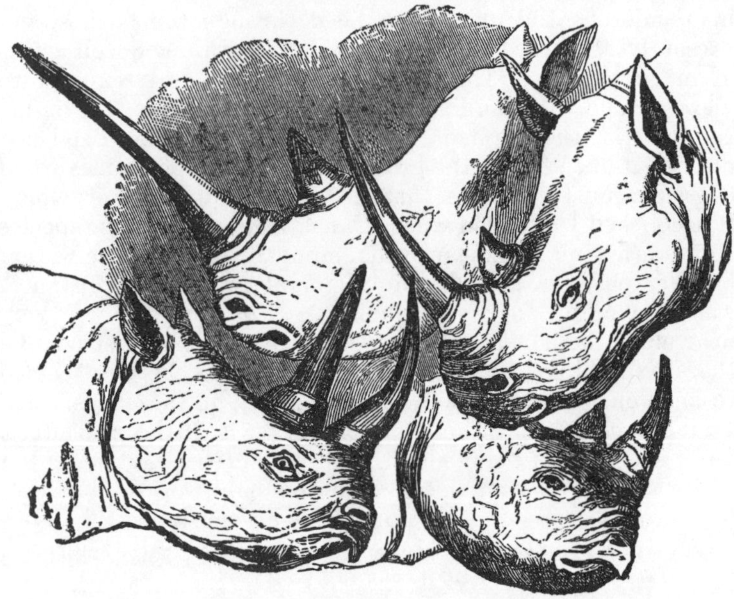

An Assortment of Rhinoceros Heads.

case) as to carry her beyond me, and I might thus be afforded a chance of escape. So, indeed, it happened; for having tumbled me over (in doing which her head and the forepart of her body, owing to the violence of the charge, was half buried in the sand), and trampled on me with great violence, her forequarter passed over my body. Struggling for life, I seized my opportunity, and as she was recovering herself for a renewal of the charge, I scrambled out from between her hind legs.

"But the enraged beast had not yet done with me. Scarcely had I regained my feet before she struck me down a second time, and with her horn ripped up my right thigh (though not very deeply) from near the knee to the hip; with her forefeet, moreover, she hit me a terrific blow on the left shoulder, near the back of the neck. My ribs bent under the enormous weight and pressure, and for a moment I must, as I believe, have lost consciousness—I have, at least, very indistinct notions of what afterward took place. All I remember is, that when I raised my head I heard a furious snorting and plunging among the neighboring bushes. I now arose, though with great difficulty, and made my way, in the best manner I was able, toward a large tree near at hand for shelter; but this precaution was needless; the beast, for the time at least, showed no inclination further to molest me. Either in the melee, or owing to the confusion caused by her wounds, she had lost sight of me, or she felt satisfied with the revenge she had taken. Be that as it may, I escaped with life, though sadly wounded and severely bruised, in which disabled state I had great difficulty in getting back to my skarm."

Andersson had sent one of his men, escorted by bushmen, to make known his approach to the natives living on the shores of the lake. This messenger shortly afterward returned, accompanied by two guides, belonging to the Betoana tribe; and the party proceeded through the almost impenetrable thorn-forest. On the third day after leaving the fountain which had been the scene of the adventure with the elephant and the rhinoceros, about noon, the cry of "Ngami! Ngami!" was raised by the men at the head of the caravan; and the explorer, looking before him, saw, glimmering in the sunshine, a sheet of water bounded only by the horizon.

The lake was at that season at its lowest stage, and was very shallow at the point where it was first seen. Its banks were overgrown with a multitude of reeds and rushes, so that, after the first excitement of catching a glimpse of it was once over, it was far from seeming an object of much admiration. The muddy stretches whence the water had receded prevented their approaching very nearly to the lake itself; and the water, a little of which was obtained by considerable exertion, was very bitter and disagreeable.

A journey of two days along the shore of the lake brought Andersson to the residence of the chief, Lecholetebe. This gentleman divided his time between soliciting presents and refusing to furnish information; so that when Andersson expressed a desire to push on toward Libebe, a place considerably north of the lake, and the chief promised to furnish him with men and canoes, the white man was most agreeably surprised.

They were first to ascend the Teoge River; the crafts furnished by the chief were two clumsy canoes, consisting of logs of wood, each about twenty feet long, pointed at both ends and hollowed out by fire. Had the logs been straight, the task of the boatmen would perhaps have been easier; as it was, they found such difficulty in guiding their rude vessels, and hugged the shore so closely, that they were three days in reaching the mouth of the river from the residence of the chief. For the first few days of the ascent, the country presented a very dreary appearance; sometimes being under water for several miles around; but as they progressed, the vegetation became profuse and varied; while animals, of all the species known to this part of the world, abounded. After twelve days' journey, they reached a village where, Lecholetebe had told him, he could obtain other men and boats for the prosecution of his journey. What the savage had not told him, was that every man in the town had gone upon a hippopotamus hunt, from which they would not return in less than a month. Lecholetebe thus secured presents for the use of his men and canoes in going and returning; since Andersson was entirely helpless.

After a month's absence, he returned to the shores of Lake Ngami, the one important result of this journey being the ascertaining of the fact that the lake received its principal supplies from the northwest. Andersson was now resolved to return home; but he had accumulated so many specimens of natural history, curiosities, ivories, and so forth, that a wagon was absolutely necessary to transport his effects. He accordingly set out for Namaqualand in order to procure one.

"During the four months that elapsed before he again reached Lake Ngami, he traveled, either alone or accompanied by a single native, sometimes on foot and at others on horseback or oxback, over more than a thousand miles of country, parts of it emulating the Sahara in scarcity of water and general inhospitality. Besides narrow escapes from lions and other dangerous beasts, he was occasionally as much as two days without tasting food; and it frequently happened that in the course of twenty-four hours he could only once or twice moisten his parched lips."

Thus it is that a brilliant journalist sums up the difficulties of the journey which he had undertaken, and which, with the return, was successfully accomplished. In the spring of

1854, he sailed from Cape Town to Europe, where he enjoyed comparative inaction for nearly four years. In 1858, Andersson again went to Africa, to explore the country near that with which he had become familiar. His object on this expedition was to explore the Cunene River; but he found, instead, a stream six hundred feet wide, the course of which was unmistakably eastward. This river, called the Okawango by the natives, and previous to Andersson's time having been known to the Portuguese as the Ouando, the discoverer believed to be a tributary of the Zambesi, then recently explored by Livingtone; he was preparing to demonstrate his belief by an expedition following the course of the stream, when he and five or six others of his party were prostrated by fever, and the project had to be given up.

Reaching the settlements after a journey which fires on the plains of grass made doubly perilous, Andersson returned to Europe and published the result of his journey. Afterward, he again went back to Africa, married a lady of Cape Town, and settled down as a farmer near Ondongo. His property suffered severely during the war between the Damaras and the Namaquas, and he was himself so severely wounded that he was obliged to go to the Cape for treatment. He had barely recovered when in May, 1866, he set out on an expedition to the Cunene, which had for its aim the establishment of a commercial treaty with the Portuguese settlers; he actually came in sight of the river of which he had dreamed for so long; but his failing strength forbade a further journey; and retracing his steps, he died before home was reached.

Between the most northern points reached by Andersson, and the 1856 route of Livingstone, westward from the mouth of the Zambesi, there lies a considerable tract of country which would have been, but for the explorations of Ladislaus Magyar, a *terra incognita*. A Hungarian by birth, he had served in the Austrian navy, in that of the Argentine Confederation, and as commander of the fleet of the negro ruler of old Calabar, before he went to South Africa, broken down in health by the coast-fever.

His starting-point was the most southern Portuguese settlement on the western coast, St. Philip de Benguela; his first objective point was the kingdom of Bihe, situated on the table-lands of the interior, in a section watered by the tributaries of the Coanza River. He was fortunate enough to secure the guidance and protection of a caravan which was going thither; and the members of this caravan esteemed

EXORCISING AN EVIL SPIRIT.

themselves fortunate to secure the presence of a white man, considering him a protection to them.

He met with great honor on account of his color; and was invited to make use of as much land as he should choose, and to build himself a house. Selecting a site which had not been appropriated by any one else, and which recommended itself to him by its beauty, he was gravely informed that a notorious wizard had been executed on the spot a year before, that ever since evil spirits had haunted the place, and that consequently he must select another place. Magyar begged one of their exorcising priests to drive away the evil spirits, and enforced his request with a fat hog and several yards of cotton cloth. The priest slaughtered a goat, marked several cabalistic figures with its blood upon Magyar's body, and having blown three blasts through a gazelle-horn, declared that the evil spirits had for ever been banished from the beautiful valley.

On another occasion, shortly after this, Magyar took advantage of the superstition of the natives. The king had confided to him that he meant to undertake an expedition against a neighboring tribe, and invited the white man to accompany him. It was dangerous to refuse, and the Hungarian accordingly accepted, hoping that he would find some loop-hole of escape before the time came round. As it drew near, and there seemed to be no such opportunity, Magyar complained of bad dreams and great bodily pains. The priests decided that evil spirits were tormenting him. Then the stranger confessed that this expedition was against the laws in his country, and they were probably punishing him for having promised to go. The news was carried to the king, who not only released Magyar from his promise, but after the evil spirit had been duly exorcised and banished, sent the white man his daughter as a wife.

It may be supposed that the explorer was now in no less dilemma than at first; but recognizing that it was impossible to refuse the honor, and being a bachelor, he married the dusky princess, who made him a very good wife.

For a while, he settled down to the cultivation of his fields, and to observation of the habits of the people; but in the spring of 1850, having resolved to penetrate still farther into the interior, he got together a large caravan for a journey to the Molumwa country, the chief object being to obtain a supply of ivory.

In the course of this journey, he came upon a peculiar race of dwarfs, whom he thus describes:

"They are not more than four feet in height, of a rusty yellow color, and with features which seem a caricature of the human face. Their legs are very thin; the round, protruding abdomen takes up one-third of the body; the lean neck sup-

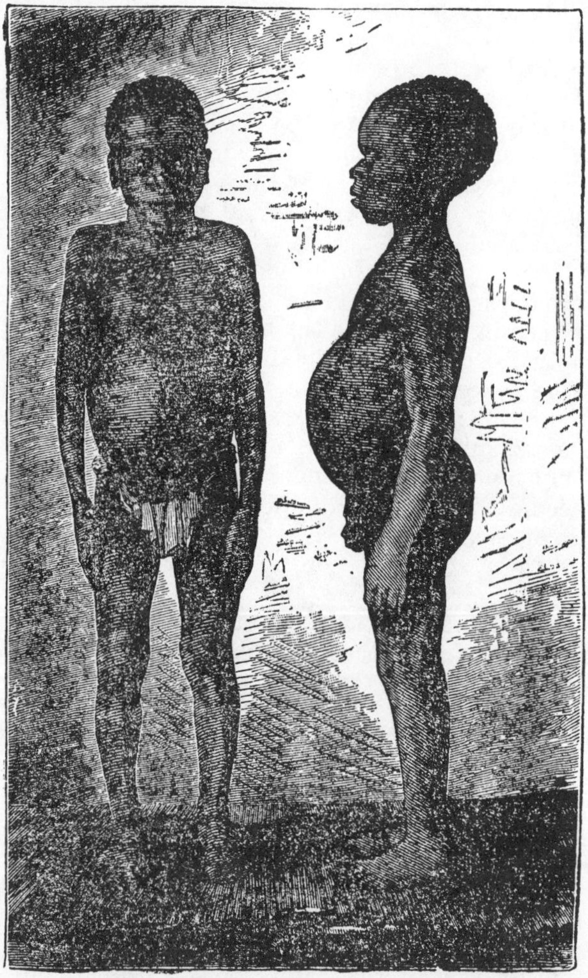

Akkas, a Dwarf Tribe of Central Africa.

ports a large head, with a perfectly flat face, in which wide mouth and nostrils and small twinkling eyes are inserted. Their ears are like flaps, and their hair is very short and woolly." If handsome is as handsome does, we must not suppose these poor creatures to be ugly, since Magyar bears testimony to their peacefulness, honesty, and faithfulness in service.

Magyar resided for more than a year among the Molumwas, whom he describes as possessed of more intelligence than any other native African tribe. Notwithstanding their intelligence, however, the grossest forms of superstition are still held among them, and even human sacrifices are offered upon certain occasions.

Returning to Bihe, Magyar made several expeditions from that kingdom as a starting-point, claiming to have reached the upper part of the Zambesi in one, and the Cunene in another; but the fact that he was unable to determine the latitude and longitude of the places which he visited, and that his geographical notes are extremely brief and unsatisfactory, renders his experiences of far less value than they would otherwise be. If to his energy and courage had been united the knowledge and technical skill of the scientist, many important geographical problems might have been solved.

CHAPTER VIII.

DU CHAILLU AND THE GORILLA COUNTRY.

WE now turn our attention to the exploration of that portion of equatorial Africa which lies west of the Congo, and follow Du Chaillu in his travels about the Ogawai river, which empties into the Atlantic at a point about one degree south of the equator.

The boundaries of the territory thus explored may be roughly described as the second parallel of latitude, north and south, and a line drawn three hundred miles from the coast. Within these limits Du Chaillu traveled nearly eight thousand miles on foot; and his contributions to our knowledge of the animal life and vegetation of equatorial Africa have never been surpassed by any explorer. The results of his journeys are indeed rather ethnographical, zoological and botanical than strictly geographical.

A French settlement had been established at the mouth of the Gaboon River in the year 1842; and following this, several missionary stations had been planted inland by the American Board of Foreign Missions. At one of these latter places, the head station, a point eight miles from the mouth of the river, Du Chaillu arrived from the city of his adoption, New York, in December, 1855. He remained there until April of the following year, in order that he might become acclimated, and to prepare for his journey inland in various ways.

Here he had ample opportunity of studying the habits of the Mpongwe tribe, whose territory lies about the mouth of the Gaboon. Their position, under the rules of African commerce, enables them to accumulate considerable wealth in the shape of "the white man's goods," and they had many singular adaptations of white men's customs and manners; while in some particulars their own ways remained wholly unchanged.

The laws of commerce to which allusion has been made are well understood and strictly regulated. The most important is, that the tribes along the coast alone have the right of trading with the white men; should a daring merchant from the interior attempt to exchange his goods directly with the Europeans, he would be liable to be sold into slavery, if not put to death at once. He must intrust his goods to some merchant of the nearest tribe, by whom they are passed onward until they reach the coast-tribe, by whom they are bartered to the whites. Of course, the middlemen, here as elsewhere, reap no small share of the profits.

While resident at this missionary station, or in its vicinity, Du Chaillu had the opportunity of witnessing the Mpongwe ceremonies on the choice of a new king; ceremonies so unique and at the same time suggestive that we here reproduce a portion of his account:

"I do not know that Njogoni [the newly elected king] had the slightest suspicion of his elevation. At any rate he shammed ignorance very well. As he was walking on the shore on the morning of the seventh day, he was suddenly set upon by the entire populace, who proceeded to a ceremony which is preliminary to the crowning, and which must deter any but the most ambitious men from aspiring to the crown. They surrounded him in a dense crowd, and then began to heap upon him every manner of abuse that the worst of mobs could imagine. Some spit in his face; some beat him with their fists; some kicked him; others threw disgusting objects at him; while those unlucky ones who stood on the outside, and could reach the poor fellow only with their voices, assiduously cursed him, his father, his mother, his sisters and brothers, and all his ancestors to the remotest generation. A stranger would not have given a cent for the life of him who was presently to be crowned. Amid all the noise and struggle, I caught the words which explained all to me; for every few minutes some fellow, administering an especially severe blow or kick, would shout out:

"'You are not our king yet; for a little while we will do what we please with you. By and by we shall have to do your will.'

"Njogoni bore himself like a man and a prospective king. He kept his temper, and took all the abuse with a smiling face. When it had lasted about half an hour, they took him to the house of the old king. Here he was seated, and became again for a little while the victim of his people's curses. Then all became silent; and the elders of the people rose and said solemnly, the people repeating after them:

"'Now we choose you for our king; we engage to listen to you and to obey you.'

"A silence followed, and presently the silk hat, which is the emblem of Mpongwe royalty, was brought in and placed on Njogoni's head. He was then dressed in a red gown, and received the greatest marks of respect from all who had just now abused him. Now followed a six days' festival. * * *"

From this account it appears that while in the United States the abuse precedes the election of an official, in the country of the Mpongwe only the successful candidate is subjected to it, and it is in the nature of corporal punishment as well as tongue-lashings.

Du Chaillu left the missionary station late in April, 1856, and proceeding about sixty miles down the coast, turned inland for about the same distance; then returned to the Gaboon. The geographical results of this journey, which occupied some three months, were not important. His journey lay chiefly in the territory of the Skeiani tribe, a people akin to the Mponwes. He describes them as subject to the most degrading superstitions, as incapable of appreciating that courage which teaches men to face their enemies openly, as treating their women very harshly, as treacherous in war and dishonest in trading. They excel as hunters, being lithe, active and cunning; their life is largely nomadic, although they have villages; for once convinced that the site of a village is bewitched, they can not be induced to remain in that neighborhood.

Bearing with him specimens of new birds and animals which he had killed, the hunter returned to the Gaboon, whence, in a few days, he set out upon a second expedition.

This second journey was begun with the intention of exploring the Muni to its head-waters, and of visiting the Sierra del Crystal. It was believed that the Congo flowed northward back of this range of mountains, and Du Chaillu was anxious to ascertain if it were true. It was necessary to obtain the assistance of the chief Dayoko before the Muni could be ascended; and when this prince was once convinced that the white man did not intend to interfere with his rights by trading with the tribes in the interior, this assistance was readily granted.

During their passage of these mountains, Du Chaillu saw, for the first time, the Ntambounay Falls, which he describes as one of the grandest sights he ever beheld, "an immense mountain torrent, dashing down hill at an angle of twenty-five or thirty degrees, for not less than a mile before us, like a vast seething, billowy sea. The river course was full of the huge granite boulders which lie about here as though the Titans had been playing at skittles in this country; and against these the angry waters dashed as though they would carry all before them; and, breaking up, threw the milky spray up to the very tops of the trees which grew along the edge."

Ascending a little farther, Du Chaillu shot an immense serpent. Very much to his disgust, his dusky companions proceeded at once to cut it up, roast and eat it. But he scarcely had time to protest before the cry was raised that gorilla tracks had been found. These were so fresh that they determined to chase the animal without farther delay; but although they caught sight of the game more than once, it finally eluded them, and escaped into the depths of the forest.

This was the first time that Du Chaillu had seen a gorilla at such close quarters; and he says that he felt like a murderer in pursuing this animal with the intention of killing it. Nor was he the only one of the party who felt that this was something more than a mere brute. The negroes of this region believe that certain gorillas are endowed with the spirits of departed negroes. In these, the intelligence of the man is united to the cunning instinct of the brute, and, joined to its activity and immense strength, enables such animals to evade pursuit and defy the hunters forever. Such a one, they told Du Chaillu, was this gorilla which had escaped them.

After three or four days' unintermitting travel, the adventurer reached the first village of the Fan tribe, distant one hundred and fifty miles, as the crow flies, from the coast. These people had never before seen a white man, or one with straight hair; and they fled in terror from the presence of the "white spirit." Re-assured as to his intentions, they were at length induced to return; and then they flocked about him in crowds. One most wonderful thing about the stranger, and something which they could not explain, was the fact that while his face was white, and his hands white and shaped like theirs, his feet were black and had no toes; for they assumed that his boots were his feet.

Although their first gorilla hunt proved unsuccessful, it is worth while to transcribe the description of a second, as showing the danger of pursuing the animal:

"Presently I noticed, ahead of us, seemingly, a noise as of

DU CHAILLU AT CLOSE QUARTERS WITH A GORILLA.

some one breaking down branches or twigs of trees. This was the gorilla, I knew at once, by the eager and satisfied looks of the men. They looked once more carefully to their guns, to see if by any chance the powder had fallen out of the pans; I also examined mine, to make sure that all was right; and then we marched on cautiously.

"The singular noise of the breaking of tree-branches continued. We walked with the greatest care, making no noise at all. The countenances of the men showed that they thought themselves engaged in a very serious undertaking; but we pushed on, until finally we saw through the thick woods the moving of the branches and small trees which the great beast was tearing down, probably to get from them the berries and fruits he lives on.

"Suddenly, as we were yet creeping along, in a silence which made a heavy breath seem loud and distinct, the woods were filled with the heavy barking roar of the gorilla. Then the underbrush swayed rapidly just ahead, and presently before us stood an immense male gorilla. He had gone through the jungle on his all-fours; but when he saw our party he erected himself and looked us boldly in the face. He stood about a dozen yards from us, and was a sight I think never to forget. Nearly six feet high (he proved two inches shorter) with immense body, huge chest, and great muscular arms, with fiercely glaring large deep-gray eyes, and a hellish expression of face, which seemed to me like some nightmare vision: thus stood before us this king of the African forests.

"He was not afraid of us. He stood there, and beat his breast with his huge fists until it resounded tike an immense bass-drum, which is their mode of offering defiance; meantime giving vent to roar after roar. The roar of the gorilla is the most singular and awful noise heard in these African woods. It begins with a sharp bark, like an angry dog, then glides into a deep bass roll, which literally and closely resembles the rumble of distant thunder along the sky, for which I have sometimes been tempted to take it when I did not see the animal. So deep is it that it seems to proceed less from the mouth and throat than from the deep chest and vast paunch.

"His eyes began to flash fiercer fire as we stood motionless on the defensive, and the crest of short hair which stands on his forehead began to twitch rapidly up and down, while his powerful fangs were shown as he again sent forth a thunderous roar. And now truly he reminded me of nothing but some hellish dream creature—a being of that hideous order, half

ELEPHANT ATTACKED BY NATIVES WITH SPEARS.

man, half beast, which we find pictured by old artists in some representations of the infernal regions. He advanced a few steps—then stopped to utter the hideous roar again—advanced again, and finally stopped when at a distance of about six yards from us. And here, as he began another of his roars and beating his breast in rage, we fired, and killed him.

"With a groan which had something terribly human in it, and yet was full of brutishness, it fell forward on its face. The body shook convulsively for a few minutes, the limbs moved about in a struggling way, and then all was quiet—death had done its work, and I had leisure to examine the huge body. It proved to be five feet ten inches high, and the muscular development of the arms and breast showed what immense strength it had possessed."

Du Chaillu had already been taught by necessity to eat roast monkey; the chief objection to which, say those who know, is that it looks unpleasantly like a child so prepared might look; but he felt repelled when the natives proceeded to cut up and eat the body of this monster, so like a man, and yet so horribly different. He was soon to find that among the Fans the flesh of the gorilla was comparatively harmless and pleasing food; for they were cannibals. Not only did they devour the flesh of enemies killed in battle, as is the custom of other anthropophagi, but they even purchased from their neighbors the bodies of those who died a natural death; and no disease was so revolting as to insure the body against being eaten.

Gorillas were not the only game hunted. Early in September Du Chaillu was invited to join in an elephant hunt, with about five hundred men of the tribe. It is their practice, at such times as this, to seek out the spots that the elephants frequent, and there cautiously twist the vines together, so as to obstruct the course of the huge animal; of course they could not hope to hold him permanently; their only aim is to entangle him in his flight until they have time to put an end to his struggles by an incessant discharge of their spears and guns. So many are the spears thrown, that the elephant not infrequently looks like a gigantic porcupine, with wooden quills quivering in his sides. On this occasion, there were four elephants killed; while by a charge of one of the infuriated beasts into the midst of the hunters, one of their number lost his life.

It was Du Chaillu's desire to penetrate still farther into the interior; but the tribes were at war, and it was unsafe to do so; he accordingly returned to the coast, and, except for short and unimportant expeditions, remained there until February, 1857. Then he again set out, this time to explore the territory known as the Camma country, extending about seventy miles north of the river of that name, and eastward from the coast about fifty miles. Here he selected for his headquarters Biagano, the town of king Ranpano, who was the ally of one of Du Chaillu's friends among a more northern tribe. He carried with him a considerable stock of articles for barter; a fact which so delighted the natives that they could scarcely be kept from hugging him. Here he built a number of huts to hold his stores and to serve him and his household for dwellings; and was so well pleased with the appearance of his town that he dubbed it Washington.

From Washington as a center, he went upon a number of hunting expeditions, and some excursions made especially for the purpose of exploration. In one of the latter, he ascended the Npoulounay, a branch of the Ogowai, and discovered the Lake of Anengue, a lake some ten miles wide, and very long in proportion to its width.

He had received a number of invitations to visit king Quengueza, at his town Goumbi; but did not accept until late in January, 1858. The town is ninety-five miles up the Fernand Vaz, which, like the Npoulounay, is a tributary of the Ogowai; and it required a month's voyage to reach it. He was graciously received by the host who had for several months awaited his coming, and introduced to the people as "the king's white man," who was not to be harmed in his person or his possessions at the penalty of their lives. From this point, Du Chaillu and the king ascended the river fifty miles farther, to the village of Obindji, a friendly chief of the Balakai. Obindji came down to the river in great state to receive his guests. He was dressed in a coat and shirt and a nice cloth, and wore a hat as the visible sign of royalty. Nor was the representative of the scepter wanting; for he carried a bell, which he rang continually. "Crown and scepter" may sound a great deal grander to our ears than "hat and cow-bell," but, after all, they are but empty signs of royalty.

Quengueza seemed bent upon doing the honors to his guest, and accompanied him even farther up the river than this town where they were received with such ceremony. Returning the last of May to Obindji's town, they found the people fairly at the point of starvation; and Du Chaillu started out upon an extensive gorilla-hunt. One of the incidents is well worth narrating in his own words:

"I gave powder to the whole party. Six were to go off in one direction for bush-deer, and whatever luck might send them; and six others, of whom I was one, were to hunt for gorillas. We set off toward a dark valley, where Gambo,

Chief Obindji and His Cow-Bell.

Igoumba's son, said we should find our prey. The gorilla chooses the darkest, gloomiest forests for its home, and is found on the edges of clearings only when in search of plantains, or sugarcane, or pineapples. Often they choose for their peculiar haunt a piece of wood so dark that even at midday one can scarcely see ten yards. This makes it the more necessary to wait till the monstrous beast approaches near before shooting, in order that the first shot may be fatal.

"Our little party separated, as is the custom, to stalk the wood in various directions. One brave fellow went off alone in a direction where he thought he could find a gorilla. The other three took another course. We had been about an hour separated when Gambo and I heard a gun fired but little way from us, and presently another. We were already on our way to the spot where we hoped to see a gorilla slain, when the forest began to resound with the most terrific roars. Gambo seized my arms in great agitation, and we hurried on, both filled with a dreadful and sickening fear. We had not gone far when our worst fears were realized. The poor brave fellow who had gone off alone was lying on the ground in a pool of his own blood, and I thought at first quite dead. His bowels were protruding through the lacerated abdomen. Beside him lay his gun. The stock was broken, and the barrel was bent and flattened. It bore plainly the marks of the gorilla's teeth.

"We picked him up, and I dressed his wounds as well as I could with rags torn from my clothes. When I had given him a little brandy to drink he came to himself, and was able, but with great difficulty, to speak. He said that he had met the gorilla suddenly and face to face, and that it had not attempted to escape. It was, he said, a huge male, and seemed very savage. It was in a very gloomy part of the wood, and the darkness, I suppose, made him miss. He said he took good aim, and fired only when the beast was about eight yards off. The ball merely wounded it in the side. It at once began beating its breasts, and with the greatest rage advanced upon him. To run away was impossible. He would have been caught in the jungle before he had gone a dozen steps.

"He stood his ground, and as quickly as he could reloaded his gun. Just as he raised it to fire the gorilla dashed it out of his hands, the gun going off in the fall; and then in an instant, and with a terrible roar, the animal gave him a tremendous blow with its immense open paw, frightfully lacerating the abdomen, and with this single blow laying bare part of the intestines. As he sank, bleeding, to the ground, the monster seized the gun, and the poor hunter thought he would have his brains dashed out with it. But the gorilla seemed to look upon this also as an enemy, and in his rage flattened the barrel between his strong jaws. When we came upon the ground the gorilla was gone. This is their mode when attacked—to strike one or two blows, and then leave the victims of their rage on the ground and go off into the woods."

After something more than a month spent in hunting, Du Chaillu decided to return to Washington; but he was prostrated here by fever, which is prevalent on that low part of the coast, and obliged to return to the higher lands about the mouth of the Gaboon to recuperate. Thence he set out, about the middle of autumn, for the country of the Ashiras. Passing through the territory which he had become acquainted with on his last trip, he came to the country of this tribe, where he was received with great honor and very striking ceremony, first by the chief men, and afterward by the king and his sons, all of whom were negroes so old that their wool and beards were snow-white. He found the Ashiras industrious and thrifty, and advanced in civilization beyond the neighboring tribes; their manufactures of grass-cloth, especially, attracted his admiring attention.

He decided to visit the Apingi tribe, living next beyond the Ashiras. To this project the king of the latter people not only assented, but appointed three of his sons to accompany the traveler to the farther country, with the people of which he kept up friendly intercourse. The white man's reception among the Apingi was in no way inferior to those with which he had already met; he was ferried across the river, escorted to the town, and lodged in the largest house there; then the king paid him a visit. But let the adventurer himself tell the story:

"He brought me two dozen fowls, and some bunches of plantains, and baskets of cassava, which being laid at my feet, he addressed me, saying:

"'I have beheld what our forefathers never saw, what I never saw before. I bid welcome to thee, O white man, O spirit! I thank your father' (turning to Minsho) 'for sending this spirit to me, for nothing greater could happen to us.'

"Then he said:

"'Be glad, O spirit, and eat of things we give thee.'

"Whereupon, to my astonishment, a slave was handed over to me bound, and Remandji said:

"'Kill him for your evening meal; he is tender and fat, and you must be hungry.'

"It took me a moment to recover from my astonishment. Then I shook my head, spat violently on the ground, and made Minsho tell him that I abhorred the people who ate human flesh, and that I and my people never did so. To which Remandji replied:

"'We always heard that you white men eat men. Why do you buy our people? Why do you come from nobody knows where, and carry off our men and women and children? Do you not fatten them in your far country, and eat them? Therefore I gave you this slave, that you might kill him, and make glad your heart.'"

Du Chaillu finally succeeded in making the king understand that he did not intend to eat this slave or any other human flesh; but it was beyond his powers to make the savage comprehend what use the slavers had for his people, if the captives were not fattened and eaten by the captors; the laws of supply and demand were beyond his capacity.

The Apingi could not show too much honor to their strange guest; and finally, at the earnest desire of Remandji himself, elected Du Chaillu their king. Their reason for so doing was, that they expected him, when thus honored, to exercise his magical powers by making them an unlimited supply of beads, by the aid of the wonderful spirit which he possessed in the shape of an old American clock. On one occasion, they gathered in great numbers to see him make a pile of beads as high as the top of a large tree; but the show did not come off.

He had arrived in his Apingi kingdom, as he styles it, a little before the middle of December, 1858; one week after his arrival, he was formally presented with the bell, which here, as among other tribes, corresponds to the scepter of more civilized nations. But they found their proposed honors not so well appreciated as they had hoped. Within less than two weeks after the investiture, he had set out toward Ashango land; but being compelled to turn back, he returned to the coast a little more than a month after he first reached their town. So ended one of the shortest reigns in history.

This was not the last of Du Chaillu's African travels, for other expeditions were made, up to the year 1865; but the later ventures were made simply to confirm the facts ascertained earlier. His statements were received with not a little distrust at first, mainly because they could not be reconciled entirely with the maps of Barth and Petermann. Many of these statements were, however, confirmed by Serval; and his assertions concerning the Fan tribe were verified by Burton; so that his reputation for accuracy may be considered established. However, as said before, Du Chaillu's contributions to our knowledge of Africa consist more largely of particlars relating to its plants and animals than to the configuration of the country and the sources and courses of its rivers.

The expedition of Serval, who verified many of the statements of Du Chaillu, was made in the year 1862. He was accompanied by the ship's surgeon, Griffen du Bellay; and was himself a lieutenant in the French navy. They ascended the Ogowai, the tributaries of which had, many of them, been explored by Du Chaillu, as far as longitude eleven degrees thirty seconds east from Greenwich. It was their purpose to ascend it to the point where two smaller streams unite to form one large river; but they were threatened by the natives in such a way that they began to doubt their ability to do so. While they were thus dubious of the result of their journey, they learned that the people of two large towns had plotted to plunder their boat and divide the spoils; under such circumstances, there was but one thing to do; and the two adventurers were very glad that they were allowed to do that. They beat a retreat in good order, and returned to the French settlements on the coast.

Twelve years later, two other Frenchmen, MM. Compiegne and Marche, ascended the Ogowai to a point two hundred miles above that reached by Serval and his companion; they were informed by the natives that the river came from four great lakes; but the hostility of the natives, as they proceeded, compelled them to give up the quest for its sources.

CHAPTER IX.

SEARCH FOR THE NILE SOURCES BY BURTON, SPEKE AND GRANT.

WE have chosen to include these three explorers in one chapter, because, although the adventures of each might fill a volume—the adventures of two, at least, have been embodied in several books—they are so intimately connected that it is difficult to dissociate them without doing much violence to the narrative.

Captain Richard F. Burton was the leader of the first expedition. He had made a brief visit to the Somali coast of Africa, and, disguised as an Arab merchant, had penetrated to the Mohammedan city of Harrar, when, in 1856, he proposed to the Royal Geographical Society an expedition for exploring the "Sea of Ujiji," as Lake Tanganyika was called. The proposition was at once taken up by the government, and a thousand pounds granted for the purpose. Captain Burton was, as above noted, made leader of the expedition, and another officer of the army, Captain John Hanning Speke, was detailed to accompany him.

They reached Zanzibar in the last month of 1856; but six months were consumed in making their final preparations for departure. The sultan of Zanzibar furnished them with an escort, consisting of an officer and thirteen soldiers; their party included, besides these, two negroes from India, two half-caste Portuguese servants from Goa, eight interpreters under an African freeman, five donkey-drivers, thirty-six porters, and nineteen others whose duties were not exactly defined —a total of eighty-eight persons.

The dominion of the sultan then extended no more than five miles from the coast; so that they were soon without the limits of his friendly sovereignty. One thing that they remarked did not add to their sense of security in this savage country. Captain Burton says:

"On the wayside appeared for the first time the Khambi, or substantial kraals, which give evidence of unsafe traveling and of the unwillingness of caravans to bivouac in the villages. In this country they assumed the form of round huts, and long sheds or booths of straw or grass, supported by a framework

Capt. Richard F. Burton.

of rough sticks firmly planted in the ground and lashed together with bark strips. The whole was surrounded with a deep circle of thorns, which—the entrance or entrances being carefully closed at night-fall, not to re-open until dawn—formed a complete defense against bare feet and naked legs."

The tribe through whose territory they first passed was the Wazaramo, a people that dress their hair by means of a pomatum of clay, moistened with castor oil. When this preparation is nearly dry, the hair is pulled out into numerous wiry twists, which point in all directions. They levy heavy taxes upon all the merchants and others who pass through the territory of their tribe, which amount to positive plunder. Their nearness to the coast has changed them, in many respects, from their natural state; they wore more clothes than are the fashion among most of the tribes of Africa; while their houses are superior, in point of "modern conveniences," to the huts of their neighbors.

The travelers arrived at the foot of the mountains near the end of July. They both suffered much from malaria, common to the coast, and were so ill that they could scarcely sit up as they rode. On the way up the mountains they saw many skeletons of those who had perished on the road, the bones picked clean by the birds of prey. As they ascended, the purer air of the mountains banished their malaria, and they recovered, to some degree, from their wasting fevers.

As they traversed a plain between two ranges of mountains, they came upon a sight which spoke more eloquently than anything else could (where human figures were lacking) of the horrors of one great African traffic. A village was completely destroyed, the houses battered or burned down, and every evidence of human habitation defaced. There were many signs of struggling, such as the earth and neighboring trees could tell; though there was no blood. The village had been attacked by slavers, and the inhabitants carried off. Two negroes lurked in the neighboring jungle, but when the travelers would have invited them to closer quarters, fled in terror. Both Burton and Speke felt the tragedy of which they beheld the scene; but not so their native attendants. To them it was a mere matter of course; they spent the night in singing and dancing, and helping themselves to whatever they could find in the ruins.

The climate of the country through which they were now passing is described as "a furnace by day and a refrigerator by night." They reached "Windy Pass," at the foot of the third range of the Usagara mountains, early in September. In spite of all that they had had to endure from the heat of the sun and the lack of water, the most difficult part of the journey was still to come. From their camp in the valley, the explorers could see the almost perpendicular face of the mountain, and wonder how they, weak and sick (for they were again troubled with ague) could ascend it. But they did not despair. The asses stumbled at almost every step, while the men were endeavoring to mount a precipice where almost every foot dislodged a rolling stone. The ascent required six hours; and Captain Speke suffered so severely from it that two days of violent delirium intervened before he was able to continue the journey, even in a hammock.

Through countries where each tribe seemed more intent on plunder (they called it presents to the chief) than the last had been, the travelers came at length to Unyamwezi, the Land of the Moon. Their approach to Tura Nullah, the first town of this country, created a sensation—literally "astonished the natives:"

"We reached a large expanse of pillar-stones, where the van had halted, in order that the caravan might make its first appearance with dignity. Then ensued a clearing, studded with large stockaded villages, peering over tall hedges of dark-green milk-bush, fields of maize and millet, manioc, gourds, and water-melons, and showing numerous flocks and herds, clustering around the shallow pits. The people swarmed from their abodes, young and old hustling one another for a better stare, the man forsook his loom and the girl her hoe, and for the remainder of the march we were escorted by a tail of screaming boys and shouting adults; the males almost nude, the women bare to the waist, and clothed only knee-deep in kilts, accompanied us, puffing pipes the while, striking their hoes with stones, crying 'beads, beads!' and ejaculating their wonder in strident expressions of 'Hi! hi!' and 'Hiu! ih!' and 'Ha! a! a!'"

The porters took possession of a considerable assemblage of vacant huts, and the two white men were assigned to a wall-less roof, bounded on one side by the village palisade. Here the mob came to behold the strangers, and from morning till night there was no cessation of their staring; when one had gazed his fill, another at once took his place.

From this point onward, we find the progress of the party even less rapid than it had been heretofore; so greatly were they delayed by sickness. Before they had passed into the country which lies nearest to Lake Tanganyika, they were obliged to dismiss those servants who had been hired for a term of six months; and it was nearly seven months after their departure that they resumed their march without these persons. It was to occupy almost two months, before they came upon the lake which it was their intention to explore. We quote again from Burton:

"On the 13th of February we resumed our travel through

screens of lofty grass, which thinned out into a straggling forest. After about an hour's march, as we entered a small savannah, I saw the the fundi running forward and changing the direction of the caravan. Without supposing that he had taken upon himself this responsibility, I followed him. Presently he breasted a steep and stony hill, sparsely clad with thorny trees. Arrived with toil, for our fagged beasts now refused to proceed, we halted for a few minutes upon the summit. 'What is that streak of light which lies below?' I inquired of Seedy Bombay. 'I am of opinion,' quoth Bombay, 'that that is the water.' I gazed in dismay; the remains of my blindness, the veil of trees, and a broad ray of sunshine illuminating but one reach of the lake bend, shrunk its fair proportions. Somewhat prematurely, I began to lament my folly in having risked life and lost breath for so poor a prize, to curse Arab exaggeration, and to propose an immediate return, with the view of exploring Nyanza, a northern lake. Advancing, however, a few yards, the whole scene burst upon my view, filling me with admiration, wonder, and delight.

"Nothing could be more picturesque than this first view of the Tanganyika lake, as it lay in the lap of the mountains, basking in the gorgeous tropical sunshine. Below and beyond a short foreground of rugged and precipitous hill-fold, down which the foot-path zig-zags painfully, a narrow strip of emerald green, never sere, and marvelously fertile, shelves toward a ribbon of glistening yellow sand, here bordered by sedgy rushes, there cleanly and clearly cut by the breaking wavelets. Farther in front stretch the waters—an expanse of the lightest and softest blue—in breadth varying from thirty to thirty-five miles, and sprinkled by the crisp east wind with tiny crescents of snowy foam. The background in front is a high and broken wall of steel-colored mountain, here flecked and capped with pearly mist, there standing sharply penciled against the azure air; its yawning chasms, marked by a deeper plum-color, fall toward dwarf hills of mound-like proportions, which apparently dip their feet in the wave. To the south, and opposite the long low point behind which the Malagarazi river discharges the red loam suspended in its violent stream, lie the bluff headlands and capes of Aguhha, and, as the eye dilates, it falls upon a cluster of out-lying islets specking a sea-horizon. Villages, cultivated lands, the frequent canoes of the fishermen on the waters, and, on a nearer approach, the murmurs of the waves breaking upon the shore, give something of variety, of movement, of life to the landscape, which, like all the fairest prospects in these regions, wants but a little of the neatness and finish of art—mosques and kiosks, palaces and villas, gardens and orchards—contrasting with the profuse lavishness and magnificence of nature, and diversifying the *coup d'œil* unbroken of excessive vegetation, to rival, if not to excel, the most admired scenery of the classic regions, the riant shores of this vast crevasse appeared doubly beautiful to me after the silent and spectral mangrove creeks on the East African sea-board, and the melancholy, monotonous experience of desert and jungle scenery, tawny rock and sun-parched plain, or rank herbage and flats of black mire. Truly it was a revel for soul and sight."

Proceeding at once to Kawele, which may be considered as the port of Ujiji, the explorers endeavored to procure a boat for the navigation of the lake; but this was no easy matter. Despairing of procuring a vessel at Kawele, Captain Speke went in a canoe, with twenty men, to Ukaranga, for the purpose of hiring a dhow from the Arab merchant there who was the possessor of the sole vessel of this kind upon the lake. The Arab detained him there by evasive answers for several days, and at last agreed to let him have it at the end of three months.

The natives had told them of a river by means of which the waters of the lake were emptied—a great river, flowing toward the west; and their eager interest was too thoroughly aroused to permit them to wait all this time inactive. They hired two canoes for an exorbitant sum, one sixty feet by four, the other about forty feet long. In such vessels, they proposed to navigate the lake which they believed to be the recipient and absorbent of the entire river system—the heart from which the great rivers, like arteries, drew their floods, and to which the vein-like smaller streams brought their constant contributions. For fifteen days they kept onward; nine days they remained at the point so reached, Uvira, and in nine days more they returned to their starting-place. Of the difficulties of the journey, Captain Burton says:

"The boating was rather a severe trial. We had no means of resting the back; the holds of the canoes, besides being knee-deep in water, were disgracefully crowded. They had been appropriated to us and our four servants by Kannena, but by degrees he introduced, in addition to the stores, spars, broken vases, pots and gourds, a goat, two or three small boys, one or two sick sailors, the little slave girl, and the large sheep. The canoes were top-heavy with the number of their crew, and

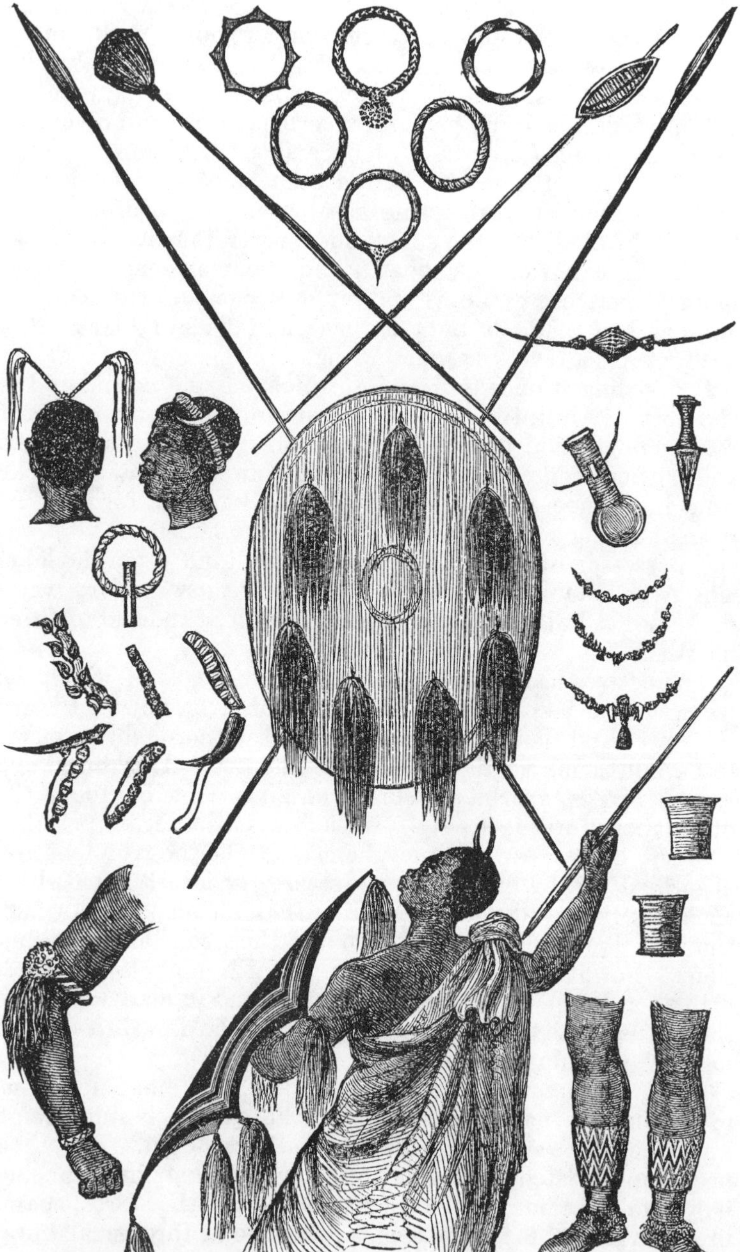

NATIVE AFRICAN WAR INSTRUMENTS AND ORNAMENTS.

the shipping of many seas spoiled our tents, and, besides, wetted our salt and soddened our grain and flour; the gunpowder was damaged, and the guns were honeycombed with rust. Besides the splashing of the paddles and the dashing of the waves, heavy showers fell almost every day and night, and the intervals were bursts of burning sunshine."

It should be remembered, in explanation of what is said above of the leaking of the canoes, that these vessels are hollowed out of logs, which soon shrink and crack; for want of caulking, they become leaky at once; and it is a regular part of the proceedings during any trip by water to bale out the boats. Narrow seats are placed across the vessel, and on each of these sit two men, managing the clumsy paddles which are their substitutes for the oars. A clear space in the middle about six feet long constitutes the hold in which, according to Captain Burton's account, so many and such various articles were stowed away. Nor was this all; from morning till night, or as long as they were engaged in paddling, the men whom they had hired for this work kept up a long, monotonous howl, varied by yells and shouts, and accompanied by the bray of horns, tomtoms, shamms, and whatever other instruments of noise are known to them; so that it was simply impossible to make calculations, to take observations, or do anything else to further the scientific objects of the expedition. Superstition forbade the boatmen to tolerate any questions, or to permit the lead to be hove; nor could the captain who had been engaged to control them dissuade them from stopping where they pleased, or from going on from a point where they did not wish to stop.

As above stated, they proceeded only a fifteen days' journey along the shores of the lake; the reason why they did not go any farther was that the captain and sailors refused to do so, although they had been hired for the whole trip. Persuasions were useless, and so were threats; they had made up their minds that they would go no farther, and the Englishmen who had suffered so much in the journey thither were compelled to turn back by the whim of a set of ignorant savages.

Burton and Speke remained at Ujiji for three months and a half; and being unable to accomplish anything more, set out on their return journey as soon as a caravan with the needful supplies had reached the lake. Their departure was taken May 26, 1858; and nearly a month later, they arrived at Kazeh, two hundred and sixty-five miles distant. Here it was determined that they should separate for a time; for they were desirous of exploring a great lake, which, the natives told them, lay some fifteen or sixteen marches toward the north. This, of course, was no other than the Victoria Nyanza, as it was named by its discoverer. Hitherto, Tanganyika and the Nyanzas, judged by the native accounts which had reached European ears, had been confused, just as, at an earlier date, the Niger and Congo had been confused. Both Burton and Speke now, however, grasped the situation; all discrepancies were explained, if this hitherto unknown basin should be proved to have an actual existence. Captain Burton was so reduced by fever that he was compelled to forego the enterprise, and Captain Speke accordingly left him at Kazeh, and pressed forward without a white companion.

After a journey of twenty days, he saw, on the 30th of July, 1858, the vast inland sea stretching before him. It was the long-sought source of the Nile, he believed; and to the lake which no white man had ever before looked upon, he gave its native name, coupled with that of the sovereign to whose service he was sworn—the Victoria Nyanza.

Returning in all haste, he reached his companion on the 25th of August, and they together set out for Zanzibar; whence they set sail, arriving in England February 9, 1859.

The two explorers were received with much enthusiasm by the Royal Geographical Society, and presented each with a gold medal, as a reward (or rather recognition) of their services. In Captain Burton's response to the speech of Sir Roderick Murchison, the President of the Society, we find the summing up of what part each had taken in the expedition:

"You have alluded, sir, to the success of the last expedition. Justice compels me to state the circumstances under which it attained that success. To Captain Speke are due those geographical results to which you have alluded in such flattering terms. While I undertook the history and ethnography, the languages and peculiarity of the people, to Captain Speke fell the arduous task of delineating an exact topography, and of laying down our positions by astronomical observations—a labor to which, at times, even the undaunted Livingstone found himself unequal."

Captain Burton's health had been so seriously affected by the African climate, and by the hardships endured on this journey, that he felt himself unequal, for the time at least, to farther efforts of this nature. Captain Speke, however, was ready to undertake the venture; and he says that this expedition "may be said to have commenced on the 9th of May,

1859, the first day after my return to England from my second expedition, when, at the invitation of Sir R. I. Murchison, I called at his house to show him my map for the information of the Royal Geographical Society. Sir Roderick, I need only say, at once accepted my views; and knowing my ardent desire to prove to the world, by actual inspection of the exit, that the Victoria Nyanza was the source of the Nile, seized the enlightened view that such a discovery should not be lost to the glory of England and the society of which he was president; and said to me: "Speke, we must send you there again."

The expedition, thus informally projected, was afterward discussed in good earnest; Captain Speke requesting that five thousand pounds be given him for the purpose. The Society thought his demand too large, however, and he finally accepted half the sum named, saying that he would pay from his own pocket whatever else was needed. It was his plan to send forward a quantity of supplies by caravans, to be lodged in certain towns awaiting his arrival; so that he should not have to travel through a thievish country with such great stores; but this intention, owing to the delays which "red tapeism" interposed, could not be wholly carried out.

Captain Grant, an old friend and fellow-sportsman, hearing of the projected expedition, requested to be allowed to accompany it; and he was formally detailed as Captain Speke's companion. The route by which they were to go was at first a matter of some doubt. Many persons said, if they wished to find the source of the Nile, the natural plan would be for them to ascend the river until they came to the head-waters; but Captain Speke urged against this that several travelers had tried it, and from some unexplained reason had failed; he preferred to proceed to Zanzibar, thence strike across the country, and, having reached the lake, explore its coasts until he came to the stream issuing from it which might be supposed to be the Nile, and descend that far enough to verify his conclusions. The nature of the return journey would have to be determined by the circumstances then encountered.

October 2, 1860, the march inland from Zanzibar began. The caravan consisted of about two hundred persons; but eleven deserted before starting. Go they must, however, because one desertion would be sure to lead to another; and go they did. The route as far as Zungemero was the same as that traversed on the previous expedition, and was followed without special incident until they reached the last district in

Ugogo, Khoko. Near this point Captain Speke met with a hunting adventure which is well worth repeating. Ninety-six men of his caravan had deserted, and it was necessary to halt

Capt. J. H. Speke.

while Sheikh Said found new recruits, laid in provisions of grain to last them eight days in the wilderness, and settled for their maintenance with the chief whose hospitality they were then experiencing.

"For this triple business I allowed three days, during which time, always eager to shoot something, either for science or the pot, I killed a bicornis rhinoceros, at a distance of five

Capt. Grant.

paces only, * * * as the beast stood quietly feeding in the bush; and I also shot a bitch-fox, * * * whose ill-omened cry often alarms the natives by forewarning them of danger. This was rather tame sport; but next day I had better fun.

"Starting in the early morning, accompanied by two of Sheikh Said's boys, Suliman and Faraj, each carrying a rifle, while I carried a shot-gun, we followed a foot-path to the westward in the wilderness of Mgunda Mkhali. There, after walking a short while in the bush, as I heard the grunt of a buffalo close on my left, I took 'Blissett' in hand, and walked to where I soon espied a large herd quietly feeding. They were quite unconscious of my approach, so I took a shot at a cow, and wounded her; then, after reloading, put a ball in a bull, and staggered him also. This caused great confusion among them; but, as none of the animals knew where the shots came from, they simply shifted about in a fidgety manner, allowing me to kill the first cow, and even to fire a

Suliman Gets into a Tree Quick.

fourth shot, which sickened the great bull, and induced him to walk off, leaving the herd to their fate, who, considerably puzzled, began moving off also.

"I now called up the boys, and determined on following the herd down before either skinning the dead cow or following the bull, who, I knew, could not go far. Their footprints being well defined in the moist sandy soil, we soon found the herd again; but, as they now knew they were pursued, they kept moving on in short runs at a time, when, occasionally gaining glimpses of their large dark bodies as they forced through the bush, I repeated my shots and struck a good number, some more and some less severely. This was very provoking; for all of them, being stern shots, were not likely to kill; and the jungle was so thick I could not get a front view of them. Presently, however, one of them with her hind leg broken pulled up on a white-ant hill, and tossing her horns, came down with a charge the instant I showed myself close to her. One crack of the rifle rolled her over, and gave me free scope to improve the bag, which was very soon done; for on following the spoors, the traces of blood led us up to another one as lame as the last. He then got a second bullet in the flank, and, after hobbling a little, evaded our sight and threw himself into a bush, where we no sooner arrived than he plunged headlong at us from his ambush, just, and only just, giving me time to present my small 40-guage Lancaster.

"It was a most ridiculous scene. Suliman by my side, with the instinct of a monkey, made a violent spring and swung himself by a bough immediately over the beast, while Faraj bolted away and left me single-gunned to polish him off. There was only one course to pursue; for in one instant more he would have been into me; so, quick as thought, I fired the gun, and, as luck would have it, my bullet, after passing through the edge of one of his horns, stuck in the spine of his neck, and rolled him over at my feet dead as a rabbit. Now, having cut the beast's throat to make him 'hilal,' according to the Mussulman usage, and thinking we had done enough if I could only return to the first wounded bull and settle him too, we commenced retracing our steps, and by accident came on Grant. He was passing by from another quarter, and became amused by the glowing description of my boys, who never omitted to narrate their own cowardice as an excellent tale. He begged us to go on in our course, while he would go back and send us some porters to carry home the game.

"Now, tracking back again to the first point of attack, we followed the blood of the first bull, till at length I found him standing like a stuck pig in some bushes, looking as if he would have liked to be put out of his miseries. Taking compassion, I leveled my Blissett; but as bad luck would have it, a bough intercepted the flight of the bullet, and it went pinging into the air, while the big bull went off at a gallop. To follow on was no difficulty, the spoor was so good; and in ten minutes more, as I opened on a small clearance, Blissett in hand, the great beast, from a thicket on the opposite side, charged down like a mad bull, full of ferocity—as ugly an antagonist as I ever saw, for the front of his head was all shielded with horn. A small mound fortunately stood between us, and as he rounded it, I jumped to one side and let fly at his flank, but without the effect of stopping him; for, as quick as thought, the huge monster was at my feet, battling with the impalpable smoke of my gun, which fortunately hung so thick on the ground at the height of his head that he could not see me, though I was so close that I might, had I been possessed of a hatchet, have chopped off his head. This was a predicament that looked very ugly, for my boys had both bolted, taking with them my guns; but suddenly the beast, evidently regarding the smoke as a phantom which could not be mastered, turned round in a bustle, to my intense relief, and galloped off at full speed, as if scared by some terrible apparition.

"Oh what would I not then have given for a gun, the chance was such a good one! Still, angry as I was, I could not help laughing as the dastardly boys came into the clearance full of their mimicry, and joked over the scene they had witnessed in security, while my life was in jeopardy because they were too frightened to give me my gun. But now came the worst part of the day; for though rain was falling, I had not the heart to relinquish my game. Tracking on through the bush, I thought every minute I should come up with the brute; but his wounds ceased to bleed, and in the confusion of the numerous tracks which scored all the forest we lost our own."

The boys were no more reliable as guides than they had been as hunting companions; for insisting that they were following the right track, they passed that which their own feet had really made, and wandered about in the pathless forest for hours. Nor was their judgment regarding the points of the compass to be relied upon; but after a night spent on the rain-soaked earth, Captain Speke could only convince them that east was not west by pointing to the rising sun.

Their absence had naturally created alarm at the camp, and volleys had been fired throughout the night. Some echoes of these had indeed reached their ears, but had been confounded with rolls of distant thunder, of which there had also been many.

Speke was surprised, on reaching the bounds of Unyanyembe, to find that changes had taken place since his previous visit; the Arabs, who had then been simple merchants, carrying on commerce between the natives and the coast, had engaged in a deadly war with the negroes, and, being victorious, lived as lords of the soil. The war was not yet over; and, in addition to its horrors, the explorers learned that a famine was here raging. These circumstances detained them for several months at Kazeh, for it was literally impossible to procure porters for the transportation of their baggage.

They improved the time by a careful study of the Wagandas. It should be remembered that the languages of this part of Africa agree in denoting, by prefixes, the variations of geographical terms. For instance, Uganda is the country, Wäganda denotes the people inhabiting it; Mganda is the designation of an individual of the Waganda; and Kiganda is the language which he speaks. It should further be noted that Nyanza, more properly written N'yanza, is a general term applied to any great body of water, either river or lake. The earliest explorers of this section of the continent made the mistake of supposing it to be a proper name, and hence arose a confusion of ideas.

It must not be supposed that they were wholly inactive during this period; they progressed somewhat, but very slowly; sickness having its due influence in hindering their advance, as well as the external circumstances which have been mentioned. They entered the rich flat district of Mininga late in March, and took up their quarters in a hut belonging to Sirboko, a broken-down ivory merchant, and the greatest man of the district. He advised them to remain there for a time; and after consultation with the chief of their own followers, they resolved to accept the advice.

Their host had lost all his property by the burning of a village in which it had been stored; and come hither, in order to avoid his creditors on the coast. He had engaged in agriculture, his operations being confined chiefly to rice, because the natives do not like it well enough to steal it.

Here they had the opportunity of doing a humane act; for one of Sirboko's slaves, recognizing Speke, told him that he had been in a fight at Ujiji, speared all over and left for dead, but then seized by the returning enemy, and sold to the Arabs. His touching appeal could not be withstood, and the explorer interceded with his master to grant him freedom. The release was effected; the freedman was newly named Farhan (Joy) and duly enrolled in Speke's service.

The two white men frequently separated for a few days at the time, Captain Speke most often making short excursions into the surrounding country, while Captain Grant remained with the caravan, recruiting his health, which had been much affected by the climate, and enjoying himself dancing with the native women. He himself furnished the sketch from which the accompanying cut is taken, so that we cannot suppose but that he was proud of his favor among the ladies.

Late in November, 1861, they reached the palace of King

SIRBOKO'S SLAVES CARRYING FUEL AND CUTTING RICE.

Rumanika, situated on the shores of a beautiful lake in the bosom of the hills, to which the discoverers gave the name of Little Windermere. Rumanika received them with cordiality, and even requested that they would take two of his sons with them when they returned to their own country, that they might be taught the white men's learning. He was the best native prince that they had yet encountered; and they were not a little pleased with his generous and eager mind.

This king sent a messenger to Mtesa, the king of Uganda, to announce the approach of the party. This embassador returned January 10, 1862, accompanied by an escort of smartly dressed men, women, and boys, to conduct the white men to the capital of Uganda. Captain Grant was unable to travel; but leaving him to follow later on, Captain Speke set out the next day with this retinue.

They crossed the equator February 7; and shortly after passing the line, they were met by some pages who came as messengers from Mtesa, to say that the king had made a vow that he would neither eat nor drink until the white men should have come to him. Speke says:

"One march more, and we came in sight of the king's kibuga, or palace, in the province of Bandawarogo, north latitude twenty-one minutes, nineteen seconds, and east longitude thirty-two degrees, forty-four minutes, thirty seconds. It was a magnificent sight. A whole hill was covered with gigantic huts, such as I had never seen in Africa before. I wished to go up to the palace at once, but the officers said: 'No, that would be considered indecent in Uganda; you must draw up your men and fire your guns off, to let the king know that you are here; we will then show you your residence, and to-morrow you will doubtless be sent for, as the king could not now hold a levee while it is raining.' I made the men fire, and then was shown into a lot of dirty huts, which, they said, were built expressly for the king's visitors. The Arabs, when they came on their visits, always put up here, and I must do the same. At first I stuck out my claims as a foreign prince, whose royal blood could not stand such an indignity. The palace was my sphere; and unless I could get a hut there, I would return without seeing the king.

"In a terrible fright at my blustering, Nyamgundu fell at my feet and implored me not to be hasty. * * * I gave way to this good man's appeal, and cleaned my hut by firing it to the ground; for, like all the huts in this dog country, it was full of fleas. Once ensconced there, the king's pages darted in to

GRANT DANCING WITH THE NATIVE WOMEN.

see me, bearing a message from their master, who said he was sorry the rain prevented him from holding a levee that day, but the next he would be delighted to see me."

The next day, word was duly sent that the stranger was awaited at court; and costuming himself for the occasion, and preparing his presents for presentation, Speke gave the signal that he was ready to proceed. * * Arrived at the ante-reception court, he found it necessary to assert his dignity in no measured terms.

"By the chief officers in waiting, who thought fit to treat us like Arab merchants, I was requested to sit on the ground outside in the sun with my servants. Now I had made up my mind never to sit on the ground as the natives and Arabs are obliged to do, nor to make my obeisance in any other manner than is customary in England, though the Arabs had told me that from fear they had always complied with the manners of the court. I felt that if I did not stand up for my social position at once, I should be treated with contempt during the remainder of my visit, and thus lose the vantage-ground I had assumed of appearing as a prince, rather than as a trader, for the purpose of better gaining the confidence of the king. To avert over-hastiness, however,—for my servants began to be alarmed as I demurred against doing as I was bid—I allowed five minutes to the court to give me a proper reception, saying if it were not conceded I would then walk away.

"Nothing, however, was done. * * The affair ended by my walking straight away home."

The Waganda stood "still as posts," unable to understand such temerity; Speke's own servants were greatly troubled for their master, not knowing what would be the consequence of his deed. Meantime Mtesa had been told of his action; and sent messengers in hot haste to beg him to return. Speke coolly shook his head and patted his heart, and walked on a little faster. Shortly after he arrived at his hut, other messengers came to say that if he would but return, he might bring with him a chair to sit upon—an unparalleled concession, since no one in Uganda but the king is allowed the dignity of such a seat. Having drank a cup of coffee and smoked a pipe, the angry prince (?) leisurely returned to the court of King Mtesa.

King Mtesa was seated on his throne to receive the guest, who, on being told to halt and sit in the burning sun, coolly put on his hat and raised his umbrella. For upwards of an hour he and the king sat silently regarding each other; Speke mute, but Mtesa pointing and remarking with those

VIEW OF KING MTESA'S PALACE.

around him on the novelty of the visitor's guard and general appearance, and even requiring to see his hat lifted, the umbrella opened and shut, and the guards face about and show their

King Mtesa and His Chief Officers.

red cloaks—for such wonders had never been seen in Uganda.

Then, inquiring by means of an interpreter if Speke had seen him, and receiving an affirmative reply, the chief arose and walked away, in what was intended to be a very majestic gait. "It was the traditional walk of his race, founded on the step of the lion; but the outward sweep of the legs intended to represent the stride of this noble beast, appeared to me only to realize a very ludicrous kind of waddle, which made me ask Bombay if anything serious was the matter with the royal person."

Speke stayed long enough in Uganda to become thoroughly well acquainted with the customs of the people. Under date of March 25, 1862, he says:

"I have now been for some time within the court precincts, and have consequently had an opportunity of witnessing court customs. Among these, nearly every day since I have changed my residence, incredible as it may appear to be, I have seen one, two, or three of the wretched palace women led away to execution, tied by the hand, and dragged along by one of the body-guard, crying out, as she went to premature death, '*Hai minange*!' (Oh, my lord!) '*Kbakka*!' (My king!) '*Hai n'yawo!*' (My mother!) at the top of her voice, in the utmost despair and lamentation; and yet there was not a soul who dared lift his hand to save any of them, though many might be heard privately commenting on their beauty."

On the arrival of Captain Grant, the queen-dowager, with whom Captain Speke was already very well acquainted, desired that the new-comer should be presented to her. Speke complied with this demand, representing Grant as his brother. Her majesty persistently ignored his claim that they were of one house, but finally gave up her attempt to extort a separate present from Grant.

For more than four months after Speke's first arrival at the capital of Uganda, Mtesa had resisted every argument and inducement to permit him to continue his journey northward. Finally, however, he became intensely jealous of Rumanika, and declared that he would show his rival that all the supplies for Uganda need not come through his country. If another route were opened, these mighty strangers would come direct to him; and he therefore promised these travelers that he would furnish them with guides to Unyoro and with boats for a voyage on the Nile.

The promise was accepted without delay, and the king was resolutely held to it. Setting out from the capital, they determined to separate, Grant going forward with the main body of the caravan to King Kamrasi's capital, while Speke skirted the borders of the lake until he should come upon the

Nile, flowing out of it. This latter intention was realized two days after their separation, July 19, 1862.

"Here at last I stood on the brink of the Nile! Most beautiful was the scene, nothing could surpass it. It was the very perfection of the effect aimed at in a highly kept park; with a magnificent stream from six hundred to seven hundred yards wide, dotted with islets and rocks, the former occupied by fishermen's huts, the latter by sterns and crocodiles basking in the sun, flowing between fine high grassy banks, with rich trees and plantains in the back-ground, where herds of the n'sunnu and the hartebeest could be seen grazing, while the hippopotami were snorting in the water, and florikan and guinea-fowl rising at our feet."

A Queen Dragged to Execution.

They marched along the left bank of the Nile, at some little distance from the river, through a country rich in many forms of vegetable and animal life. They reached the Isamba Rapids on the 25th, Ripon Falls on the 28th of the month; but paused only a short time at either place. Here we have come to the point where the results of the expedition may be summed up, in the words of its leader:

"The expedition had now performed its functions. I saw that old Father Nile without any doubt rises in the Victoria Nyanza, and, as I had foretold, that lake is the great source of the holy river which cradled the first expounder of our belief. * * * I had seen full half of the lake, and had information given me of the other half, by means of which I knew

SPEKE INTRODUCING GRANT TO THE QUEEN DOWAGER OF UGANDA.

all about the lake, as far, at least, as the chief objects of geographical importance are concerned.

"Let us now sum up the whole and see what it is worth. Comparative information assured me that there was as much water on the eastern side of the lake as there is on the western—if anything, rather more. The most remote waters, or top head of the Nile, is the southern end of the lake, situated close on the third degree of south latitude, which gives to the Nile the surprising length, in direct measurement, rolling over thirty-four degrees of latitude, of above 2,300 miles, or more than one-eleventh of the circumference of our globe. Now from this southern point, round by the west, to where the great Nile stream issues, there is only one feeder of any importance, and that is the Kitangule River; while from the southernmost point, round by the east, to the strait, there are no rivers at all of any importance; for the traveled Arabs one and all aver that from the west of the snow-clad Kilimandjaro to the lake where it is cut by the second degree, and also the first degree of south latitude, there are salt lakes and salt plains, and the country is hilly, not unlike Unyamuezi; but they said there were no great rivers, and the country was so scantily watered, having only occasional runnels and rivulets, that they always had to make long marches in order to find water when they went on their trading journeys; and farther, those Arabs who crossed the strait when they reached Usoga, as mentioned before, during the late interregnum, crossed no river either."

Returning to the point at which he had first struck the Nile, Speke and his party fashioned five boats out of five planks each, bound and caulked with mbugu rags. His destination was Unyoro, the country of Kamrasi, to whom messages regarding him had been sent by Mtesa. They arrived here September 4, and found "the worst royal residence since leaving Uzinza." They were lodged in dirty huts at some distance from the palace; and for several days the king was too drunk to entertain any complaints about their lodging.

At length, however, he "sobered up," and received the message that they wished to see him. No answer was received; and Speke sent another messenger to say that if his majesty did not receive them, they would cut off their hair and blacken their faces, so that he would no longer be afraid of them, for fear must be the reason why he had delayed so long. "This message acted like magic; for he fully believed that we would do as we said, and disappoint him altogether of the sight of

KAMRASI'S FIRST LESSON IN THE BIBLE.

us as pure white men. The reply was, Kamrasi would not have us disfigured in this way for all the world; men were appointed to convey our traps to the west end at once; and Kidgwiga, Vittagura and Kajunju rushed over to give us the news in all haste, lest we should execute our threat, and they were glad to find us with our faces unchanged." This terrible danger being averted, Kamrasi received them very graciously, and showed himself, when sober, friendly enough to accept presents. He was particularly impressed with Speke's exposition of the account of the Ethiopians found in the Bible; but could not resist the temptation, when the book was put in his hands, of counting the leaves. Concluding that each one represented a year since the creation, he was anxious to ascertain how old the world might be considered; but his patience gave out when he had counted about one quarter.

Kamrasi demanded, on the very first interview, a many-bladed knife of which his officers had told him. Only a few days more, and he decided that he wished to have a chronometer, which the explorers valued at about fifty pounds sterling. Speke explained that he needed this—to tell him when it was time to eat his meals, among other things. Whereupon Kamrasi generously offered to send it to him, three times a day, that he might know. Told something of the value of the article, he concluded that it must possess magic powers, since no one in his senses would give five hundred cows simply to be told when to eat his dinner. Evidently, in Unyoro, time is not money.

The whole autumn and almost all of the winter were consumed in the journey down the Nile, from Unyoro to Gondokoro. They reached the latter point on the fifteenth of February, and here had the pleasant surprise of meeting Samuel White Baker, who had not yet earned the title by which he is better known, and who had come up this far with three completely equipped vessels, to search for the explorers, or to learn where and how they had perished. Their difficulties were substantially at an end; and although the journey down to Alexandria was not without adventure, such experiences pale into insignificance when compared to those through which they had previously passed.

A few of those who had been employed as attendants when the expedition left Zanzibar remained faithful to the end, and accompanied Speke down the river. They numbered eighteen men, besides Bombay, the trusted servitor who had accompanied Burton and Speke on their first expedition, and who

SPEKE'S FAITHFULS.

was appointed captain of the "Faithfuls." They were suitably rewarded for their fidelity, receiving a year's pay in addition to their regular earnings, an order for a grand freeman's garden to be established for their benefit at Zanzibar, and an order for a dowry of ten dollars for the bride of each, when she should be selected.

Let us again review, with Speke, the information which had been gained by the expedition, this time with respect to the affluents of the Nile:

"The first affluent, the Bahrel Ghazal, took us by surprise; for, instead of finding a huge lake, as described in our maps, at an elbow of the Nile, we found only a small piece of water resembling a duck-pond buried in a sea of rushes. The old Nile swept through it with majestic grace, and carried us next to the Geraffe branch of the Sobat River, the second affluent, which we found flowing into the Nile with a graceful semicircular sweep and good stiff current, apparently deep, but not more than fifty yards broad.

"Next in order came the main stream of the Sobat, flowing into the Nile in the same graceful way as the Geraffe, which in breadth it surpassed, but in velocity of current was inferior. The Nile by these additions was greatly increased; still, it did not assume that noble appearance which astonished us so much, immediately after the rainy season, when we were navigating it in canoes in Unyoro.

"Next to be treated of is the famous Blue Nile, which we found a miserable river, even when compared with the Geraffe branch of the Sobat. It is very broad at the mouth, it is true; but so shallow that our vessel was with difficulty able to come up to it. It had all the appearance of a mountain stream, subject to great periodical fluctuations. I was never more disappointed than with this river; if the White River was cut off from it, its waters would all be absorbed before they could reach Lower Egypt.

"I had now seen quite enough to satisfy me that the White River which issues from Nyanza at the Ripon Falls is the true or parent Nile; for in every instance of its branching, it carried the palm with it in the distinctest manner, viewed, as all the streams were by me, in the dry season, which is the best for estimating their relative perennial values."

The discoverers were received with great honors at home; nor was their own country the only one which recognized the value of their services to science. In addition to the gold medal which the Royal Geographical Society conferred upon each of them, the king of Italy forwarded similar tributes; France had, at the end of the previous expedition, recognized the services of Captains Burton and Speke by gifts of the same nature.

It forms a singular parallel to the case of Bruce, that Speke should have passed through the dangers of an African exploring expedition, and yet die by accident at home. Going out for a day's shooting in September, 1864, he accidentally wounded himself in such a manner that he died from the effects of it.

CHAPTER X.

SIR SAMUEL W. BAKER AND HIS HEROIC LADY.

WE have already spoken of the meeting between Captain Speke and his friend Mr. Baker; it remains to trace the journey of the latter to that far-off point on the Nile where they met; then to follow the footsteps of the later explorer on other expeditions.

Mr. Baker had heard so much of explorers being hampered by the instructions which were given them, and the unsuitability of the stores which were in some cases provided against their protests, that he determined to risk failure from no such causes. He intended to venture upon an African exploring tour; but everything should be as he wished it; the sole glory, if glory there were, should be his; if he failed, none should have the right to criticise his actions. In short, he determined to pay the whole cost of the expedition himself.

At Cairo, he met with a new traveling companion, who proved to be of much service to him, assisting him in keeping his scientific records, and filling many other offices, such as most African explorers can only dream of. This was a young Swedish lady, whom he married shortly before leaving Cairo, and who insisted upon sharing his dangerous journey. Clear-headed, courageous, and of decision which quickly manifested itself in action when emergency required, few women could have performed the duties which she took upon herself, and which she did so well.

The expedition left Cairo in April, 1861; about half a year after Speke had left Zanzibar. That it had only reached Gondokoro by the time that Speke and Grant arrived there, by a much longer and more difficult route, is explained by the fact that Mr. Baker found it would be necessary, before proceeding very far, to acquire a knowledge of the Arabic. He accordingly spent a year in exploring the Atbara and the Blue Nile, and in the study of this tongue. June 11, 1862, he was at Khartoom, armed with a sufficient knowledge of Arabic to carry him through his intercourse with the native tribes, and ready to prosecute his journey up the White Nile.

Sir Samuel White Baker.

Some incidents of the journey may well be repeated here, as showing the character of the country through which they passed, and giving some idea of the fauna of the region. These incidents are best told in Baker's own words, prefaced only by such brief explanation as may be necessary to show the circumstances which are supplied, in the original work, by the natural course of the narrative.

Passing over the long journeys through the desert, we take

Lady Baker.

up the narrative at the time when they were engaged in exploring the Atbara; and follow their fortunes as rhinoceros hunters. The following account is in the words of Baker, although some unnecessary statements are omitted to save space:

"We were returning home through alternate plains and low open forests of mimosa, when Taher Sherif, who was leading the party, suddenly reined up his horse, and pointed to a thick bush, beneath which was a large gray but shapeless mass. He whispered, as I drew near, '*Oom gurrini!*' ('mother of the horn,' *i. e.*, rhinoceros). I immediatety dismounted, and advanced as near as I could. As I drew near, I discovered two rhinoceros asleep beneath a thick mass of bushes; they were lying like pigs, close together, so that at a distance I was unable to distinguish any exact form. I was compelled to advance with the wind direct from me to them; they were suddenly disturbed by the scent of an enemy; for without the least warning they sprang to their feet with astonishing quickness, and with a loud and sharp whiff, whiff, whiff, one of them charged straight at me. I fired my right-hand barrel in his throat, as it was useless to aim at the head protected by two horns at the nose. This turned him, but had no other effect, and the two animals thundered off together at a tremendous pace.

"Without waiting to reload, I quickly remounted my horse Tetel, and with Suleiman in company, I spurred hard to overtake the flying Arabs. The ground was awkward for riding at full speed, as it was an open forest of mimosas, which, although wide apart, are very difficult to avoid, owing to the low crowns of spreading branches; these, being armed like fish-hook thorns, would have been serious on a collision. I kept the party in view, until in about a mile we arrived upon open ground. Here I again applied the spurs, and by degrees I crept up, always gaining, until at length I joined the aggageers.

"The two rhinoceros were running neck and neck, like a pair of horses in harness, but bounding along at tremendous speed within ten yards of Taher Sherif, who, with his sword drawn, and his long hair flying wildly behind him, urged his horse forward in the race, amidst a cloud of dust raised by the two huge but active beasts, that tried every sinew in the horses. Roder Sherif was second; Abou Do was third. There were seven of us; and passing Abou Do, whose face wore an expression of agony at finding that his horse was failing, I quickly obtained a place between the two brothers, Taher and Roder Sherif. There had been a jealousy between the two parties of aggageers, each striving to outdo the other; thus Abou Do was driven almost to madness at the superiority of Taher's horse, while the latter, who was the renowned hunter of the tribe, was determined that his sword should be the first to taste blood. I tried to pass the rhinoceros on my left, so as to fire close into the shoulder my remaining barrel with my right hand, but it was impossible to overtake the animals, who bounded along with undiminished speed. With the greatest exertion of men and horses we could only retain our positions within about three or four yards of their tails—just out of reach of the swords. The only chance in the race was to hold the pace until the rhinoceros should begin to flag. The horses were pressed to the utmost; but we had already run about two miles, and the game showed no signs of giving in. At length the party began to tail off, and only a select few kept their places. We arrived at the summit of a ridge, from which the ground sloped in a gentle inclination for about a mile toward the river; at the foot of this incline was thick thorny nabbuk jungle, for which impenetrable covert the rhinoceros pressed at their utmost speed. Never was there better ground for the finish of a race; the earth was sandy, but firm; and as we saw the winning-post in the jungle that must terminate the hunt, we redoubled our exertions to close with the unflagging game. Suleiman's horse gave in—we had been for about twenty minutes at a killing pace. Tetel, although not a fast horse, was good for a distance, and he now proved his power of endurance. Only four of the seven remained, and we swept down the incline, Taher Sherif still leading, and Abou Do the last! His horse was done, but not the rider; for springing to the ground while at full speed, sword in hand, he forsook his tired horse, and, preferring his own legs, he ran like an antelope, and for the first hundred yards I thought he would really pass us, and win the honor of first blow. It was of no use; the pace was too severe, and, although running wonderfully, he was obliged to give way to the horses. Only three now followed the rhinoceros. The excitement was intense—we neared the jungle, and the rhinoceros began to show signs of flagging, as the dust puffed up before their nostrils, and with noses close to the ground, they snorted as they still galloped on. Oh for a fresh horse! 'A horse! a horse! my kingdom for a horse!' We were within two hundred yards of the jungle; but the horses were all done. Tetel reeled as I urged him forward, Roder pushed ahead; we were close to the dense thorns, and the rhinoceros broke into a trot; they were done! 'Now, Taher, for-r-a-a-r-r-d! for-r-a-a-r-r-d, Taher!' Away he went—he was close to the very heels of the beasts; but his horse could do no more than his present pace; still he gained upon the

SIR SAMUEL W. BAKER AND LADY ON AN AFRICAN JOURNEY.

nearest; he leaned forward with his sword raised for the blow—another moment, and the jungle would be reached! One effort more, and the sword flashed in the sunshine, as the rearmost rhinoceros disappeared in the thick screen of thorns, with a gash about a foot long upon his hind-quarters. Taher Sherif shook his bloody sword in triumph above his head; but the rhinoceros was gone. We were fairly beaten, regularly outpaced; * * * he had ridden splendidly, and his blow had been marvelously delivered at an extremely long reach, as he was nearly out of his saddle when he sprang forward to enable the blade to obtain a cut at the last moment. He could not reach the hamstring, as his horse could not gain the proper position. * * * The other aggageers shortly arrived, and as the rival Abou Do joined us, Taher Sherif quietly wiped the blood off his sword without making a remark; this was a bitter moment for the discomfited Abou Do."

It is exciting enough to chase a rhinoceros, as the above extract will prove to the inexperienced reader; but it is even more exciting to be chased by a rhinoceros. Here is what Baker says about such an unpleasant experience:

"We were passing through a mass of kittar or thorn-bush, almost hidden by the immensely high grass, when, as I was ahead of the party, I came suddenly upon the tracks of rhinoceros. These were so unmistakably recent that I felt sure we were not far from the animals themselves. As I had wished to fire the grass, I was accompanied by my Tokrooris, and my horsekeeper, Mohammed. It was difficult ground for the men, and still more unfavorable for the horses, as large disjointed masses of stone were concealed in the high grass.

"We were just speculating as to the position of the rhinoceros, and thinking how uncommonly unpleasant it would be should he obtain our wind, when whiff! whiff! whiff! We heard the sharp whistling snort, with a tremendous rush through the high grass and thorns close to us; and at the same moment two of these determined brutes were upon us in full charge. I never saw such a scrimmage; *sauve qui peut!* There was no time for more than one look behind. I dug the spurs into Aggahr's flanks, and clasping him round the neck, I ducked my head down to the shoulder, well protected with my strong hunting-cap, and I kept the spurs going as hard as I could ply them, blindly trusting to Providence and my good horse, over big rocks, fallen trees, thick kittar thorns, and grass ten feet high, with the two infernal animals in full chase only a few feet behind me. I heard their abominable whiffing close to me, but so did the good horse also, and the good old hunter flew over obstacles that I should have thought impossible, and he dashed straight under the hooked thorn bushes and doubled like a hare. The aggageers were all scattered; Mohammed was knocked over by a rhinoceros; all the men were sprawling upon the rocks with their guns, and the party was entirely discomfited. Having passed the kittar thorn, I turned, and seeing that the beasts had gone straight on, I brought Aggahr's head round, and tried to give chase; but it was perfectly impossible; it was only a wonder that the horse had escaped in ground so difficult for riding. Although my clothes were of the coarsest and strongest Arab cotton cloth, which seldom tore, but simply lost a thread when caught in a thorn, I was nearly naked. * * * * All the men were cut and bruised, some having fallen on their heads among the rocks, and others had hurt their legs in falling in their endeavors to escape. Mohammed was more frightened than hurt, as he had been knocked down by the shoulder and not by the horn of the rhinoceros, as the animal had not noticed him; its attention was absorbed by the horse.

Let us now follow through the excitement of an elephant hunt the same party that chased the rhinoceros:

"We had ridden about a mile, and were beginning to despair, when suddenly we turned a sharp angle in the watercourse, and Taher Sherif, who was leading, immediately reined in his horse, and backed him towards the party. I followed his example, and we were at once concealed by the sharp bend of the river. He now whispered, that a bull elephant was drinking from a hole it had scooped in the sand, not far from the corner. Without the slightest confusion, the hunters at once fell quietly into their respective places, Taher Sherif leading, while I followed closely in the line, with my Tokrooris bringing up the rear; we were a party of seven horses.

"Upon turning the corner, we at once perceived the elephant, that was still drinking. It was a fine bull; the enormous ears were thrown forward, as the head was lowered in the act of drawing the water up through the trunk; these shaded the eyes, and with the wind favorable, we advanced noiselessly upon the sand to within twenty yards before we were perceived. The elephant then threw up its head, and with the ears flapping forward, it raised its trunk for an instant, and then slowly, but easily, ascended the steep bank and retreated. The aggageers now halted for about a minute to confer together, and then followed in their original order up the crumbled bank. We were now on most unfavorable ground; the fire that had cleared the country we had hitherto traversed had been stopped by the bed of the torrent. We were thus plunged into withered grass above our heads, unless we stood in the stirrups; the ground was strewed with fragments of rock, and altogether it was ill adapted for riding. However, Taher Sherif broke into a trot, followed by the entire party, as the elephant was not in sight. We ascended a hill, and when near the summit, we perceived the elephant about eighty yards ahead. It was looking behind during its retreat, by swinging its huge head from side to side; and upon seeing us approach, it turned suddenly around and halted. 'Be ready, and take care of the rocks!' said Taher Sherif, as I rode forward by his side. Hardly had he uttered these words of caution, when the bull gave a vicious jerk with its head, and with a shrill scream it charged down upon us with the greatest fury. Away we all went, helter-skelter, through the dry grass, which whistled in my ears, over the hidden rocks, at full gallop, with the elephant tearing after us for about a hundred and eighty yards at a tremendous pace. Tetel was a sure-footed horse, and being unshod, he never slipped upon the stones. Thus, as we all scattered in different directions, the elephant became confused, and relinquished the chase; it had been very near me at one time, and in such ground I was not sorry when it gave up the hunt. We now quickly united, and again followed the elephant, that had once more retreated. Advancing at a canter, we shortly came in view. Upon seeing the horses, the bull deliberately entered a stronghold composed of rocky and uneven ground, in the clefts of which grew thinly a few leafless trees, the thickness of a man's leg. It then turned boldly toward us, and stood determinedly at bay.

"Now came the tug of war! Taher Sherif came close to me and said:

"'You had better shoot the elephant, as we shall have great difficulty in this rocky ground.'

"This I declined, as I wished to end the fight as it had been commenced, with the sword; and I proposed that he should endeavor to drive the animal to more favorable ground.

"'Never mind,' replied Taher, '*Inshallah* (please God) he shall not beat us.'

"He now advised me to keep as close to him as possible, and to look sharp for a charge. The elephant stood facing us like

A CLOSE CHASE.

a statue; it did not move a muscle beyond a quick and restless action of the eyes, that were watching all sides. Taher Sherif and his youngest brother Ibrahim now separated, and each took opposite sides of the elephant, and then joined each other about twenty yards behind it; I accompanied them until Taher advised me to keep about the same distance upon the left flank. My Tokrooris kept aloof from the scene, as they were not required. In front of the elephant were two aggageers, one of whom was the renowned Roder Sherif with the withered arm. All being ready for action, Roder now rode slowly towards the head of the cunning old bull, who was quietly waiting an opportunity to make certain of some one who might give him a good chance.

"Roder Sherif rode a bay mare, that, having been thoroughly trained to these encounters, was perfect at her work. Slowly and coolly she advanced towards her wary antagonist, until within about eight or nine yards of the elephant's head; the creature never moved, and the *mise en scene* was beautiful; not a word was spoken, and we kept our places amidst utter stillness, which was at length broken by a snort from the mare, who gazed intently at the elephant, as though watching for the moment of attack. One more pace forward, and Roder sat coolly upon his mare, with his eyes fixed upon those of the elephant. For an instant I saw the white of the eye nearest to me.

"'Look out, Roder! He's coming!' I exclaimed.

"With a shrill scream, the elephant dashed upon him like an avalanche! Round went the mare as though on a pivot, and away, over rocks and stones, flying like a gazelle, with the monkey-like form of little Roder Sherif leaning forward, and looking over his left shoulder as the elephant rushed after him. For a moment I thought he must be caught. Had the mare stumbled, all were lost; but she gained in the race after a few quick bounding strides, and Roder, still looking behind him, kept his distance so close to the elephant that its outstretched trunk was within a few feet of the mare's tail.

"Taher Sherif and his brother Ibrahim swept down like falcons in the rear. In full speed they dexterously avoided the trees, until they arrived upon open ground, when they dashed up close to the hind-quarters of the furious elephant, who, maddened with the excitement, heeded nothing but Roder and his mare, that were almost within its grasp. When close to the tail of the elephant, Taher Sherif's sword flashed from its sheath, as grasping his trusty blade he leaped

THE ELEPHANT'S LAST CHARGE.

nimbly to the ground, while Ibrahim caught the reins of his horse; two or three bounds on foot, with the sword clutched in both hands, and he was close behind the elephant; a bright glance shone like lightning, as the sun struck upon the descending steel; this was followed by a dull crack, as the sword cut through skin and sinews, and settled deep in the bone, about twelve inches above the foot. At the next stride, the elephant halted dead short in the midst of its tremendous charge. Taher had jumped quickly on one side, and had vaulted into the saddle with his naked sword in hand. At the same moment, Roder, who had led the chase, turned sharp around, and again faced the elephant as before; stooping quickly from the saddle, he picked up from the ground a handful of dirt, which he threw into the face of the vicious looking animal, that once more attempted to rush upon him. It was impossible! The foot was dislocated, and turned up in front like an old shoe. In an instant Taher was once more on foot, and again the sharp sword slashed the remaining leg. The great bull elephant could not move; the first cut with the sword had utterly disabled it; the second was its death-blow; the arteries of the leg were divided, and the blood spouted in jets from the wounds. I wished to terminate its misery by a bullet behind the ear, but Taher Sherif begged me not to fire, as the elephant would quickly bleed to death without pain, and an unnecessary shot would attract the Base, who would steal the flesh and ivory during our absence. We were obliged to return immediately to our far distant camp, and the hunters resolved to accompany their camels to the spot on the following day. We turned our horses' heads and rode direct toward home, which we did not reach till nearly midnight, having ridden upwards of sixty miles during the day. * * * * * *

"On the following day, the hunters started towards the dead elephant with camels and sacks, but they returned at night thoroughly disgusted; the nimble Base had been before them, most probably attracted to the carcass by the cloud of vultures that had gathered in the air. Nothing remained but the bones and the skull of the elephant; the flesh and the ivory had been stolen. The tracks of a great number of men had been left upon the ground, and the aggageers were fortunate to return without an attack from overwhelming numbers."

But it is not enough that we follow the explorer through his hunting adventures. Let us be with him as he looks for the first time upon some of the wonders of Nature. Here is his description of the whirlpool at the Royan Junction:

14

THE GREAT WHIRLPOOL OF THE ROYAN JUNCTION.

"The entire course of the Royan was extremely rapid, but at this extremity it entered a rocky pass between two hills, and leapt in a succession of grand falls into a circular basin of about four hundred yards diameter. This peculiar basin was surrounded by high cliffs, covered with trees; to the left was an island formed by a rock about sixty feet high; at the foot was a deep and narrow gorge through which the Settite River made its exit from the circle. This large river entered the basin through a rocky gap, at right angles with the rush of waters from the great falls of the Royan, and as both streams issued from gorges which accelerated their velocity to the highest degree, their junction formed a tremendous whirlpool; thus, the basin which was now dry, with the exception of the single contracted stream of the Settite, was in the rainy season a most frightful scene of giddy waters. The sides of this basin were, for about fifty feet from the bottom, sheeted with white sand which had been left there by the centrifugal force of the revolving waters; the funnel-shaped reservoir had its greatest depth beneath the mass of rock that formed a barrier before the mouth of the exit. From the appearance of the high-water mark upon the rock, it was easy to ascertain the approximate depth when the flood was at its maximum."

This whirlpool is in north latitude fourteen degrees, fifteen minutes, and east longitude thirty-six degrees, fifty-five minutes. The Royan is a small stream, not laid down upon most maps, which flows into the Settite, itself one of the rivers which unite to form the Atbara. Let us follow through one more hunting adventure, and then briefly sum up the results attained by this journey. The scene is a point on the Atbara, nearly due southwest of the whirlpool just described:

"I had been observing the country for some time from my high station, when I suddenly perceived two rhinoceros emerge from a ravine; they walked slowly through a patch of high grass, and skirted the base of the hill on which we were standing; presently they winded something and they trotted back and stood concealed in the patch of grass. Although I had a good view of them from my present position, I knew that I should not be able to see them on their covert, if on the same level; I therefore determined to send to the tent for my other horses, and to ride them down, if I could not shoot them on foot; accordingly, I sent a man off, directing him to lead Tetel from the peak, and to secure him to a tree at the foot of the hill, as I was afraid the rhinoceros might observe the horse upon the sky line. This he did, and we saw the man tie the horse by

A GOOD HORSE IN DANGER.

the bridle to the branch of a tree below us, while he ran quickly towards the camp. In the mean time I watched the rhinoceros; both animals lay down in the yellow grass, resembling masses of stone. They had not been long in this position, before we noticed two pigs wandering through the grass directly to windward, towards the sleeping rhinoceros; in an instant these animals winded the intruders, and, starting up, they looked in all directions, but could not see them, as they were concealed by the high grass. Having been thus disturbed, the rhinoceros moved their quarters, and walked slowly forward, occasionally halting, and listening; one was about a hundred yards in advance of the other. They were taking a direction at the base of the hill that would lead them directly upon the spot where Tetel was tied to the tree. I observed this to Taher Noor, as I feared they would kill the horse.

"'Oh, no,' he replied, 'they will lie down and sleep beneath the first tree, as they are seeking for shade—the sun is like fire.'

"However, they still continued their advance, and upon reaching some rising ground, the leading rhinoceros halted, and I felt sure he had a clear view of the horse, that was now about five hundred yards distant, tied to the tree. A ridge descended from the hill, parallel with the course the animals were taking; upon this, I ran as quickly as the stony slope permitted, keeping my eye fixed upon the leading rhinoceros, who, with his head raised, was advancing directly toward Tetel. I now felt convinced that he intended an attack. Tetel did not observe the rhinoceros, but was quietly standing beneath the tree. I ran as fast as I was able, and reached the bottom of the hill just as the wilful brute was within fifty yards of the horse, which now for the first time saw the approaching danger; the rhinoceros had been advancing steadily at a walk, but he now lowered his head, and charged the horse at full speed.

"I was about two hundred yards distant, and for the moment I was afraid of shooting the horse, but I fired one of the Reilly No. 10 rifles; the bullet, missing the rhinoceros, dashed the sand and stones into his face, as it struck the ground exactly before his nose, when he appeared to be just into the unfortunate Tetel. The horse in the same instant reared, and breaking the bridle, it dashed away in the direction of the camp, while the rhinoceros, astonished at the shot, and most likely half blinded by the sand and splinters of rock, turned round, and trotted back upon the track by which he had arrived. He passed me at about a hundred yards distance, as I had run forward to a bush, by which he trotted with his head raised, seeking for the cause of his discomfiture. Crack! went a bullet against his hide, as I fired my remaining barrel at his shoulder; he cocked his tail, and for a few yards he charged towards the shot; but he suddenly changed his course, and ran round several times in a small circle; he then halted, and reeling to and fro, he retreated very slowly, and lay down about a hundred yards off. Well done, Reilly! I knew that he had had his quietus, but I was determined to bag his companion, who in alarm had now joined him, and stood looking in all quarters for the source of danger; but we were well concealed behind the bush. Presently the wounded rhinoceros stood up, and walking very slowly, followed by his comrade, he crossed a portion of rising ground at the base of the hill, and both animals disappeared. * * * * * I waited a long time, until at length the two grays, Aggahr and Gazelle, arrived with my messenger from the camp. I tightened the girths of the saddle upon Aggahr, and had just mounted, when my eyes were gladdened by the sight of Hassan cantering toward me on Tetel, but from the exact direction the rhinoceros had taken.

"'Quick, quick!' he cried; 'come along! One rhinoceros is lying dead close by, and the other is standing under a tree not far off.'

"I immediately jumped on Tetel, and taking the little Fletcher rifle, as lighter and handier than the heavy No. 10, I ordered Taher Noor and Hassan to mount the other horses, and to follow me with spare rifles. I found the rhinoceros lying dead about two hundred yards from the spot where he had received the shot, and I immediately perceived the companion, that was standing beneath the small tree. The ground was firm and stony, all the grass had been burnt off, except in a few small patches; the trees were not so thick together as to form a regular jungle.

"The rhinoceros saw us directly, and he valiantly stood and faced me as I rode up within fifty yards of him. * * * I was unable to take a shot in this position, therefore I ordered the men to ride round in a half-circle, as I knew the rhinoceros would turn towards the white horses; and thus expose his flank; this he did immediately; and firing well, and right at the shoulder, I dropped him as though stone dead. * * The rhinoceros lay kicking upon the ground, and I thought he was bagged. But the bullet had not force to break the massive shoulder bone, but had merely paralyzed it for a moment; up he jumped, and started off in full gallop. * * * Spurring hard, I shot up to him at full speed until within twenty yards, when round he came with astonishing swiftness, and charged straight at the horse. I was prepared for this, as was my horse also; we avoided him by a quick turn, and again renewed the chase. * * * Thus the hunt continued for about a mile and a half, the rhinoceros occasionally charging, but always cleverly avoided by the horse. * * * The pace began to tell upon his wounded shoulder; he evidently went lame, and I felt that it would shortly be a case of "stand still." In this I was correct, and, upon reaching the deep and crumbling soil, he turned sharp round, made a clumsy charge that I easily avoided, and he stood panting at bay. Taher Noor was riding Gazelle; this was a very timid horse, and useless as a hunter, but, as it reared and plunged upon seeing the rhinoceros, that animal immediately turned towards it with the intention of charging. Riding Tetel close to his flank, I fired both barrels of the little Fletcher into his shoulder; he fell to the shots; and stretching out his legs convulsively, he died immediately."

Baker explored thoroughly, during the course of this expedition, the whole country drained by the Blue Nile, through which Bruce had passed more than a half century before. But the earlier traveler could not do more than find the fountains of the stream; the later explorer traced its whole course, and that of the kindred river, the Atbara. Thus, when he met Speke and Grant, with their records of the great Lake from which the White Nile flows, the three were ready to teach the world the geography of the Nile.

A brief description of that meeting, to which allusion has been made at the close of the last chapter, will not be out of place here. As usual, we give the words of the explorer himself:

"When I first met them [Speke and Grant] they were walking along the bank of the river towards my boats. At a distance of about a hundred yards I recognized my old friend Speke, and with a heart beating with joy I took off my cap and gave a welcome hurrah! as I ran towards him. For the moment he did not recognize me; ten years' growth of beard and moustache had worked a change; and as I was totally unexpected, my sudden appearance in the center of Africa appeared to him incredible. I hardly required an introduction to his companion, as we felt already acquainted, and after the transports of this happy meeting we walked together to my diahbiah, my men surrounding us with smoke and noise by keeping up an unintermitting fire of musketry the whole way. We were shortly seated on deck under the awning, and such rough fare as could be hastily prepared was set before these two ragged, careworn specimens of African travel, whom I looked upon with feelings of pride as my own countrymen. * * * Speke appeared the more worn of the two; he was excessively lean, but in reality he was in good tough condition; he had walked the whole way from Zanzibar, never having once ridden during that wearying march. Grant was in honorable rags; his bare knees projecting through the remnants of trousers that were an exhibition of rough industry in tailor's work. He was looking tired and feverish; but both men had a fire in the eye that showed the spirit that had led them through.

When Speke and Grant had told their story of what had been accomplished, Baker was disappointed that there was nothing left for him to do; the source of the Nile had already been discovered.

"Does not one leaf of the laurel remain for me?" he cried.

The answer was such as to satisfy even the thirst of such a man as Baker for adventure and achievement in this difficult field; although there was proof that the Nile flowed out of one great lake, the Victoria Nyanza, it must receive an additional supply from an unknown lake, the Luta Nzige. Baker at once resolved to continue the explorations which Speke and Grant had begun; and made arrangements with Debono's party, which Speke and Grant had accompanied, to go with them back to Falore, and farther if they could be induced to continue the journey.

But these arrangements were hardly made before they were unmade; for the traders were not anxious that this country should be explored. Baker at length persuaded seventeen of his own men, whom he had brought thus far at very great expense, to follow him; and the kindness of Mrs. Baker to the little child of an Arab merchant was eventually the means of securing a measure of good-will from the father. At the first halt, however, Baker's men mutinied; the captain declared that not a man should stir to load the camels. For answer, Baker struck him a blow on the jaw that felled him to the ground, while his gun flew into the air. The Englishman then rushed in among the others, and seizing them, some by the throat, he marched them to where the camels were awaiting their loads, and bade them do their work. They did it.

It was not long before Baker had won the admiration of those with whom he was associated; and after the final desertion of the rebellious captain, together with two or three others, he does not seem to have had any serious trouble of this nature. It added not a little to the respect which those who were left had for their master, that, when two of the deserters had been killed in a skirmish between their new masters and the natives, and their guns had been brought to Baker, he knew, from the numbers on the weapons, to what men they had been entrusted. He repeated the names aloud and added, impressively:

"Where are the men who have deserted from me? All gone! Food for vultures!"

His influence after this was almost unbounded; and he was treated with great respect, not only by the men who were in his pay, but by the Arabs under whose protection he was traveling.

But the rainy season had now set in; and both Mr. and Mrs. Baker suffered severely from fever. For several months they were inactive, save for one expedition of Baker's to the Asua, a stream of which the natives had told him. Finally, they recovered sufficiently to take up the line of march again, and about a year after the meeting with Speke at Gondokoro, they arrived at Kamrasi's capital. From this point they desired to start for the lake of which they had heard; but Kamrasi managed to delay them, on one pretext or another, for a considerable time. At last, at a meeting which was ostensibly for the purpose of arranging for their departure, Kamrasi told Baker that he was at liberty to go when he pleased, but that he must leave his wife with Kamrasi. To this very modest condition the traveler gave such an answer as might be expected; and when Mrs. Baker added her ideas upon the subject, "with a countenance almost as amiable as the head of Medusa," her husband declares, the savage king was ready to apologize. He was in the habit of giving his visitors pretty wives, he said, and expected to present one to Baker; he had not thought that his present guest would object to making such an exchange. As it was, there was an end of it, and he would never mention the subject again. Baker refused to accept any apology, however, and bade the king a very cold adieu. Kamrasi, to make amends, ordered his people to carry the traveler's baggage, and sent an escort of six hundred yelling natives to accompany them.

On the fourth day they came to the Kafoor River, which

THE START FOR THE LAKE WITH KAMRASI'S SATANIC ESCORT.

they were obliged to cross in a curious manner. The stream is covered with a network of floating weeds, strong enough to bear up a running man, although one moving slowly would sink through them. Baker started across, begging his wife to follow him as quickly as she could. He looked back, and saw her sinking through the weeds. Just as he started to her rescue, she fell headlong. She had been sunstruck; and was insensible when they got her, with many exertions, to land. All efforts to restore her to life were for a time useless; but at length, after three days of insensibility, she moved and spoke. But to the dreadful quiet, so like death, had come the no less dreadful energy of delirium, which lasted for seven days. It was not until the next week after the return of her senses that they were able to progress by slow degrees.

On the sixteenth day after leaving Kamrasi, they arrived at Parkani. A range of lofty mountains had been visible to them on the previous day, and the explorer felt assured that beyond them lay the goal of his journey; but on his arrival at Parkani he learned that he was nearer to it than he had thought. These mountains were the western boundary of the Nzige, and if he started early in the morning he might reach it by noon. Such a hint was not to be neglected; and bright and early on the morning of the 14th of March, 1864, they set out. The ascent proved too steep for their beasts of burden, and Mrs. Baker was worn out by sickness; but leaning on her husband's shoulder she, with undaunted resolution, accompanied him up the slope. At last they reached the summit of a pass, and saw, fifteen hundred feet below them, the great lake shining in the sunlight; to the south and southwest there was but one great stretch of waters, apparently boundless as the ocean; to the west, the lake appeared to be about sixty miles wide, and bounded by mountains at least seven thousand feet high. Regarding this scene, Baker says:

"Long before I reached this spot, I had arranged to give three cheers with all our men in English style in honor of the discovery, but now that I looked down upon the great inland sea lying nestled in the very heart of Africa, and thought how vainly mankind had sought these sources through so many ages, and reflected that I had been the humble instrument permitted to unravel this portion of the great mystery when so many greater than I had failed, I felt too serious to vent my feelings in vain cheers for victory, and I sincerely thanked God for having guided us and supported us through all dangers to the good end. I was about fifteen hundred feet above

A STORM ON THE ALBERT NYANZA.

the lake, and I looked down from the steep granite cliff upon those welcome waters—upon that vast reservoir which nourished Egypt and brought fertility where all was wilderness—upon that great source so long hidden from mankind; that source of bounty and of blessings to millions of human beings; and as one of the greatest objects in nature, I determined to honor it with a great name. As an imperishable memorial of one loved and mourned by our gracious queen, and deplored by every Englishman, I called this great lake the Albert Nyanza. The Victoria and the Albert lakes are the two sources of the Nile."

Some time was spent in exploring the surrounding country, particularly the connecting stream between the two Nyanzas; but both the travelers were quite worn out by sickness. At one time, Baker had his headman carefully instructed what to do with his maps and memoranda when he should die; for his wife he had no fear, for she was at least as sick as he.

They were now in a village of Kamrasi's country; and they found that the desertion of their men, and the starvation with which they were threatened, were due to Kamrasi's orders. Baker therefore sent a messenger to the king, demanding that an escort should be sent him. Kamrasi complied, only demanding the rifle which Baker always carried, his compass and his watch. This demand was promptly refused; whereupon Kamrasi invited the traveler to visit him. The savage expected to see him in rags, and was prepared to insult him in every possible way; what was his surprise, then, to see a man in the gorgeous costume of a Scotch Highlander, plaid, kilt, sporran, and bonnet! Baker had worn this when he lived in Perthshire many years before, and had saved it for some occasion like the present; it was a fortunate thing that he possessed it, for his other clothes were all in rags. As it was, the wonderful resources of the white man, who had these fine clothes when all thought he was destitute, appalled Kamrasi, who was not sure how much of it might be due to magic; and the strangers were duly provided with the necessary food.

In February, 1865, they set out for Gondokoro. They found that they had long been given up for dead by those who knew the dangers of the way. Reaching Suez about the middle of August, they found themselves once more in an English hotel. "What an Elysium! The beds had sheets and pillow-cases!" So exclaims the traveler who had been wholly unused to these luxuries for several years.

Mr. Baker found letters from home awaiting him at Cairo;

the first that he opened contained the information that, while still uncertain whether he were alive or dead, the Royal Geographical Society had awarded him the Victoria gold medal. "This appreciation of my exertions was the warmest welcome I could have received on my first entrance into civilization after so many years of savagedom; it rendered the completion of the Nile sources doubly grateful, as I had fulfilled the expectations that the Geographical Society had so generously expressed by the presentation of the medal before my task was done."

On their arrival in England, the travelers were received with much enthusiasm. Royal recognition of his services followed the Geographical Society's honor, and Mr. Baker became Sir Samuel White Baker, a title by which he is now better known than by the simpler one that he first bore. It is but just to add that Captain Speke would also have been knighted, but for his premature death.

Of a later expedition of Sir Samuel Baker's, we shall have more to say when we come to consider the slave trade, and what has been done for the abolition of the infamous traffic.

CHAPTER XI.

SCHWEINFURTH IN THE HEART OF AFRICA.

DR. Georg A. Schweinfurth was a native of Riga, who, being influenced by one of his earliest teachers, the son of an African missionary, early felt a great interest in the exploration of the southern continent. He was yet but a young man when, in 1863, he spent some time in Egypt, botanizing along the course of the Nile. He went as far as Khartoom, skirted the shores of the Red Sea, and visited the highlands of Abyssinia, returning after a stay of two years and a half.

Speke, Grant, and Baker were then the heroes of the day, their works on African exploration being but recently published. But their work had been largely confined to an investigation of the topography of the country; it is true, that Captain Grant had made careful notes of the new plants, and of the flora generally; but to Schweinfurth, this was the main thing to be accomplished. He was a botanist, and he naturally thought more of the botany of the country than of anything besides.

He submitted to the Royal Academy of Science at Berlin a plan for the botanical exploration of the equatorial districts lying west of the Nile, which was readily accepted. A grant was made to him for this purpose from the funds of the Humboldt Institution of Natural History and Travels; and in July, 1868, he found himself once more on the soil of Africa.

Instead of making the long voyage up the Nile, as Baker had done, Schweinfurth decided to proceed to Khartoom from Suez by way of Suakim and Berber. He made the journey in a leisurely way, reaching Berber October 7, and Khartoom on the first of the following month.

This was his real starting-point. It was not his intention to fit out an expedition with native soldiers and porters, as he feared that such a party would be only a hindrance to his plans; it would arouse the hostility of the native princes, and the jealousy of the traders and merchants. He decided, therefore, to attach himself to the train of the ivory merchants who came to Khartoom; and while he would thus be confined to the territory which they chose to visit, he considered that this would afford ample range for his botanical investigations.

Dr. Georg A. Schweinfurth.

The ivory merchants of this part of Africa have systematized the trade very thoroughly. They maintain a great number of settlements in districts as near the ivory countries as possible, the natives being brought into a state of complete subjection, and the country regularly portioned out among the various merchants. These depots are palisaded villages, called seribas. At each one is an agent of the merchant in whose territory it is located; while a superintendent has general charge of the district. These agents command the soldiers that the merchant maintains for the defense of his goods, and impose taxes for their support upon the subject natives; they decide the number of bearers which the natives must furnish when a distant expedition is planned; carry on war or make peace with the chiefs of the ivory country; and once a year send the collected stores of ivory to their master at Khartoom.

It will thus be seen that the ivory merchant is more powerful than any of the native chiefs; and that a traveler under the protection of one may safely journey through the wilds of Africa. Schweinfurth could more readily follow such leaders as the caravans of these men than if he were engaged on a strictly geographical expedition; the flora will be substantially the same throughout a district; and ten miles to the right or the left cannot matter as much as if the source of a river were in question.

Leaving Khartoom January 5, 1869, Schweinfurth, in company with a party of men in the employ of Ghattas, a Coptic Christian ivory dealer, and attended by six Nubians who were in his own pay, sailed up the Nile toward the country of the Shillooks. This territory was then but little known, even to the Egyptians, who completed its subjection some two years after Schweinfurth visited it. From data then obtained, the traveler's impressions were verified; he found it to be a densely populated country, everything which contributes to the exuberance of life here finding a concentrated field. The huts in their villages were so closely huddled together as to remind him of a thick mass of fungus. He reckoned that there must be nearly a hundred districts containing from fifty to one hundred villages each. This estimate was found to be too great, when the Egyptian government came to enumerate the villages and the people; of the former, it was found that there were three thousand, with about one million two hundred thousand inhabitants. It is the most densely populated part of Africa known to us, not even the Valley of the Nile being excepted.

Like most African tribes which wear but scanty clothing, the Shillooks spend much time and care upon their head-dress; the aim of all being, apparently, to render themselves as ridiculous-looking as possible. This result is attained in various ways, the wool being sometimes fashioned into the shape of a helmet, sometimes of a comb or a fan. Occasionally the traveler found a man with several combs arranged in parallel lines upon his head.

The White Nile is formed by the confluence of two streams,

ASCENDING THE NILE.

the Bahr-el-Ghazal and the Bahr-el-Gebel. The latter was considered by Speke and Baker as the main stream of the Nile; the first-named explorer speaking of the Bahr-el-Ghazal, or Gazelle River, as an unimportant stream. This judgment Schweinfurth condemns, believing that it is the Gazelle which is the main branch, draining a country of about one hundred and fifty thousand square miles. This difference in judgment is perhaps due to the difference of the seasons at which the two travelers viewed the rivers in question.

The Gazelle is unnavigable by reason of the grass-tangle, which, beginning in the White Nile below the mouth of this affluent, is so thick that, at the point where the Gazelle debouches, Schweinfurth was six days in pushing his way through it into the tributary stream; and increasing in density as the Gazelle is ascended, it finally renders navigation of any kind absolutely impossible.

This point, where the expedition must take to land whether or no, is the point from which the march begins. The destination was some seribas of Ghattas, two hundred miles in the interior. The caravan numbered nearly four hundred, of whom half were armed men—surely a sufficient force to overawe the natives in any numbers.

Their route lay through the country of the Dinkas, whom Schweinfurth considers the foremost of native people. They occupy such a wide extent of territory, that they vary materially in their ethnological standing; but one and all are lovers of cattle. Their one idea is to acquire a large herd. Not for food; far from it; they think too much of their cattle to slaughter them; only those that die a natural death are eaten; and the owner usually feels too severely his loss to join in the feast which his friends and neighbors make to celebrate such an event. Single cattle-yards sometimes hold as many as 10,000 cattle, the owners of which profess themselves entirely satisfied if only their cows get fat and look nice.

The caravan arrived at Ghattas' chief seriba March 30, and the explorer now had considerable leisure for an investigation of the flora of the surrounding country, and for getting into shape those notes and specimens which had been procured on the way. Two neatly built huts had been prepared for him, and of these he at once took possession, leaving them only for strolls in a country of almost idyllic beauty. The early rains had begun, and the ground was fairly covered with plants, the beauty of which rivalled anything which the botanist had ever seen.

A NIAM-NIAM MINSTREL.

During this time, he made a pretty thorough exploration of the sources of the Dyoor River, one of the most important tributaries of the White Nile system. He has, in this connection, carefully noted the characteristics of the Dyoor tribe, a branch of the Dinkas. His time was further occupied in the care of a garden, which he planted with corn from New Jersey, tobacco from Maryland, and other plants from various countries. Of the corn, he remarks that not only did the amount reaped answer his highest expectations, but that the quality surpassed that of the seed.

After an excursion into the country of the Bongo, whom he found better housed than any tribe which he had yet seen, but whose customs in eating disgusted him, he accepted the invitation of another ivory-merchant's representative, to accompany a caravan into the country of the Niam-Niams. It was under the protection of this merchant's people that he was enabled to reach the upper Shari, more than eight hundred miles from Khartoom; and thus open fresh districts to geographical knowledge and establish the existence of some enigmatical peoples. The expedition set out January 29, more than a thousand souls in the caravan, four hundred of whom were soldiers. On the fourth day the country of the Niam-Niams was entered. At first the natives fled from the caravan; but as the caravan was recognized as that of Abou Sammat, they became more friendly. The stranger found these people tall and well-proportioned, intelligent, warlike, and impatient of restraint. They are extremely fond of music, and have wandering minstrels, who perform on a kind of stringed instrument, and accompany this music with a song. Their affection for their wives is unusual among African peoples; and their whole bearing is almost chivalrous. There is a dark side to the picture, of course; and these models of chivalric savages are cannibals, whose war-cry is "Meat!" Their language contains no equivalent for God or prayer, and their only religion is a belief in magic.

"Their curiosity appeared to be insatiable, and they never wearied in their inquiries as to my origin. To their mind the mystery was as to where I could have come from; my hair was the greatest of enigmas to them; it gave me a supernatural look, and accordingly they asked whether I had dropped from the clouds or was a visitor from the moon, and could not believe that anything like me had been seen before. * * * * When they came to see me, I had to provide for their entertainment, and in this respect I was greatly assisted by my

KING MUNZA IN FULL STATE.

matches, as the marvel of my being able to produce fire at pleasure was an inexhaustible source of interest. If ever I handed over a lucifer and let them light it themselves, their rapture surpassed all bounds; they never failed to consider that the power of producing flames resided in me, but their astonishment was very greatly increased when they discovered that the faculty could be extended to themselves. Giving the white man credit for being able to procure fire or rain at his own pleasure, they looked upon the performances as miracles unparalleled since the dawn of creation."

As the journey continued, Schweinfurth was not a little puzzled by the varying directions which the puny streams appeared to take; he could not, for some time, make out the point of the compass to which they flowed, or even to what great river they were tributary. It was no small wonder; for, as he discovered before many days had passed, he was on the watershed of the Nile, and was the first European who, coming from the north, had yet reached that point. Finally, after a journey of nearly two months, they reached the Welle, which Schweinfurth regards as the upper course of the Shari. This was crossed in Monbuttoo boats, and the next day they entered the territory of this tribe, of which Munza was the king.

The merchant in whose caravan Schweinfurth was traveling was a sworn brother of this monarch, according to rites which obtain among savage peoples; and the stranger was therefore introduced at court under the most flattering auspices. Notwithstanding this, he was compelled to wait a full hour after he presented himself in the great hall (for the Monbuttoos excel other African tribes in their architecture), and allow the king time to make his toilet. Of his appearance, when he finally entered and seated himself in his chair of state, Schweinfurth says:

"I could now feast my eyes upon the fantastic figure of this ruler. I was intensely interested in gazing upon the sovereign of whom it was commonly reported that his daily food was human flesh. With arms and legs, neck and breast, all bedizened with copper rings, chains, and other strange devices, and with a great copper crescent at the top of his head, the potentate gleamed with a shimmer that was to our ideas unworthy of royalty, but savored too much of the magazines of civic opulence, reminding one almost unavoidably of a well-kept kitchen. His appearance, however, was decidedly marked with his nationality, for every adornment that he had about him belonged exclusively to Central Africa, as none but the fabrications of his native land are deemed worthy of adorning the person of a king of the Monbuttoo. Agreeably to the national fashion, a plumed hat rested on the top of his chignon, and soared a foot and a half above his head; this hat was a narrow cylinder of closely plaited reeds; it was ornamented with three layers of red parrots' feathers, and crowned with a plume of the same; there was no brim, but the copper crescent projected from the front like the vizer of a Norman helmet. The muscles of Munza's ears were pierced and copper bars as thick as the finger were inserted in the cavities. The entire body was smeared with the native unguent of powdered camwood, which converted the original bright brown tint of the skin into the color which is so conspicuous on ancient Pompeian halls. With the exception of being of an unusually fine texture, his single garment differed in no respect from that worn throughout the country; it consisted of a single large piece of fig-bark impregnated with the same dye that served as his cosmetic, and this, falling in graceful folds about his body, formed breeches and waistcoat all in one. Round thongs of buffalo hide, with heavy copper balls attached to the ends, were fastened around the waist in a huge knot, and like a girdle held the coat, which was neatly hemmed. Around the king's neck hung a copper ornament made in little points which radiated like beams all over his chest; on his bare arms were strange-looking pendants which in shape could only be compared to drum-sticks with rings at the end. Halfway up the lower part of the arm and just below the knee were three bright, horny-looking circlets cut out of hippopotamus hide, likewise tipped with copper. As a symbol of his dignity Munza wielded in his right hand the sickle-shaped Monbuttoo scimetar, in this case only an ornamental weapon, and made of pure copper. * * I could hardly help marveling at the composure of this wild African, and wondering where in the world he could have learned his dignity and self-possession."

Schweinfurth was the first white traveler who had ever penetrated to the country of the Monbuttoo, which lies between the parallels of three degrees and four degrees north, and the meridians twenty-eight degrees and twenty-nine degrees east from Greenwich. The area is not more than four thousand square miles, but the population amounts, according to this traveler's estimate, to not less than a million; and the degree of progress which they have made in civilization and its arts, renders them remarkable among the nations of Central Africa.

It is a remarkable physical feature of the race, that in addition to the fact that their color is lighter than that of any other natives of this part of the continent, many of them have light hair.

The people of this tribe use a great deal of fat, both as a cosmetic, rubbed in with the paint with which they color their skin, and in cooking. For the latter purpose, they use palm-oil and the oil prepared from the bodies of white ants; besides a fat which is even more revolting—they are cannibals, and human fat is universally employed among them. Schweinfurth says that "the cannibalism of the Monbuttoo is unsurpassed by any nation in the world."

But the discovery which has rendered this explorer's name more famous than any other achievement has done, was that of the pygmies. For two thousand years, there had been stories told of a pygmy race living in the interior of Africa; but modern enlightenment had set them down as mere idle fables of antiquity and ignorance. But at the court of Munza, the German found actual specimens of the Akka tribe, men scarcely four feet and a half high, whom the Monbuttoo king, to whom the tribe was tributary, had compelled to settle in his neighborhood, that he might have such curiosities at his court. These dwarfs, however, proved so shy that it was impossible to obtain much information regarding them, their customs, or their country. The most definite information he could obtain was that four days' journey from Munza's capital, in a direction south of southeast, would bring him to the first village of the Akkas.

After a couple of weeks spent at the capital of Munza, the ivory merchant became convinced that he had all the stores which that king possessed; it was commercial wisdom, therefore, to waste no more time here, and he proposed to visit those tribes living farther to the south. But Munza did not wish to lose the monopoly of the ivory trade, and therefore refused his co-operation. Without him, nothing could be done; and much to the chagrin of Schweinfurth, they were obliged to return. Something of his disappointment may be realized, when we state that he was actually not more than four hundred miles from Livingstone's most northern terminus. He was almost within sight of the hills bounding the Albert Nyanza; the solution of the Nile question, so long unsolved, was nearly within his grasp; but without soldiers, such as accompanied the Speke expedition, without the funds which might have made it possible for a solitary traveler to

KING MUNZA DANCING BEFORE HIS WIVES.

make his way through the country, he realized that he had reached the southernmost limits of his journey.

The caravan broke camp on the 12th of April, and after a comparatively uneventful journey, reached the head seriba of the merchant early in July. From this point, Schweinfurth pressed on toward Egypt; but was detained for some time by various circumstances. It was an irreparable loss when a most disastrous fire destroyed all his botanical and entomological collections, as well as his journals and registers. Having lost his pedometers in the fire, he actually counted all his steps in order to ascertain the distance over one whole expedition. They numbered more than a million and a quarter. This was in an effort to map out the district of the upper Gazelle. When his ink failed, he drew and made his memoranda with chicken's blood.

In the absence of these notes which were destroyed by the fire, the results of Schweinfurth's journey, from a geographical point of view, may be thus briefly summed up: he crossed the water-shed between the Nile and the tributaries of Lake Tchad, and thus proved that the basin of the Gazelle was of considerably less extent than Livingstone had supposed.

CHAPTER XII.

DR. HOLUB, THE AUSTRIAN HUNTER AND EXPLORER.

DR. Holub was an Austrian physician, who, in 1872, resolved to go to South Africa and make such explorations as a lengthy residence in the country would permit. He remained in this portion of the continent for seven years, the greater part of which time was spent in traveling through the country so little known to Europeans.

He was not over-burdened with this world's goods; he naively remarks, having occasion to mention that his cabin was not the first, that he had not the money to take any but a second-cabin passage to Cape Town; and he further informs us that on landing, after having paid the duty on his gun and revolver, he had but two dollars and a half remaining in his pocket. Under such circumstances, it was necessary for him to remain at Cape Town for some little time, in order to recruit his exhausted finances, which he did by the practice of his profession. Having paid his medical visits, he would set out on long excursions into the surrounding country, which would occupy the remainder of the day; and in this way, four weeks passed away, at Cape Town and Port Elizabeth. In the beginning of August, 1872, he set out for Fauresmith, where he hoped to enter upon a practice which would maintain him for a while. In this, however, he was disappointed; and accepted the advice of a new-found friend, to push on toward the diamond fields.

Here, two courses lay open to him; he must dig for diamonds, or secure a medical practice. He chose the latter; and established himself in a rude hut containing two rooms; here he kept bachelor's hall, with all the discomforts implied in that term. Servant he had none, and his housework was done after night and by stealth, that his professional dignity might not suffer. Yet even his poverty did not secure him from attempts at theft. Countries where wealth may possibly be accumulated suddenly, as in rich mines of every kind, are infested with many disorderly characters; and here, in addition to those who came from the various countries of Europe, were the natives who had learned the white man's vices, without losing any of their own, or acquiring any of his virtues. Police supervision was so slight that once, at least, he had occasion to eject from his hut a thief whose arms showed that he was prepared to commit a greater crime than theft, if such should be necessary to attain his end.

Dr. Emil Holub.

The whole of the diamond-fields of South Africa may be divided into three districts. The oldest fields are on the Vaal River, and extend from Bloemhof to the confluence of the Vaal and the Harts; the next are the so-called dry-diggings, where the "pebbles" were originally obtained by sifting the earth, instead of washing it; of this district the town of Kimberley is the center; and here it was that Dr. Holub was established; the third district lies in the Orange River Free State. His residence here was shortly after the palmiest days of the mines, which were in 1870 and 1871. It is not that the aggregate profits have diminished, but while the yield has largely increased, the cost of working has also increased. Since this period, however, when a swaggering adventurer would sometimes light his pipe with a five-pound note, the rush of adven-

Bouncing a Midnight Thief.

turers eager for sudden wealth has largely given way to the application of steady and systematic industry; the mode of obtaining the diamonds has gradually become more skilled and scientific, and the authorized rules and regulations for the protection of the diggers and the merchants have materially improved the condition of both. Law and order have gradually gained control, and the large numbers of reckless characters who flocked thither during the wild excitement which followed the first discovery of precious stones, have been forced to give way to a better class of inhabitants.

Dr. Holub's medical practice increased so rapidly that he was soon able to pay the debts which he had incurred, and to lay by considerable sums toward the undertaking on which he had resolved. He purchased a wagon and many requisites for traveling, invited three friends to join him, and in February, 1873, set out on his first long journey, which, he says, was to be mainly one of reconnoissance.

His main object was to ascertain by actual experience what amount of provisions and other articles it would be necessary to carry with him for a prolonged expedition into the interior. His goal was the country of the Batlapins, living up the Harts

African Explorers Trading with Natives.

valley. He found these people friendly enough, and ready to admire all the articles of European manufacture which the travelers had with them and were willing to take the time to exhibit.

The time of the travelers was spent in alternate hunting and journeying, the hunting being done not only with a view to obtaining food, but from an interest in the strange animals themselves; nor was botany neglected. Perhaps a description which Holub gives of the journey just after leaving Bloemhof may illustrate some of the difficulties of traveling in this part of the world, even when there is no danger of attack from hostile natives:

"Ever since we had left Klipdrift the weather had been remarkably fine, with only a few occasional exceptions; but as we quitted Bloemhof we observed that the horizon was ominously heavy; and as evening drew on, the rain began to fall, and it became so dark that it was quite impossible to see more than a few yards ahead. I regretted that I had not come to the determination of passing the night in the town.

"For a while one or two of us tried to walk in front of the team, to give confidence to the Koranna who was leading the foremost pair of bullocks by the bridle, declaring every minute that he could not distinguish the path from the ground by the side; but the rain was so drenching, and the wind so pitiless, that we were obliged to give up, and get what shelter we could in the wagon. After slipping and sliding for about a hundred yards or so more, the bullocks all came to a standstill, and I could not help fearing that we had got on to a declivity, which would lead down to the river; and knowing that further progress under such circumstances would be dangerous, I came to the conclusion that we must stay where we were until daylight.

"Notwithstanding the pouring rain, I went out twice to reconnoiter our situation. The second time I went farther than before, and made a discovery which rather startled me. Not many yards in front of us I observed a large dark spot, which it struck me must be a deep hollow in the ground. I called to the driver to watch with me, and wait for the next flash of lightning, that we might ascertain what it really was. The lightning was not long in coming, and revealed close at our feet the bed of a rain-torrent, that of course went right to the river. Only a few more steps and the consequences must have been most disastrous; for when daylight came, we found that the walls of the ravine were not only very precipitous, but not less than sixteen feet in depth."

Wonderfontein, a name which the Boers apply to the caves and grottos which distinguish the district lying along the Mooi River, was the farthest point reached in this first journey. Their visit was limited to three days, during which time the adventurer explored the caves as far as possible; lamenting that he was not permitted to enlarge certain passages which would have enabled him to explore what he supposed must be much longer and loftier rifts in the rocks.

Their return route was the same, as far as Bloemhof, as that by which they came. Passing over minor hunting adventures, we come to one the scene of which is laid in the Maquassie

Hills; an account of which we quote, as it was told to Holub:

"The northern passes of the hills were being terribly ravaged by four lions, that none of the Boers would venture to attack. At last, one day, a farmer's son, having gone out to fetch home three of his horses, came riding back in great excitement, with the intelligence that he had found their carcasses all lying half-eaten in the grass. The foot-marks all around left no doubt that the lions had been the perpetrators of the deed.

Dangers of Midnight Traveling.

"The announcement stirred the Boers to action, and they determined to make up a party to hunt them down. Accordingly, the farmer and six others, of whom Schmitt was one, mounted their horses; the son who had discovered the tracks being elected leader. The lion-track was soon found; it led through a valley, across one hill, then another, and finally on to a level plain, where, not only was the grass very short, but the soil was so hard that the vestiges of the beasts could no longer be distinguished. After some hesitation, it was agreed that there was no alternative but to abandon the chase; and it is very probable that most of the party had found their ardor

ARROUSING A LIONESS FROM HER AMBUSH.

somewhat abated by their exertions, and were quite content to acquiesce in the proposal to return home. They broke up close to Schmitt's house, one of the party remaining behind a minute to talk. All at once, to their vast surprise, they spied out, close to the farm, a lion and lioness, evidently lurking in ambush. Without losing an instant they rode towards them, their horses behaving bravely in the presence of their natural foes. In order to get a better aim at the beasts when they rose, Schmitt dismounted and led his horse a few steps by the bridle, then raising his gun to be ready to fire, he called to his partner to do the same. On turning his head, however, he found that his friend, instead of following him, had retreated for a good fifty yards, so that here he was alone confronting a couple of lions, with very likely several more in the rear. What could he do but retreat also? As he retired he kept his eye fixed upon the lions, who kept steadily following him, till just as he joined his companion, they suddenly turned tail and made off towards one of the rock-funnels where the bushes were very thick.

"The rest of the party had hardly got out of earshot, and were soon summoned back. Off they started, and determined to explore the hollow, taking especial care to watch the side nearest the hills for which the lions were almost sure to make. After a continuous holloing and throwing of stones, the lioness was ultimately aroused from her retreat. She did not rush straight towards the hills, as had been expected, but took a devious course, which, however, happened to bring her within range of no less than three of her pursuers. Simultaneously three shots rang in the air. Despite her efforts to escape, the lioness very soon sunk to the earth. Every shot had taken effect."

Arrived at Bloemhof, they started off again for the famous Hallwater Salt-pan, near the Vaal, and nominally in the Transvaal Republic, but virtually under the power of the native tribe of the Korannas. From this point they pursued a path nearly parallel to the river, intending to explore the Hebron hills.

They arrived at Hebron, once an important place, but now merely a village containing a shop or two, a hotel, a smithy, a slaughter-house and a prison. The state of their finances made it necessary for them to push on without an hour's delay, although the day was Easter Sunday. Because it was a holiday, the ferryman refused to set them across the river; all his men were tipsy; so that Holub resolved to try his luck

A DANGEROUS FORD.

crossing the river by a ford. One of his companions went reconnoitering, and returned with the information that there was a ford about two miles down the stream. They started off at once.

"Though the water was shallow, the current was strong; the river-bed, too, was covered with rocks, which even in the open road would sorely have tried the strength of our oxen. Before we got one-third of the way across, we found ourselves carried considerably below the ford, and our position rapidly becoming critical.

"Our black drivers exerted themselves to the uttermost. They shouted, they flogged, they pulled; but quite in vain; the oxen were utterly unable to stir, and distressed by the strength of the current, they began to be restive and to pull at their yokes and bridles. This caused the foremost pair to sink deeper and deeper, and it seemed only too certain that they must be drowned. Prompt action was necessary. I had hurt my hand and was incapacitated from rendering much help; but I sprang from the wagon, followed by one of the rest; and although we could do nothing to rescue the vehicle from its situation, we succeeded in unharnessing the oxen, who struggled to the opposite side with the greatest difficulty. By the most arduous exertions, we went backwards and forwards carrying the most valuable part of my collection ashore; but the wagon itself we were obliged to leave with a large portion of its contents, in the bed of the river, until further assistance could be procured. Our labor entailed such fatigue that before darkness came on we were all ready to drop. The uncertainty about our wagon and property made us pass an anxious night, and it was a great relief in the early morning to hear a distant cracking of whips, announcing that aid was at hand. Four Koranna wagons, drawn by six or eight pairs of oxen, soon appeared, and made their way quickly to our side of the river. A bargain was concluded, by which our wagon was to be brought to land for the sum of ten shillings, and the maneuver was accomplished without difficulty or farther accident."

A little more than a month after this adventure, the party arrived at their original starting-point; and Dr. Holub once more set himself to work to procure funds for a second journey, much longer, but still partaking somewhat of the nature of a trial trip. This second journey was begun Nov. 3, 1873; the party consisted of Holub, three German friends, a Griqua driver, nine dogs, a saddle-horse, and eight oxen. The first stage of the journey was from Dutcitspan to Musemanyana;

and they had traveled but a very few days when the first of their adventures befell them:

"Proceeding east by north we soon came to a region where we could well believe our guide that not a drop of rain had fallen for months, and the further we advanced the more parched and yellow did the grass become; though the spring was coming on, we saw but few sprouting blades, and as we went on we found fewer still; the young leaves of the amaryllis, too, that had sprung up here and there were quite withered by the drought. * * * A light breeze swayed the tall grass stems like a field of corn, and was hailed by us with delight as it moderated the heat, and gave a sort freshness to our fevered lips. The oxen had not tasted water for thirty hours; their languor was excessive, and up hill they could climb only at a snail's pace. * * * While we were looking about us, we saw a thick cloud overhanging the plains. Every one, natives included, settled that it was a huge swarm of locusts. I was occupied with my own matters, and soon forgot all about it. A sudden cry from one of the people in the wagon very shortly afterward recalled my attention to what we had seen, and on looking again I beheld a sight that could not fail to fill me with amazement and alarm. The plain right in front of us, over which we were on the point of passing, was one sheet of flame. The cloud that we had observed turned out to be a volume of smoke among the bushwood, that was all on fire. The conflagration was perhaps five miles from us, but it was exactly across our path, and we might well feel dismayed."

"The first among us to regain composure was our temporary guide, who pointed out that the wagon-tracks of which he had spoken were hardly twenty yards ahead; at least, we could reach them. We looked to the right; we looked to the left; on the right the ground was level, but it only led to a chain of hills, the base of which was already licked by the flames; on the left was a hollow which was just beginning to catch fire, and beyond it a little hillock some forty feet high. Our perplexities seemed only to increase; the oxen were too weary to allow us to think for one moment of retreating; they could not hold out a mile; and yet something must be done; the fire was manifestly advancing in our very face. We discussed the possibility of setting fire to the bushwood close in front of us, and thus, as it were, forestalling the flames; but the scheme was not to be thought of; the wagon, which contained some thousands of cartridges, three hundred pounds of gunpowder, besides a quantity of spirits, was already so heated by the sun that we could scarcely lay our hands upon it; a single spark of fire would in an instant involve it in complete destruction.

"My eye still rested upon the little hill. I saw that the wind was blowing the flames in a direction away from it, and aware that delay would be fatal, and that some action must be taken, I gave my decision that at all hazards we must make for it. Every one agreed that I was right, and, rushing to their posts, did what they could to urge on the bullocks without a moment's loss of time. Mounting my horse, I hurried on in front, but on reaching the hollow that had to be crossed before the place of safety on the hill could be gained, I almost gave a cry of despair on seeing its character; it was not only overgrown with bushwood and very steep, but was strewn in all directions with huge blocks of stone; if only the wagon-wheel should strike against one of these, who could doubt the consequences?

"With all his might, Boly cracked his whip and shouted vigorously, and succeeded in making the oxen drag the wagon with unexpected speed; they were all flecked with foam as they pulled their oscillating load behind them; every moment it seemed as if it must overbalance. At the bottom of the hollow it was absolutely necessary to take a rest; the beasts must have time to recover from their exertions; they were all more or less torn by the bushes, and my friends, too, were much scratched about the hands and face. The heat was becoming intense. My horse was not naturally a nervous animal, but it trembled until it could scarcely stand, and the hardest part of our struggle was yet to come.

"A flake of fire fell within fifteen yards of us, and warned us that it was time to be on the move. '*Hulloh an! Hulloh an!*' roared the driver, and the bullocks once again strained themselves to their work. Scarcely, however, had they gone ten paces, when the smoke puffed against their eyes, and bewildered, they swerved into a track where the wagon must inevitably have been overturned; it was a critical moment, but happily one of my party, who was walking by my side, saw the danger, and rushing at the heads of the leaders, turned them by a desperate effort into the right direction. The instinct of self-preservation now redoubled every one's efforts; onwards we pushed through clouds of smoke, amidst falling ashes, amongst fragments of red-hot bark, till we were within fifty yards of a place of safety. So heated was the atmosphere, that I momentarily expected to see the canvas of the wagon break out into a blaze.

A HEADLONG FLIGHT FROM THE FLAMES.

"The bullocks once more gasped and tottered beneath their yoke; with painful toil they made their way for another thirty yards; it was doubtful whether they could accomplish the remaining twenty.

"One more moment of rest, followed by one more frantic paroxysm of exertion, and all was safe! Just in time we reached a hill that overlooked a hollow, beyond which was the expanse of black burnt grass."

The next day brought a pouring rain, which effectually ended all danger of fire for that season. A few days after this adventure with the prairie-fire, they had another, which was laughable when they had recovered from the annoyance. They were fairly mobbed by the natives, who demanded that they should sell them brandy:

"They had brought all manner of things to barter for spirits. One man held up a jackal's hide, another a goat-skin; another offered us bullock-thongs; yet another had brought out a bullock-yoke; and some of them had their home-made wooden spoons and platters to dispose of to us. It was a most disgusting scene. We tried to treat the whole matter with contempt, and to take no notice of their demand; but when we attempted to drive on, their importunities waxed louder than ever. They caught hold of the bridles, and pushed the oxen back, becoming ever more and more clamorous. One of the men made what he evidently thought would be an irresistible appeal, by offering me a couple of greasy shillings. They next tried to bribe us with some skins of milk which the women were made to bring out from the huts, and they were driven to despair when they found that the offer of a goat which they dragged forward was not accepted. Their screechings and shoutings were of no avail; not a drop of fire-water was to be extorted from me. We had almost to beat them off before they would allow us to proceed. A few persevered in following us to the ford, and made a final effort to secure one bottle by a private negotiation, out of sight of their neighbors. They confidently offered five shillings for the bottle; but I was inexorable."

The next stage of their journey was from Musemanyana to Moshaneng. It was during this part of their trip that they found the natives especially alarmed by the fear of lions, who had committed many depredations. It appeared that the savage beasts preferred domestic animals to any other; they were incredibly bold, being so accustomed to the sight of men and the sound of fire-arms that they ventured very close to

A RUSH FOR FIRE-WATER.

the kraals. The chief with whom, among others, they talked, told them that he had lost many cattle, and several of his people; and two of his men, who had gone out to search for a missing bullock, had come suddenly upon a colony of lions, eight in number, including cubs, devouring the animal; and had scarcely had time to scramble into the branches of an immense tree to save themselves from this veritable lions' den.

"He related a distressing incident that had occurred on one of the neighboring rivers. A party of natives were on their way from Maraba, in the Makalaka country, to the diamond fields, a distance of eight hundred miles. It was by no means unusual for such parties to quit their homes with simply a hide and an assegai, quite prepared, during their long and arduous journey, to live on nothing but roots, wild fruit, and occasionally a small head of game. The spectacle they would present to any traveler who might meet them was very piteous. Sometimes they would be almost destitute of food of any sort for days together, and be reduced well-nigh to skeletons. Their progress would become more and more painful; and they would endeavor to mitigate the pangs of hunger by drawing in the waistbands which with a strip of hide formed clothing. The ordinary custom was for them to travel in single file, the strongest first, then the less robust, followed by the weakest; so that an invalid would often be quite by himself, a long way in the rear. In the party of which the chief was speaking there were two brothers, one of whom, on account of his feeble condition of health, had for more than a week been obliged to take his place last in the procession. Arriving at the bank of the Sitlagole, the party halted to search for some roots, not unlike turnips, which were known to grow there, and which they hoped to cook and enjoy for supper. They found the roots in such abundance that it was resolved to spend the night on the spot, and they kindled a fire to prepare their meal. On closing in, it was soon ascertained that the sick comrade was absent. They looked at each other with much perplexity; but the brother of the missing man, without losing a moment, snatched up his own and his brother's share of the roots which had been gathered, fastened them to a strap upon his shoulder, seized his assegai, and started off. The rest drew closer in, enjoyed their supper, lighted up several additional fires as a protection from attack, and laid themselves down under the bushes to sleep.

"The missing Bechuana was a Batloka, and the evidence went to show that the poor fellow had been compelled to rest

TREED BY LIONS.

so often and so long from his weakness, hunger and sore feet, that he had fallen far into the rear; and missing his way, had strayed into a rocky valley full of bushes that were notoriously the haunt of lions. Here no doubt he had been pounced upon and killed, for the brother had not gone far before he could trace the spot where the proper path had been left, and proceeding onward he soon observed a lion's footprints in the sand. Instead of turning back, he had apparently caught sight of his brother's stick, straw hat, and gourd bottle, lying on the ground, and trusting to his assegai, had resolved to venture on alone.

"'But what was an assegai,' exclaimed Shebor, 'in the face of a lion which had just tasted human blood?'

"It was clear that before he reached his brother's corpse the lion had sprung from its concealment, and secured him as a second victim.

"Finding next morning that both the men were absent the whole party was in consternation, too truly fearing the worst. They applied for help at a Barolong farm close at hand, and following the tracks were not long in discovering the two mangled bodies close to each other. The marks on the ground were quite distinct, and left no doubt that a lion had just quitted the spot. Probably it had only been scared away by their own approach, and they determined to continue the chase. After they had made their way for about five hundred yards along the bank, they caught sight of a tawny object in a thicket just ahead. They hardly dared to hope that it was the creature of which they were in pursuit; but simultaneously a number of them fired, and great was their triumph when they discovered amongst the bushes the carcass of a large lion pierced by six bullets."

They were not destined, for the present, to fall in with any lions; but after listening to the old chief's cautions, profited by the words of advice, and took a path which was not infested by these animals. The road by which they traveled led them through a country where the rain-pools were frequented by large herds of gnus, which Holub had some success in hunting; although his hunts were not attended by any events of special interest. The progress of their wagon frequently alarmed the herds of blessbocks and zebras. Some of these made their way through the thickets in the glades, while others scampered off across the open plain to more distant shelter; the natives, who chanced to be with Holub's party temporarily, following in hot pursuit; while the Europeans,

THE FINDING OF THE LOST BROTHER.

dismounted, followed eagerly on foot at a distance, to get a shot at the animals which the mounted Bartotongs were threatening with their assegais.

Dr. Holub was not a little interested in the religion of the native tribes; or, rather, their lack of religion, for he says that they seem to have had no faith of their own, before the introduction of Christianity. Here, as elsewhere throughout Africa, the people trust much to magic, and fear much the magic which is opposed to them. In spite of the efforts of the missionaries, this fear clings to many of them. By others, again, charms and incantations are viewed in their true light. Holub gives an instance of this, which occurred in 1866, among the Bechuanas of Shoshong. The word "moloi" means a magician or wizard, and is applied to one whose supposed power is exerted to work evil only:

"King Sekhomo was so jealous of the exceeding popularity of his son Khame that he determined to kill him. For this purpose he secretly engaged some moloi to go by night and enact their deadliest enchantments in front of Khame's house. Awakened by the gleam of a fire just beyond his enclosure, Khame crept out and stood quietly viewing the preparations. One of the performers of the mysteries happened to look round, and catching the sight of Khame's face in the glare, gave a loud cry of surprise; this so startled his companions that they took to their heels. The young man came forward, smashed up all the magic apparatus, threw it as so much lumber upon the fire, which he stopped carefully to extinguish, and the next morning, to the chagrin of the king and the discomfiture of the moloi, made his appearance in the kotla as well and hearty as ever."

From this little story it appears, that before you voodoo your enemy, you had better find out if your enemy is a good subject for such proceedings.

Among the Bechuanas, he found two distinct tribes of slaves; the Makalahari and the Masarwas. The former are generally employed as domestic servants, but the Masarwas are perpetually engaged as hunters, a pursuit in which they are greater adepts than their masters. Like the Bushmen, between whom and the Bantu family they appear to be a link, they use bows and arrows, to which Bechuanas are little accustomed; they are very adroit also in the use of poisoned assegais, with which they will attack almost any animal. Indeed, a naked Masarwa, armed only with a couple of these poisoned darts, will not hesitate to face a lion.

We have not space to note the reception which Holub met with from Sechele and other chiefs whom Livingstone had taught Christianity and civilization. Stirring adventures and curious customs fill the bulk of his two volumes, and we cannot pause for that which is of lesser interest. We stop here to note a custom which obtains among the Bantu:

Spoiled Magic.

"Held as of the highest importance by the heathen Bechuana is the rite of circumcision; until it has been submitted to, no youth is supposed to have arrived at man's estate, and no woman is considered of marriageable age. * * * * Called the '*boguera*,' the observance is put into force upon boys after they have reached their ninth year. The ceremony is

Facing a Lion with an Assegai.

performed at intervals varying from two to five years, according to the strength of the tribe; the period of its enactment being held to be a time of great festivity in the towns. If the boys do not present themselves voluntarily, they are brought under compulsion, and as a preparatory office they are smeared all over with a solution of chalk; the girls wear nothing but belts made of pieces of reed or aprons of genets' tails, their breasts and faces being also whitened with chalk. The solemnization of the rite takes place outside of the town, old men acting as operators with the boys and old women with the girls.

Training Bechuana Boys.

"The *boguera* happened to be celebrated at the time of my visit to Shoshong, so that I had the best opportunity of becoming acquainted with its details. Singing as they go, the young people of both sexes accompanied by the *linyakas* [medicine men] proceed beyond the town to the appointed spot, where the boys are put through a drill in manly exercises, and the girls are formally initiated into domestic duties, such as carrying wood and fetching water; throughout their performances they keep up their monotonous chant; and as their figures are all white by the application of chalk, nothing can be imagined much more grotesque than the appearance they present as they go through their series of gymnastics.

"The boys are next marched off in detachments to the kotla, where they all have to be beaten with rods. Bare of all clothing, except their little girdle and their sandals, which they are permitted to hold in their hands, they are placed in two rows, back to back, and made to kneel down whilst a man, generally their next of kin, stands in front of each and proceeds to deliver his lashes, which the lads parry as best they can by the dexterous manipulation of their sandals; they are required to keep on singing, and to raise each foot alternately, marking the measure of the chant.

"All the youths who submit to the *boguera* at one time are formed into a company, and the more sons a Bechuana can bring to the ceremony, the prouder he is. A chief will generally try to introduce a son of his own or of a near relative to take command of the troop, and an *esprit de corps* is frequently excited which sometimes has a beneficial effect upon the quarrels which arise at court. The friendship thus formed often remains unbroken, in spite of the commander avowing himself a Christian and being baptized.

"The girls, so long as the ceremonial lasts, are not allowed to sleep; to keep them awake, they are made to spend the night sitting upon wooden corn-pounders of which the equilibrium is so unstable that the first attempt to get a wink of sleep sends the damsel toppling over.

"The real object of the entire ceremonial is to discipline and harden the young, particularly the boys; the rite is followed by a succession of hunting excursions, organized and kept up for several successive years; the members of a company are told off into sets, and under the guidance of an experienced hunter are taken out first to chase antelopes and gazelles, and in course of time to pursue elephants and buffaloes. On these expeditions they are designedly exposed to many hardships; they are compelled to make long marches through districts where there is no water; only in exceptional cases are they allowed to approach the fire even in the severest weather, and they are forced to experience the long-continued pangs of hunger."

While Dr. Holub's hunting adventures had, up to this time, been chiefly in the pursuit of the smaller game, and more for the purpose of making scientific observations than for the sake of sport, he was a diligent collector of the experience of others; and from the stories which he tells "as 'twas told to him," we select and condense these two:

In the year 1870, a Shoshong merchant sent two wagons to Zeerust, in charge of three colonial half-breeds and a Bamangwato slave. One of their resting-places was near the mouth of the Notuany River; here, indeed, they halted a longer time than was necessary for the mere repose of men and beasts; for the heat of the day was excessive. One of the half-breeds, however, was not to be deterred from action by any such fear of discomfort; and followed by a pack of dogs, he set out on a short hunting-trip. Pressing along the shore, he was followed for a while by his four-footed friends, but they soon deserted him; they had scented game, and yelping wildly they dart-

The Lion at Bay.

ed away. He paid no attention to them at first, but when it appeared that all were following the same scent with equal eagerness, he noted the direction, and cautiously followed them. Thick bushwood covered a portion of ground; here and there was a tree of larger dimensions, and some open spaces, covered with tall grass. The barking sounded clearer and clearer, and he quickened his pace. After a quarter of an hour, he found himself in the very presence of the game, and just in time to witness the beginning of the action. Surrounded by a yelping pack of dogs, a few feet away, stood a full-grown, dark-maned lion, turning his majestic head first to this and then to that side, as the hoarse war-cry of the dogs, here and there, reached him. The hunter, under cover of the bush, crept up within fifty feet of the lion, where he could hear the gnashing of his teeth, varied by a low growl. He raised his gun and took aim; but at that very moment, the largest dog, known in Shoshong as Hyena-killer, sprang forward to attack the king of the forest. A lightning stroke of the lion's paw felled the dog to the earth, the under part of his body showing a gaping wound from which the entrails protruded. Alarmed at the fate of their leader the dogs scattered in all directions. The hunter's hand trembled perceptibly; he was obliged to kneel, and with all his strength to press his gun to his shoulder and cheek in order to obtain a sure aim. The lion rose and snuffed at his quivering victim; at that instant the bullet pierced his heart, and the royal beast fell on the very spot where he had killed his heroic assailant.

Two friends, Boer farmers, went on a hunting expedition into the country infested by the tsetse fly. They came upon a herd of elephants which retreated at once. The hunters pursued, and found that the trail divided. Fourier, one of the farmers, with a Matabele slave, followed the trail of the larger number, while his friend followed the tracks of a single large male. He was the first to catch a glimpse of his game, after half an hour's progress through the wilderness. Fourier heard his shot as he fired at the elephant, and after fruitless endeavors to find the larger herd, returned to his friend only to find him a corpse, his face covered with the blood that had flowed from mouth, nose and eyes. His gun lay beside him, the stock burst, and about thirty feet away, under a tree, was the body of the elephant. The same charge which had sent the four-ounce bullet speeding on its way had caused the death of the hunter who held the imperfect weapon.

Shoshong was the most northern point reached in this second trip. Returning thence, the adventurer again found it necessary to engage in the practice of medicine before he could set out on that journey which had been his real aim. He was now thoroughly well acquainted with the country as far as he had traveled; he had become inured to the peculiar hardships of South African travel, and he had learned by experience what supplies were needed. His third, last and greatest trip extended as far north as the Zambesi River.

As far as Shoshong, the course need not be followed; it was but a repetition of previous journeys. At this place, however, he visited a place of interest which he had not seen before; this was the field where Khame had fought his father and

A DEADLY ENCOUNTER.

brother. Sekhomo had been king at the time of his previous visit, and Khame, the same young man who had risen above the power of a malevolent parent's magic, his heir apparent. Sekhomo had been indefatigable in promoting heathen orgies, and had been the most determined enemy of every reform that had tended to introduce the benefits of civilization. Two of his sons, Khame and Khamane, having refused to take part in the *boguera*, he fairly drove them from his country for a while. Khame took refuge with Sechele, and the contest that ensued ended in the deposition of the father, and the recognition of the son as king. Of course Sekhomo was banished; but it was not long before Khame regretted this severe sentence, and allowed his father to return to Shoshong, on condition of keeping the peace. The ex-king returned, but did not hold to the condition; Khame was ultimately deposed, and went into a sort of voluntary exile to a point on the Zooga River, where being followed by great numbers of the people, he established a settlement. But the locality was marshy, and his followers were decimated by fever. He boldly announced that on a certain day he would return to Shoshong. Sekhomo made ready to receive the exile, who could only come as an enemy. His forces were divided into two bodies, one of which was to protect the town, while the main body was to intercept Khame's advance. His army was about equal to that of his son, although a considerable part of it was composed of allies from the Matabele country. These fugitive Makalakas proved utterly treacherous; for while they professed allegiance to Sekhomo, they secretly sent word to Khame that they would hold themselves in readiness to welcome him at the Shoshong pass. Khame's attack was so sudden that Sekhomo's men were completely demoralized; and before they had time to recover themselves and begin a retreat, Khame led his men to where the Makalakas were posted. These soldiers of fortune thought that Khame had been worsted and turned their weapons upon him in behalf of Sekhomo, whom they had voluntarily offered to betray. Khame's men discharged a single volley at these utterly unscrupulous traitors, and then rushed at them, and felled them with clubbed muskets. Khame was restored to the royal power; his exiled followers returned with him; and he set to work to root out many evils which had been tolerated by his father. His great reform was the prohibition of the sale of of brandy, a regulation which in Africa as well as elsewhere struck at the root of many disorders.

KHAME DEFEATS THE TRAITORS.

Khame gave the traveler a guide northward to the great salt lakes, or to the Zambesi, should he desire to go so far; and furthered his journey in every possible way. Under this native's guidance, the way was free from adventure of an unpleasant kind. The country through which they passed, however, was not free from danger; an extract from his second volume will give an idea of the kinds of game with which they fell in:

"On our way we passed a tree, the bark of which was torn in a way which showed that it had been used by lions for sharpening their claws; the boughs of the tree were wide-spreading, branching out like a candelabrum, and forming what struck me as a convenient perch. Here I resolved to keep a long watch of ten or twelve hours. I was determined if I could to see the lions for myself. Accordingly, just before sundown, I took Niger, and accompanied by Pit I returned to the tree, and having made myself comfortable in my concealment, I sent Pit back to the wagon in time for him to arrive while it was still tolerably light. * * * * * * The nights were now extremely cold, and appeared especially so in contrast to the high temperature of the day, and I took the precaution of tying myself to one of the strongest boughs, in case I should fall asleep; to tumble off might bring me in closer contact with the monarchs of the forest than might be agreeable. * * * * Amongst the first of the sounds to arrest my attention was the sonorous "quagga, quagga" of the male zebras; they were on the grass-plains, keeping watch over their herds; with this was soon mingled the melancholy howl of the harnessed jackal, awaking the frightful yell of its brother, the gray jackal; the beasts, I could not doubt, were all prowling round the enclosure of our camp. For some hours the various noises seemed to be jumbled together, but towards midnight they became more and more distinct, so that I could identify them separately, and fancied that I could count the beasts that made them. After a while a peculiar scraping commenced, caused by rhyzaenas hunting in the sand for worms and larvæ; it went on all night except during the brief interval when the busy little creatures were temporarily disturbed by some movement near them.

"The gazelles and antelopes came down quite early to lick at the salt mud in the Nata-bed; they evidently were accustomed to get back to their haunts in the open lands before the beasts of prey quitted their lairs in the woods. Some of the little steinbocks (those most graceful of African gazelles) came-down so cautiously along the track that it was only through accidently looking down that I was aware of their being near me. I think there were three or four of them. They were followed by some other gazelle, of which the movements were so light and rapid that I failed to catch a glimpse of it. After a considerable time an antelope passed beneath me, of another species larger than the others, making a succession of short leaps, then pausing and bounding on again, but I could not recognize what kind it really was.

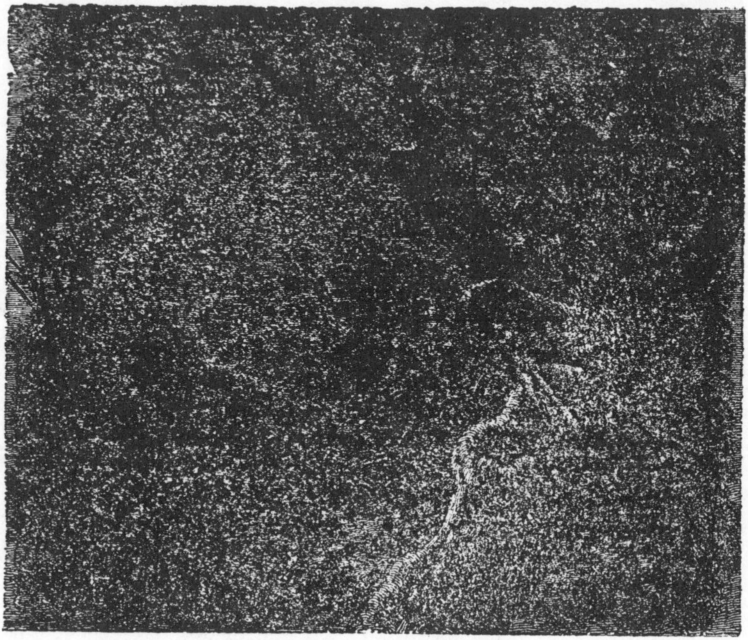

A Fruitless Night Vigil.

"The slow, steady tramp of a large herd on the other side of the bank proceeding towards the salt pools, and in the direction of the one fresh-water pool, could not be mistaken; moreover, the crashing of their horns against the wood in the thickets left no doubt of the approach of a number of koodoos. While I was listening to their movements I heard another tread on the game-path beside the river; straining my eyes in that direction I saw a dark form stealthily making its way towards the descent; it was about the size of a young calf, and I could have little doubt that it was a brown hyena;

it sniffed the air at every step, and after stopping a few seconds just beyond the channel started off at a brisk trot.

"As the hours of the night waned away I began to think that I should see or hear nothing of the monarch of the forest. I had not, however, to wait much longer before the unmistakable roar, apparently about half a mile away, caught my ear. I could only hope that the beast was on its way once more to sharpen its claws upon the accustomed tree. I had now no heed to give to any other sound; neither the barking of our own dogs beside the wagon, nor the yelling of the jackals around our encampment could distract my attention, and I listened eagerly about half an hour before the roaring was repeated; it was now very much nearer; I listened on, and it must have been nearly twenty minutes before I distinguished its footsteps almost within gunshot. The lion was not in the ordinary track, as I expected, but right in the long grass in the rain-channel. Its strides were generally rapid, but it paused frequently. I could only hear its movements; it was too dark for me too see. I was sure that it could not be more than about fifteen yards from me, and could hardly restrain myself from firing. I feared, however, that a random shot would only be fired in vain, and with no other effect than that of driving the lion away. Accordingly I waited on. It came still nearer and crouched down somewhere for about another quarter of an hour without stirring an inch. At last I became convinced that it had caught sight of me; I saw the bushes shake, and the great brute looked out as if uncertain whether to make a spring towards me or to effect its escape. It was a terrible mistake on my part not to fire then and there, but my moment of hesitation was fatal to my design; the lion made a sudden bound, and in an instant had disappeared for good. It was no use to me that Niger's frantic barking made me aware what direction it had taken. My chance was gone. I was much mortified, but there was no help for it. With the cold night air and my cramped position I was stiff all over, and much relieved when daylight dawned, and Pit appeared with Niger to accompany me back to the warmth and shelter of the wagon."

His way from Tasetze to the Chobe was through the heart of an elephant country; and although they found many signs of the presence of the huge beasts, and more than once followed the trail of a considerable herd, they were not successful in killing any themselves.

An interesting episode during this journey was his visit to

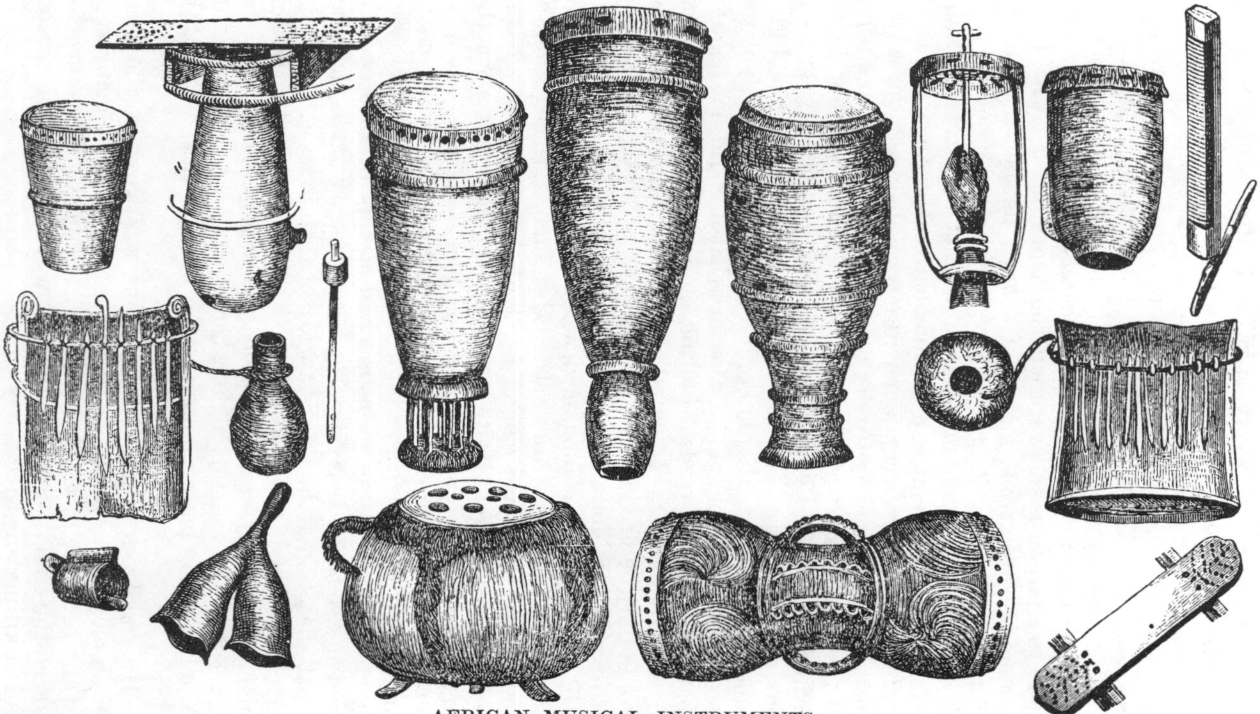

AFRICAN MUSICAL INSTRUMENTS.

the Marutse kingdom, a territory lying around the Zambesi River. The king, Sepopo, had heard of his traveling through the country, and had many times inquired of those around him when the *nyaka* (doctor) was coming, to travel through the country like Monari (Livingstone). Since the visit of the great explorer he had seen at least fifteen white men, but he determined to give Holub a more imposing reception than any of them. The reason for such a determination is not made clear; perhaps he had just got educated up to the point of liking white men.

"The most notable part of the procession was the royal band; on either side of the king were myrimba players bringing out the most excruciating sounds with a pair of short drumsticks from a keyboard of calabashes suspended from their shoulders by a strap; these were preceded by men with huge tubular drums, upon which they played with their fingers, accompanying the strains with their voices."

The Marutse kindom is of considerable extent, and claims as tributaries several of the neighboring tribes. Dr. Holub remained some days with Sepopo, then took up his journey towards the river which flows through this kingdom, and which was the bound of his journey—the Zambesi. On his way, he fell in with two English travelers, Capt. M'Leod and Fairley, with whom he joined company. He later became, along with these officers, member of a party of European traders, with whom he visited Victoria Falls, as the great cataract of the Zambesi had already been named by its discoverer. But we need not linger over his description of this grand spectacle; we follow him, as he returns, on another visit to the Marutse kingdom.

While again at the court of Sepopo, he noticed a commotion one morning, and learned that four lions had made an attack upon the royal herd the night before, and a party was being organized for pursuing the robbers. Holub, with a young Englishman, Cowley, joined the hunters, who numbered about a hundred and seventy, although only four were provided with guns.

It was decided that the track of the largest lion should be followed. A few natives and a couple of dogs were put on the trail, and the chief, together with the two white men, came next. The bushes, however, were so thick that no regular order could be kept up, and the hunters advanced as best they might.

For more than an hour they followed the tracks, but with-

THE LIONESS SPRINGS OUT OF CONCEALMENT.

out once catching sight of the game. The negroes began to joke about the lion, averring that he was ashamed to show his face; and the white men felt not a little disappointed. From this point, let Holub tell the story in his own way:

"On leaving the next hollow the dogs commenced growling angrily, and made a rush into another hollow beyond again, about ten feet deep and thirty feet wide. The condition of the trail satisfied us that the lion was concealed here close at hand. We made the crowd of natives halt, Maranzian [the chief] and I hastened round to the farther side and prepared to fire, Cowley staying on the nearer side, and sending the dogs into the reeds; but we schemed to no purpose; the baying of the hounds made us aware that the lion had got round behind us, and we were obliged to change our position.

"Followed by the throng, we proceeded to the open space beyond the reeds, close to the spot in which we imagined that the lion was now concealed, and having chosen our places where we thought we had the best chance of firing at it on its escape, we made the whole crowd shout at the top of their voices, and threw in bits of wood; and when that proved ineffectual we ordered them, whether they liked it or not, to go into the thicket and rummage about with their spears.

"It was a very pandemonium. The screaming and yelling of the negroes was quite unearthly, and the noise seemed to grow louder and more frightful as their courage increased at not finding any lion to alarm them. Maranzian, with his four men that had guns, was standing about twenty yards in front of me. We were beginning to think that we were again balked, when, like a flash of lightning, a lioness made a tremendous spring out of its concealment, and then another spring as sudden into the very midst of the excited crowd of hunters. There were so many of them scattered about between me and the angry brute that it was out of the question to think of firing, and it made another bound, and disappeared into another thicket close behind; it knocked over several of the men, but fortunately it did not hurt any of them seriously.

"Without the loss of a moment, Maranzian sent his men to drive the lioness to the very extremity of her new retreat. It rather surprised us to find the dogs perfectly silent as we followed them into the thicket, but before long we heard them barking vehemently in the open ground beyond; they had driven out the brute, and were in full pursuit.

"As he saw the lioness bounding away in the distance, with the dogs at her heels, Cowley was terribly chagrined at having abandoned his former position, and sighed over his lost chance of adding to his rising renown as a lion-hunter. * * * * The climax was now at hand, and full of excitement it was. Again the lioness took refuge in a triangular thicket, with its vertex farthest from us. Close beside it was a sand-bank, some ten feet high. Maranzian, with a number of men, placed himself on the right side of the thicket; I took up my position on the left, Cowley stationing himself on the sand-bank at a point where he conceived the lioness when pressed by the negroes would try to escape. By encouraging words, and where words failed by the use of a stout stick, Maranzian made a lot of men go and ransack the reeds, and as they tumbled about they gave the place almost the aspect of a battlefield. The excitement became more intense when there remained but one little corner to be explored. Now or never the lioness must be found. Suddenly there was an angry growl, and the beast leaped forward toward the pursuers. A shot was fired at that moment, but it only struck the sand; the negroes, taken by surprise, fell back, some of them disappearing altogether, a few of them desperately hurling their spears. Once again the lioness retreated, and when the natives had recovered themselves, they saw her crouching down as if prepared for another spring. Here was my chance; catching sight of her head, I took deliberate aim and fired; my shot took good effect, and at the same time a couple of spears hit her on the side. One more growl, and she was dead."

It was now Holub's desire to make a trip up the Zambesi, and for this purpose four of the royal canoes were lent to him. Three of these were required to transport his baggage, and the fourth was reserved for his personal use, his servant being obliged to travel on foot. He was to accompany a party of queens who where taking a trip to the Barotse country; and his path was thus clear of all unpleasantness that could arise from the displeasure of the natives.

All went well until they came to the Mutshila Aumsinga Rapids, which are formed by a considerable slope in the river bed, combined with the projection of numerous masses of rock above the water. The chief danger in crossing them, however, arises from another cause. Between a wooded island and the left-hand shore are two side-currents about fifty yards broad, formed by some little islands at their head; and as no part of the rapids is shallow enough for the boats to be lifted across them, the strength of the rowers has to be put to the test by pulling against the full force of the stream.

"The boat in which I was sitting happened to be the third in the order of procession. It carried my journals, all my beads and cartridges, and the present intended for native kings and chiefs. Like all my other boats, it was too heavily laden, and not adequately manned. The second boat just ahead of me carried my gunpowder, my medicines and provisions, and all the plants and insects that I had collected at Shesheke, the bulk of my specimens having been left with Westbeech to send back to Panda ma Tenka. Observing that the

Capsized in the Rapids.

crew were experiencing the utmost difficulty in holding their own against the current, I shouted to them to catch hold of the branches of some over-hanging trees; I was most anxious to see them at least keep the bow in the right direction. My voice was lost in the roar of the waters. I could see that the oars of the men were slipping off the surface of the rock that was as smooth as a mirror, and that the men, although obviously aware of their peril, were paddling wildly and to no purpose at all. My heart misgave me. Nothing could save the boat; still I could not bring myself to believe that fate was about to deal so hardly with me. I could not realize that just at the time that a threatening fever made me especially require my medicines, I was about to lose them all. I could not face the contingency of having my stock of provisions, on which I depended not only for the prosecution of my journey, but for my very maintenance, totally destroyed; neither could I resign myself to the loss of all the natural curiosities that I had labored for so many days to accumulate. I called vehemently upon my own crew to hasten to the rescue; but they, in their alarm at the desperate plight of the others, were quite powerless; they were utterly bewildered, and were letting themselves drift into the fury of the current; but happily they were within reach of the drooping branches of a tree, which they clutched only just in time to make their boat secure. By this time, the boat in front had twisted around, and presented its broadside to the angry flood. Nothing could save it now. Heedless of the state of fever I was in, I should have flung myself into the current, determined to help if I could, had not the boatmen held me back. Not that any assistance on my part could have been of any avail, for in another moment I saw that the paddles were all broken, the men lost their equilibrium, and to my horror the boat was overturned.

At the greatest risk, by the combined exertions of both crews, the capsized canoe was after some time set afloat again, and a few trifling articles were gathered up, but the bulk of my baggage was irrecoverably lost. Thus ended all my schemes; thus ended all my visions for the future."

An hour after this misadventure, they landed near a Mabunda village, called Sioma, where they collected and arranged as a shelter the roofs of seven deserted huts. The natives, anxious for them to move on, told many stories of lions haunting the neighborhood, and ravaging the village night after night; but finding that the stranger was not alarmed by the prospect, became more hospitable.

The accounts of the Mabundas had not been without a very substantial foundation, however; and the adventurer found it necessary to protect his collection of huts every night by means of a number of fires, around which his boatmen sat, spears in hand, awaiting the coming of the lions whose roar they could plainly hear, less than a hundred and fifty yards away.

They were detained some time at Sioma, by the illness of Holub. At one time, he was convinced that he could not live through the night; but time disproved this. He became no better, however, and at last decided that he must return to Sesheke, the capital of Sepopo. He gave orders that the boats should be made ready, and learned that they were prepared for the journey down the river. He was at first angry on hearing that his servants had presumed to do this without orders; but his anger cooled down when he was told that they had received strict orders from Sepopo to consider the white man's health above everything else; he was a doctor, a magician, and great harm might befall Sepopo and his people if Holub were to die while under their protection.

A Boer's Wife Defending Her Wagon from Kaffirs.

But even the return to Sesheke did not effect a cure; and very reluctantly, the physician was obliged to admit to himself that he could not recover in this country. He accordingly set out on his return, the first stage of his journey being performed by means of boats descending the Zambesi. Joined by one of the ivory-traders with whom he had become acquainted at Sepopo's capital, an Englishman named Westbeech, the trip was continued in wagons.

His return route as far as Shoshong was a little different

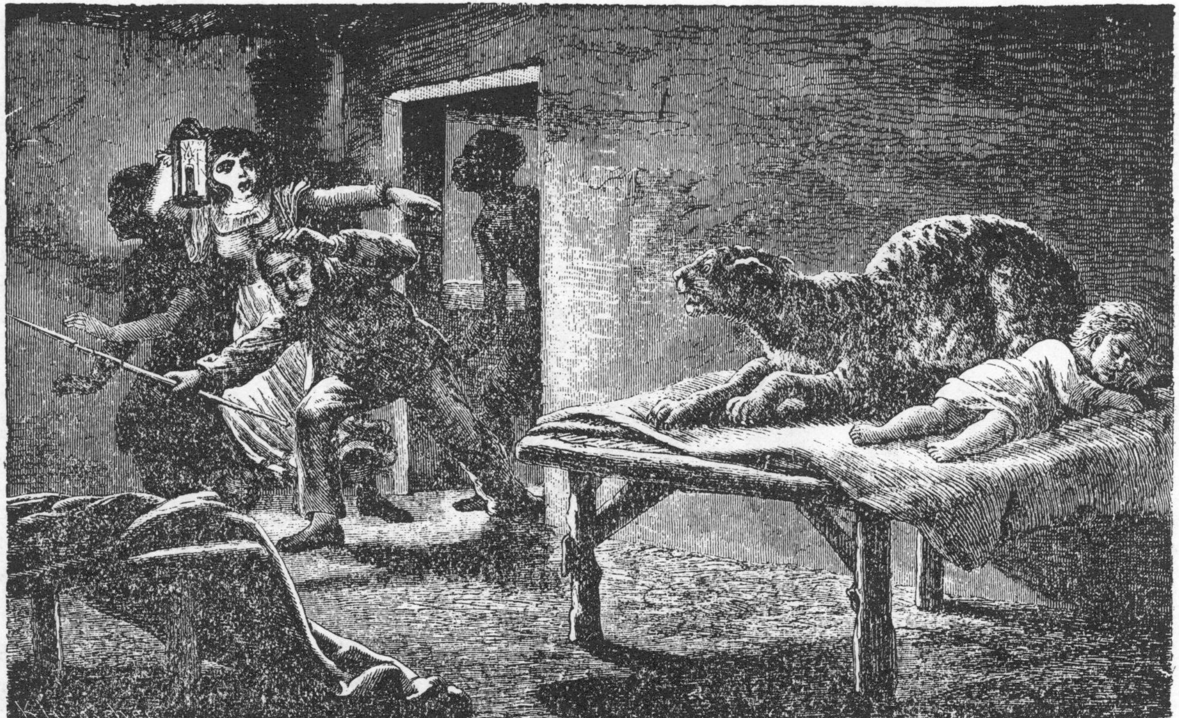

A TERRIBLE INTRUDER.

from that by which he had traveled northward; lying farther toward the east, it led him more among the Zulus and the outlying dwellings of the Boers, where the contest between these two peoples is rarely quieted. He learned there why the Boers have not been driven from the country by these determined savages: the Boer women can fight as well as the men when necessity demands it.

An incident which occurred at Tati may well be recorded here, as it is quite significant of what may be expected in this country, even in such settlements as might be thought reasonably safe:

Pit Jacobs, who had accompanied Holub on a former expedition, had gone on a hunting trip with his two sons, leaving his wife, his daughter, two little boys, and a Masarwa servant in the house. The dwelling contained but two rooms, the inner one of which was the sleeping apartment of the family. Mrs. Jacobs had put her two little boys to bed, and was lying down beside one of them. The daughter's fiance had called for an evening visit, and they were sitting in the living-room, where the window was open, and a kitten lying on the window-sill.

A leopard was known to be lurking about the village, and every fence ought to have been carefully guarded; but by some means it had obtained access to Jacobs' enclosure, and made a spring at the kitten. Its intended prey saw it in time to leap from the window sill and hide under the sewing-machine; but the leopard had already sprung, and going too far, landed in the middle of the room where the lovers were sitting.

The beast was as much alarmed at finding itself there as the people were to see it; and made for the bed-room, which seemed to it a haven of refuge. Mrs. Jacobs caught up the child that was lying on her arm, and dashed out into the other room with it, demanding to know what animal it was; for in the imperfect light she could not tell. She would at once have returned for her other child, but they held her by force from what seemed a hopeless attempt.

Such weapons as were at hand were hastily got hold of; the most available was an old assegai, which belonged to the servant. The lover took the spear, and followed closely by the others with a lantern, entered the bedroom. The beast was lying beside the child, who was sleeping as sweetly as if none but his mother and his brother were near. Seeing the light, the animal sprang at the man who was approaching it; its claws fastened in his throat; the impetus of the spring was such that he lost his balance and fell backward, bearing the women to the floor in his fall. The leopard, bewildered at such a state of things, and seeing the way for escape clear, bounded through the open door and the window, and was seen no more.

The human participants in this adventure picked themselves up, and congratulated themselves that the really terrible danger was past.

The journey from Shoshong to the diamond fields was without special adventure, although toward the last they were obliged to travel night and day, through storm as well as good weather, to reach their destination before the rivers should have become entirely impassable from the rains. They reached Kimberley late in November, 1877, Dr. Holub being quite prostrated from the fever, which had never wholly left him through all this weary return journey from Shesheke.

Here he was obliged to remain for some time, the reason being that which had frequently detained him from adventure before—the lack of money. A gift from the Emperor of Austria of a thousand florins, from the Bohemian National Society of £60, of two hundred florins from the Svatabor Club, and a loan of one thousand florins from a lady, placed him in a position to leave the diggings much sooner than he had expected to be able to do so. Yet it was only in August, 1879, that he finally embarked for Europe.

Holub traversed a country which had previously been explored, and which was visited by white traders; his travels, then, have added nothing to our knowledge of the topography of Africa. But his persistent scientific zeal has taught us more of the botany and zoology of this section of the continent than we have derived from any other source. His ethnological specimens were collected from about thirty different tribes; and his natural history collection amounted to more than thirty thousand different articles. A selection of 12,500 of the latter was exhibited in Vienna shortly after his return to his native country.

Added to this service to science, his volumes give us a clearer picture of the condition of the country at a comparatively recent date than can be obtained from any other single authority. It is mainly for this reason that we have included so much in the present volume from his first work, "Seven Years in South Africa."

But Dr. Holub was not content with what he had done; he

was anxious to explore, as well as to note new botanical and zoological forms. Accordingly, in November, 1883, he again sailed for the Cape, accompanied by his wife, who was not yet twenty. Six other Europeans accompanied the expedition, to which the Emperor of Austria and several scientific societies contributed funds. The greater part of the expense, however, was borne by the explorer himself; but notwithstanding the variety of sources from which the money was derived, there was not enough to fit out the expedition properly, and many of their difficulties were owing to their poverty; servants were parted with for the lack of money with which to pay them; and they had not always the means of conciliating the native chiefs by presents which the dusky rulers thought appropriate to their condition.

They were delayed for several months in Cape Colony by various circumstances, but at last made their way through Bechuana-land. It was Dr. Holub's intention to explore the country around the Zambesi, hoping that his previous intercourse with the Marutse chiefs had paved the way for success in this enterprise. But he found the Marutse engaged in wars among themselves, and with neighboring tribes.

Sixty oxen had been purchased at the Cape, and were to be used for the transportation of the party and of the specimens which were collected. Their diligence in scientific research may be judged by the fact that before many months had elapsed, before indeed the main difficulties were encountered, twenty-five cases of botanical and zoological specimens were sent home to Vienna.

Half of their oxen died, either from the bite of the tsetse or from eating the poisonous machau plant; the leader and his companions were attacked with malaria in its worst form, African Fever; three of them succumbed; the five who were left alive suffered from diphtheria, dysentery, and rheumatism, the after effects of the fever. Mrs. Holub, brave and energetic little woman that she was, became so ill that she was utterly unable to go on, and begged them to leave her there to die, since a longer stay might result in the death of all the party; but weak and sick as they were, they toiled along, carrying the lady until she was once more able to ride and walk. Eight months were spent on the south bank of the Zambesi, during which time but little was accomplished because of sickness.

Three weeks were spent at Victoria Falls, after the members of the expedition had been restored to comparative health; and thence, after considerable difficulty in obtaining carriers, they pushed on toward the Luenge.

In this new country, however, they found that their troubles were increased. Dr. Holub had relied greatly upon his medical skill as a means of conciliating the natives; but these tribes were inclined to look upon it as a sort of magic, which could not be altogether trusted. Many of their goods were stolen; and when they invoked the aid of the chief in recovering them, they found that gentleman extremely apathetic regarding their loss. Later investigations disclosed that half the stolen goods had been made over to him by the thieves, as the price of his consent to their actions.

Mrs. Holub.

Not content to share in these ill-gotten spoils, this chief, Niambo, coveted what was left to the explorer; perhaps he admired Mrs. Holub. At any rate, some milk which he furnished them had a queer taste; some of it was given to a dog, by way of experiment; in a few minutes the dog was dead.

This was an unmistakable hint to leave; and they lost no time in doing so. In their haste to be gone secretly, they were unable to ascertain a safe road, and were lost in a marsh not far from Niambo's village. From this they were guided by some natives, more compassionate than their neighbors. The representations of these people were to the effect that at two days' journey distance there was a Portuguese settlement. It was therefore decided that Dr. Holub and his wife should push on toward it, and obtain help there for the others. After a toilsome journey of the required length, they learned that the Portuguese settlement was two days' journey from the boundaries of the Marutse kingdom, and these boundaries were still at an indefinite distance. Footsore and weary, they retraced their steps, to find that the camp was even then being attacked by the Mashukulumbe. They managed to reach their party, and Dr. Holub's first thought was how to save his diaries. Thirty-two precious volumes were in his hut, but of these he was able to save but fourteen.

Even when attacked unprovoked, it was no part of his plans to massacre the natives. Throughout the journey, the members of the party had been strictly forbidden to fire upon the people, unless in self-defense; and up to this time, not a gun had been discharged at any but the lower animals. Now, the order was given: "Wound, but do not kill," and scrupulously obeyed. The Mashulukumbe were finally driven off, but probably only to return with a larger force while the camp was asleep. The white man therefore determined to beat a retreat; the party crept through the reeds to the river-bank; but how to cross the stream? A small boat was visible on the opposite side, but the river was full of crocodiles, and the men shrank from the danger. At last, however, for the bribe of a gun, one of the native servants agreed to swim the stream and bring the canoe across. Accomplishing the dangerous part of his task in safety, he discovered a larger boat, which had not been visible from the other bank, and the two were appropriated by the fugitives. In three hours after reaching the bank, they were all safely across the river.

It was now certain that they could not attempt to explore the country between the Zambesi and Bangweolo, as Holub had wished to do; and they bent all their efforts toward reaching civilization again. In miserable plight, their feet wounded by the rough road, they reached the Zambesi August 22, 1886. The natives of the village of Mala showed them a short cut, but, nevertheless, they were three months in descending the Zambesi, following its course on land. Arrived at the settlement, Westbeech, an English trader with whom, it will be recollected, Dr. Holub had had some acquaintance on his previous trip, lent them a span of oxen with which to make their journey to the Cape.

These animals, however, were bitten by the tsetse before they reached their destination; and this fact, together with other causes, made their journey to Shoshong occupy a period of seventy days. Thence the way was easy to Cape Town. They sailed for Europe in August, 1886, and reached Vienna in safety, ready to arrange and prepare their specimens of plants and animals, and then, probably, to leave for Africa again; for the man once imbued with the enthusiasm of the explorer is rarely content to end his days in peace at home.

CHAPTER XIII.

CHRISTIAN MISSIONS IN AFRICA.

THE forms of religious beliefs professed by the inhabitants of Africa may be classed under three heads—Christian, Mohammedan, and pagan. The second form of faith was propagated in this continent at a very early period of Mohammedan history; and we find professors of it among many tribes which are not far removed from a state of savagery. These, however, are only nominally Mohammedans; in their gross superstitions, their ignorance, and their revolting practices, they are really pagans; and their profession of belief in the Prophet of Islam only serves to bring contempt upon his teachings, as too many who call themselves by a holier name bring contempt, by the manner of their lives, upon the religion which they profess.

It is difficult to speak in general terms of the faiths which are classed under the head of pagan. Some tribes appear to have a confused and gross belief in a future life; others declare that death ends all. Others, again, believe in the transmigration of souls, and hold certain animals in reverence, as inhabited by the souls of dead friends. The negroes on the equatorial western coast of Africa believe that the souls of men frequently pass into gorillas, and that such animals are too cunning for the hunter. Some people have a well defined belief in a superior Being, who is good and beneficent; others, again, while they believe in spirits, cannot imagine one that is not malevolent; and are perpetually in terror of all supernatural agencies. But whatever rank these various religions may hold in point of purity or approach to reason, there is one thing in which they all agree: all teach a belief in magic, by whatever name it may be called; and the sorcerer is a person to be feared, the diviner to be honored.

One particular form of this belief in magic is Fetichism, or the belief in charms. A European explorer of recent years relates that on one occasion, when he had become unconscious from the effects of fever, he found, upon recovering his senses, that he was almost literally covered with the charms which his faithful servitors had believed would restore him to health. But it was not even an opportunity for a faith cure; for he cast aside the antelope's horns, elephant's teeth and similar articles, and took a dose of quinine. The present writer is not prepared to say what are the peculiar virtues of the various fetiches, or whether the Africans are so ridiculous as to hang a horse-shoe over the stable-door for luck, and carry a horse-chestnut in the pocket (those of them who wear clothes) to ward off rheumatism.

From their universal belief in spirits, and that prevailing

Natives Worshiping a Clay Idol.

impression that spirits cannot be beneficent, arises what has been styled devil-worship. Much of that to which this name is applied is properly so called, since it is an effort to propitiate bad spirits; it may be that ignorance of their language and customs has caused some genuine worship of a Good Being to be so designated; since the stranger would suppose the god so worshipped to be, necessarily, a false one.

We have already had occasion to speak of the evangelization of Abyssinia; in connection with that, we have alluded to the efforts of the Portuguese missionaries. These followed close upon the earliest explorers—indeed, in many cases the explorers were missionary monks, who were willing to brave every danger and hardship for the extension of their faith. As in later days, they were met with bigoted persecution by the Mohammedans, and with an appalling indifference by the natives. The pagans would sometimes, it is true, embrace the proffered faith readily enough, to all outward seeming; but when it came to the test, and they were required by their religious teachers to give up some old practice, like polygamy or idolatry, they would relapse into paganism.

In 1481, the king of Portugal sent ten ships with five hundred soldiers and one hundred laborers, together with "a proper complement of priests," to Elmina. The mission thus founded lingered on for a period of 241 years, but does not seem to have made any impression upon the natives, except those who were immediately dependent upon the whites at the station. Finally, in 1723, the mission of the Capuchins at Sierra Leone was given up, and they disappeared altogether from West Africa. Whatever influence they may have had at the time has left no permanent traces.

An effort was made by the same authority to establish a mission station at the mouth of the Congo; but the natives proved too thoroughly wedded to their immoral practices to be really desirous of a purer mode of life. Somewhat of the story might be told, did our space admit; but the end is wrapped in darkness; vessels came from Portugal, and found that the missionaries had disappeared, and no one could or would tell them how.

Portuguese missionaries also penetrated as far as Abyssinia, and succeeded in effecting a temporary conversion of the rulers to their faith; but as the Abyssinians professed Christianity before the advent of these strangers, a history of their effort hardly belongs in an account of African missions.

The earliest Protestant efforts for the evangelization of Africa were made in 1736. In that year the Moravians determined to send out a missionary to the southern part of this great continent. The next year, George Schmidt arrived at the mouth of Sergeant's River. Though opposed and persecuted both by the government of the colony and by the native chiefs, he persevered, and at last succeeded in establishing a mission at Genadenthal, one hundred and twenty miles north of the Cape. The results of nine years' labor showed that forty-seven families had professed Christianity, and received baptism. He then returned to his native Holland, to seek for assistance; but not only did he find no others who would join him, but for some unexplained reason, he was not allowed to return. He passed the remainder of his days as a poor day-laborer in Germany, "with his heart in that southern land which he was never to see again."

In 1792, the Brethren obtained permission to resume the work in South Africa, and in that year three artisans were sent to the same place. They found the walls of Schmidt's house still standing, and among the first to welcome them was a poor old blind woman, who had been a pupil and convert of Schmidt's fifty years before, and who now brought to them the Testament which she had cherished since the departure of the missionary. If the Moravian Brethren had been disposed to regard the work lightly, this would have been enough to kindle their zeal. The good work went on. More missionaries were sent out. Other stations were opened. In less than a century after the re-establishment of the mission at Genadenthal, the Brethren had forty-three missionaries, with two hundred native helpers, in this part of Africa. They have also numerous schools and colleges in successful operation, with between eight and nine thousand adults and children under pastoral care.

On the west coast, the efforts of the Moravians were less successful. Beginning there at the same time that Schmidt went to South Africa, five different attempts were made to establish missionary stations; but they were made at the cost of eleven lives. Finally, in 1770, the effort was given up.

The Methodists were the next to seek to occupy the field. In the Minutes of the Conference for 1792, we find Africa, for the first time, set down as one of the missionary stations, Sierra Leone being the point selected. Four years later, the names of A. Murdoch and W. Patten are set down as missionaries to the Foulah country.

In 1798, the London Missionary Society sent out four missionaries, who arrived at the Cape the next year. Of these the most remarkable was Dr. Vanderkemp, who for years endured great hardships in his work of preaching the gospel to "his beloved Hottentots." But the most notable (with one great exception) of the missionaries sent out by this society was Robert Moffat

He was a young man of but twenty-two when he offered himself for the work. Of his early training we have not space to say much; but volumes are told of the influences which had surrounded him at home, in the answer of his parents when he asked their consent to engage in this work: "We have thought of your proposal to become a missionary; we have prayed over it; and we cannot withhold you from so good a work." He never had any formal theological training; and seems, indeed, to have had but slight acquaintance with schools generally.

Rev. Robert Moffat.

Great Namaqua-land was to be the scene of his earliest labors; a region where there had already been some effort at evangelization, so that the chief Africaner was thought to give evidence that would warrant a hope of his conversion. The missionary, of course, had landed at Cape Town; and the journey across Cape Colony was both toilsome and adventurous. It was late in January, 1818, when he arrived at Africaner's kraal, on the banks of the Orange River.

No sooner was he told that a white man had come, than Africaner appeared and demanded if Moffat were the missionary who had been promised. Receiving an answer in the affirmative, he turned to two women standing by, and commanded them to build a house for the missionary at once.

Moffat Preaching to the Natives.

They went to work with an alacrity that showed how pleasing the task was; and in an hour's time the "house" was finished. It is true that it was not a very substantial edifice; composed of native mats hung on poles, it was a shelter from neither rain nor sun, and frequently required extensive repairs after a storm. A dog could push aside the mats and enter at will; sometimes such an uninvited visitor would help himself to the missionary's stock of provisions for the next day. "Nor were these all the contingencies of such a dwelling; for as the cattle belonging to the village had no fold, I have been compelled to start up from a sound sleep, and try to defend myself and my dwelling from being crushed to pieces by the rage of two bulls which had met to fight a nocturnal duel."

But the hut, rude and unsubstantial as it was, was the best that they knew how to build; and Moffat felt himself more than repaid for such slight evils as bodily discomfort when the chief Africaner became an earnest Christian, and zealously seconded the efforts of the young missionary to teach his people not only the Gospel, but those lessons of industry and cleanliness which so powerfully assist the missionary in all countries to emphasize the blessings which his religion would teach the world.

Several efforts were made to find a place which would be more suitable for a missionary station than Africaner's kraal; it was desired to reach other peoples more directly; but these efforts were not successful. Finally, it was decided that Africaner's two brothers, who proved to be able and willing assistants, should conduct the services at the kraal when Moffat found it necessary to absent himself on missionary tours. These he made frequently. The missionary rode a borrowed horse, to the back of the saddle of which was tied a blanket, in which was wrapped his Bible and hymnbook. His guide rode an ox. They were not encumbered with useless baggage; they carried only a pipe, some tobacco, and a tinder-box—for it was before the days of matches. Their living they managed to get wherever they might be. After a day's ride through the hot sun, they would ask a drink of milk at the village to which they came; and then, assembling the people in a corner of the cattle-fold, the missionary would tell the glad tidings he had come so far to bring. His sermon done, and some talk held with the people individually, the preacher would lie down on a mat in the corner of a hut for the night. After another address in the morning, the preacher and his companion would ride on toward another village, where the same thing would be repeated. Often their only breakfast was a drink of milk and sometimes, on arriving in the evening at a point where they had expected to find a village, they would discover that lack of grass and water had compelled the inhabitants to drive their flocks and

African Superstition—
A Sham Devil.

herds, and remove their rude huts and few belongings to some other point.

Moffat spent forty years in this work; and lived to see the missionary stations pushed as far as the head-waters of the Limpopo, in twenty-four degress south latitude; Kolobeng being then the farthest station in the interior. His daughter became the wife of the most famous African missionary—David Livingstone. It is useless here to follow his work in detail, since the country which he traversed has been explored by travelers who have noted more closely than he the characteristics of the country, because they were less concerned with the welfare of the people. Moffat was, above all else, a missionary; that work, in his eyes, far transcended anything else in importance; hence there is but little space for him in a volume on the history of African exploration.

In regard to the missionary labors of Livingstone, we shall here say nothing; but when he returned to England after his first great journey and long residence in Africa, his account of his experiences gave a greater impulse to the missionary effort for this part of the world than anything else had ever done. It is in place to sum up the results of ninety years' labor by the emissaries of the London Missionary Society in Africa. There are about twenty principal stations, with fifty-two branches, including the Tanganyika mission in Central Africa. One of the chief stations, Kuruman, seven hundred and fifty miles due north from the Cape, was founded by Moffat and Hamilton in 1817; it was here that Livingstone found a church-house, a well-stocked garden, and a printing-press—evidences of civilization that surprised the newly arrived missionary not a little. It was here, too, that he found Mary Moffat, who had not then (1840) dreamed that she would one day become Mary Livingstone.

Twenty-five English missionaries and something more than a hundred native preachers carry on the work so nobly begun, and the stations of the society now have forty-two schools, with more than two thousand pupils. The communicants number nearly twenty-five thousand.

The Dutch Reformed Church is naturally, from the number of Boers there resident, a strong one in South Africa; and from the settlements as a basis, missionaries have gone out among the surrounding tribes, until between four and five thousand of the aborigines have been brought into the church, while more than twenty thousand others are under instruction.

In addition to these agencies, the Methodist Missionary Society, another English association, has done much work in South Africa, beginning in 1815. Its circuits now present an unbroken chain of coast stations from the Cape to Zululand. Their adherents number nearly a hundred thousand, of whom about one-fifth are communicants. They are also largely represented in the Orange Free State and the Transvaal.

Grave of Bishop Mackenzie, with Cross Made of Slave-Yokes.

The Glasgow Missionary Society, which, like the London association of a similar aim, was intended to represent the work of Christians irrespective of denominational differences, began its work in South Africa in 1821, when two missionaries were sent out. Two years later, the most notable of their missionaries, Rev. John Ross, began those ministrations which only ceased with his death in 1878. The work of the society's successors is carried on chiefly in Kaffraria. Frequent outbreaks among hostile tribes have greatly impeded the work of the missionaries, and the Kaffir War was a serious hindrance.

But still it has been carried on, and extended into Zululand.

When Livingstone had aroused enthusiasm in England in regard to African mission work, the two great universities, Oxford and Cambridge, resolved to institute a mission at the mouth of the Zambesi. Bishop Mackenzie was selected to take charge of it; and accompanied by six Englishmen, and five colored men from the Cape, he arrived at the scene of his intended labors in 1861. But he was not long to work here. He became entangled in the terrible slavery broils, and made frequent trips to a country far from healthful; he contracted a fever through these journeyings, which was neglected because the press of his duties was so great. He sank rapidly, and died in the hut of a native, situated on the edge of a dark forest. His companion read the burial service over his body; but in a few days more, he too was cut down by the terrible fever, and was buried in that strange land. Another and another fell victims to the climate, and in 1862 the attempt was, for the time, given up. It has since been revived, however, and a mission instituted, with head-quarters at Zanzibar, and twelve laborers in the field, with as many assistants.

Shortly after the death of Livingstone, the Free Church of Scotland resolved to establish a memorial mission. Livingstonia was adopted as the name, and the southern end of Lake Nyassa as the site. Ten thousand pounds was the sum subscribed, and the Free Church of Scotland, the Established Church of Scotland and the United Presbyterian Church united in the enterprise. The work received a severe blow when Dr. Black, a young man of great promise, died; his last words were: "Africa must not be given up, though it should cost thousands of lives." True to this watchword, the work in this section has been carried on with unextinguishable zeal; and a companion mission station called Blantyre established some two hundred miles from Livingstonia.

We now return to West Africa, which was, as we have seen, the scene of the earliest missionary efforts in the continent. The missions extend from the mouth of the Gaboon to the mouth of the Senegal, including Senegambia, Liberia, Sierra Leone, the Gold Coast, Dahomey, and Lower Guinea. The most northern part, that originally settled by the French, is occupied by the Paris Evangelical Society. South of this the English Wesleyans and the Church Missionary Society have established themselves in flourishing missions. Liberia, with its coast line of about six hundred miles, is occupied chiefly by Americans of various denominations. The Gold

Coast and Ashantee missions have about fourteen thousand communicants. It is no small evidence of the success of the missions in this section, that natives should have been fitted for carrying on the work. The Rev. Samuel Crowther was, we believe, the first African who received a thorough theological education in Europe. He was ordained by the Bishop of London as a missionary to Sierra Leone, and went immediately to his field of labor. He preached his first English sermon in Africa in the last month of the year 1843; and at the begin-

Rev. Henry Johnson, Archdeacon of the Upper Niger.

ning of the following year established a service in the language of the country. It was Mr. Crowther who laid the foundations for the great scheme of the Niger Mission, the success of which is attested by the fact that a native of this section has become arch-deacon. Crowther was consecrated bishop in later years, and has proved an able and worthy director of the evangelistic effort.

South of this territory occupied by the Church of England, we find the old Calabar Mission of the United Presbyterian Church of Scotland, and still farther south, the field occupied by the members of the same denominations living in the United States.

The American Board for Foreign Missions began its work on the west coast of Africa in 1834, by establishing a station at Cape Palmas.

The same point has been chosen as a station by the American Episcopalians, who have also stations at other places not far distant.

The efforts of the Baptists of this country have been most vigorous in Liberia and the Yarriba country, where churches and schools have been established, and much good has been accomplished among the natives of the vicinity.

The Rhenish Missionary Society, which was established at Barmen, Prussia, in 1828, chose the southern part of Africa for its field of labor; and its missionaries are now found in the country occupied by the Hottentots, the Bushmen, the Namaquas and the Hereros. A distinguishing feature of this mission is, that it is nearly or quite self-supporting.

The Berlin Missionary Society, four years older than that just mentioned, has its most flourishing missions among the people of the Transvaal, the Bapedi and other Basuto tribes; although its stations are spread over an area of five hundred by one thousand miles. Dr. Krapf, the well-known missionary, has always been specially interested in the work of this society, and was for several years the president of its college at Berlin.

Egypt was the scene of many efforts at missionary labor, but has not proved an encouraging field. Only the United Presbyterian Church of the United States has really been successful in maintaining missions there. Two English societies have made efforts to convert the Abyssinians from that corruption of faith which is derived from the Greek Church, but greatly changed during the many centuries since they held converse with other Christians. Two missionaries were sent there in 1829; but one of them died the following year; and the other, finding the country so disturbed by tribal wars that nothing could be accomplished, returned to England. He went back again, however, in 1834, and, with a colleague, translated the New Testament into the Abyssinian language; but beyond this but little progress was made. Shortly before this, Dr. Krapf had reached the northeast coast, and engaged in the work of reviving the mission there. Their labors, although unfruitful in other respects, have given the people the Bible in their own language.

Since the French occupation of Liberia in 1830, that military settlement has been the base of several missions by the French priests. In 1846, Cairo became the starting-point of an exploratory mission which professed to include Nubia from Khartoom, Kordofan, and the whole Soudan. In 1878, almost the first act of Pope Leo XIII. was to issue a rescript to the Algerian missions, directing them to evangelize the whole breadth of Central Africa from Zanzibar to the mouth of the Congo, which the International Association is exploring. Lake Nyassa, Lake Tanganyika, Kabebe and the North Congo were fixed upon as missionary centers. The Jesuits have made similar attempts on the Upper Zambesi, but at a terrible expense of money and life.

Of the International Society for the Evangelization of Africa, of which the king of the Belgians is the head, we need not speak here; since an account of that will more properly come in the history of its leading spirit, Henry M. Stanley. It is sufficient to say, as an apology for the briefness with which much important work is mentioned in the foregoing pages, that there are no less than thirty-three distinct missionary agencies at work in Africa at the time of the present writing. By consolidation the work may be carried on more systematically than ever.

There is yet one portion of Africa, if an outlying island can be called a portion of a continent, which has not yet been mentioned. The history of missions in Madagascar is a story well worth the telling, were it only for the intense dramatic interest which clothes it. The first missionaries were two Welshmen, David Jones and Samuel Bevan, who went out, with their families, in 1818. Unfortunately, however, they landed at such an unhealthy spot that all took the fever so common there; and Jones was the only survivor of the party. He went back to England; but returned in 1820. The king, Radama I., was not a Christian, but he saw the benefits which Christianity and civilization brought to a country, and was determined that Madagascar should share them. It was he who invited the missionaries there; he took great interest in their efforts to reduce the native tongue to a written language, preparatory to making a translation of the Bible; and even issued a proclamation that no letter of the new alphabet should have more than one sound. In less than ten years, the work of translation had been accomplished, and fifteen thousand native youths were able to read their own language. Many of these had been converted to Christianity.

But the death of the great and good heathen king, Radama, brought dark days for the infant Church. His nephew and heir was suspected by the nobles of a leaning toward Christianity; they therefore concealed Radama's death as long as they could; and finally placed his senior wife, Ranavalona, on the throne. She has been called "the Bloody Mary of Madagascar;" during her reign, from twenty to thirty thousand persons each year fell victims to her rule. Her reign lasted thirty-two years, and during that time nearly one-half of the population was swept away. War was declared against the Christians in 1834; up to that time they had been tolerated because they taught the people to become good artisans; but now, one month was given them, in which to recant. The missionaries left the island; the people, deprived of their teachers, met by stealth in their houses or in lonely glens and on mountain-tops. Open persecution began. A young woman was the first martyr; she was dragged to execution August 14, 1837. Of the effect of this upon the people, we need only say that it was what such martyrdoms have ever produced; some recanted; others believed the more firmly because of her constancy.

Five years passed by, and the persecution continued. Then a friend was raised up, in the person of Radama, the prince royal. He interceded for those condemned to die, and succeeded in securing a commutation of the sentence. But after his first effort, the persecutions went on again. Those who were condemned had their mouths stuffed full of rags, to prevent their speaking to the people of their faith. Four were burned alive; fourteen others were carried to the edge of a cliff, three hundred feet high, situated near the palace and called Ampamarinana, and hurled over its edge. All save one of them shared this fate. This one was a young woman named Ranivo. She was entreated to take the oath, but refused, and demanded that she should be allowed to suffer martyrdom. They quailed before her heroism, and her life was saved. The people were astonished at such devotion; and for a time even the queen gave them a brief respite.

In 1853, Radama was appointed prime minister; and used his power for the amelioration of the condition of the Christians. The London Missionary Society sent out two missionaries, who could do nothing beyond confirming and encouraging the party favoring Christianity. That which was opposed to the religion of the cross was still too strong to be opposed with much success.

A fourth persecution was brought about by a seditious effort of a Frenchman, whose attempt to dethrone the queen, although it had no connection with the party favoring Christianity, was made the pretext for renewed severities. But at last, in July, 1861, the long and terrible reign of Ranavalona came to an end; and Radama II. ascended the throne. Before the sun had set on the day of his accession, he had proclaimed liberty throughout the land, unto all the inhabitants thereof. The brightest hopes were entertained; but they were not to be realized. Radama gave himself up to dissipation; and after a reign of little more than a year, his mind became unsettled, and finally he was strangled by a party of desperadoes.

His widow, Rascherina, succeeded him, and reigned for five years. Under her rule, there was complete religious liberty; and at the request of the queen of England, she agreed that there should be no more persecution of the Christians.

This queen was succeeded by her husband's sister, Ranavalona II., the first Christian ruler of Madagascar. Under her rule, idolatry has fallen into a state of general decay. It is worthy of mention that four memorial churches have been erected upon spots consecrated by the death of the martyrs, one upon that very cliff which has already been mentioned, and one on the place where the first Christian martyr was put to death.

But great as the progress has been—and we leave the story unfinished, having nothing more than the barest outlines—the island is not yet wholly Christian. Far from it. The great majority of the inhabitants are still heathens—ignorant and superstitious as that word implies. The reformation has chiefly been confined to the middle division of the island; and it is from thence, that portion which has churches and schools and printing-presses and teachers, that evangelists are constantly being sent out for the conversion of these people. One of the memorial churches sent out twenty missionaries in one year; another sent out eleven; and so the good work goes on.

Brief and bare is the story as told above; if you would read more, the volumes of Mears, of Ellis, of Mullens, of Mrs. Parker, tell the tale more at length. It is the martyr church of our own century; and here have been repeated the cruelties of the early Roman emperors and the constancy of the early Christians.

Most of the American missions are on the west coast of Africa. The first established was that of the American Baptist Missionary Union, in Liberia, in 1821. After eleven years, this was followed by the establishment of another station in the same locality by the American Presbyterian Board of Missions. The same year (1832) the Methodist Episcopal Missionary Society sent a missionary to Liberia, who died shortly after reaching that country. The good work was carried on, however, and others followed him to the dangerous charge, but without suffering the same fatal results from the climate. The work is now carried on chiefly by native workers, who are less liable to the dreaded African Fever than strangers; and the work is under the charge of a colored bishop (Taylor).

The "American Board" of Missions began its African work in 1834 at Cape Palmas; and two years afterward, the Protestant Episcopal Church of the United States established a station at the same point. This church sent out three missionaries, who worked faithfully among the dense population of the surrounding country. Not a little of their success was due, speaking from a purely secular point of view, to the fact that one of these missionaries was a physician, and was enabled to win the confidence of the natives by attending to their physical ills. Native helpers have been trained, schools have been established and a newspaper is published in the interests of the mission.

In 1842 the American Missionary Association established a station in the Sherbro country, where the usual difficulties in regard to climate were encountered and finally overcome.

In 1848, the Baptist Missionary Society extended its labors to West Africa, and stations were established in the island of Fernando Po and also on the banks of the Cameroons, in the Bight of Benin. In 1858, the Baptist missionaries were expelled from Fernando Po by the Spanish government, when Spain took possession of the island on the termination of its agreement with England. The work on the mainland went on and took deep root, the unrestricted religious liberty allowed by the native chiefs being a great aid to its success. A year after Stanley descended the Congo, this same society established a mission in that country.

But the Baptists are not the only denomination to establish missions in this vast territory. The basin of the Congo comprises an area of nine hundred thousand square miles, filled with a large population. To give one missionary to each hundred square of this tract would require the services of nine thousand workers. Nothing daunted by the immensity of the task, two agencies have set to work to effect what good can be done by the means within their reach. One of these is undenominational, and the other is Baptist; called respectively the Livingstone Inland Congo Mission, and the Arthington Mission of the Baptist Church. These have established themselves at Leopoldville, one to the right and one to the left of the station. It has been a well-contested race to the great goal; the Baptists were the first to win the race to Stanley Pool; Dr. Sims, of the Livingstone Inland Congo Mission, was the first to navigate any portion of the waters of the Upper Congo. The Baptists were the first to occupy a station above Stanley Pool; but soon after, the Livingstone Mission had arranged for a station even at the equator. The Baptists were the first to launch a steamer; but the Livingstone Mission were engaged in building their steamer at Leopoldville at the time that the other was launched. It has been a singular religious duel between two missions of the Protestant Church; both mission chiefs alternately have gained the advance post, and have exhibited remarkable aptitude for their work. Of course, both have experienced dark days, and have been sorely afflicted; but each month the horizon has been clearing, and the prospect is infinitely brighter before them to-day than they could have anticipated when the difficulties of the work first became known by experience.

CHAPTER XIV.

LIVINGSTONE THE MISSIONARY.

LIVINGSTONE'S own account of his early life is so graphic, and yet so modest, that we reproduce it for our readers:

"At the age of ten I was put into the [cotton] factory as a 'piecer,' to aid by my earnings in lessening her [his mother's] anxiety. With a part of my first week's wages I purchased Ruddiman's 'Rudiments of Latin,' and pursued the study of that language for many years afterward, with unabated ardor, at an evening school, which met between the hours of eight and ten. The dictionary part of my labors was followed up till twelve o'clock, or later, if my mother did not interfere by jumping up and snatching the books out of my hands. I had to be back in the factory by six in the morning, and continue my work, with intervals for breakfast and dinner, till eight o'clock at night. I read in this way many of the classical authors, and knew Virgil and Horace better at sixteen than I do now. * * * * In reading, everything that I could lay my hands on was devoured except novels. Scientific works and books of travel were my delight.

"Great pains had been taken by my parents to instil the doctrines of Christianity into my mind; * * * but it was only about this time that I really began to feel the necessity and value of a personal application of the provisions of that Atonement to my own case. * * * * In the glow of love which Christianity inspires, I soon resolved to devote my life to the alleviation of human misery. Turning this idea over in my mind, I felt that to be a pioneer of Christianity in China might lead to the material benefit of some portions of that immense empire; and therefore set myself to obtain a medical education, in order to be qualified for that enterprise. * * * * My reading while at work was carried on by placing the

David Livingstone

book on a portion of the spinning-jenny, so that I could catch sentence after sentence as I passed at my work. I thus kept up a pretty constant study undisturbed by the roar of the machinery. To this part of my education I owe my present power of completely abstracting the mind from surrounding noises, so as to read and write with perfect comfort amid the play of children or near the dancing and songs of savages. The toil of cotton-spinning, to which I was promoted in my nineteenth year, was excessively severe on a slim, loose-jointed lad, but it was well paid for; and it enabled me to support myself while attending medical and Greek classes in Glasgow in winter, as also the divinity lectures of Dr. Wardlaw, by working with my hands in summer. I never received a farthing of aid from any one, and should have accomplished my project of going to China as a medical missionary, in the course of time, by my own efforts, had not some friends advised my joining the London Missionary Society on account of its perfectly unsectarian character. It 'sends neither Episcopacy, nor Presbyterianism, nor Independency, but the Gospel of Christ to the heathen.' This exactly agreed with my ideas of what a missionary society ought to do; but it was not without a pang that I offered myself, for it was not quite agreeable to one who was accustomed to work his own way to become in a measure dependent upon others; and I would not have been much put about had my offer been rejected."

But the offer was not rejected; and the self-helpful student was finally, by the aid of the Missionary Society, admitted as a Licentiate of Faculty of Physicians and Surgeons. China was then closed to the outside world; but the young missionary hoped to gain access to the empire as a physician. The opium war, however, was then raging; and the Society deemed it inexpedient for him to go. There was no immediate prospect of a peace with China, and, on the other hand, Moffat's work in South Africa was beginning to have some effect upon English interest in that part of the world. Livingstone's original intention was thus changed; and in place of becoming a missionary to China, he went to that continent with which his name must ever be indissolubly associated in the minds of all who read about missions or explorations.

After a somewhat more extended course of theological training in England, he set sail for the Cape, where he arrived after a voyage of three months. From this point he embarked for Algoa Bay; and thence proceeded overland to Kuruman, the farthest inland station of the Society. From this point, his instructions bade him turn to the north. Waiting only to recruit the oxen, he proceeded from this point to the Bakwain country, and found Sechele, with his tribe, located as Shokuane. The visit was a short one; and after resting three months at Kuruman, the missionary decided that he could only do his work well if he spoke the language of the people. Accordingly, for six months he shut himself off from all intercourse with Europeans, and studied the Bakwain language. He now began at Lepolole, a point some fifteen miles south of Shokuañe, to make preparations for gardening, by arranging for irrigation. Having dug his canals, he occupied his time in excursions to the surrounding country, a great part of his journeys being performed on foot, because his oxen were sick. Some of the natives, who did not know how conversant he was with their language, remarked:

"He is not strong; he is quite slim, and only appears stout because puts he himself into those bags (trousers); he will soon knock up."

This aroused his spirit of opposition; he was determined that he would not knock up; and he kept them at the top of their speed for days together, until he heard them express a little higher opinion of his physical powers.

He selected the valley of Mabotsa as the site of a missionary station, and removed thither in 1843; he had arrived at the Cape in 1840. He found the Bakatla of this village much annoyed by the lions, which would even attack the herds in broad day. Here occurred one of his most famous adventures.

"The people believed that they were bewitched—'given,' as they said 'into the power of the lions by a neighboring tribe.' They went once to attack the animals, but being rather a cowardly people compared to Bechuanas in general on such occasions, they returned without killing any.

"It is well known that if one of a troop of lions is killed, the others take the hint and leave that part of the country. So, the next time the herds were attacked, I went with the people, in order to encourage them to rid themselves of this annoyance by destroying one of the marauders. We found the lions on a small hill about a quarter of a mile in length, and covered with trees. A circle of men was formed round it, and they gradually closed up, ascending pretty near to each other. Being down below on the plain with a native school-master, named Mebalwe, a most excellent man, I saw one of the lions sitting on a piece of rock within the now closed circle of men,

Mebalwe fired at him before I could, and the ball struck the rock on which the animal was sitting. He bit at the spot struck, as a dog does at a stick or stone thrown at him; then leaping away, broke through the circle and escaped unhurt. The men were afraid to attack him, perhaps on account of their belief in witchcraft. When the circle was re-formed, we saw two other lions in it; but we were afraid to fire lest we should strike the men, and they allowed these beasts to break through also. If the Bakatla had acted according to the custom of the country, they would have speared the lions in the attempt to get out. Seeing we could not get them to kill one of the lions, we bent our footsteps toward the village; in going round the end of the hill, however, I saw one of the beasts sitting on a piece of rock as before, but this time he had a little bush in front. Being about thirty yards off, I took a good aim at his body through the bush, and fired both barrels into it. The men then called out: 'He is shot! He is shot!' Others cried: 'He has been shot by another man, too; let us go to him!' I did not see any one else shoot at him, but I saw the lion's tail erected in anger behind the bush, and turning to the people, said: 'Stop a little, till I load again.' When in the act of ramming down the bullets, I heard a shout. Starting and looking half round, I saw the lion just in the act of springing upon me. I was upon a little height; he caught my shoulder as he sprang, and we both came to the ground below together. Growling horribly close to my ear, he shook me as a terrier dog does a rat. The shock produced a stupor similar to that which seems to be felt by the mouse after the first shake of the cat. It caused a sort of dreaminess, in which there was no sense of pain nor feeling of terror, though quite conscious of all that was happening. It was like what patients partially under the influence of chloroform describe, who see all the operation, but feel not the knife. This singular condition was not the result of any mental process. The shake annihilated fear, and allowed no sense of horror in looking round at the beast. This peculiar state is probably produced in all animals killed by the carnivora; and if so, is a merciful provision by our benevolent Creator for lessening the pain of death. Turning round to relieve myself of his weight, as he had one paw on the back of my head, I saw his eyes directed to Mebalwe, who was trying to shoot him at a distance of ten or fifteen yards. His gun, a flint one, missed fire in both barrels; the lion immediately left me, and attacking Mebalwe, bit his thigh. Another man, whose life I had saved before, after he

THE MISSIONARY AT THE MERCY OF A LION.

had been tossed by a buffalo, attempted to spear the lion while he was biting Mebalwe. He left Mebalwe and caught this man by the shoulder, but at that moment the bullets that he had received took effect, and he fell down dead. The whole was the work of a few moments, and must have been the paroxysms of his dying rage. * * * Besides crunching the bone into splinters, he left eleven teeth wounds in the upper part of my arm."

Livingstone had attached himself to that division of the Bechuanas which is known as the Bakwains. The chief of this tribe was named Sechele; and from the very first, he manifested an interest in Christianity. The missionary was a great favorite with him; and he never lost an opportunity of pressing him to read the Bible to him.

Seeing Livingstone's anxiety to convert the people, he once said to him:

"Do you imagine that these people will ever believe by your merely talking to them? I can make them do nothing except by thrashing them; and if you like, I will call my head men, and with our litupa (whips of rhinoceros hide) we will soon make them all believe together."

It is needless to say that this offer of help in evangelizing the Bakwains was declined. Sechele continued to listen to the missionary's teaching, and for the space of two years and a half endeavored, by other means than whips of rhinoceros hide, to impress his people with a belief in it. He himself still clung to his many wives; because they were the daughters of sub-chiefs who had helped him against domestic enemies, and if he sent them back, he would appear ungrateful to those who had done so much for him in his adversity.

Finally, however, he made up his mind to this; and sent each one back to her parents, with such presents as were suitable for the occasion. Then he and his children were baptized, great numbers coming to see the ceremony.

But the example of the chief was not followed by many of his tribe. The country had, ever since Livingstone's arrival there, suffered from terrible droughts, which made it nearly impossible to obtain food by any means but hunting; and the people believed this to be the result of his coming among them. Under such circumstances, it is small wonder that the ignorant Bakwains refused to listen to him.

In consequence of the drought, the tribe removed to a point on the Kolobeng, the missionary accompanying them. Here Livingstone persuaded the chief to have a canal for irrigating

THE HOPO, OR TRAP FOR DRIVING GAME.

his garden dug; the experiment succeeding admirably during the first year; but failed with the drought in the second and third. Sechele himself was a noted rain-doctor, but forbore to use his supposed powers after his conversion; although he had firmly believed in them himself, and assured the missionary that this was the hardest part of the old belief to give up. But his people protested loudly against this refusal to exercise his powers; and considered Livingstone responsible.

Under these circumstances, it was necessary for the women of the tribe to sell their ornaments in order to purchase grain of more fortunate tribes. The children scoured the country for roots and bulbs; while the men hunted industriously. A favorite method of securing a large quantity of game was by means of the trap called the *hopo.* This consisted of two very high hedges in the form of the letter V, thick near the angle; but instead of an angle, there is a lane about fifty yards long, formed by the continuation of these hedges. At the end of this lane is a pit, six or eight feet deep, and about twelve or fifteen feet square. Trunks of trees are laid across the margin of the pit, and carefully decked with short green rushes. The hedges are about a mile long, and the opening is equally wide. The men of the tribe, making a circuit throughout the surrounding country, and gradually closing up, are almost sure to drive a large quantity of game into the *hopo*; and pursuing the animals with shouts to the narrow lane mentioned, men secreted there throw their javelins into the affrighted herds, which rush into the pit concealed by the rushes. The men wild with excitement, spear the animals that are on the surface of the mass; while those beneath are crushed by the weight of their fellow-victims. The Bakwains often kill between sixty and seventy head of large game at one of these traps at a time; and rich and poor partake alike of the flesh.

Here at Kolobeng, Livingstone built a house for himself, the third that he had erected. A native smith had taught him how to weld iron; he had received many valuable hints in building from his father-in-law, Mr. Moffat, as well as in carpentering and gardening; and he was becoming handy at almost any trade, as well as doctoring and preaching. He says that at this time, he and his wife came "nearly up to what may be considered indispensable in the accomplishments of a missionary family in Central Africa, namely, the husband to be jack-of-all-trades without doors, and the wife maid-of-all-work within." He further says:

"You want bricks to build a house, and must forthwith pro-

THE PIT AT THE END OF THE HOPO.

ceed to the field, cut down a tree, and saw it into the planks to make the brick-moulds; the materials for doors and windows, too, are standing in the forest; and if you want to be respected by the natives, a house of decent dimensions, costing an immense amount of manual labor, must be built. The people cannot assist you much; for though most willing to labor for wages, the Bakwains have a curious inability to make or put things square; like all Bechuanas, their dwellings are made round. In the case of three large houses, erected by myself at different times, every brick and stick had to be put square by my own right hand."

Livingstone also assisted the natives to build a square house for their chief, and a building for a school. But he could not succeed in convincing them that he was in no way responsible for the drought. Another source of trouble was the behavior of the Boers. These were not the farming class, but rather fugitives from justice, English deserters, and every variety of bad characters, who had attacked the surrounding tribes, and made slaves of as many as they could capture. These persons did not hesitate to misrepresent Livingstone to the Bakwains as a spy of their enemies; and might have done him great harm if Sechele's faith in him had been less persistent.

With the troubles between Sechele and these Boers we have here nothing to do; it is our place rather, to follow Livingstone as he journeys from Kolobeng farther into the interior. In the effort to benefit the native tribes, he twice made a journey of about three hundred miles to the eastward of Kolobeng; Sechele lamenting that he could not accompany him, since the Boers were such bitter enemies. His independence and love of the English had excited their hatred against him. He gave Livingstone two servants, however, to accompany him and be his (Sechele's) arms to serve him.

"Suppose we went north," suggested the missionary; "would you come then?"

It was the first conception of the journey which resulted in the discovery of Lake Ngami. But even northward Sechele could not go; for he feared to leave his tribe without a chief in case it should be attacked by the Boers. Learning of Livingstone's intentions, two English travelers, Messrs. Oswell and Murray, asked to accompany him; and June 1, 1849, the party set out on the journey along the outskirts of the great Kalahari Desert. They had gone but a few days' journey, when they found that there was but little water for their horses and oxen. A few hollows like those made by buffaloes

ELEPHANTS IN DIFFICULTY AT THE STEEP BANK OF A RIVER.

and rhinoceros when they roll themselves in the sand appeared, and in the corner of one of these was a little water, which the dogs would have quickly drank up if they had not been held back. Nothing daunted by the prospect, their guides bade them have patience; and rapidly scooped out holes in the sand, so as to form pits six feet deep and as many broad. Into these the water flowed slowly at first, but more rapidly toward morning; and they had sufficient for their needs.

This method of obtaining water answered only in certain localities; and Livingstone supposes, from the indications of the surrounding country, that these places were the beds of what had once been rivers; and that the water thus procured would have otherwise been conducted by underground filtration to a lower level. They were soon beyond these easily dug wells, and suffered much for the lack of water. On one occasion, however, they captured a Bushwoman, and bribed her to conduct them to a spring. She accepted their gift, and walked before the wagon no less than eight miles before reaching the water.

On the fourth of July, the travelers reached the Zouga. The natives confirmed what they had already heard, that by following this stream they would reach Ngami; and added that perhaps they would be a moon on the way. They ascended the river for about ninety-six miles, traveling along the banks in the wagons which they had crossed the desert in; and at that point, Ngabisane, left all the wagons except the smallest, and continued the ascent in the canoes of the natives.

The people in whose territory they now were possess one peculiarity—they never fight. Livingstone calls them the "Quakers of the body politic of Africa;" the Bechuanas call them Bakoba, a name which retains something the meaning of slaves. They regard their canoes, hollowed out of the trunk of a tree, as the Arab does the camel; and prefer sleeping in them to spending the night on land.

While ascending the beautifully wooded river, they came to a mouth of a considerable tributary; and the missionary inquired concerning its source.

"It comes from a country full of rivers—so many no one can tell their numbers," was the reply; "and full of large trees."

This effectually disproved, to his mind, the theory that had been entertained, that the country beyond was not a "large sandy plateau."

Twelve days after their departure from Ngabisane, they came

NATIVES HARPOONING HIPPOPOTAMI.

to the northeast end of Lake Ngami. The first sight was a disappointment, for he had dreamed of a great highway for commerce in the heart of this untraveled country; he found a body of water, which, according to the natives' account of it, could not be more than seventy-five miles in circumference, and so shallow that he saw a native punting his canoe over seven or eight miles of the northeast end.

Livingstone's chief object, however, was not to see Lake Ngami, but to see Sebituane, the chief of the Makololo. In order to do this, he must procure guides and permission from Lecholetebe, Chief of the Batanana, a half-tribe of the Bamangwato. But Lecholetebe was not willing to grant these favors; if the white men reached the country of Sebituane, that chief would be able to procure muskets, and his own supremacy would therefore be endangered. It was in vain that Livingstone represented himself as an agent of peace; the savage could not understand anything of the kind; and the travelers were obliged to return to the south again.

They witnessed many sights peculiar to this part of the world. One occurrence that particularly excited their curiosity was the behavior of a herd of elephants when drinking at the river. These huge animals would play like so many children in the water, throwing great quantities of it over each other, and screaming with delight at the fun. On finishing their sport and endeavoring to leave the water at a point where the bank was quite steep, a comical sight ensued of their desperate struggles to get out. The elephants about Ngami, they observed, were much smaller than farther south, the variation in height being as much as three feet.

Several new kinds of animals were observed; and many different species of fish. The natives living along the Zouga are determined fishermen, for much of their food is drawn from the water. They use nets knotted like those of other countries; and also spear the fish with javelins having a handle so light that it readily floats on the surface. They show great dexterity in harpooning the hippopotamus; and the barbed blade of the spear being attached to a rope made of the young leaves of the palmyra, the animal cannot rid himself of the canoe, attached to him in whale fashion, except by smashing it, which he frequently does with his teeth or by a stroke of his hind foot.

Returning to Kolobeng, Dr. Livingstone started upon a second trip to Ngami in April, 1850, accompanied by his wife, three children, and the chief Sechele. The Zouga was ascended by means of wagons this time, although with immense labor, since the trees along the route had often to be cut down to make the road passable for the wagon. On approaching the confluence of the Tamunakle, another difficulty beset them; they were informed that the fly called tsetse abounded on its banks. This insect is not much larger than the common house-fly, and is of nearly the same color as the ordinary honey-bee; the after part of the body has three or four yellow bars across it. It is remarkably alert at the ordinary temperatures; but during the cool of the morning and evening is less agile. Its peculiarity is, that its bite is fatal to horses, oxen, and dogs, but not to man and wild animals; even calves, as long as they continue to suck the cow, are safe from its bite. Although the travelers were not aware of any great number having at any one time lighted upon their cattle, they lost no less than forty-three fine oxen by the bite of this deadly insect. It is remarkable that its bite does not produce instant death, but acts as a slow poison, sometimes requiring months for its development. In some cases, the animal's brain seemed to be acted upon by the virus, and it was affected with staggering and blindness.

The districts where the tsetse is found are defined by sharply drawn boundaries; and in this case, the travelers were able to escape its ravages simply by crossing the Zouga. But although Lecholetebe yielded to Sechele's persuasions, and agreed to furnish the missionary with guides to Sebituane's dominions, the traveler was again foiled. Two of his children were taken sick with fever; on the next day, all their servants were down; there was but one sure cure—change of air; and he was obliged to return with his embryo hospital to the purer air of the desert.

On their return, they met Mr. Oswell on the banks of the Zouga. He had been elephant hunting, and had greatly distinguished himself in the eyes of the natives, because his great success was achieved without the aid of dogs. He was known to have killed four large male elephants in one day, the value of whose tusks would be fairly estimated, at that time, at about five hundred dollars of our money. Two years later, when the Livingstone family visited the Cape, the missionary wearing a coat which had been in his outfit in 1840, and his wife and children clad in such costumes as her ingenuity could devise out of next to nothing, they found that Mr. Oswell had ordered an outfit for them costing about a thousand dollars. When remonstrated with, he replied that Mrs. Livingstone had a right to the proceeds of the game of her own preserves.

They returned once more to Kolobeng, whither they were soon followed by messengers from Sebituane himself, with a gift of thirteen cows to Sechele, and a request that that chief would assist the missionary in his efforts to reach Sebituane's country. A similar present and request had been sent to Lecholetebe and another chief, Sekomi; but it was the policy of all, in accordance with that law of African commerce which has already been stated, to prevent the white men from reaching Sebituane's country.

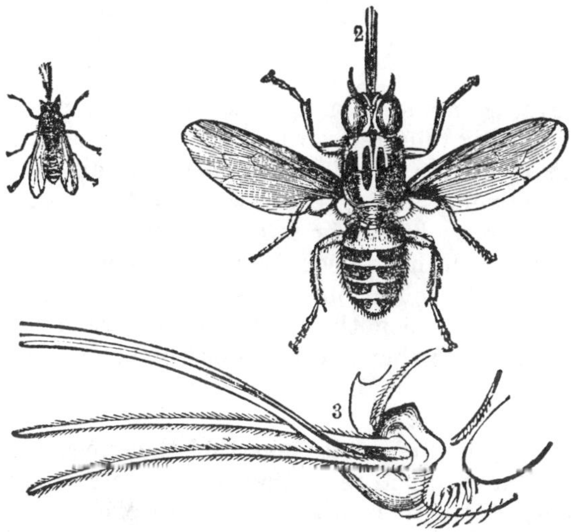

1. *The Tsetse Fly.* 2. *The Same Magnified.* 3. *The Proboscis.*

A third effort to reach his territories proved more successful; the chief himself coming a hundred miles to meet them.

But the chief did not live long to befriend them. He was taken down, shortly after their arrival, with inflammation of the lungs; he had had previous attacks, it seemed, and now trusted to the same "doctors." Livingstone decided that it was best not to interfere, so long as he was not requested to do so; since if the chief died (and he was a doomed man from the first) the consequences would be great danger to the missionary and his family. The chieftainship devolved upon a daughter of Sebituane's, named Ma-mochisane, who was twelve miles away when her father's death occurred. She sent word that the white travelers were free to visit any part of her dominions. In accordance with this permission, Livingstone and Oswell, having previously arranged to leave Mrs. Livingstone and the children in the care of their new friends, proceeded one hundred and thirty miles to the northeast, to Sesheke; in the end of June, 1851, they were rewarded by the discovery of the Zambesi.

This was indeed a discovery: for it was not known that this great river proceeded from a point so far inland; indeed, the direction of its source from its mouth was uncertain. On the Portuguese maps, which were then the best authority for this portion of Africa, conjecture had placed it far to the east of this point.

They saw the river at the end of the dry season, when it was at its lowest stage; yet Oswell, whose Indian experience made his opinion worth having, declared that even in the far East he had never seen a stream equal to this, with its breadth of from three to six hundred yards of deep, flowing water. Had they seen it during the highest floods, when the depth of the water is twenty feet greater than at this season, and it covers the country fifteen or twenty miles on each side of its banks, what would have been their judgment concerning it?

It had been the intention of Livingstone to establish a missionary station between the Chobe and the Zambesi, but the country over which they traveled was obviously so unhealthful that the project was abandoned. Even the natives had been cut off by fever.

These being the first white men that the tribes living around the Upper Zambesi had seen, they were visited by great numbers. Some of the men who came were clad in garments of gaudy cotton, which the explorers saw at once must have come from Europe. In answer to inquiries, the wearers said that these vestments were received in exchange from the Mambari, a tribe living near Bihe, who acted as middlemen between the Portuguese and the interior races. The price of each gown had been a boy about fourteen years old, who had been bought from the Makololo or the Barutse. The natives explained that this traffic was a very recent thing; and comparing their statements with his own movements, Livingstone found that Sebituane and his people had only begun to trade in slaves after the time of the missionary's first attempt to reach his country; had that been successful, the good man reflected with much regret, this traffic might never have been begun.

Livingstone now returned to Kolobeng; but as the Boers would not permit the peaceable instruction of the natives there, and it was next to impossible for a European to live in the protected portion of Sebituane's country on account of the prevalent fever, he resolved to send his family to England, and to return and explore the country alone, in search of a healthy region where a missionary station could be established. The directors of the London Missionary Society cordially approved of this plan, and left the details to be arranged by him. Accordingly, he took his wife and children to the Cape, placed them on a homeward-bound vessel, and early in June, 1852, turned his steps once more to the interior.

His journey northward was a slow one, delayed as he was by an accident to his wagon and by the ravages of tsetse upon his oxen. It was the last day of the year when he arrived at Kolobeng. He found that Sechele and his tribe had been attacked by the Boers of the mountain, and had suffered considerable loss. The news of this attack had reached him while he was on the way; indeed, it was in consequence of the resolute defense of the Bakwains that he was unable to get servants at Kuruman. Forty miles north of this place, he met Sechele, who told him that he was on his way to the queen of England. A former wife and two of her children had been captured by the Boers; and Sechele, who had imbibed a very high opinion of the justice and generosity of England, wished to lay this case before the queen, that the Boers might be compelled to restore the captives. It was in vain that the missionary and others attempted to teach him what difficulties beset the journey; he had no conception of the distance, and resolutely pressed on. Poor fellow! He found his resources exhausted when he got to the Cape; there was none to help him, for the governor had his own theory about dealing with the Boers and the native tribes; and the chief sadly turned away from the sea, to begin his weary return journey of a thousand miles to his own country.

Sechele had left orders that his people were not to undertake any act of revenge during his absence; but some of his young men had disobeyed this, and attacked the Boers. The latter became alarmed, and thinking that the Bakwains meant to begin a guerrilla war, sent four embassadors to ask for peace. One condition was made: That Sechele's children should be returned to him; this was eagerly acceded to, and when the chief arrived, he found that his appeal would have been needless.

Leaving Kolobeng on the fifteenth of January, they skirted the edge of the Kalahari Desert again; but the preceding rainy season an unusual quantity of rain had fallen, and con-

A LION NARROWLY MISSES MR. OSWELL.

sequently they did not suffer for water as before. This was a country much frequented by lions, and Mr. Oswell, who again accompanied the missionary, found much sport in hunting them. Upon one occasion, his sport came near ending more fatally for himself than for the lion. He had exhausted the loads in his gun without any effect except to wound the lion, which, enraged by the pain, sprang upon the hind-quarters of his horse as he turned to fly over the plain. The rider was dragged from his saddle by the thorns of an overhanging tree, and the fall rendered him insensible. The hunter's dogs attacked the lion, which soon fell dead from the effects of the previous wound.

A little farther on, they came across many indications of the presence of ostriches. Livingstone says of this bird:

"The ostrich is generally seen quietly feeding on some spot where no one can approach him without being detected by his wary eye. As the wagon moves far along to the windward he thinks it is intending to circumvent him, so he rushes up a mile or so from the leeward, and so near to the front oxen that one sometimes gets a shot at the silly bird. When he begins to run, all the game in sight follows his example. I have seen this folly taken advantage of when he was feeding quietly in a valley open at both ends. A number of men would commence running, as if to cut off his retreat from the end through which the wind came; and although he had the whole country hundreds of miles before him by going to the other end, on he madly rushed to get past the men, and so was speared. He never swerves from the course he once adopts, but only increases his speed.

"When the ostrich feeds, his pace is from twenty to twenty-two inches; when walking, but not feeding, it is twenty-six inches; and when terrified, as in the case noticed, it is from eleven and a half to thirteen and even fourteen feet in length. Only in one case was I at all satisfied of being able to count the rate of speed by a stop-watch, and if I am not mistaken, there were thirty in ten seconds; generally one's eye can no more follow the legs than it can the spokes of a carriage-wheel in rapid motion. If we take the above number, and twelve feet stride as the average pace, we have a speed of twenty-six miles an hour. It cannot be very much above that, and is therefore slower than a railway locomotive. They are sometimes shot by a horseman making a cross cut to their undeviating course, but few Englishmen ever succeed in killing them."

OSTRICH HUNTING.

If was May before they arrived at the banks of the Chobe, at a point some thirty miles below Linyanti, the capital of the Makololo. Here they turned to the north, and on the twenty-third of that month reached Linyanti, where Sekeletu, the son of Sebituane, was now chief. On his previous journey, Livingstone had seen Ma-mochisane, the daughter of Sebituane, recognized as that chief's successor; but she had found that the chieftainship was not what she had anticipated; and voluntarily resigned that bad eminence to her eighteen-year-old brother, saying that she would rather be like other women, married and have a family.

While at Linyanti, Livingstone was taken with the fever. Anxious to ascertain if the natives had any cure for this disease with which he was not acquainted, he gave himself up to the treatment of one of the Makololo doctors. The result was not encouraging. "After being stewed in their vapor-baths, smoked like a red herring over green twigs, and charmed *secundum artem*, I concluded that I could cure the fever more quickly than they."

Livingstone proposed to teach the Makololos to read, but they declined the offer at first; the chief alleging, as a reason, that to learn to read might make him content with one wife, like Sechele. Finally, however, this objection was overcome; some of the under chiefs put themselves under instruction, and when Sekeletu saw that it did them no particular harm, he began to study.

After remaining at Linyanti for about a month, Livingstone set out to ascend the river, Sekeletu, who had volunteered to accompany him, being his companion, together with about one hundred and sixty of his tribe. They traveled on land for some distance, but finally took to the canoes, of which thirty-three were required for the transportation of their party.

The river was one which had never been explored by a white man thus far from the coast; and Livingstone could not sufficiently admire its grandeur. Along the banks were villages and fields which gave evidence of an industrious and prosperous people. They met with no particular difficulties in the ascent except at the cataract of Gouye, where the canoes had to be carried overland for more than a mile. The river was sufficiently high to make it possible to pass the rapids without portage.

But his investigations regarding the nature of the country did not lead to anything satisfactory; he found no place at

RECEPTION OF LIVINGSTONE BY SHINTE.

which it would be wise to establish a missionary station; and therefore returned to Linyanti, having ascended the Zambesi to its confluence with the Leeba. He determined to cross the continent to Loanda, and resisted all attempts of the "doctors" to persuade him that such a course would be fatal. He left Sekeletu's town November 11th, and reached Sesheke on the 17th. Forty days later, they arrived at the confluence of the Leeba and the Leeambye, traveling mainly overland. They found the Makololo extremely friendly wherever they went, the missionary and his attendants being the messengers of peace in their estimation. It is remarkable that this warlike tribe values peace so highly; probably, like many a great soldier, they had seen enough of war to make them desire peace.

As he went on, he found that many of the chiefs were women. One of these, Manenko, received him with special honors, and insisted that he should visit her brother, Shinte or Kabampo, the greatest Balonda chief in this part of the country. Livingstone was not very willing to do this, as it took him out of the more direct route; but his followers were not disposed to encounter the hostile tribes that lived farther up the river, so that he was obliged to yield. Manenko headed the numerous party which escorted them to the residence of her brother, and decided upon the lucky moment for an entrance to his town.

"We were honored next day with a grand reception by Shinte about eleven o'clock. * * * The kotla, or place of audience, was about a hundred yards square, and two graceful specimens of a species of banyan stood near one end; under one of these sat Shinte, on a sort of throne covered with a leopard's skin. He had on a checked jacket, and a kilt of scarlet baize edged with green; many strings of large beads hung from his neck, and his limbs were covered with iron and copper armlets and bracelets; on his head he wore a helmet made of beads closely woven together, and crowned with a great bunch of goose feathers. Close to him sat three lads with large sheaves of arrows over their shoulders.

"When we entered the kotla, the whole of Manenko's party saluted Shinte by clapping their hands, and Sambanza did obeisance by rubbing his chest and arms with ashes. * * * When all had come and were seated, then began the curious capering usually seen in pichos. A man starts up, and imitates the most approved attitudes observed in actual fight, as throwing one javelin, receiving another on the shield, springing to one side to observe a third, running backward or forward, leaping, etc. This over, Sambanza, the spokesman of Nyamoana, stalked backward and forward in front of Shinte, and gave forth, in a loud voice, all that they had been able to learn, either from myself or people, of my past history and connection with the Makololo; the return of the captives; the wish to open the country to trade; the Bible as a word from heaven; the white man's desire for the tribes to live in peace; he ought to have taught the Makololo that first, for the Balonda never attacked them, yet they assailed the Balonda; perhaps he is fibbing, perhaps not; they rather thought he was; but as the Balonda had good hearts, and Shinte had never done harm to any one, he had better receive the white man well, and send him on his way. When nine speakers had concluded their orations, Shinte stood up, and so did all the people. He had maintained true African dignity of manner all the while, but my people remarked that he scarcely ever took his eyes off me for a moment. About a thousand people were present, according to my calculation, and three hundred soldiers."

Livingstone remained here ten days, being detained by another attack of fever; when he left, Shinte furnished him with eight men to assist in carrying his baggage, but could only provide guides for a short distance. After traveling five days, they came to a country so full of branches and feeders of the Leeba, and so largely under water; that the traveler could only keep his watch dry by carrying it in his arm-pit.

Their journey, however, was not attended by any special adventure until they reached Njambi, a village of the Chiboque. They arrived here on Saturday, and the missionary expected to spend the ensuing Sunday in talking to the people. But his expectations were not fulfilled. The chief refused the gift of the hump and ribs of an ox which Livingstone had killed, and demanded that the traveler should present him with a man, an ox, or a gun. Oxen they had none to spare; of guns they had but five; and the missionary had no notion of leaving one of his faithful servants in slavery. The young Chiboque brandished their weapons threateningly, but Livingstone was firm. He declared that he and his people would not strike the first blow, but that if attacked they would defend themselves.

"It was rather trying for me, because I knew that the Chiboque would aim at the white man first; but I was careful not to appear flurried, and, having four barrels ready for instant action, looked quietly at the savage scene around. * * * The chiefs and counselors, seeing that they were in more danger than I, did not choose to follow our decision that they should begin by striking the first blow, and then see what we could do, and were perhaps influenced by seeing the air of cool preparation which some of my men displayed, and the prospect of a work of blood."

A compromise was finally effected, and the party passed on. But their experience here was only an earnest of what would await them in the country to the west. The slave-trade is there vigorously prosecuted; and it was because they were accustomed to make such demands and see them complied with that the Chiboque of Njambi had asked a slave from this explorer. Livingstone therefore resolved to alter his course, and take a direction north-northeast, in the hope that he might find some point from which the Portuguese settlements might be reached without having to face this danger. Crossing several tributaries of the Kasai, they found themselves in a country to which the traders had more frequently penetrated, and where, therefore, a white man was less of a curiosity. It was less difficult, in some respects, to make their way here than it had been through the more secluded country.

Just beyond the Quilo they found a well-beaten path, which they were told would lead them to the Portuguese settlement of Cassange, the farthest inland station of that nation on the western coast of Africa. Following this for some time, they at last emerged from the gloomy forest, and beheld a magnificent prospect which made them feel "as if a weight had been lifted off our eyelids." This was the valley of the Quango, into which they descended.

Some few difficulties remained to be overcome before they actually reached the bank of this river and were ferried across; but once on the other side, they were within Portuguese territory, and there remained no further obstacle to their journey. On the 31st of May, they entered the city of Loanda; and after an incessant tramp of nearly six months, Livingstone found himself again enjoying the "luxurious pleasure of a good English bed" in the house of the only Englishman in the city of twelve thousand inhabitants.

Here he remained for four months; for not only must he make preparations for the return journey, but he was prostrated by several successive attacks of fever. In the meantime his Makololo attendants improved the time by becoming acquainted with the wonders of European architecture. They had been unable to comprehend how a house could be two stories high; since their huts are made by sticking the poles in the ground so as to form a cone, and covering that with skins

A ZEBRA CHASE.

or thatch, they could not understand how the poles for the second story were provided with a foundation, or what use the second floor would be, with the peak of the lower hut projecting above its floor. One of them, who had seen Livingstone's house at Kolobeng, described it as a mountain with several caves in it. Now, however, they all understood this much. The English vessels in port were another source of wonder; and they gravely pronounced these "towns;" designating them particularly as "towns that you climb into with a rope." The statement that these vessels, with their huge guns, were used to put down the slave-trade, afforded the poor creatures unalloyed gratification.

The Portuguese merchants resident at Loanda so heartily sympathized with Livingstone's aims that they gave him handsome presents for distribution among the peoples of the interior; and the Board of Public Works sent a present to Sekeletu. These gifts were accompanied by letters from the bishop and the merchants.

Livingstone left Loanda September 20, 1854; and went by sea to the mouth of the Bengo. They did not reach Cassange until the middle of January, 1855, having delayed to visit a group of curious rocks on the way. Crossing the Quango February 28, Livingstone resolved to leave his old route and accompany the Portuguese traders as far as Cabongo, in the Londa country. This would lead him much farther eastward than the former route, but it would be no longer in the end, and he would avoid contact with the hostile Chiboques. Much sickness delayed them; for if one carrier was sick, the others could not be induced to share his burden among them.

This change in route became the means of correcting a mistake into which Livingstone had fallen, in regard to the course of the rivers. He says:

"I became fully persuaded that the Quilo runs into the Chikapa. As we now crossed them both considerably farther down, and were greatly to the eastward of our former route, there can be no doubt that these rivers take the same course as the others, into the Kasai, and that I had been led into a mistake in saying that any of them flowed to the westward. Indeed, it was only at this time that I began to perceive that all the western feeders of the Kasai, except the Quango, flow first from the western side toward the center of the country, then gradually turn, with the Kasai itself, to the north; and after the confluence of the Kasai with the Quango, an immense body of water, collected from all these branches, finds its way out of the country by means of the River Congo or Zaire on the west coast."

Some of the difficulties of traveling through an African forest are succinctly stated in the following lines:

"We passed on through forests abounding in climbing plants, many of which are so extremely tough that a man is required to go in front with a hatchet; and when the burdens of the carriers are caught, they are obliged to cut the climbers with their teeth, for no amount of tugging will make them break. The paths in all these forests are so zigzag that a person may imagine he has traveled a distance of thirty miles, which, when reckoned as the crow flies, may not be fifteen."

On the evening of June 2, they reached the village of Kawawa, a Balonda chief; who at first received them very cordially. But as they were preparing to leave, he decided that they ought to present him with an ox; and told them that they should not leave until they had done so. If they refused an ox, they must give a man.

"Kawawa came in the coolest manner possible to our encampment after sending this message, and told me that he had seen all our goods, and must have all he asked, as he had command of the Kasai in our front, and would prevent our passing it unless we paid this tribute. I replied that the goods were my property and not his; that I would never have it said that a white man paid tribute to a black, and that I should cross the Kasai in spite of him. He ordered his people to arm themselves, and when some of my men saw them rush, ing for their bows, arrows and spears, they became somewhat panic-stricken. I ordered them to move away, and not to fire unless Kawawa's men struck the first blow. I took the lead and expected them all to follow, as they usually had done, but many of my men remained behind. When I knew of this, I jumped off the ox, and made a rush to them with the revolver in my hand. Kawawa ran away among his people, and they turned their backs too. I shouted to my men to take up their luggage and march; some did so with alacrity, feeling that they had disobeyed orders by remaining; but one of them refused, and was preparing to fire at Kawawa, until I gave him a punch on the head with the pistol, and made him go too. I felt here, as elsewhere, that subordination must be maintained at all risks. We all moved into the forest, the people of Kawawa standing about a hundred yards off, gazing, but not firing a shot or an arrow. * * * * Kawawa was not to be balked of his supposed rights by the unceremonious way in which we had left him; for, when we had reached the ford of the Kasai, about ten miles distant, we found that he had sent four of his men, with orders to the ferrymen to refuse us passage. We were here duly informed that we must deliver up all the articles mentioned, and one of our men besides. This demand for one of our number always nettled every heart. The canoes were taken away before our eyes, and we were supposed to be quite helpless without them, at a river a good hundred yards broad, and very deep. Pitsane stood on the bank, gazing with apparent indifference on the stream, and made an accurate observation of where the canoes were hidden among the reeds. The ferrymen casually asked one of my Batoka if they had rivers in their country, and he answered with truth, 'No, we have none.' Kawawa's people then felt sure we could not cross. I thought of swimming when they were gone; but after it was dark, by the unasked loan of one of the canoes, we soon were snug in our bivouac on the southern bank of the Kasai. I left some beads as payment for some meal which had been presented by the ferrymen; and the canoe having been left on their own side of the river. Pitsane and his companions laughed uproariously at the disgust our enemies would feel, and their perplexity as to who had been our paddler across. They were quite sure that Kawawa would imagine that we had been ferried over by his own people, and would be divining to find out who had done the deed. When ready to depart in the morning, Kawawa's people appeared on the opposite heights, and could scarcely believe their eyes when they saw us prepared to start away to the south. At last one of them called out: 'Ah, ye are bad!' to which Pitsane and his companions retorted: 'Ah, ye are good, and we thank you for the loan of your canoe.'"

The plain which had been covered with water when they crossed it going westward, was now dry, the water remaining only in a few scattered pools. During their second day on this plain, Livingstone records that he suffered from his twenty-seventh attack of fever. The next day, however, he considered himself well enough to travel; and June 8, they forded the Lotemba to the northwest of Dilolo, and regained their former path.

Now they were among friends; for they had conciliated all the chiefs in whose countries they had traveled, except the two that have been mentioned. Their reception at Libonta, where they arrived July 27, was particularly cordial; for they were looked upon as men risen from the dead; the most skilful

THE BOAT CAPSIZED BY A HIPPOPOTAMUS ROBBED OF HER YOUNG.

diviners having long before declared that they had perished. The missionary's means, acquired in Loanda, had all been spent, during a journey in which many delays had occurred, but this made no difference to the natives whose love had been won long before. They knew that Livingstone had been engaged in an effort to open the country to trade, and to suppress the slave-trade, and that was enough for them. Even Livingstone's men said: "Though we return as poor as we went, we have not gone in vain."

One of the adventures of the party shortly after they left Libonta is worth recording, as a characteristic accident:

"I left Naliele on the 13th of August, and when proceeding along the shore at midday, a hippopotamus struck the canoe with her forehead, lifting one-half of it quite out of the water, so as nearly to overturn it. The force of the but she gave tilted Mashauana out into the river; the rest of us sprang to the shore, which was only about ten yards off. Glancing back, I saw her come to the surface a short way off, and look at the canoe, as if to see if she had done much mischief. It was a female, whose young one had been speared the day before. No damage was done except wetting person and goods. This is so unusual an occurrence, when the precaution is taken to coast along the shore, that my men exclaimed: 'Is the beast mad!' There were eight of us in the canoe at the time, and the shake it received shows the immense power of this animal in the water."

Long before this, Livingstone had heard that a party of Matabele had brought a number of parcels to the south bank of the Zambesi, and left them there in the care of the Makololo. The two tribes are sworn enemies, and the Makololo would not believe that Mr. Moffat had sent these goods to Dr. Livingstone, as the bearers told them. The Matabele answered:

"Here are the goods; we place them now before you, and if you leave them to perish the guilt will be yours."

After much divination, and with fear and trembling, the Makololo, who feared some attempt to bewitch them, built a hut over the parcels, and there Livingstone found them safe on his return in September, 1855, exactly a year after they reached that destination. Among other things, there was a copy of an address by Sir Roderick Murchison before the Royal Geographical Society, in which he stated his conviction that the interior of Africa was not a vast plateau, but a vast basin, flanked by mountains and highlands. This was the very

THE VICTORIA FALLS OF THE ZAMBESI.

same conclusion to which Livingstone had come, although with infinitely more difficulty:

"In his easy-chair he had forestalled me by three years, though I had been working hard through jungle, marsh, and fever, and since the light dawned upon my mind at Dilolo, had been cherishing the pleasing idea that I should be the first to suggest the idea that the interior of Africa was a watery plateau of less elevation than flanking hilly ranges."

From this point they went directly to Linyanti, where the men who had accompanied him were at last able to tell their own people of the wonderful things that they had seen. They had gone to the end of the world, and had only turned back when there was no more land.

"Then you reached Ma-Robert (as Mrs. Livingstone was called by them, because her eldest child was named Robert)?" asked one eagerly.

Then the recounters of wonders were obliged to admit that she lived a little beyond the end of the world to which they had gone.

The presents which had been sent gave great satisfaction; and when Sekeletu appeared at church in the uniform which he had received, it attracted more attention than the sermon. Livingstone was soon overwhelmed with offers to accompany him to the east coast. Finally, the chief selected a party of those who were most anxious to go, and dispatched them under the care of an Arab trader, to learn how to trade.

Livingstone remained at Linyanti until the latter part of October; for it would have been extremely unhealthful and uncomfortable traveling so near the close of the dry season, when the thermometer sometimes stood at one hundred and thirty-eight degrees in the shade. He had nothing to pay the men who were to accompany him, but was re-assured by the Makololo; he was to take all the ivory in the country, and Sekeletu would furnish men to carry it. Such was the affection which he had excited among them by his actions toward them.

Escorted by Sekeletu and his followers as far as the island of Kalai, two days' journey below the mouth of the Chobe, he determined to visit the great cataract of the Zambesi to which he has given an English name—Victoria Falls:

"Of these we had often heard since we came into the country; indeed, one of the questions asked by Sebituane was, 'Have you smoke that sounds in your country?' They did not go near enough to examine them, but viewing them with awe

THE TRAVELING PROCESSION INTERRUPTED.

at a distance, said, in reference to the vapor and noise, '*Mosi oa tunya*' (smoke does sound there). It was previously called Shongwe, the meaning of which I could not ascertain. The word for a pot resembles this, and it may mean a seething caldron, but I am not certain of it. Being persuaded that Mr. Oswell and myself were the very first Europeans who ever visited the Zambesi in the center of the country, and that this is the connecting link between the known and the unknown portions of that river, I decided to use the same liberty as the Makololo did, and gave the only English name I have affixed to any part of the country. * * * * After twenty minutes' sail from Kalai we came in sight, for the first time, of the columns of vapor appropriately called 'smoke,' rising at a distance of five or six miles, exactly as when large tracts of grass are burned in Africa. Five columns now arose, and, bending in the direction of the wind, they seemed placed against a low ridge covered with trees; the tops of the columns at this distance appeared to mingle with the clouds. They were white below, and higher up became dark, so as to simulate smoke very closely. The whole scene was extremely beautiful; the banks and islands dotted over the river are adorned with sylvan vegetation of great variety of color and form. * * * * The falls are bounded on three sides by ridges 300 or 400 feet in height, which are covered with forest, the red soil appearing among the trees. * * * * I did not comprehend it until, creeping with awe to the verge, I peered down into a large rent which had been made from bank to bank of the broad Zambesi, and saw that a stream of a thousand yards broad leaped down a hundred feet and then became suddenly compressed into a space of fifteen or twenty yards. * * * * On the left side of the island we had a good view of the mass of water which causes one of the columns of vapor to ascend, as it leaps quite clear of the rock, and forms a thick unbroken fleece all the way to the bottom. Its whiteness gave the idea of snow, a sight I had not seen for many a day. As it broke into (if I may use the term) pieces of water, all rushing on in the same direction, each gave off several rays of foam, exactly as bits of steel, when burned in oxygen gas, give off rays of sparks. The snow-white sheet seemed like myriads of small comets rushing on in one direction, each of which left behind its nucleus rays of foam. I never saw the appearance referred to noticed elsewhere. It seemed to be the effect of the mass of water leaping at once clear of the rock, and but slowly breaking up into spray."

Livingstone selected a spot near the falls, the soil of which was perpetually moistened by the spray from the columns of vapor; and planted there a number of peach and apricot seeds, and also coffee-beans. This done, he cut his initials and the date, 1855, on a tree near by.

It was nearly the end of November when Sekeletu parted from him and returned home; Livingstone then turned toward the north, and traveled for a few days over a beautiful but uninhabited district. There was a great abundance of game here, and on several occasions the lions approached unpleasantly close to their camp, but did no damage.

Crossing the Mozuma early in December, they found themselves among the Batonga. Their route now lay almost directly eastward, and mainly through hostile tribes. They managed, however, to escape conflict with the natives, and reached the banks of the Zambesi once more a few days after Christmas. The confluence of the Loangwa and the Zambesi was reached January 14, 1856. They had just passed Zumbo when the traveling procession was interrupted in a manner that is well worth description:

"Tsetse and the hills had destroyed two riding oxen, and when the little one that I now rode knocked up, I was forced to march on foot. The bush being very dense and high, we were going along among the trees, when three buffaloes, which we had unconsciously passed above the wind, thought that they were surrounded by men, and dashed through our line. My ox set off at a gallop; and when I could manage to glance back, I saw one of the men up in the air about five feet above a buffalo, which was tearing along with a stream of blood running down his flank. When I got back to the poor fellow, I found that he had lighted on his face, and though he had been carried about twenty yards on the horns of the buffalo before getting the final toss, his skin was not pierced nor was a bone broken. When the beasts appeared, he had thrown down his load and stabbed one in the side. It turned suddenly upon him, and before he could use a tree for defense, carried him off. We shampooed him well, and in about a week he was able to engage in the hunt again."

They reached Tette March 3; here they rested for some time, the missionary making preparations, not only for continuing his own journey, but for sending back most of his Makololo friends to their own country. One of them, Sekwebu, was to accompany him to England. The bearers set off on their return trip, and Livingstone, with his one attendant, sailed down the Zambesi to Quillimane, the Portuguese point situated at its mouth. From this point, he went by sea to Mauritius, embarking July 12. But poor Sekwebu's brain was literally turned with all the wonders that he beheld; he became insane. Livingstone quieted him by telling him that they were going to Ma-Robert; but this was not a sufficient medicine for the mind diseased, after a time or two. He became violent, and finally plunged overboard and was drowned.

Livingstone was hospitably received at Mauritius, and remained there until he had recovered from the after effects of his African fevers. In November he came up the Red Sea; and finally, on the 12th of December, 1856, landed in England, after an absence of seventeen years, and nearly five years after he had parted from his wife and children at Cape Town.

CHAPTER XV.

LIVINGSTONE THE GREAT EXPLORER.

DURING the course of his first journey (if that may be called one journey which included so many miles of travel, first north, then west, then east, with different goals in view) Livingstone had become thoroughly well acquainted with the slave-trade as carried on in the interior of Africa. He believed the great remedy for the existing evil would be the opening up of the country to commerce; if the tribes of the interior could trade directly with the white man, and exchange their ivory and other articles of produce for the cloths and manufactured goods which they covet, there would be no temptation for them to capture slaves and trade them for these desired articles. It was for this reason that, having failed to find a suitable place for the establishment of a missionary station, he gave up that idea, and made his way across the continent to Loanda, and then back again to the mouth of the Zambesi. Returning to England, his narrative of the time which he had spent in Africa aroused men to a longing to increase the missionary aid sent to that continent.

But Livingstone had advanced beyond the position of a missionary; his views had broadened so that he was no longer content to spend his days in one place, teaching the people around him; he was eager and anxious to put down the slave-trade, by showing the people who supplied the market that a more lucrative business could be established in the development of the agricultural and mineral resources of their country. The government and the Royal Geographical Society lent him their heartiest aid; and the expedition to the Zambesi was undertaken very soon after his return to England.

Livingstone was made consul, which, of course, gave this undertaking a semi-national character, and enabled him to deal with other powers to much better advantage. The most liberal provision was made in the way of supplies, which even included a small steam-launch, named the "Ma-Robert." This was sent out from England in sections, and put together at the mouth of the Zambesi.

Dr. Livingstone's brother, Rev. Charles Livingstone, who had been living for some years in the United States, was a member of the expedition; also Dr. Kirk, the celebrated botanist. They left England March 10, 1858, and reached the mouth of the Zambesi in May. Their instructions were to extend the knowledge already attained of the geography and mineral and agricultural resources of Eastern and Central Africa; to improve their acquaintance with the inhabitants, and to endeavor to engage them to apply themselves to industrial pursuits and to the cultivation of their lands with a view to the production of raw materials to be exported to England in return for British manufactures. Their first object was to explore the Zambesi, its mouths and tributaries, with a view to their being used as highways for commerce and Christianity to pass into the vast interior of Africa. They entered the River Luawe first, because its entrance is so smooth and deep that the vessel could easily go in without a boat sounding ahead. Here the Ma-Robert was screwed together, and launched as the proper vessel for these coast explorations.

They found the Luawe unnavigable at a short distance above its mouth, by reason of the vegetable matter in the channel; after ascending about seventy miles, it ended in a marsh, being only a tidal river after all. They now resolved to try the East Luabo, as the main stream of the Zambesi is called. This proved to be the river which they sought, although it was not then known that the Zambesi has four separate mouths.

The Pearl, the vessel in which they had come from England, accompanied the Ma-Robert as far as the Island of Simbo; when finding that the river was becoming too shallow for her draught (9 feet 7 inches) she steamed down the river, after having landed the goods belonging to the expedition on a small island; and the expedition to the Zambesi was fairly launched on its independent career.

The country around the mouth of the Zambesi had long been in the possession of the Portuguese; but their maps of it had been anything but reliable. It is charged that they had represented the Quillimane as the true mouth of the Zambesi, in order to promote and protect the slave trade; if the British vessels, and those of other nations, sent out to watch for slavers, could be persuaded to keep a close lookout on the Quillimane, as the outlet of the Zambesi, the slavers could readily sail down the true Zambesi and get safely out to sea before they should be discovered. Be this as it may, it is certain that one official Portuguese map had the mouth of the Mazaro, a narrow creek which in time of flood communicates with the Quillimane, as the point at which the Zambesi began to discharge its waters into the more northern river. As a fact, this creek is some six or eight feet above the level of the Zambesi, except, as mentioned, during periods of very high water.

Arrived at the mouth of this creek, the members of the expedition found that they had run into a veritable hornets' nest. A half-caste named Mariano or Matakenya had built a stockade near the mouth of the Shire, and carried on his trade as a slave-hunter. So long as he confined his depredations to the tribes of the interior, the indignation of the Portuguese settlers was not aroused; but he was allowed to send his kidnapped victims in chains to Quillimane, thence to be sent to the French Island of Bourbon. But as soon as Mariano began to practice violence on the people nearer at hand, under the very guns of the fort, the whites began to protest. Mariano paid no attention; and Dr. Livingstone was told, by a gentleman of the highest standing, that it was no uncommon occurrence for a slave to rush into the room where the informant's family was at dinner, pursued by one of Mariano's men with spear in hand to murder him.

War was declared against Mariano, and a force was sent to take him. He resisted for a time; but knowing that Portuguese governors have small salaries, and are amenable to bribery, he went down to Quillimane to "arrange" with the governor. But that official was of a different stamp from most of his predecessors; and clapped the atrocious murderer into prison. When the English explorers came into the country, Mariano's brother, Bonga, was at the head of the rebel forces; and the contest was waging fiercely.

The fact that they were Englishmen proved to both parties at once what were their opinions regarding the slave trade; yet they were regarded as friends by Bonga's forces as well as by the Portuguese. On more than one occasion, they were almost in the midst of a fight; but happily escaped unharmed, and able to preserve their neutrality.

The right bank of the Zambesi is held by the Landeens or Zulus, to whom the Portuguese pay a pretty heavy annual tribute. Regularly every year the Zulus come to Senna and Shupanga to collect this tribute, which is really paid by the few wealthy merchants of Senna. They submit to pay two hundred pieces (sixteen yards each) of cloth, besides beads and brass wire, etc., to secure themselves from being plundered in

Zulu Girls in Dancing Dress.

war. The Zulu is like the Irish landlord of tradition; the more his tenants cultivate, the higher tribute he demands. On asking some of the Portuguese why they did not try to

ZULUS, WHO LIFT TRIBUTE OF THE PORTUGUESE AT SENNA, EXHIBITING WAR EXERCISES.

raise certain highly profitable products, the Englishmen received this characteristic reply:

"What's the use of our cultivating any more than we do? The Landeens would only come down on us for more tribute."

They arrived at Tette Sept. 8, and Dr. Livingstone at once went ashore. He was received by the Makololo with the most affecting joy; tempered with a ludicrous respect for his new clothes. Some were hastening to embrace him; when others cried out:

"Don't touch him; you will spoil his new clothes."

Dr. Livingstone had heard, while he was in England, that his Makololos who had not returned to their own country were to receive from the Portuguese government a sufficient support; but he found now that no such rumor had ever reached Africa; they had been given hoes and land sufficient for gardens by a generous officer of that government, but it had been a gift paid for out of his own pocket; and they had maintained themselves by means of these gardens, and by cutting and selling wood. These now readily attached themselves to the expedition; and the leader was only too glad to have assistants whose faithfulness had been tried.

Ascending the river, they carefully examined the Kebrabasa Rapids. After making their way seven or eight miles up through the swift current, they saw that this was not feasible until they knew what was to come next; and anchoring the little steamer below the rapids, proceeded to ascend the bank of the stream on foot. The stones upon the path were so hot that the soles of the Makololo's feet were blistered; but still they continued to advance. The Makololo told Dr. Livingstone that they had always thought that he had a heart, but that now they knew he had none; and appealed to Dr. Kirk to return, since the leader must have gone mad before he determined to go where no living foot could tread. Unfortunately for the Makololo, Dr. Kirk did not understand a word of their language; and Dr. Livingstone, knowing him to be as anxious as himself to explore the Kebrabasa, did not think it worth while to translate.

At last, however, they arrived at the cataract of Morumba, which is a sloping fall of about twenty feet in thirty yards. It is sufficient to stop all navigation except in the highest floods, when the river sometimes rises eighty feet above the level of the dry season.

They retraced their footsteps, then; although not exactly over the same path; they crossed Mount Morumba, which rises very near the fall, and camped on its side the first night of their return journey. As their guide had told them, the people were very ready to sell them provisions as long as they appeared to be leaving the country; in fact the ignorant people manifested the most unreasoning opposition to an expedition the objects of which were beyond their comprehension. The story is told that shortly after their departure from Tette, the river rose a foot and became turbid. A native Portuguese went to the governor with a grave face and complained that that Englishman was "doing *something* to the river."

Finding that it was impossible to take their steamer of only ten-horse-power through Kebrabasa, and convinced that, in order to force a passage when the river was in flood, much greater power was required, due information was forwarded to her majesty's government, and application made for a more suitable vessel. In the mean time, they turned their attention to the River Shire, a northern tributary of the Zambesi, which joins it about a hundred miles from the sea. The Portuguese could tell them nothing concerning this stream, except that it was covered with a mass of aquatic plants, which they pronounced impassable. They received a hint, however, that it was not the duckweed, but the hostility of the natives which had caused the one Portuguese expedition for the exploration of this river to return without making any considerable progress.

Their first trip to the Shire was in January, 1859. A considerable quantity of duckweed floated on the river for the first twenty-five miles, but not enough to obstruct navigation. They met with the first obstruction at the village of a chief named Tingane. This chief had always been the barrier to all intercourse between the Portuguese black traders and the natives farther inland; but on the explorers telling him that they had come neither to take slaves nor to fight, but only to open up a path by which their countrymen might come to purchase cotton or anything else that he had to sell (except slaves) he became at once quite friendly, and the men who had been dodging behind trees to take aim at the strangers with their poisoned arrows, came out and listened to the words of the missionary.

They ascended the Shire for a distance of about one hundred miles from its mouth; although the windings of the river are such that this distance represents about two hundred miles of actual travel. At this point, their further progress was stopped by the rapids, the first of which was named by them Murchison Falls. During the time that they were ascending the river, the natives kept a strong guard on the bank, night and day; apparently distrusting the strangers. The general opinion which the natives of this portion of Africa entertain in regard to white men does not speak well for the Portuguese, the first whites with whom they became acquainted.

A second trip up the Shire was begun about the middle of March. Thanks to their conciliating behavior on the previous journey, they found the natives extremely well disposed toward them. Leaving the banks of the river about ten miles below the falls, Drs. Livingstone and Kirk, with a number of Makololo, started on foot for Lake Shirwa. They traveled in a northerly direction over a mountainous country, among people who did not seem to be well-disposed, and with guides who were far from being trustworthy. This unreliability was partly due to their ignorance of the country and the language; they asked to be led to "Nyanja Mukulu," or Great Lake, meaning thereby Lake Shirwa; but since the word Nyanja, or Nyanza, means a lake, river, marsh, or even a rivulet, the guides did not clearly understand them, and conducted them to the Great Elephant Marsh.

From this point, the party pressed on without guides, or with crazy ones. Regarding these, Dr. Livingstone says:

"They were often under great obligations to the madmen of the different villages; one of these honored them, as they slept in the open air, by dancing and singing at their feet the whole night. These poor fellows sympathized with the explorers, probably in the belief that they belonged to their own class; and uninfluenced by the general opinion of their countrymen, they really pitied, and took kindly to the strangers, and often guided them faithfully from place to place, when no sane man could be hired for love or money."

The perseverance of the party was finally crowned with success; for on April 18 they discovered Lake Shirwa, a body of bitter water, having no outlet, and containing leeches, fish, crocodiles and hippopotami. Their point of view was at the base of Mount Pirimiti or Mopeupeu, on its south-southwest side. Thence the prospect northward ended in a sea horizon with two small islands in the distance; a larger one, resembling a hill-top and covered with trees, rose more in the foreground. Ranges of hills appeared on the east, and on the west stood Mount Chikala. The shore, near which they spent two nights, was covered with reeds and papyrus.

HUNTING ON THE GREAT ELEPHANT MARSH OF THE SHIRE VALLEY.

From the people living near the lake, they gathered that there was a much larger one to the north, separated from Shirwa only by a tongue of land. But they considered that enough had been done for one expedition; it would be better to return from this point, and, having gained the confidence of the natives as far as this, make another trip for the exploration of countries beyond. They accordingly went back to their vessel on the Shire.

They reached Tette June 23, and from that point proceeded to the Kongone for the necessary repairs upon their vessel. They again ascended the Zambesi in August, and about the middle of that month reached the mouth of the Shire, which they proposed to ascend once more, and make, from the head of navigation, an overland trip to Lake Nyassa.

They found the banks lined with hippopotamus traps; for the animals were evidently very plentiful, if the tracks on the bank were any guide. The hippopotamus feeds only on land, and crops the grass as short and even as a mowing machine. The trap consists of a beam five or six feet long, armed with a spear-head or hard-wood spike, covered with poison, and suspended from an overhanging branch by a cord, which, coming down to the path, is held by a catch, to be set free when the brute treads on it. Being wary beasts, they are very numerous, even where these traps are plentiful. One got frightened by the ship as she was steaming close to the bank. In its eager hurry to escape it rushed on shore, and ran directly under a trap, when down came the heavily weighted beam on its back, driving the poisoned spear-head a foot deep into its flesh. In its agony it plunged back into the river, to die in a few hours, and afterward furnished a feast for the natives. The poison on the spear-head affects only that part of the flesh which is directly around the wound, and this is always thrown away. In some places the descending wood is weighted with heavy stones, but in others the hard, heavy wood needs no extra weight.

As they passed the neighborhood of the Great Elephant Marsh, they saw many elephants; but these sagacious animals soon learned that the puffing monster was a thing to be avoided, and fled in terror before the approach of the steamer. They succeeded, however, in catching a fine young elephant alive, as he was climbing up the bank to follow his dam; but after he was drawn on board, he was wounded by one of the men, and died in a few days.

They left ship August 28, 1859, for the discovery of Lake

Nyassa. The party numbed four whites, thirty-six Makololo, and two guides. The party was unnecessarily large, but it was thought that the strength of numbers would prevent attack from natives inclined to be hostile, and command respect from others. For the same reason, each one carried a musket, although many of the Makololo had never drawn a trigger. They were a week in crossing the highlands in a northerly direction; and having reached the Upper Shire valley, some 1200 feet above the sea-level, they were detained for some days by the sickness of one of the white men.

Hippopotamus Trap.

They found that the natives of this region were considerably advanced, in respect to their manufactures. They weave cotton cloth, by painfully slow processes; make pottery, and dig the iron ore out of the hills and make it into good axes, spears, needles, arrow-heads, bracelets, and anklets. Every village has its charcoal-burners, its smelting-house, and its blacksmiths. They weave neat baskets from split bamboos, and make fish-nets of a plant-fiber from their hills.

These people, judging from the old men and women who came to look on the white men, are generally long-lived; but they do not owe their longevity to cleanliness; an old man told them that he remembered to have washed once in his life, but it was so long ago that he had forgotten how it felt. They were much annoyed by one man, who persisted in preceding them from village to village and proclaiming that they had wandered; that they did not know where they were going. Persuasions and remonstrances were alike in vain; finally, he was informed that they were going to take him down to the river and wash him; he disappeared and was seen no more.

The language here was so unlike those dialects with which Dr. Livingstone was acquainted, that they were obliged to have recourse to an interpreter. This man, Masakasa, had an unbounded faith in anything that was said in a book; on one occasion, this faith served them well. The natives had persistently asserted that there was no such lake as that of which they were in search; but Masakasa knew that the lake was mentioned in a book, and grew indignant accordingly.

"There is a lake," said he to the natives, "for how could the white men know about it in a book if it did not exist?"

Then they admitted that there was a lake; and were probably not a little impressed by the white man's magical knowledge of things he had never seen. They pressed on, and discovered Lake Nyassa a little before noon of September 16, 1859. They could make out that there were hills on both sides of the lake, looking from their point of view at the southern end; but the haze from burning grass prevented their seeing very far. They learned afterward that they preceded a German explorer, Dr. Roscher, by about two months in the discovery of this lake. The only results of his discovery, however, were told in the depositions of his servants after they arrived at the Cape; for he was murdered by the natives shortly after reaching the lake.

They were now among the Ajawa, who furnished a large number of slaves to the market, and are more debased in this traffic than most other tribes, since they sell each other. The chief with whom they remonstrated seemed ashamed of selling his own people, but apologized by saying that he sold only

AFRICAN BLACKSMITH AT WORK.

those who were bad. The party made but a short stay at Lake Nyassa, being, as usual, anxious to persuade the natives that they had no other object in view than to see the country. After a land-journey of forty days, they returned to the vessel October 6. It was necessary to send two of their number across the country from the Shire to Tette; and Dr. Kirk and Mr. Rae, the engineer, undertook the journey. But during their absence, the vessel began to leak so badly that they were obliged to go to the Kongone again for repairs. The steel plates were defective, and had been damaged by some chemical action shortly after the vessel was launched, so that they were full of minute holes. It leaked so badly that they were frequently compelled to mop up the cabin floor, and the engines proved so unsatisfactory that the Ma-Robert was re-christened the "Asthmatic." Returning from the sea, it was nearly the end of April, 1860, before they again reached Tette.

As they proceeded up the Zambesi toward the country of the Makololo, they found that many of the Makololo, who had descended the river with Dr. Livingstone in 1856, deserted them; the reason of this was, that these men had formed new ties in Tette; marrying slave-wives, they could not take their wives or children with them, and gradually deserted the party until all who had married in Tette had left. Yet at setting out, they had declared that they wished to return to their own country.

They of course left the Asthmatic below, as she could not ascend the Kebrabasa; this was no matter of regret to the Makololo who had been compelled to cut the wood for her fires on the former journeys. One of them laughingly exclaimed in broken English:

"Oh, Kebrabasa good, very good; no let shippee up to Sekeletu, too muchee work, cuttee woodyee, cuttee woodyee; Kebrabasa good."

They arrived at the Chicova plains, the level country above the Kebrabasa hills, June 7, and at Zumbo, on the left bank of the Loanwa, on the 26th. Here they had some difficulty in getting ferried across the river; the ferrymen were all tipsy, and did not come when they were expected. Having a waterproof cloak, which could be inflated into a small boat, they sent one of their attendants across in this improvised canoe. At the summons thus delivered, three men brought them the shaky canoes, lashed together. Five men were all that could be taken at a trip; and after four trips, the ferrymen began to

A NATIVE DOCTOR ADMINISTERING "MEDICINE."

clamor for drink. The travelers had none to give; and they became insolent, declaring that not another man should cross that day. One of the Makololo began to remonstrate with them, when a loaded musket was presented at him by one of the trio. In an instant the gun was out of the rascal's hands, a rattling shower of blows fell on his back, and he took an involuntary header into the river. He crawled up the bank a sad and sober man, and all three fell at once from the height of saucy swagger to a low depth of slavish abjectness. The musket was found to have an enormous charge, and might have blown the Makololo to pieces but for the promptitude with which his companions administered justice in a lawless band. They were all ferried safely across the river by eight o'clock in the evening.

On the 4th of August they reached Moachemba, the first of the Batoka villages which then owed allegiance to Sekeletu. From this point, they could see distinctly, with the naked eye, the columns of vapor rising from Victoria Falls, although the cataract was twenty miles away. Here they learned that many of the Makololo had been regarded as dead, not having been heard of since they accompanied Dr. Livingstone to the sea. They also learned that a recent effort to establish a missionary station at Linyanti had proved a failure and been abandoned. On the 9th, they set out to visit the falls, in the canoes of a native named Tuba Mokoro, who was said to possess the best "medicine" for ensuring safety in the rapids above the falls. This important personage forbade all talking while in the canoes, as it might impair the power of the medicine; and the white men, fearing to distract the steersman's attention when it might be critically necessary for him to attend to his business, obeyed unhesitatingly. They found that the hippopotami had trodden down the fruit trees which Dr. Livingstone had planted on his previous visit; and now erected a strong hedge for protection to newly sown seeds. There was not much hope, however, but what the same animals would break down the hedge.

Arriving at the town of Sekeletu, they found that, as they had been told, the chief was afflicted with the leprosy. He had been treated by several different doctors of his own tribe, and was now under the care of an aged negress who had come from some distance especially to take this case. Sekeletu, however, insisted upon placing himself at once under the care of the white doctor; and Drs. Livingstone and Kirk gave him the best remedies, internal and external, that their store of medicines afforded. He considered that his disease was the result of enchantment practiced by one of his enemies, and could not be persuaded otherwise. It was the opinion of his white physicians that the disease was rather due to the inordinate quantities of matokwane, or Indian hemp, which he smoked; and they could hardly induce him to give it up while he was under their treatment.

They found, indeed, that many of the natives are slaves of this pernicious habit, which makes the smokers feel strong in body, but weakens and finally destroys the mind. Both men and women indulge freely in its use; although the men do not like their wives to follow their own example, and sometimes forbid it entirely.

Dr. Livingstone determined now to go to Linyanti, in order to procure some medicines and other articles which he had left there in his wagon, eight years before. He found them all intact, and the wagon in fairly good condition, although the cover was, as might be expected, very rotten. The people inquired affectionately after "Ma-Robert" and her children, and asked why he had not brought them.

"Are we never more to know anything of them but their names?" asked the affectionate creatures, whose love had been won years before.

Returning to Sesheke by a trip which required three days, the party left that point September 17, 1860, taking with them a number of Makololo who were to return with additional medicines for Sekeletu. The path now pursued was a little nearer the river than that by which they had come, in order to see Kalunda and the Moamba Falls. They passed over a rugged country, with many hills and perennial streams, of which the Sindi was the finest for irrigation. They encamped on the Kolomo on the 1st of October; and on the 5th, after crossing some hills, rested at the village of Simariango.

A considerable part of their journey eastward was made by water; and in at least one instance, their attendants showed their faithfulness. Entering the narrow gorge called Karivua, the huge waves of the mid-current began at once to fill the canoes. With great presence of mind, and without the least hesitation, two men lightened each by jumping overboard; they then ordered a Batoka to do the same.

"I cannot swim," he replied.

"Jump out, then, and hold on to the canoe," they answered him; "for the white men must be saved."

Swimming alongside, they guided the swamping canoes

down the swift current to the foot of the rapid, and then ran them ashore to bale them out. Thanks to the bravery of these poor fellows, nothing was lost, although everything was well soaked. A few hundred yards brought them to another rapid; but as this was worse than the first, the canoes had to be unloaded, and the goods carried about a hundred yards.

They continued their voyage down the river, not leaving their canoes until they arrived at Kebrabasa; here their bearers complained much about having to carry the goods, and wished that they had tried the rapids. This difficulty over, they reached Tette early on the morning of the 23rd of November, having been absent a little over six months. The Zambesi being unusually low, they remained at Tette till it rose a little, and then left on the 3rd of December for the Kongone. Here their vessel was laid up for repairs; but the attempt was useless. New leaks broke out every day; the engine-pump gave way; the bridge broke down; three compartments filled at night. On the morning of the 21st the vessel grounded on a sandbank and filled; she could neither be emptied nor got off; the river rose during the night, and all that could be seen of her the next morning was about six feet of her two masts. Thus ended the Ma-Robert, otherwise the Asthmatic.

On the 31st of January, 1861, their new ship, the Pioneer, arrived from England, and anchored outside the bar of the Kongone; but the weather being stormy, she did not venture into the harbor until five days later. Two cruisers came at the same time, on board one of which were Bishop Mackenzie and his assistants, for the Universities' Missions.

The bishop desired them to take him and his colleagues up the Shire as far as Chibisa's, supposing that that would be a suitable place to establish the mission; but Dr. Livingstone, remembering the fate of the station at Linyanti, and fearful that, as there were no medical men on the bishop's staff, they might fall victims to the African fever, objected very strongly to this plan. In addition to this reason, was another: the Portuguese government refused to open the Zambesi to the ships of other nations, and it was therefore impolitic to expend so much labor at this point, when others that were equally important and more easily accessible were neglected. Finally, it was decided that the bishop should accompany the Zambesi expedition to the Rovuma, which their new instructions bade them explore, and ascertain whether the country around its headwaters was suitable for the establishment of a

GANG OF CAPTIVES ON THEIR WAY TO TETTE.

station. The other members of the mission were to proceed, in one of the cruisers, to Johanna, and there await the orders of their superior.

Arriving at the mouth of the Rovuma toward the end of February, it was not until the 11th of March that they proceeded up the river, which had fallen four or five feet while they were delayed at the mouth, awaiting the arrival of the bishop; for he had chosen to go this far in the cruiser Lyra. But the river fell rapidly as they ascended, and as the March flood is the last of the season, they saw that the only thing to save the Pioneer from being hopelessly grounded was to get her back to salt water as quickly as possible. Had the expedition been absolutely unincumbered, they would have left the ship and pushed on in boats or on foot, and done what they could toward the exploration of the river and Lake Nyassa, from which it was supposed to flow; but they were anxious to advance the work of the mission, and therefore decided to return to the Shire, see the mission party safely settled, and afterward explore Lake Nyassa and the Rovuma from the lake downward. Fever broke out on board the Pioneer at the mouth of the Rovuma, and the vessel was soon left, through the illness of the officers, to the management of Dr. Livingstone.

They arrived at the mouth of the Zambesi after a prosperous voyage, and steamed up to the mouth of the Shire without any special adventure. Their vessel, however, was not well adapted for their purpose in one particular: her draught was too great, being five feet, for the Shire. Much of their time was spent in getting her off sand-bars, and she could not venture down the river until a rise had increased its depth.

Arrived at Chibisa's village, they left the river, July 15, and with a sufficiently strong party, went inland to show the bishop a suitable station for the mission. Halting at the village of Mbame, they were told that a slave party on its way to Tette would presently pass through. "Shall we interfere?" they asked of each other. The question was a difficult one to answer, for all of their valuable goods had been left at Tette, and if they were to interfere to free these slaves, the owners of them might retaliate by procuring the destruction of these stores. But the slave-hunters had taken advantage of the expedition's opening the country to white men, and had persistently dogged their footsteps in places where they had never dared to venture before. The Englishmen therefore resolved to run all risks and put a stop, if possible, to the slave-trade, which had followed on the footsteps of their discoveries. A few minutes after Mbame had spoken to them, the slave party, a long line of manacled men, women and children, came wending their way around the hill and into the valley, on the side of which the village stood. The black drivers, armed with muskets, and bedecked with various articles of finery, marched jauntily in the front, middle, and rear of the line; some of them blowing exultant notes out of a long tin horn. They seemed to feel that they were doing a very noble thing, and might proudly march with an air of triumph; but the instant the fellows caught a glimpse of the English, they darted off like mad into the forest—so fast, indeed, that they caught but a glimpse of their red caps and the soles of their feet. The chief of the party alone remained, and he, from being in front, had his hand tightly grasped by a Makololo. He proved to be a well-known slave of the late commandant at Tette, and for some time the Englishmen's attendant while there. On asking him how he obtained these captives, he answered that he had bought them; but on inquiry being made of the people themselves, all, save four, said they had been captured in war. While this inquiry was going on, he bolted, after his men.

The captives knelt down, and in their way of expressing thanks, clapped their hands with great energy. They were thus left entirely on the hands of the whites, and knives were soon at work, cutting the women and children loose. It was more difficult to cut the men adrift, as each had his neck in the fork of a stout stick, six or seven feet long, and kept in by an iron rod which was riveted at both ends across the throat. With a saw, luckily in the bishop's baggage, one by one the men were sawn out into freedom. The women, on being told to take the meal they were carrying and cook breakfast for themselves and the children, seemed to consider the news too good to be true; but after a little coaxing, went at it with alacrity, and made a capital fire by which to boil their pots with the slave sticks and bonds, their old acquaintances through many a sad night and weary day. Many were mere children of five years and under. One little boy, with the simplicity of childhood, said to one of the liberators:

"The others tied and starved us; you cut the ropes and tell us to eat; what sort of people are you? Where did you come from?"

The stories that the captives had to tell were heart-rending: two women had been shot the day before for attempting to untie the thongs; this, the rest were told, was to prevent them from attempting to escape. One woman had her baby's brains knocked out because she could not carry the load and it; and a man was dispatched with an axe because he had broken down with fatigue. Eighty-four, chiefly women and children, were liberated; and on being told that they were now free, and might go wherever they wished, or remain with their liberators, they all chose to stay; and the bishop decided that they should be attached to the mission, to be educated as members of a great Christian family.

They proceeded next morning to Soche's with their liberated party, the men cheerfully carrying the bishop's goods. As they had begun, it was of no use to do the thing by halves, so eight others were freed in a hamlet on their path; but a party of traders, with nearly a hundred slaves, fled from Soche's on hearing of these proceedings. Dr. Kirk and four Makololo followed them with great energy, but they got off clear to Tette. Six more captives were liberated at Mongazi's, and two slave-traders detained for the night, to prevent their carrying information to a still larger party in the front. Of their own accord they volunteered the information that the governor's servants had charge of the next party; but the Englishmen did not choose to be led by them, though they offered to acts as guides to his excellency's own agents. Two of the bishop's black men from the Cape, having once been slaves, were now zealous emancipators, and volunteered to guard the prisoners during the night. So anxious were these heroes to keep them safe, that, instead of keeping watch and watch, both kept watch together till toward four o'clock in the morning, when sleep stole gently over them both, and the wakeful prisoners, seizing the opportunity, escaped. One of the guards, perceiving the loss, rushed out of the hut, shouting:

"They are gone! The prisoners are off! And they have taken my rifle with them, and the women, too! Fire! Everybody fire!"

The rifle and the women, however, were safe enough, the slave-traders being glad to escape alone. Fifty more slaves were freed the next day in another village; and, the whole party being stark naked, cloth enough was left to clothe them, better probably than they had ever been clothed before. The head of this gang, whom the liberators recognized as the agent of one of the principal merchants of Tette, said that they had the license of the governor for all that they did. This was no news to the Englishmen, who were convinced that it was quite impossible for any enterprise to be undertaken there without the governor's knowledge and connivance.

They now approached the Manganja country, where they had seen such evidence, on the previous journey, of progress in manufactures. The country was now desolated by a war between the inhabitants and the Ajawas; the villages were all deserted; the stores of corn were poured out in cartloads, and scattered all over the plains, and all along the paths, neither conquerors nor conquered having been able to convey it away. About two o'clock they saw the smoke of burning villages, and heard triumphant shouts, mingled with the wail of Manganja women, lamenting over their slain. The bishop then engaged the company of Englishmen in fervent prayer; and on rising from their knees, they saw a long line of Ajawa warriors, with their captives, coming round the hill-side. The first of the returning conquerors were entering their own village below, and were welcomed back by the women with "lilliloo-ings." The Ajawa head man left the path on seeing the whites, and stood on an ant hill to obtain a good view of their party. They called out that they had come to have an interview with his people, but some of the Manganja, who followed them, shouted:

"Our Chibisa is come!"

Chibisa being well known as a great conjurer and general. The Ajawa ran off, yelling and screaming:

"*Nkondo! Nkondo!*" (War! War!)

The whites heard the words of the Manganja, but did not think of them at the moment as neutralizing all their own expressions regarding peace. The captives threw down their loads on the path, and fled to the hills; and a large body of armed men came running up from the village, and in a few seconds were all around the whites, though mostly concealed by the projecting rocks and long grass. In vain the Englishmen protested that they had not come to fight, but to talk with them. They would not listen, having good reason in the cry of "Our Chibisa." Flushed with recent victory over three villages, and confident of an easy triumph over a mere handful of men, they began to shoot their poisoned arrows, sending them with great force upward of a hundred yards, and wounding one of the Makololo through the arm. The slow withdrawal of the English up the ascent from the village only made them more eager to prevent their escape; and in the belief that this retreat was the evidence of fear, they closed upon the little party with bloodthirsty fury. Some came within fifty yards, dancing hideously; others, having quite surrounded them, and availing themselves of the rocks and long grasses hard by, were intent on cutting them off, while others made off with their women and a large body of slaves. Four were armed with muskets; and the Englishmen were obliged in self-defense to return their fire and drive them off. When they saw the range of the rifles, they very soon desisted and ran away; but some of them shouted to the whites from the hill the consoling intimation that they would follow, and kill them where they slept. Only two of the captives escaped to the Englishmen, but probably most of those made prisoners that day fled elsewhere in the confusion. The whites returned to the village which they had left in the morning, after a hungry, fatiguing, and most unpleasant day.

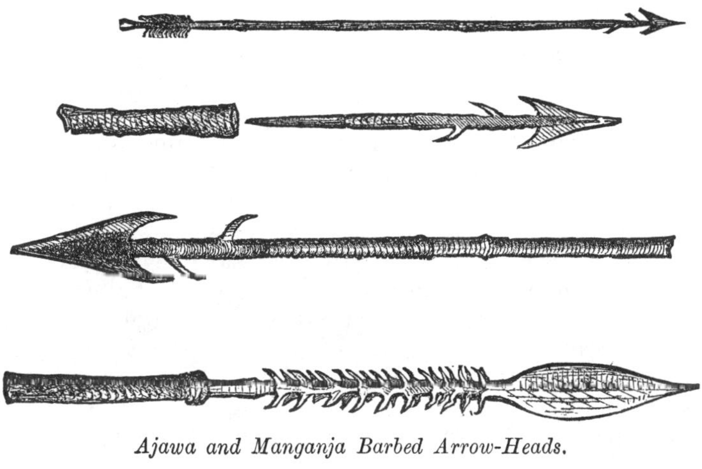

Ajawa and Manganja Barbed Arrow-Heads.

Though the explorers could not blame themselves for the course which they had pursued, they felt sorry for what had happened. It was the first time they had ever been attacked by the natives or had come into collision with them; though they had always taken it for granted that they might be called upon to act in self-defense, they were on this occasion less prepared than usual, no game having been expected here. The men had only a single round of cartridge each; their leader had no revolver, and the rifle he usually fired with was left at the ship, to save it from the damp of the season. Had they known better the effect of slavery and murder on the temper of these blood-thirsty marauders, they would have tried messages and presents before going near them.

The bishop, feeling as most Englishmen would at the prospect of the people now in his charge being swept off into slavery by hordes of men-stealers, proposed to go at once to the rescue of the captive Manganja, and drive the marauding Ajawa out of the country. All were warmly in favor of this save Dr. Livingstone, who opposed it on the ground that it would be better for the bishop to wait, and see the effect of the check the slave-hunters had just experienced. On the bishop inquiring if in the event of the Manganja asking aid against the Ajawa, it would be his duty to accede to the request:

"No," replied Dr. Livingstone, "you will be oppressed by their importunities, but do not interfere in native quarrels."

It would have been better if the bishop had followed this advice, which he mentions in his journal.

The members of the mission now having proceeded far enough to be able to form their own opinion of the country, the Zambesi expedition left them, and returned to the ship. A few days after their return, a party consisting of Dr. Livingstone, Dr. Kirk, and Charles Livingstone started for Lake Nyassa with a light four-oared gig, a white sailor, and a score of attendants. They hired people along the path to carry the boat past the forty miles of the Murchison Cataracts for a cubit of cotton cloth a day. This was such magnificent pay, that twice the required number of men eagerly offered their services; crowds followed them; and it was only by taking down the names of the porters engaged in the morning that they could dispute claims made by those who had only helped during the last ten minutes of the evening.

After passing the cataracts, they launched their boat upon the broad and deep waters of the Upper Shire, and were virtually on the lake, for the gentle current shows but little difference of level. The natives regard the Upper Shire as a prolongation of Lake Nyassa; for where what the explorers called the river approaches Lake Shirwa, a little north of the mountains, they said that the hippopotami, "which are great night travelers," pass from one lake into the other. There the land is flat, and only a short land journey would be necessary.

The geographical features of the lake which they now entered have become comparatively well known since that day, so that it is unnecessary here to enlarge upon the subject; nor were they impressed, as other discoverers have been, with the grandeur of the scene before them when they first came in sight of it. At this second entrance into Lake Nyassa, as on the previous occasion, the air was full of smoke from burning grass, and their view was consequently extremely contracted.

By Chitanda, near one of the slave-crossing places, they were robbed for the first time in Africa, and learned by experience that these people, like more civilized nations, have expert thieves among them. It might have been only a coincidence, but they never suffered from imprudence, loss of property, or were endangered, unless among people familiar with slaving. They had such a general sense of security, that never, save when they suspected treachery, did they set a watch at night. Their native companions had, on this occasion, been carousing on beer, and had removed to a distance of some thirty yards, that their free and easy after-dinner remarks might not be heard by their employers. Two of the whites had a slight touch of fever. Between three and four o'clock in the morning some light-fingered gentry came, while the explorers slept ingloriously—rifles and revolvers all ready—and relieved them of most of their goods. The boat's sail, under which they slept, was open all around, so that the feat was easy. One of them felt his pillow moving, but, in the delicious dreamy state in which he lay, thought it was one of the attendants adjusting his covering, and so, as he fancied, let well enough alone.

Their consternation on awaking in the morning and finding their clothing, beads, and rice gone, may well be imagined. Their first question to each other was: "Is the cloth gone?" For the loss of that would have been equivalent to all their money. Fortunately, the parcel had been used as a pillow that night, and thus was safe. The rogues left on the beach a pair of boots and the aneroid barometer, also some dried plants and fishes; but they carried off many other specimens which had been collected, some of the notes of the journey, and nearly all of their clothing. They could not suspect the people of the village where they lay; they had probably been followed by the thieves for several days, watching their opportunity.

They found that the northern end of the lake was the scene of lawlessness and bloodshed. So threatening did the various parties of natives appear, that the attendants of the explorers, who were making the journey by land, while the white men kept to the boat, became afraid to go on, unless a white man should join their party; and indeed, the danger was not small.

Dr. Livingstone accordingly left the boat, and having taken the first morning's journey along with them, and directing the boat to call for him at a bay in sight, both parties proceeded north. In an hour Dr. Livingstone and his party struck inland, on approaching the foot of the mountains which rise abruptly from the lake. Supposing that they had heard of a path behind the high range which there forms the shore, those in the boat held on their course; but it soon began to blow so fresh that they had to run ashore for safety. While delayed for a couple of hours, two men were sent up the hill to look for the land party, but they could see nothing of them, and the boat party sailed as soon as it was safe to put to sea, with the conviction that the missing ones would regain the lake in front.

The boat passed a couple of parties, evidently lake pirates, who assured them that there was a path behind the hills. Pursued by another party of pirates, they put their boat to its utmost speed to escape; and after sailing twelve or fifteen miles north of the point where Dr. Livingstone had left them, a gale compelled them to seek shelter in a bay. A succession of gales prevented their advancing or going back to the point whence they had started.

In the meantime, Dr. Livingstone and his party had tried the path behind the hills, and found it so bad as to be almost impassable. They therefore turned back to the coast, expecting to find the boat; but only saw it disappearing away to the north. They pushed on as briskly as possible after it, but the mountain-flank which forms the coast proved excessively tedious and fatiguing; traveling all day, the distance made, in a straight line, was under five miles. As soon as day dawned the march was resumed; and after hearing at the first inhabited rock that their companions had passed it the day before, seven Mazitu suddenly appeared before them. These demanded presents, and became boisterous; but the quiet persistence of Dr. Livingstone made them retreat. Their presence showed that there was more or less danger to be encountered. The next night was spent, unconsciously, on the very brink of a precipice; the party having traveled during every moment of daylight, and fearing to kindle a fire lest it should attract the attention of the Mazitu. The next night was also spent without fire, except a little for cooking the flesh of a goat which they killed. The next day, Dr. Livingstone was delighted to see the boat coming back, having been separated from his companions for four days.

Their exploration of the lake extended from the 2nd of September to the 27th of October, 1861; and having expended or lost most of the goods they had brought, it was necessary to go back to the ship. They reached the vessel November 8, in a very weak condition, having suffered more from hunger than on any previous trip. Bishop Mackenzie came down to the ship to visit them, and gave a glowing account of his success at the mission. It was hoped that it could soon be made self-sustaining to a considerable degree.

The river was rapidly and steadily falling; and they were obliged to wait until it should begin to rise, before the Pioneer could cross the bars. Not until January 7 did they leave their anchorage at Ruo, reaching the Zambesi on the 11th. Arrived at Tette, they expected to be called to account, in some way, for liberating the slaves; but beyond a mere mention of the fact by one of the owners of the liberated captives, nothing was said; all the others seemed to be ashamed to speak of it.

Descending the Zambesi, they anchored in the Great Luabo mouth; and here, January 30, the British vessel Gorgon arrived, bringing Mrs. Livingstone and some ladies who were to join their relatives connected with the Universities' Mission. This vessel also brought out the sections of a new iron steamer intended for the navigation of Lake Nyassa, called the Lady of the Lake, or Lady Nyassa. Owing to the rivers being in flood, their progress up stream was extremely slow; and they were finally obliged to put the hull of the Lady Nyassa together, and tow her up to Murchison Falls.

They were naturally anxious, as they progressed, to receive news of the mission; but it was some time before they were able to learn anything of it. At last, however, they learned that the bishop and Mr. Burrup had both died, from the consequences of exposure during a trip undertaken to rescue some of their "Mission family" of liberated slaves, who had been recaptured. The bishop's sisters and Mr. Burrup's wife had arrived on the Gorgon, and just reached the Shire in time to learn the sad news of the two deaths.

Shortly after this, the surviving members of the mission decided to remove to the lower Shire valley—a course which had the fatal consequences that Dr. Livingstone foresaw.

Many members of the Zambesi expedition were prostrated by the fever, which seems to have raged with unusual virulence this year; and they noticed that an extraordinary number of natives wore the stripes of palm-leaf which are their sign for sickness and mourning. In April, Mrs. Livingstone

THE GRAVE OF MRS. LIVINGSTONE.

was taken down; and after a few days' illness, died April 27, 1862. She had come out again to Africa, thinking to assist her husband in his work as she had done before; but was taken before she could reach those who affectionately remembered "Ma-Robert." She was buried at Shupanga, under the shade of a wide-spreading baobab tree.

After many delays, the Lady Nyassa was launched on the 23rd of June. In accordance with their customs, the natives hotly discussed the question of what would be the result of putting so much iron in the water; some affirming that it would go to the bottom at once, others asserting that the white men had powerful medicine that would enable them to keep even iron from sinking. Dr. Livingstone frequently notes the warm discussions which the negroes of this part of Africa hold over any question upon which they chance to differ; these discussions often ending in laying wagers as to the event of a given course. When the discussion cannot be settled this way, one party will challenge the other to a foot-race, and the winner is held to have been in the right.

The Portuguese officials threw so many obstacles in the way of ascending the Zambesi, that they at last concluded to explore the Rovuma, at least until the water of the Zambesi should be at a stage which would not assist these officers in their efforts to detain them. They accordingly sailed for the mouth of the Rovuma. The first people with whom they met were inclined to be hostile; but as they ascended the river, they found them more friendly. At last, after traveling about a hundred and forty miles by the river's course from the sea, or nearly two degrees of longitude in a straight line from the coast, they were obliged to stop. The river was narrow and full of rocks, with a rapid divided into such narrow passages that only a native canoe could pass through them. The natives reported a worse place above their turning-point, the passage being still narrower. They now saw that their easiest path to Nyassa was by way of the Shire, even with the Portuguese officials in the way; and they decided to return and try that path again. They reached the Pioneer October 9, and put to sea nine days later.

Their destination was the Zambesi, but their fuel failed, and they were obliged to put into Quillimane. The delay thus occasioned brought them to the Zambesi so late in the season, that that river was very low, and their progress was correspondingly impeded. While waiting the March rise, they unscrewed the Lady Nyassa at a point about five hundred yards below the first cataract, and began to make a road over the thirty-five or forty miles of land portage by which to carry her up piecemeal.

The valley of the Shire had been well populated when they saw it on their former expeditions; but now, the results of the slave-trade, combined with those of a famine induced by drought, had turned the once smiling country into a wilderness. Everywhere that they turned, they saw desolation; and the living were not enough to bury the dead. Decaying corpses poisoned the atmosphere, or floated down the river in too great numbers for the over-gorged crocodiles to consume. The effect upon the spirits of the explorers may be imagined; and when to this feeling was added sickness, it was judged best that the two who suffered most severely physically, should return home. These were Dr. Kirk and Charles Livingstone. The parting took place May 19; and with them went all the whites that could be spared.

On the 2nd of July, a dispatch was received from Earl Russell, containing instructions for the withdrawal of the expedition. The attempt to open up this portion of Africa to trade was regarded as practically hopeless, while the Portuguese government maintained such an attitude—counteracting the effect of its open instructions to its officials by actual private instructions, or by allowing abuses of authority which practically nullified the laws made in Lisbon. In the then condition of the river, however, it was useless to attempt a return to the sea.

They accordingly decided to make an exploratory journey on foot to the northward. Crossing the country to the southern shores of Lake Nyassa, they skirted the western coast of that body of water almost half-way to the northern end; then, by a three days' journey to the westward, reached a village on the banks of a tributary of the Loangwa. It was now the latter part of September; and if they were to take advantage of the winter floods, they could not afford to go farther. From this point, their path was, with slight variations, that by which they had come. Reaching the ship, they took advantage of a rise about the middle of January to sail down the Shire, and, after some delays, occasioned by waiting to take on board some members of the helpless "Mission family" of Bishop Mackenzie, the mission having now been abandoned, they reached Zanzibar April 16, 1864; and after two weeks spent there, directed the course of the Lady Nyassa to Bombay. Early in June, after sailing more than twenty-five hundred miles, they sighted Bombay; the expedition to the Zambesi had come to an end.

Hercules Falls, South Africa.

CHAPTER XVI.

LIVINGSTONE'S LAST JOURNEY.

THE Zambesi expedition was substantially a failure; and no one felt this more keenly than its illustrious leader. Not only had he spent thousands of pounds of the Government's money and of his own, without attaining any appreciable result, or at least any such result as had been expected, but his failure had brought the whole subject of African exploration into disfavor with his countrymen. He returned to England, a disappointed man. But although the popular feeling was now as much against the exploration of Africa as at the close of the first journey it had been in favor of it, there were some whose interest was not lightly to be changed. The president of the Royal Geographical Society still held the work as of the same importance; and it was Sir Roderick Murchison who, almost as soon as he had returned, proposed that the explorer should undertake a third journey, for the purpose of fixing the true water-shed of Inner Southern Africa. After much difficulty, Sir Roderick persuaded the Government to advance five hundred pounds for this purpose; the Council of the Royal Geographical Society subscribed as much more; and "a valued private friend" of Dr. Livingstone's placed a further thousand pounds at his disposal.

The expedition was organized at Bombay, and proceeded thence to Zanzibar. From this point, Livingstone sailed down the coast to Mikindany Bay, near the mouth of the Rovuma River; thence they were to proceed overland to Lake Nyassa.

His attendants numbered thirty-six. Of these, three had been with him on the previous trip, employed, not at the beginning, but after the arrival of the Pioneer; of these we shall have occasion hereafter to single out Susi by name. Two of his attendants were among the slaves liberated by the party when Bishop Mackenzie was with it; of these, Chuma is the one whose name has been perpetuated by what he did for his master.

Six camels, two buffaloes and a calf, two mules, and four donkeys, were the animals attached to the expedition. It should be noted that while the bite of the tsetse is fatal to the horse and to cattle, it does not affect the donkey or the mule any more than it injures the wild beasts or man. This fact will explain the reason for selecting these animals.

They reached Rovuma Bay March 22, 1866; and landed April 6, at the point chosen. Then the march began, nearly due west, as they followed the course of the river. The journey to the lake is marked only by misfortunes. The camels proved as vulnerable to the tsetse as cattle, and all died from the bites. The mules and three donkeys succumbed to the ill-usage of their drivers. The thirteen Sepoys mutinied, and then proved so worthless that Dr. Livingstone was obliged to dismiss them; the ten Johanna men deserted in a body; one of the nine Nassick boys died, and another met some of his friends and concluded to remain with them. Thus the expedition of thirty-seven which had left Zanzibar had dwindled down to a little group of twelve persons.

The first hundred pages of his journal of this expedition are melancholy reading; containing, as they do, little beyond the record of events which would have discouraged a less determined explorer to the point of retracing his footsteps and giving up the effort; and of devices for easing the pangs of hunger; for which the folly and laziness of the attendants themselves were largely responsible. But Livingstone's was too great a mind to be shaken by such adverse winds as these; and he pressed steadily forward.

There is yet another element of sadness in these early pages of his journal. Even in the first stages of his journey, there was again laid bare to his eyes "the great open sore of the world," as the slave-trade has fitly been styled. In a little more than two months after leaving the coast, the first indications that they were on the track of the slave-traders appeared. First, they passed by a woman tied by the neck to a tree, and dead; the people of the surrounding country explained that she had been unable to keep up with the other slaves in a gang, and her master had determined that she should not become the property of any one else if she recovered after resting a time. They saw others tied up in a similar manner, and others lying in the path shot or stabbed, a pool of their own blood surrounding them. The explanation which the traveler

SLAVE-TRADERS REVENGING THEIR LOSSES.

invariably received was that the Arab who owned these victims was enraged at losing his money by the slaves becoming unable to march, and vented his spleen by murdering them. Dr. Livingstone remarks that the traders are quite well aware that such an example as this spurs the others to renewed endeavors to keep up with the march, even when their strength is rapidly failing them. In other cases, they found slaves who were dying of starvation, having been abandoned because they could not go on, or because the trader found his stock of provisions insufficient for those under his charge.

On the 8th of August, he again reached the shores of Lake Nyassa, this time at the mouth of the Masinje River. "It was as if I had come back to an old home I never expected again to see," he writes; "and pleasant to bathe in the delicious waters again, hear the roar of the sea, and dash in the rollers." He remained at this point for several days, taking observations, and writing up his journal fully. Then he skirted the southern shore of the lake, reaching the western borders September 25.

It had been his intention to strike directly north-west from Nyassa for the exploration of Lake Tanganyika; but the intervening country was filled with hostile Mazitu, and it was not safe for his little party to attempt to cross it. He therefore resolved to journey directly west until he reached the Zalyanyama Mountains, and then to proceed nearly due north until the lake was reached.

Most of the country crossed in this westward journey was lowland, of the kind known in Africa as "sponges." Whereever a plain sloping toward a narrow opening in hills or higher ground exists, we have the conditions requisite for the forming of an African sponge. The vegetation, not being of a peat-forming kind, falls down, rots, and then forms a rich black loam. In many cases, a mass of this loam, two or three feet thick, rests on a bed of pure river sand, which is revealed by crabs and other aquatic animals bringing it to the surface. In the dry season, the black loam is cracked in all directions, and the cracks are often as much as three inches wide, and very deep. The whole surface falls down and rests on the sand; but when the rains come, the first supply is nearly all absorbed in the sand. The black loam forms soft slush, and floats on the sand. The narrow opening prevents it from moving off in a landslip, but an oozing spring rises at that spot. All the pools in the lower portion of this spring-course are filled by the first rains, which happen south of the equator

FANTASTIC AFRICAN HEAD-DRESSES.

when the sun goes vertically over any spot. The second, or greater rains, happen in his course north again, when all the bogs and river-courses being wet, the supply runs off, and forms the inundation. This was certainly the case which Livingstone had observed on the Zambesi and the Shire; and, taking the different times for the sun's passage north of the equator, he considered that it explained the inundation of the Nile.

It may be inferred that traveling over ground of this nature was not the easiest thing in the world; but so long as the little party was not thrown among hostile tribes, it did not matter so much. The people through whose territory they were passing were Manganja, a very industrious race, combining agriculture and hunting with nets with various handicrafts, such as weaving and working in iron.

The Manganja are very ceremonious in their demeanor toward each other; and were very friendly to the strangers. In return for the food and native sweet beer with which the chiefs generally provided them at each stopping-place, Livingstone usually gave a "cloth," (two yards of unbleached muslin), and so little clothing is worn in this country that this was considered quite a munificent payment. Owing, however, to the raids and forays of the Mazitu, food was very scarce in some localities, and more than once the caravan was almost on the verge of starvation.

They crossed the Loangwa, the great northern tributary of the Zambesi, the middle of December; and reached the Chambeze late in the following January (1867). But before they got to the banks of this latter river, they had met with a loss which affected the whole after history of the expedition; and the editor of Livingstone's Last Journals has advanced the statement that this loss materially hastened his death, by leaving him without the means of counteracting fever, and thus allowing his constitution to be undermined.

The desertion of so large a number of his men in the very outstart of the expedition had made him dependent upon the people of the country through which he passed for porters and for guides; the Johanna men had been intended chiefly for the latter purpose.

They were traveling through the forest near the Lobo, having just set out from Lisunga.. Their guides were two Waiyau who had joined them some time before, and who were considered perfectly trustworthy because of their uniform good conduct ever since they had joined the caravan. A boy named

CHITAPANGWA RECEIVING DR. LIVINGSTONE.

Baraka, who was very careful, had charge of the medicine box, which was packed with a parcel containing five large cloths and all Baraka's clothing and beads. The Waiyau offered to exchange burdens for a while with Baraka, his own being the lighter (his real reason was that his own contained no cloth). Baraka consented. The fugitives watched their chance, and suddenly disappeared in the dense forest. Besides Baraka's package, they took all the dishes, a large box of powder, some flour, for which a high price had been paid, the tools, two guns, and a cartridge-pouch. The loss of these things was bad enough, but the great loss was the medicine. Livingstone says: "I felt as if I had now received the sentence of death, like poor Bishop Mackenzie," whose medicines had been wetted and rendered worthless by the upsetting of a boat.

The caravan returned to Lisunga, and men were at once sent out to scour the surrounding country for a trace of the fugitives. Livingstone was aware that they could attach no value whatever to the medicine-chest, but would throw it and its precious contents away as soon as they had got the clothing and beads out of the parcel.

They remained for two days at Lisunga, and then, having bought all the provisions which the chief had to sell, were obliged to push forward in spite of the rain. For the next few days, they had much difficulty in obtaining food; but looked forward to great plenty when they should have reached the village of the powerful Chitapangwa.

This was called Molemba; and they came to it about noon of the last day of January. It was surrounded by a triple stockade, the inner being defended also by a deep, broad ditch and a hedge of a thorny shrub, resembling the tomato or nightshade family. Chitapangwa sent to inquire if they desired an audience; and the messenger informed them that they must take something in their hands the first time they went to see so great a man. Dr. Livingstone was tired from marching, and sent word that he would not come until evening. About five o'clock he sent notice of his coming. They passed through the inner stockade, and then to an enormous hut, where sat Chitapangwa, with three drummers and ten or more men, with two rattles in their hands. The drummers beat furiously, and the rattlers kept time to the drums, two of them advancing and receding in a stooping posture, with rattles near the ground, as if doing the chief obeisance; but still keeping time with the others. The traveler declined to sit on the ground, and so an enormous tusk was brought for him. The chief saluted courteously. He had a fat, jolly face, and legs loaded with brass and copper leglets. Dr. Livingstone mentioned his losses by the desertion of the Waiyau, but as power is merely nominal, Chitapangwa could do nothing. After talking a while, he conducted his guest to a group of cows, and pointed out one.

"That is yours," he said, politely.

The tusk on which the explorer had sat was also sent after him to his quarters, as being his. Before they separated, Chitapangwa put on the cloth which Livingstone had given him, as a token of acceptance; and further showed his gratitude by sending two large baskets of sorghum to the stranger's hut after dark. The gift of the cow, however, proved a delusion and a snare; for when the traveler would have it killed the next day, a man interfered, and pointed out a much smaller one; an appeal to the chief ended in his having to pay Chitapangwa about four times the value of the animal in cloth, and then the savage was not satisfied.

Sending a number of letters from this point by means of a small party of Arab slavers, who were on their road to Zanzibar, Dr. Livingstone remained at this village about three weeks. This stay was partly on account of illness, as he was taken down with the fever, which he had no means of curing. But much of the time was spent in negotiating for food with Chitapangwa.

About the middle of March, they met with an enemy who had not before been encountered. Dr. Livingstone says:

"A shower of rain set the driver-ants on the move, and about two hours after we had turned in we were overwhelmed by them. They are called kalandu, or nkalanda. To describe this attack is utterly impossible. I wakened covered with them; my hair was full of them. One by one they cut into the flesh, and the more they are disturbed, the more vicious are their bites; they become quite insolent. I went outside the hut, but there they swarmed everywhere; they covered the legs, biting furiously; it is only when they are tired that they leave off."

They reached Lake Tanganyika the 1st of April, viewing it from the summit of the ridge two thousand feet above its level, which forms the southern boundary of its cup-like bed. The village at this point, Pambete, is surrounded with palm-oil-trees, tall and graceful as those found upon the west coast.

But the leader of the expedition was too weak and ill to make journeys about the lake. At one time, he was unconscious for several hours from the effects of fever; and finally his faithful servants hung a blanket before the entrance to his hut, that the curious natives might not be witnesses of his weakness. Nor could he learn anything by inquiry of the people. Either they were wholly ignorant, or they mistrusted him so much that they would give no information.

They remained at this village a month, before the leader was able to travel; and then he was far from being well. Toward the end of May, they arrived at Chisaka, Chitimba's village, and here they were detained for more than three months, owing to trouble between a party of Arab traders and a native chief, Nsama. Dr. Livingstone frankly says he heard but one side of the story, that of the Arabs, and hence cannot pretend to state the case truly; but the fact that the native chiefs generally condemned Nsama seemed to indicate that he was in the wrong. About the middle of September, however, the Arabs having lost about fifty men and Nsama probably twice as many, negotiations for a peace were entered upon; and as was often the case among civilized nations in other days, this peace was to be cemented with a marriage, Nsama promising to give one of his daughters to Hamees, one of the Arabs, as a wife. She came riding pick-aback on a man's shoulders into the village where her future lord was for the time, "a nice, modest, good-looking young woman, her hair rubbed all over with nkola, a red pigment made from the cam-wood, and much used as an ornament. She was accompanied by about a dozen young and old female attendants, each carrying a small basket with some provisions, as cassava, ground-nuts, etc. The Arabs were all dressed in their finery, and the slaves, in fantastic dresses, flourished swords, fired guns, and yelled. When she was brought to Hamees' hut she descended, and with her maids went into the hut. She and her attendants all had small, neat features. I had been sitting with Hamees, and now rose up and went away. As I passed him, he spoke thus to himself: 'Hamees Wadim Tagh! see to what you have brought yourself?'"

Nsama had been a great conqueror in his time, and with bows and arrows as the arms of his enemies, he was invincible; but the Arabs had of course been provided with fire-arms, and it was to the supremacy of weapons, not of generalship, that he had been obliged to yield so far as to consent to a peace. Dr. Livingstone visited his village, Itawa, and found

THE ARRIVAL OF HAMEES' BRIDE.

the people particularly handsome. Nsama was very gracious, and promised guides and porters; but showed so much distrust that the traveler finally decided to go on without the proffered assistance.

Keeping to the north of Nsama's country after this brief visit, the party moved westward until it reached the north end of Moero. This was Nov. 8; it was the rainy season again, and the explorer was obliged to be very careful where he traveled, lest he again fall a victim to that fever against which he was now defenseless.

Their next visit of note was to a chief of Lunda, called the Casembe. This word, which means simply a general, has been applied as a proper name both to the chief and to the village where he lives. The Portuguese had used it in the latter sense; and their various observations as to the location of the village Casembe did not agree very closely, for the simple reason that each Casembe, as he came into office, removed the village from its previous site to one which pleased him better. The town at the time of Livingstone's visit was situated on the east bank of the lakelet Mofwe, and one mile from its northern end. The plain extending from the Lunde to the town of Casembe is level, and studded pretty thickly with red-ant hills, from fifteen to twenty feet high. Casembe had made a broad path from his town to the Lunde, a distance of about a mile and a half. The town consisted of a space a mile square, dotted over with cassava plantations, in the midst of which were the huts. The court or compound of Casembe was surrounded by a hedge of high reeds, ornamented with about sixty human skulls. Before the gigantic hut within this enclosure, which was Casembe's abode, the chief sat on a square seat placed on lion and leopard skins; he was dressed in a coarse blue and white print edged with red baize, arranged in large folds "so as to look like a crinoline put on wrong side foremost." His arms, legs, and head were covered with sleeves, leggings, and cap made of various colored beads arranged in patterns; a crown of yellow feathers surmounted his cap, and he considered himself a model of royal magnificence.

While at this village, Dr. Livingstone was provided with food on a liberal scale; and his presents seemed to be fully appreciated. His first gift to the chief consisted of eight yards of orange-colored serge, a large striped table-cloth, another large cloth, and a large richly gilded comb for the hair, such as ladies wore about 1820. As Lunda fashions in coiffure are various, this could not fail of being a welcome gift.

Casembe showed himself very friendly, although the traveler, remembering the skulls, and noting that many of his attendants had their ears cropped or their hands lopped off in token of their master's displeasure, could not trust him entirely. Although the Portuguese had visited this country, it is to be noted that Casembe thought there were only two sovereigns in the world, Queen Victoria and the sultan of Zanzibar.

A Lunda Toilet.

As they came down the watershed toward Tanganyika, they entered an area of the earth's surface still disturbed by internal igneous action. A hot fountain in the country of Nsama, they found, was often used to boil cassava and maize. Earthquakes are no rarity in this section of the country, and one was experienced which shook their hut, and set the fowls to cackling, in the middle of the night. The most remarkable effect of this earthquake was, that it changed the rates of the chronometers, and stopped one entirely.

Dr. Livingstone was so affected by the climate that he was unable to leave Casembe's town until late in June, 1868, although he had arrived there in the previous autumn. His desire was to explore Lake Bangweolo, but the shores of it were so marshy, and the intervening country so overflowed during the wet season that it was highly imprudent for him to attempt it.

It was on the 18th of July, 1868, that Dr. Livingstone discovered this lake, one of the largest in central Africa. It is extraordinary to note the total absence of all pride and enthusiasm as, almost parenthetically, he records the fact in these few brief words:

"Reached the chief village of Mapuni, near the north bank of Bangweolo. On the 18th I walked a little way out, and saw the shores of the lake for the first time, thankful that I had come safely hither."

His intention to explore the lake was not carried out for a week, a strong and unfavorable wind detaining him on shore. But his return was much delayed by the condition of the country. We have already referred to that contest between Nsama and the Arab traders, which was apparently settled by the marriage of Hamees to Nsama's daughter. But this alliance did not accomplish this result; for the lady, hearing what seemed to her an indication that her father was to be attacked by her husband's people, departed quietly from her new home, and was seen no more. The other native chiefs, beginning to be alarmed at the encroachments of the Arabs, joined forces and attempted to storm the stockade of one of their leaders. They suffered a severe defeat in this attempt; and the whole country was thrown into turmoil and confusion. For several months travel or exploration was impossible; and several times the life of the stranger was in imminent danger. During this period, he occupied his time in writing out an exceedingly valuable treatise on the subject of the periodical floods which drain the enormous cistern-lakes of Central Africa. It would manifestly be out of place to transfer that treatise to these pages; and the reader who would study the subject is referred to the work of which the present chapter is substantially an abridgment—"The Last Journals" of David Livingstone in Central Africa.

At last, a cruel outrage perpetrated by one of the Arabs on the natives of Kizinga so exasperated the latter that they declared war; and although badly defeated in the first instance, soon compelled the slave-traders to leave the country. With a party of these, led by Mohammed Bagharib, Livingstone started to Ujiji on December 11. The march to the nearest point on Lake Tanganyika occupied just two months, but was entirely uneventful, except that just before reaching the lake, Livingstone had an attack of pneumonia, accompanied by spitting of blood and distressing weakness. He had to be carried for sixteen days, during part of which time he was insensible, and lost count of the days of the week and the month. And this was the man who at the start, had been able to outstrip all his companions in walking, and was often obliged to loiter on the way because the caravan could not keep up with his swift, steady pace.

He had arranged for a quantity of goods to be sent from Zanzibar to Ujiji by one of the caravans trading along this route; and fully expected to find at this point, not only cloth and beads for propitiating the natives along his way, but a supply of the sorely needed medicines. Unfortunately, the goods had been intrusted to a scoundrel, who had helped himself most liberally to them. Sixty-two out of eighty pieces of cloth had been stolen, and most of his best beads. Medicines, wine, and cheese had been left at Unyanyembe, thirteen days' journey east of Ujiji. Nor was the distance the only difficulty; the way was blocked by a Mazitu war, so that he must wait at Ujiji until the governor of Unyanyembe should have an opportunity of forwarding the goods in safety.

At Ujiji, however, he found a supply of flannel, which was very beneficial worn next to the skin, in his present condition. He also received a present of Assam tea from Calcutta, and his own supply of coffee and a little sugar had not been stolen.

The next month was occupied in writing letters home; and on the 27th of April he records that he had finished forty-two. He had great difficulty in persuading any one to undertake to deliver these at Zanzibar; the probability is, that even those who were not directly implicated in the theft of his goods were afraid that they would be accused of it; at last, however, he found messengers who promised to take them; and to their charge the documents were confided. That is the end of the history of the letters then written; for they never reached their destination.

July 12, he set out to explore the Manyuema country, hitherto a country wholly unknown. Securing canoes, he skirted the edge of the lake for a short distance, then crossed it, and struck along the coast on foot. They passed through Uguha, or the country of the Waguha, and came to the territory occupied by the Manyuema.

Late in October, 1869, being thoroughly rested, he determined to cross the country to the Lualaba, and buy a canoe for its exploration. It is scarcely necessary to say that at the period of which we write, the course of this river was shrouded in mystery. Their route was west and south-west, through a country of beauty so great that he seems never tired of praising it. But they found the people far from friendly. A slave-trader had been through there, and had treated the people with great severity; in spite of the difference of color, they persisted in looking upon Dr. Livingstone as akin to the Arab. Owing to this state of feeling, they found it impossible to buy a canoe in which to cross the Luamo, the banks of which they reached November 17. Finally the party returned to Bambarre.

A second trip was begun the day after Christmas, the route being slightly altered, so that they struck the Luamo at a higher point than before. Their course from Bambarre for a number of days was nearly due north. They found the people civil, as a rule, but like noisy children, all talking and gazing when they entered a village. But weakness and sickness delayed them, and it was a month and more before they reached the Lualaba.

The incidents of the next few months need not be recorded in detail. He made but little progress, and even after reaching the banks of the Lualaba he turned aside, to visit Arab traders who had come for ivory, and with whom he was good friends. Under the date of June 26, we have this entry:

"Now my people failed me; so, with only three attendants, Susi, Chuma and Gardner, I started off to the north-west for the Lualaba."

But this was another false start. For the first time in his life his feet failed him; and learning that the Lualaba took a great bend to the west-south-west, he gave up the quest, and limped back to Bambarre with his three faithful servants. Fairly baffled by the difficulties in his way, and sorely troubled by the demoralized state of his men, who had been seduced by the Arabs to a more lucrative employment, the explorer turned back from this point. He was laid up for some time with the sores on his feet, which became irritable eating ulcers, so painful that sometimes he could not sleep.

While he was thus rendered helpless, the few men that had not deserted him occupied much of their time in hunting. The chief game about this point was the soko, a species of the chimpanzee which has sometimes been identified with the gorilla; but no white scientist has ever seen the soko, and those Africans who came to England after the death of Dr. Livingstone failed to recognize the gorilla, stuffed, which is in the British

HUNTERS KILLING SOKOS.

Museum, as a soko. Nor do the descriptions of soko-hunts lead us to believe that they are the same as that powerful and ferocious animal of Western Equatorial Africa, which Du Chaillu has described. The soko is represented by some to be extremely knowing, successfully stalking men and women while at their work, kidnapping children and running up trees with them; he seems to be amused by the sight of the young natives in his arms, but comes down when tempted by a bunch of bananas, and as he lifts that, drops the child. One man was cutting honey from a tree, when a soko suddenly appeared and caught him, and then let him go. Another man was hunting, and missed in his aim when he attempted to stab a soko; it seized the spear and broke it, then grappled with the man, who called for help to his companions; it bit off the ends of his fingers and escaped unharmed. Another still was caught by a soko while hoeing; he roared out, but the soko giggled and grinned, and left him as if it had attacked him in play. A child caught up by a soko is often abused by being pinched and scratched and let fall.

His friend Mohammed, the chief of the ivory traders, offered to go with him to see the Lualaba; the explorer explained that it would not be sufficient for him to see it, he must descend the stream and see whither it flowed. Mohammed then offered to provide him with men; and this offer was accepted, the equivalent of two hundred and seventy pounds sterling being paid as amends for the injury to his ivory trade which the loss of these men would occasion.

Eighty days had passed since Dr. Livingstone first knew that his feet had failed him, before he was able to use them them again. He was, by the journey which he was now beginning, entering upon the solution of a vexed geographical problem. It was a vexed problem, because the assumption of a point as true had caused errors which could not be corrected as long as this error obtained. This mistake was in identifying the Chambeze with the Zambesi. The map of Africa which Dr. Livingstone carried with him upon this expedition contained this error; the map-maker showing the river as running up-stream, and between three and four thousand feet uphill, in order to reach the Zambesi which was known through Livingstone's former expedition, as well as by the settlements of the Portuguese.

Upon this trip, the explorer departed from the course which he had previously marked out for himself, to give no European name to any natural feature; this rule had been broken

A DANGEROUS PRIZE.

but once before, when he gave to the great cataract of the Zambesi the name of Victoria Falls; he now gave English names to the lakes which are the head-waters of the Congo—Palmerston Fountain, Frere Fountain, and Lake Lincoln, thus perpetuating, in the interior of Africa, the names of three men who had been, in his own day, most prominent in their efforts to suppress slavery.

But his effort to descend the Lualaba was not without hindrance. Under date of December 10, 1870, he says:

"I am sorely let and hindered in this Manyeema. Rain every day, and often at night. * * * This is the sorest delay I ever had."

While detained thus at Bambarre, Dr. Livingstone became acquainted with a curious disease—the strangest disease which he had seen in that country, he declared. Freemen who were taken as slaves died without any assignable cause, the only pain which they suffered being in the region of the heart. He regarded their death as due to that much scoffed-at trouble, a broken heart.

Late in December, the traveler's goat, on which he depended for milk, was killed by a leopard. A gun set for the animal went off at ten o'clock at night. The next morning, some of the attendants of the explorer set off on a hunt, and tracked him to his lair. The ball had broken both hind-legs and one fore-leg; yet he sprang viciously upon the foremost of the hunters, and bit him badly. Speared by the comrades of the man attacked, he proved to be a splendid specimen of his kind, being six feet eight inches from tip of nose to end of tail.

They left Bambarre February 16, but progressed very slowly. Their way lay across a great bend of the Lualaba, and they traveled on foot. After a journey lasting about six weeks, they came once more to the bank of the Lualaba, a mighty stream, at least three thousand yards broad, and so deep that the people living near by declared it could never, at any time of the year, be forded. The current, he found to be about two miles an hour.

But having reached the banks of this mighty river, the traveler found that he could go no farther, for the present at least; the suspicions of the natives prevented him from obtaining canoes either for descending or for crossing it. Here he remained from March 31 until July 20, hoping day by day to be able to obtain canoes; getting bits of uncertain information now and then from the people about the rivers of the surrounding country, and striving to teach those with whom he

MASSACRE OF THE MANYUEMA WOMEN AT NYANGWE.

came in contact. Finally, there was a terrible fight at this point, which was a market-place for the whole surrounding country. A quarrel between the natives and a slave of the ivory-traders who had come hither was taken up by all interested, and between three and four hundred persons killed. Livingstone, powerless to prevent the slaughter, could only look on at the affrighted people struggling in the river into which they had plunged for safety, and, when the fight was over, intercede for those who had fled to him for safety. So far had the people been carried by their anger, that after it was all over, no one could give a connected account of the reasons for the fight. They had seen their friends fighting, and had joined in.

On July 20, he started back to Ujiji; but the journey back was different from anything that this old traveler had yet experienced. The ivory-traders had passed through this country, and maltreated the natives to such an extent that the whole country was aroused; and Dr. Livingstone being constantly taken for an Arab, was in perpetual danger of his life. Three times in one day (August 8) was he delivered from impending death.

In passing along the narrow path, with a dense wall of vegetation touching either hand, the party came to a point where an ambush had been placed, and trees cut down to obstruct their passage while the assailants speared them; but for some reason it had been abandoned. Nothing could be detected; but by stooping down toward the earth and looking up toward the sun, a dark shade could sometimes be seen; this was an infuriated savage, and a slight rustle in the dense vegetation meant a spear. A large spear from Livingstone's right lunged past, and, almost grazing his back, stuck firmly in the soil. The two men from whom it came appeared in an opening in the forest only ten yards off, and bolted, one looking back over his shoulder as he ran. As they are expert with the spear, the traveler could only account for its missing by supposing that the man had been too sure of his aim, and by attributing his safety to the protecting care of his Father.

Shortly after this, another spear was hurled at him, missing him by about a foot in front. Guns were fired into the thick forest, but with no effect, for nothing could be seen; but they heard the savages jeering and denouncing them close by. Two of Livingstone's men were killed by them.

The third danger was not from concealed spearmen. Coming to a part of the forest cleared for cultivation, the explorer

THE MANYUEMA AMBUSCADE.

noticed a giant tree, made to appear still taller by growing out of an ant-hill twenty feet high; it had fire applied near its roots. Dr. Livingstone heard a crack, which told that the fire had done its work in felling the tree; but he felt no alarm until he saw the mass of wood sway and then descend directly toward him. He ran a few paces back, and down it came to the ground within a yard of where he paused; breaking into several lengths, it covered him with a cloud of dust. Had the branches not been rotted off previously, he could scarcely have escaped.

His attendants, who had been scattered in all directions, regarded this as a good omen, taken in connection with his other escapes that day, and came running toward him, crying out:

"Peace! Peace! You will finish all your work in spite of these people, and in spite of everything!"

Reaching Ujiji October 23, he found that all his goods had been sold by an Arab, Shereef, to his friends, at nominal prices. In spite of the protests of other traders, more than three thousand yards of calico and seven hundred pounds of beads had been thus sacrificed. Shereef had the assurance, however, even after this was fully made known to Dr. Livingstone, to come to shake hands with him; and when the long-suffering traveler rebelled against such behavior at last, and refused to do so, the Arab assumed an air of displeasure, as if he had been badly treated. He afterward came twice a day with his salutation of "*Balghere* (good luck)!" until Livingstone told him that if he were an Arab, his (Shereef's) hand and both ears would be cut off for thieving; and the traveler wanted no salutations from him.

He was now utterly destitute, and with no prospect of further supplies for months to come; for letters must be dispatched to the coast before such would be sent to him; and how to pay the bearers of such letters, except in promises, he could not tell. He had made up his mind, if he could not get people at Ujiji, to wait until men should come from the coast; but to wait in beggary, was what he had never contemplated; and he "now felt miserable."

The few simple words are significant enough, if we consider the patience of the man. Livingstone's journals are unlike those of every other African traveler in the brevity and lack of enthusiasm with which the events are chronicled; the cold and undemonstrative nature of the Scotchman shows itself most plainly in this way; and especially in respect to his own sufferings But in this case, we must remember that it is something more than natural reluctance to enlarge upon his feelings; it is even more than the manly reticence regarding personal physical pain, which is shown by the great majority of the explorers; it is the patience of the Christian, who sees in all the suffering and trouble which come upon him, the trial which is to fit him for his Master's purpose.

Just as his spirits had reached their lowest ebb, the dawn began to break; an Arab merchant, who said that he himself had no goods, offered to sell some ivory, and give the goods so obtained to the stranger. This was encouraging; but Livingstone felt that he was not yet at the point of accepting such an offer.

"Not yet, but by and by," he said to the Arab.

He had still a very few goods for barter remaining, goods which had been left in the care of another Arab than the one who had stolen his new stock, which he had deposited before going to Manyuema, in case of returning in extreme need. These he was now resolved to use, to get to the coast a letter, if possible. He had been full two years without any tidings from Europe whatever; he had sent dispatches during that time, but as we have seen, they had not reached the coast.

Such were the circumstances surrounding this great explorer when his servants brought him word that an Englishman was approaching the town. Susi came running to his master at the top of his speed, and in great excitement. He breathlessly gasped out:

"An Englishman! I see him!"

In an instant he was off. Dr. Livingstone followed him to the door, and saw the caravan approaching the town. Bales of goods, a tin bath, huge kettles, cooking-pots, tents, and all the paraphernalia of a well-equipped traveler through a country where few or no conveniences were to be expected, struck him with a sense of the difference between himself and the approaching stranger.

"This must be a luxurious traveler," he told himself, "and not one at his wit's end like me."

The first glance at the caravan had showed him that Susi had been mistaken in one particular—this was not an Englishman, for at the head of the caravan floated the flag of England's eldest daughter, the United States. The stranger was Henry M. Stanley.

Of the meeting, we need not here give details. Overwhelmed as Livingstone was by surprise at the coming of this man, sent by a stranger through the heart of Africa especially to find him if alive, and to bring back his bones if he were dead, we could hardly expect that his narrative of the meeting would be clear and succinct; he was too bewildered, probably, in spite of his Scotch coolness of head, to remember just what took place. Little by little the whole wonderful story came home to him, and he realized that he was once again in communication with the outer world. And with this realization, came renewed vigor; he was no longer the broken-down old man, spiritless, bitterly disappointed at the failure to reach the points which he had endeavored to attain, heart-sick at the duplicity which had left him well-nigh without resources in the heart of this great continent; a new life seemed to fill his veins, and emotions that had lain dormant in Manyuema revived at the tidings that he had to tell. But while struggling to express the flood of feeling which so nearly overwhelmed him, these are the words he uses:

"I really do feel extremely grateful, and at the same time I am a little ashamed at not being more worthy of the generosity."

Mr. Stanley brought news that Sir Roderick Murchison most earnestly desired that Lake Tanganyika should be fully explored, and accordingly, after a little more than two weeks spent at Ujiji, the whole party set out for the north of the lake. The start was made November 16, but a cruise to the head of the lake failed to reveal any passage into the Nyanza, or any stream flowing out of Tanganyika; the natives appeared to know nothing of any large lake to the north, and they returned to Ujiji a month after they had left it.

Directly after their return, they made ready for a journey towards the east to secure Dr. Livingstone's goods, the English government having granted one thousand pounds for supplies for the explorer, in addition to the assistance which Mr. Bennett had commissioned Stanley to bring. Owing to the illness of the younger traveler, however, they did not leave Ujiji until two days after Christmas. The same cause which had detained them at Ujiji delayed their journey somewhat after they had started; and during one stage, Mr. Stanley had to be carried on a cot. After a march of fifty-four days, they reached Unyanyembe, over three hundred miles away.

Mr. Stanley was extremely anxious to have Dr. Livingstone return to England with him, to recruit his strength; but the old explorer was by no means ready to do so. His own judgment told him:

"All your friends will wish you to make a complete work of

the exploration of the sources of the Nile before you retire."

His daughter Agnes had written:

"Much as I wish you to come home, I would rather that you finished your work to your own satisfaction than return merely to gratify me."

In spite of the persuasions of his newly found friend, then, he resolved to remain until this work should be accomplished. Probably, in the enthusiasm which had been re-awakened in his breast, and the return of a measure of good health, he did not realize what inroads upon his constitution had been made by the fever from which he had suffered so much after the theft of his medicines. Feeling so much better, he fancied himself a strong man again.

They remained at Unyanymebe until the 14th of March, Dr. Livingstone preparing dispatches and letters for the outer world to which his companion was so shortly to return. On the date mentioned, they separated; communication between them was kept up for some time; and it was arranged that Mr. Stanley was to procure men for Dr. Livingstone in Zanzibar, and send them forward to Unyanyembe, where he was to await them. The time thus spent in waiting was utilized by completing many calculations which lack of time had caused him to leave unfinished, and by planning his work for the future. Briefly stated, it was his intention to allow the remainder of the year 1872 (at that time, five months,) for the journey to his new field of exploration; devote the whole of 1873 to his work, and return in 1874 to home and a well-earned repose.

It was the middle of August before the caravan of porters arrived at Unyanyembe. They numbered fifty-seven. Besides these new men, of whom John and Jacob Wainwright are to be remembered, Dr. Livingstone had five old servants with him—Susi, Chuma and Amoda, who had been employed by him during the Zambesi expedition, and Mabruki and Gardner, two of the Nassick boys who had left Zanzibar with his caravan at the beginning of the present journey.

Leaving a sufficient quantity of goods with Sultan bin Ali to secure their return journey from Unyanyembe to the coast, the caravan set out August 23. A week later, the two Nassicks had, "from sheer laziness," allowed all the cows to stray; they were found a long way off, but one was missing, and was never recovered. One cow, their best milker, had been lost three days after starting. Two of the pagazi, engaged at a village on their road, deserted, taking with them a quantity of calico belonging to the men. Thus the story goes on.

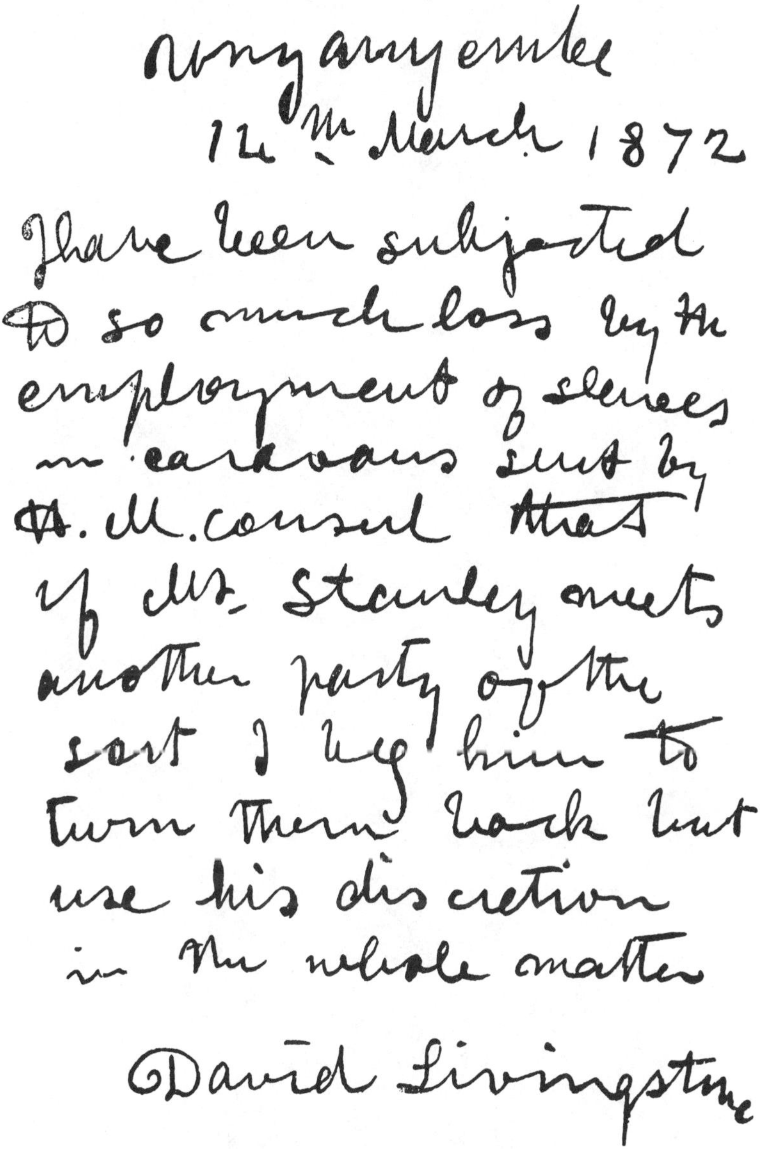

Unyanyembe
14th March 1872

I have been subjected to so much loss by the employment of slaves in caravans sent by H. M. consul that if Mr. Stanley meets another party of the sort I beg him to turn them back but use his discretion in the whole matter

David Livingstone

Autograph Fac-Simile Letter from Dr. Livingstone.

The latter half of September, they were much delayed by sickness, both of the leader and of his followers. They came in sight of Tanganyika October 8, and slowly approached the

"THE MAIN STREAM CAME UP TO SUSI'S MOUTH."

lake from which so short a distance seemed to divide them. Their course was nearly due south to Fipa, as that was the town to which their steps were now directed; they had been many times assured in Unyanyembe that the route to this point was much shorter and less difficult than that to Ujiji.

From this point they skirted the shores of the lake; and early in November came within sight of the Luazi. For some time past, Livingstone had been tormented by doubts about the Lualaba; he was in search of the ultimate sources of the Nile, not considering that the discovery of the two Nyanzas had settled this vexed question; what if, after all, the Lualaba should prove to be a tributary of the Congo? The question occurs more than once in his journal, even before the meeting with Stanley, showing that the idea was gaining hold upon his mind. Still, he pressed on, resolved to find out for himself what was the destination of this great river.

The journey now turned toward the southwest, for he wished to visit Lake Bangweolo again, and ascertain what connection it might have with a great river-system. The journey was without special incident; there was the same old story of natives angered by the outrageous treatment of Arab traders, and consequently jealous of all strangers; of efforts to get food, sometimes unavailing because of this jealousy; of sickness of the men; and finally, here and there we find the simple word "ill" among the entries in his journal, coupled sometimes with a statement of the length of time during which his illness had continued. Occasionally, the feeble writing testifies more plainly than words that his strength was failing.

February 13, they arrived within sight of Lake Bangweolo; the plain surrounding the lake was under water, and it was necessary to obtain canoes to make their way along the shore of the enlarged lake. Halting at the village of a chief named Matipa, they entered into negotiations for these vessels. Matipa showed himself at first very friendly, but on one pretext or another, put off the arrival of the canoes in a sufficient number to serve their purpose. At last, they found that he was deliberately acting treacherously; Dr. Livingstone then took possession of Matipa's own hut, fired his pistol through the roof, and left ten men to guard the village. Matipa fled to another village, while his people sent off and brought a number of canoes, so that Livingstone's men were enabled to embark at once. Later intercourse showed that Matipa was thoroughly frightened by the warlike demonstration, and became once more very friendly.

THE LAST MILE OF LIVINGSTONE'S TRAVELS.

An entry under date of March 24 will give some idea of the hardships endured at this time, when the end was so rapidly approaching:

"We punted six hours to a little islet without a tree, and no sooner did we land than a pitiless, pelting rain came on. We turned up a canoe to get shelter. We shall reach the Chambeze to-morrow. The wind tore the tent out of our hands, and damaged it, too; the loads are all soaked, and with the cold, it is bitterly uncomfortable. A man put my bed into the bilge, and never said 'Bale out,' so I was safe for a wet night, but it turned out better than I expected. No grass, but we made a bed of the loads, and a blanket fortunately put into a bag."

It is interesting, in this portion of his journal, to note what care Susi and Chuma took of their master. He does not seem to realize it himself, yet from his own record we see that, day by day, their watchfulness over him was increasing, as they saw his strength diminishing. It was on this journey that, for the first time, he was unable to wade the streams which they crossed on foot; and all the way to Bangweolo, wherever they came to a sponge or a river, Chuma carried his master on his strong and willing shoulders, even though the main stream came up to Susi's mouth as they waded along.

The voyage over this overflowed land was far from easy sailing. On the 7th of April, he records that they were lost for five hours on the grassy prairies, which were covered with from three to five feet of water. The next morning they obtained guides from a village within hearing, who caused them to take their large canoe along a course where the water was sometimes but fifteen inches deep; and although the men put all their strength to her, she stopped at every haul with a jerk, as if in a bank of adhesive plaster.

But exertion and exposure had further weakened him; and a few days later we find the entry that he was so weak he could hardly walk, but tottered along nearly two hours, and then lay down quite done over. At this resting-place, he made coffee—the last of his stock—and tried to go on again; but in an hour's time was compelled to give it up. Even then, he was very unwilling to be carried, but, "on being pressed," allowed the men to help him on by relays to Chinama, a highly cultivated region.

From this point forward we cease to refer to his journals, giving a fac-simile of the two last pages; and carrying the story forward by means of the narration of his two faithful

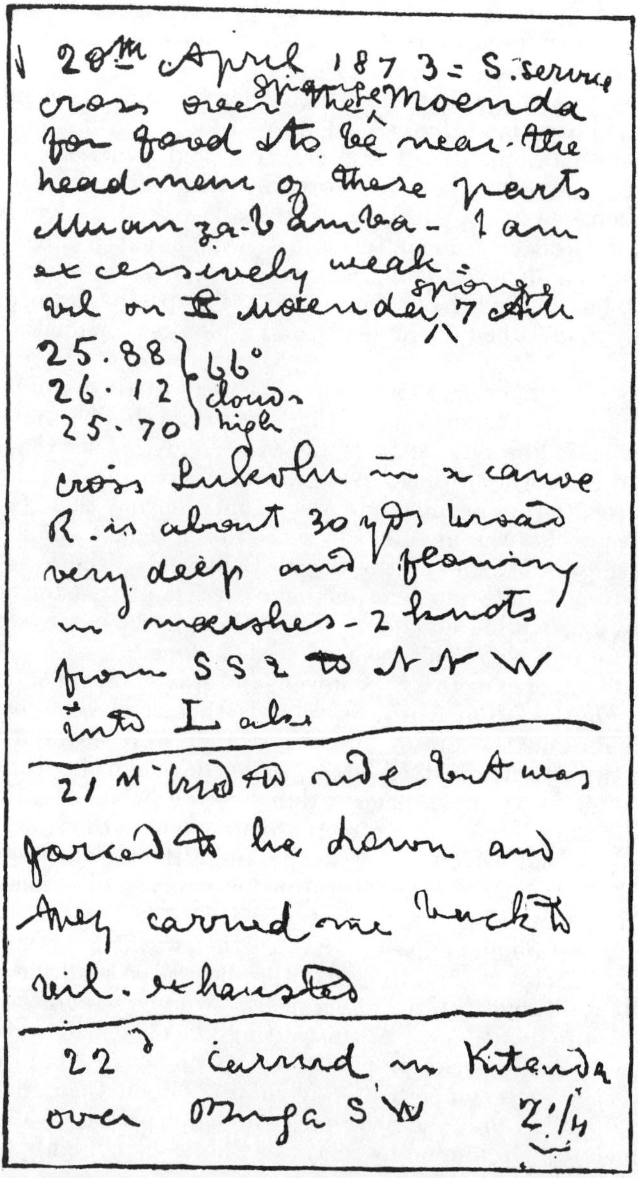
20th April 1873 = S. service
cross over the sponge of the Moenda
for food & to be near the
head men of these parts
Muanza-bamba - I am
excessively weak =
vil on R Moenda sponge 7 Ath
25.88 } 66°
26.12 } clouds
25.70 } high
cross Lukolu in a canoe
R. is about 30 yds broad
very deep and flowing
in marshes - 2 knots
from SSE to NNW
into Lake
21st tried to ride but was
forced to lie down and
they carried me back to
vil. exhausted
22d carried in Kitanda
over Buga SW 2 1/4

Autograph Fac-Simile from Livingstone's Last Journal.

servants. April 21, he tried to ride the donkey, but was so weak that he fell to the ground utterly exhausted and faint.

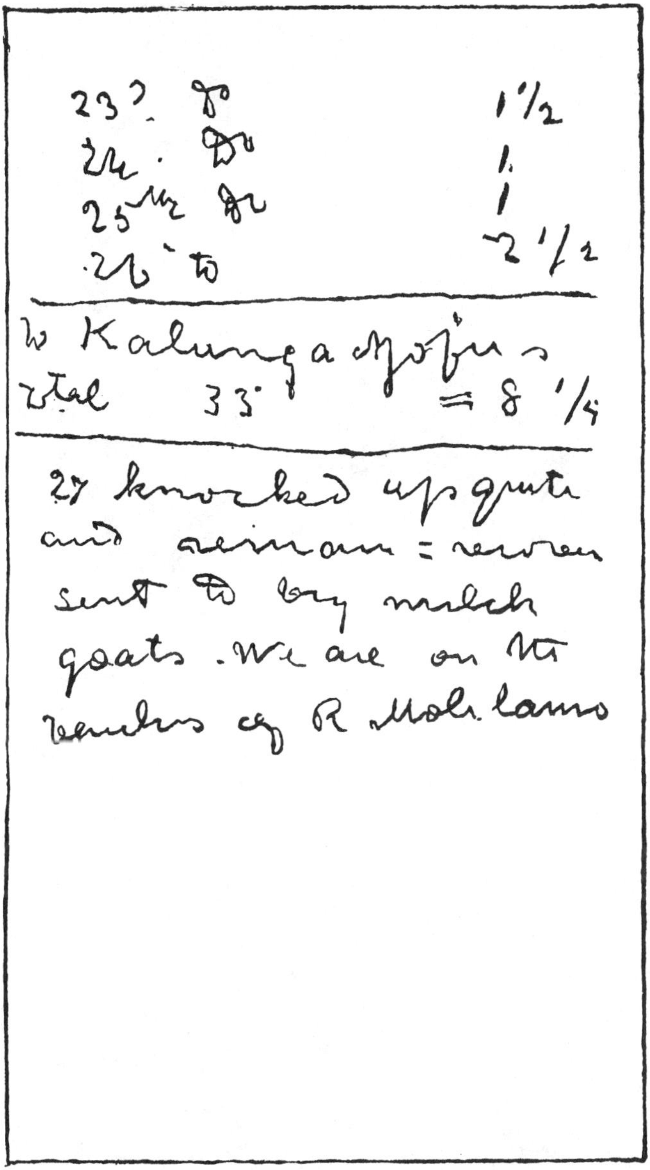
23rd do 1½
24 do 1
25th do 1
26 to 2½
to Kalunganjovu's
total 33 = 8¼
27 knocked up quite
and remain = recover
sent to buy milch
goats. We are on the
banks of R. Molilamo

Autograph Fac-Simile from Livingstone's Last Journal.

Chuma carried him back to the village which they had just left, and placed him in his hut. The next day, they contrived a

THE LAST ARRIVAL ON EARTH.

sort of litter, known to the natives as a kitanda, a framework covered with grass, and having a blanket laid upon it. On this he was placed, while Chuma walked by his side, to steady the sick man when the bearers stopped; for he was so weak that he could not otherwise have kept from falling off.

They arrived at the village of Kalunganjova, on the banks of the Molilamo, April 27. From this point, they sent out to buy food. The effort was unsuccessful, for the Mazitu had made raids through that country, and taken everything. The chief, nevertheless, made them a substantial present of a kid and three baskets of ground-nuts; and those who had food were quite willing to sell it for beads. The chief visited Dr. Livingstone on the morning of the 29th, and assured him that he would personally accompany the caravan to the crossing-place of the river, in order to be sure that canoes were furnished as he wished them to be.

But when they were ready to set out, Dr. Livingstone was too weak to walk from his bed in the hut to the kitanda at the door. It was therefore necessary, because the door was so narrow, to break down one of the frail walls of the hut; through the breach thus made, the bearers brought the litter close to the sick man's bed, and he was carefully lifted upon it.

With almost incredible gentleness, when we remember that only love had taught them how to deal with the sick, these men, who had until the last few years been rude and untaught savages, lifted him from the kitanda into the canoe, and again into the litter when they had crossed the river; for the canoe was not wide enough to admit the kitanda with the sick man upon it. Susi hurried on ahead of the caravan, that a hut might be built at Chitambo's village, which was their present destination, by the time that his master arrived.

The natives stood in silent wonder as he was helped from his litter into the hut, for his praises had reached them long ago. This was the "good man," as he was emphatically called by the tribes that knew him best; and they watched him till he was lost to their view inside the hut.

The next day, the chief paid a visit of ceremony to his guest; but Dr. Livingstone was obliged, after an effort to talk to him, to send him away, telling him to come again the next day, when he hoped to have more strength. The day wore on, and night came; some of the men took to their huts; it was the duty of others to keep watch. The boy who was appointed to sleep just within his master's hut, summoned Susi about eleven o'clock; Livingstone asked a few questions, first about noises that he heard outside, and then about distances, the latter showing that his mind was wandering. An hour later, the man was again summoned, and attended to his master's wants, getting the medicine which was required.

"All right; you can go out now," said the white man.

The hours passed on; it was not yet dawn when the boy came to Susi again, this time in fright:

"Come to Bwana; I am afraid; I don't know if he is alive."

Susi called his immediate companions, and six men went to the doctor's hut. A candle, stuck by its own wax to a box, was burning at the head of the rude bed; the light showed their master's form, kneeling by the side of the bed, his head buried in his hands upon the pillow. He gave no sign of hearing them; one of them gently touched his cheek; it was quite cold; at some time between midnight and dawn, of the 1st of May, 1873, David Livingstone had knelt in prayer, and died upon his knees.

They laid him reverently upon his couch, and went out to consult as to what should be done. As they went out, the cocks crew, fixing the hour as that of dawn. Before daylight the men were quietly told in each hut that they were to assemble because their master was dead. They knew that Jacob Wainwright could write, and Chuma and Susi asked him to make a list of the things that they should find in the boxes, and, all being present when these boxes were opened, all would be responsible if any money or valuables should be missing when they arrived at the coast. What difficulties were to attend them in their proposed journey, only God could know; but they bravely faced them all, and resolved to take their master's body back to his friends. Chuma and Susi were chosen captains of the caravan, and all promised to obey them as their chiefs.

Finding it impossible to keep the secret from Chitambo, whose superstition they had dreaded, they were agreeably surprised when the chief made no objections to their preparing the body by a rude sort of embalming and taking it to Zanzibar. The burial service of the English church was read by Jacob Wainwright, and for fourteen days this process of preparing the body continued. Then, they wrapped it in muslin, and stripping from a myonga tree a large piece of bark, made a cylinder of it, in which the body was placed, and which was covered with a piece of sail-cloth and lashed securely to a pole, so as to be carried by two men. Jacob Wainwright, at the request of Susi and Chuma, who seem to have forgotten nothing, carved an inscription on a large mvula tree which stood near the hut where the body rested; they also erected two high, thick posts, with a heavy cross-piece, like a lintel and door-posts in form, which they painted thoroughly with tar.

Susi and Chuma.

The homeward march was then begun; but they were so affected by the hardships which they had previously undergone, that on the third day after setting out they were obliged to halt; half their number were positively unable to go on. It was nearly three weeks before they were able to proceed. Then, fortunately, the rains were over, so that there was less danger of sickness.

With the events of this journey, we have nothing to do, so far as they relate to the adventures of the men themselves. It was weeks after their starting that they learned from an Arab caravan that the news of their master's death had already been reported in Unyanyembe.

Livingstone's Body Carried to the Coast.

A second caravan assured them that this news was true, and that Dr. Livingstone's son, with two other Englishmen and a quantity of goods, was at Unyanyembe. Arrived at Baula,

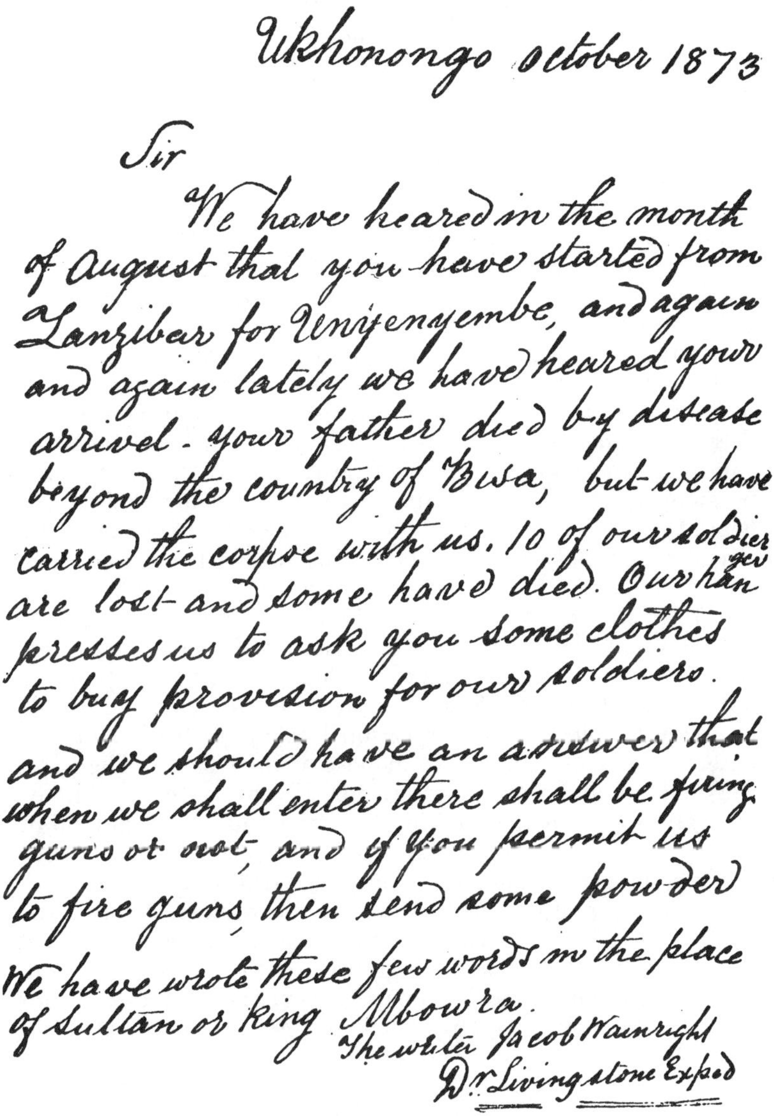

Ukhonongo october 1873

Sir

We have heared in the month
of August that you have started from
Zanzibar for Unyenyembe, and again
and again lately we have heared your
arrivel - your father died by disease
beyond the country of Bisa, but we have
carried the corpse with us. 10 of our soldier
are lost and some have died. Our hunger
presses us to ask you some clothes
to buy provision for our soldiers.
and we should have an answer that
when we shall enter there shall be firing
guns or not, and if you permit us
to fire guns, then send some powder
We have wrote these few words in the place
of Sultan or king Mbowra.
The writer Jacob Wainwright
Dr. Livingstone Exped

Autograph Fac-Simile of Wainwright's Letter Announcing Death of Livingstone.

Jacob Wainwright was commissioned to write an account of the doctor's death, and Chuma, taking three men with him, pressed on in advance to deliver it to the English party. Arriving at Unyanyembe, he found that the report of Mr. Oswell Livingstone's being one of the party was erroneous; but his letter was delivered and his story told to the chief of the Livingstone Search Expedition, Lieut. Cameron.

It was this officer's idea that perhaps Dr. Livingstone would have wished to be buried in Africa, since there his wife's remains lay; but the faithful servants who had brought his body so far in order that it might be taken to his own country thought that it was right, at all risks, to attempt to bear their master home; and he did not press them to bury him at Kwihara, whither the Search Expedition had come from Unyanyembe to met them.

But the natives showed themselves hostile because they had with them a corpse; their superstition could not permit them to allow such men a free passage through the country. It was therefore necessary to resort to stratagem. Some distance beyond Unyanyembe, when they finally decided that it was impossible to advance any farther with the body carried as it had been, they made a fagot of mapira-stalks of such shape and size as to simulate a dead body when properly covered; and sent six men with this toward Unyanyembe, letting it be known that they had given up the original plan, and had sent their master's body back to be buried there. The body was then transferred to another package, which, when made up, could not be told from one of the ordinary traveling bales. The six messengers held on their way until fairly past all chance of detection, and then began to dispose of their load. The fagot was undone, and the sticks scattered by being thrown one by one far away into the jungle; the wrappings were got rid of in the same way. They then went on some little distance farther, and first one, then another, leaped from the path into the long grass, so as to leave no clear trace of where the party had left the path, and no trace at all that they had turned back. They made their way to their comrades again by different routes; and the natives never suspected that they had not gone on to Unyanyembe with the body of their master.

Thus at last the sea was reached; and their precious burden consigned to the care of the acting British consul, Captain Prideaux. Arrangements were quickly made for transporting the remains of Dr. Livingstone to the island of Zanzibar, whence they were taken to England and interred in Westminster Abbey.

Just one year before the day that he died, the record in his journal shows that he had finished a letter to the New York Herald, trying to enlist American zeal to stop the east-coast slave-trade. The concluding words of this letter were as follows:

"All I can add, in my loneliness, is, may Heaven's rich blessing come down on every one, American, English, or Turk, who will help to heal the open sore of the world."

It was felt that nothing could better represent the man, and these words have consequently been inscribed on the tablet at his grave in Westminster.

CHAPTER XVII.

HOW STANLEY FOUND LIVINGSTONE.

IN the year 1840, there was born, near the town of Denbigh, in Wales, a boy, who was named after his father and grandfather, John Rolland, or Rowlands, as the name is sometimes anglicized. His father died when he was but two years old; his mother married again, not many years afterward. He was for several years a pupil at the poor-house of St. Asaph, where he procured the best education that that institution of learning could afford. Leaving this, he was employed for a year as a teacher at Mold, in Flintshire; but finding this quiet life very little to his taste, he made his way to Liverpool, and there shipped as cabin-boy in a vessel bound for New Orleans. There, while looking for employment, he came into contact with a wealthy, childless merchant named Stanley. This gentleman liked the boy so well that he employed him about various parts of his extensive business, promoting him rapidly; and finally adopted him as his own son, promising to provide liberally for him.

But the youth had a restless spirit, and could not be prevailed upon to settle down and enjoy the good things of this life unless a great deal of the spice of variety could be added to them. He wandered away into the wildest parts of Arkansas; thence he made his way overland to California, making friends with many of the Indians on the way, and sitting gravely by their council fires when it so pleased him to do. At last, he returned to New Orleans. His adopted father had given him up as dead, and welcomed him as one who had come back from beyond the grave.

The trial of thus losing his adopted son, as he thought that he had, had been a severe one to Mr. Stanley; but he was not destined to suffer again from the young man's roving disposition. Shortly after his return, the elder Stanley (for of course his adopted son had assumed his name) died suddenly; investigation showed that he had left no will; and the angry relatives whom young Rollant-Stanley was to have supplanted as the heir, inherited all his fortune. The young man was turned adrift, receiving from the affectionate adopted father nothing but the name of Henry Moreland Stanley.

Very shortly afterward, the war between the States broke out; and young Stanley, being in New Orleans, and surrounded by Confederate influences, enlisted in the Southern army. After various adventures and some hair-breadth escapes, he was captured by the enemy, and held as a prisoner of war. The case was a hopeless one; there was no chance of regaining his late comrades; and the soldier promptly took the oath of allegiance to the United States and enlisted in the United States navy. It would seem that he had none of the qualities which would recommend him for promotion on board of a man-of-war where the discipline was peculiarly rigid, as it was on the iron-clad Ticonderoga; but in a few months' time we find him acting ensign.

After the war was over, his ship was sent to the Mediterranean. Here he obtained leave, and, with two of his comrades, started on a pedestrian tour of a part of Syria. They were attacked by Turkish brigands, and only with great difficulty were they able to make their way back to Constantinople, there to appeal to the American minister for assistance and redress. But for the excellent generalship of Stanley, they would never have reached the Turkish capital.

It is a little doubtful whether this adventure occurred before or after he had left the United States service; although the probabilities are that it was previous to doffing his uniform. Whatever the truth may be in the case, he left the navy about this time, and before he revisited his native place, a very few months after his Turkish adventure.

Returning to America, he was employed as special correspondent of the New York *Herald*, and given a roving commission. His duties first took him to Abyssinia, where the British were then waging war against King Theodore. It is, (or was) an article of firm belief in England that the government receives the earliest news from the seat of war, and gives out the information to the newspapers; and that newspaper correspondents are simply to fill up the outlines thus kindly furnished by the authorities. Mr. Stanley somewhat astonished the people of the War Department by providing the London newspapers with information which had not then reached the office of the Minister. It was one evidence of the energy which was derived in part from Mother Nature, and in part learned from the people of his adopted country.

The war over, he returned to the United States, and was attached, still in the capacity of special correspondent of the *Herald*, to the Indian Commission of 1867. In 1868-9, we find him in Spain, following the fortunes of the royal forces and those of the republicans, as the latter strove to dethrone Isabella II. While he was portraying the situation for the benefit of the readers of the *Herald*, he received, October 16, 1869, a dispatch from Paris. It ran thus:

"Come to Paris on important business,"

and was signed by James Gordon Bennett, Jr., the manager of the New York *Herald*. The telegram reached him at ten A. M.; he at once proceeded to make ready; his pictures and books were packed in a hurry; his laundress was not given time to finish drying his clothes; by noon he was ready, having only to say good-bye to his friends.

At three in the afternoon, that being the hour at which the first express left Madrid after the receipt of the telegram, he was on his way, arriving in Paris the following night. He went straight to the Grand Hotel, and knocked at the door of Mr. Bennett's room.

A voice bade him enter; he found Mr. Bennett in bed.

"Who are you?" was the first question.

"My name is Stanley," was the reply.

"Ah, yes, sit down; I have important business for you."

Throwing over his shoulders his robe de chambre, Mr. Bennett asked:

"Where do you think Livingstone is?"

"I really do not know, sir," rejoined the subordinate, rather taken aback (if Stanley ever was taken aback) at the suddenness of the question.

"Do you think he is alive?"

"He may be, and he may not be."

"Well, I think he is alive, and that he can be found, and I am going to send you to find him."

"What!" ejaculated Stanley; "do you really think that I can find Dr. Livingstone? Do you mean me to go to Central Africa?"

"Yes, I mean that you shall go and find him wherever you may hear that he is, and to get what news you can of him; and perhaps"—delivering himself thoughtfully and deliberately—"the old man may be in want; take enough with you to help him, should he require it. Of course you will act according to your own plans, and do what you think best—but FIND LIVINGSTONE."

The subordinate wondered at the cool order of sending one to Central Africa to search for a man whom most men believed to be dead; and asked:

James Gordon Bennett.

"Have you considered seriously the great expense you are likely to incur on account of this little journey?"

"What will it cost?" asked the chief, abruptly.

"Burton and Speke's journey to Central Africa cost between three thousand and five thousand pounds, and I fear it cannot be done under two thousand five hundred pounds."

"Well, I will tell you what you will do. Draw a thousand pounds now; and when you have gone through that, draw another thousand, and when that is spent, draw another thousand; and when you have finished that, draw another thousand, and so on; but, FIND LIVINGSTONE."

He was not to go directly to Africa; or at least not to the part where he might expect to find Livingstone. He was to go first to the inauguration of the Suez Canal; then proceed up the Nile, find out what he could about Baker's expedition under the authority of the Khedive (the celebrated Englishman was then just starting for Upper Egypt), write up a practical guide for Lower Egypt, go on to Jerusalem, visit Constantinople, the Crimea and its battle-grounds, cross the Caucasus to the Caspian Sea, write up Persepolis and Bagdad, get to India by a journey across Persia, and thence start to Zanzibar, if news of Livingstone had not been received in the meantime. Having mapped out this little program, Mr. Bennett told him that this was all, and bade him good-night.

He followed out his instructions to the letter, arriving in India in August, 1870; on October 12, he sailed from Bombay to Mauritius, the journey occupying thirty-seven days; and at last arrived at Zanzibar, January 6, 1871. Here he was well received by the United States consul, Captain Webb; and had the good fortune, as he then esteemed it, to meet with Dr. Kirk, the coadjutor of Dr. Livingstone during the Zambesi expedition.

Naturally enough, the conversation turned upon the subject of African exploration; and Mr. Stanley, whose plans had not yet been made public, asked, with apparent carelessness:

"Ah, yes, Dr. Kirk, about Livingstone—where is he, do you think, now?"

"Well, really, you know," was the answer, "that is very difficult to answer; he may be dead; there is nothing positive whereon we can base sufficient reliance. Of one thing I am sure, nobody has heard anything definite from him for over two years. I should fancy, though, that he must be alive. We are continually sending something up for him. There is a small expedition now at Bagamoyo about starting shortly. I really think the old man should come home now; he is growing old, you know, and if he died, the world would lose the benefit of his discoveries. He keeps neither notes nor journals; it is very seldom he takes observations. He simply makes a note, or dot, or something on a map, which nobody could understand but himself. Oh, yes, by all means, if he is

Zanzibar.

alive he should come home, and let a younger man take his place."

"What kind of a man is he to get along with, Doctor?" asked the deeply interested listener.

"Well, I think he is a very difficult man to deal with, generally. Personally, I have never had a quarrel with him; but I have seen him in hot water with fellows so often, and that is principally the reason, I think, that he hates to have any one with him."

"I am told that he is a very modest man; is he?" again queried the *Herald* attache, anxious not to change the subject.

"Oh, he knows the value of his own discoveries; no man better. He is not quite an angel," was the reply, with a laugh.

"Well, now," persisted Stanley, "supposing I met him in my travels—I might possibly stumble across him if he travels anywhere in the direction I am going—how would he conduct himself toward me?"

"To tell you the truth," answered Livingstone's former companion, "I do not think he would like it very well. I know if Burton, or Grant, or Baker, or any of those fellows were going after him, and he heard of their coming, Livingstone would put a hundred miles of swamp in a very short time between himself and them. I do, upon my word I do."

This was not very encouraging; and so the embryo explorer felt it; his ardor was rather damped by the interview with Livingstone's old companion; but there was no going back without a positive disobedience of orders, and that was what he had no notion of doing. Dr. Kirk, still in ignorance of Stanley's actual object, promised to afford him every assistance in his power; this, unfortunately, was *nil*.

Of course the presence of a correspondent of the New York *Herald* in Africa must have some reason assigned; and Mr. Stanley gave out that he had come to explore the Rufiji River to its source. The great American public and all the other readers of the *Herald* were supposed to be burning with curiosity to know whence the Rufiji flowed; perhaps some of them would not have been able to tell on what continent it could be found; but Mr. Stanley said nothing of this little circumstance.

Many questions now occurred to the traveler, which he had no means of answering. They were such as these: How much money is required? How many pagazis, or carriers? How many soldiers, free black men, natives of Zanzibar, or freed slaves from the interior? How much cloth? How many beads? How much wire? What kinds of cloth are required for the different tribes? He studied the volumes of

African travels at his command, chiefly Burton, Speke, and Baker; but information such as he sought was not to be found in them. Even the hints in Baker's "Ismailia" were not available, for the materials for that volume had not yet been collected; and Baker does not answer there such questions as these.

He decided it was best to hunt up an Arab merchant who had been engaged in the ivory trade, or who was fresh from the interior. Sheikh Hashid was a man of note and wealth in Zanzibar. He had himself dispatched several caravans into the interior, and was necessarily acquainted with several prominent traders who came to his house to gossip about their adventures and gains. Of all men Sheikh Hashid was the man to be consulted, and he was accordingly invited to visit Mr. Stanley at the consulate. From the venerable-looking sheikh, the new-comer elicited more information about African currency, the mode of procedure, the quantity and quality of stuffs required, than he had obtained from three months' study of books upon Central Africa; and from other Arab merchants to whom the ancient sheikh introduced him, he received valuable suggestions and hints, which enabled him at last to organize an expedition.

The reader must bear in mind that the traveler requires only that which is sufficient for travel and exploration; that a superfluity of goods or means will prove as fatal to him as poverty of supplies. Mr. Stanley's informants gave him to understand that for one hundred men, 10 doti, or forty yards of cloth *per diem*, would suffice for food. The proper course to pursue, he found, would be to purchase 2,000 doti of American sheeting, 1,000 doti of Kaniki, and 650 doti of the colored cloths, such as Barsati, a great favorite in Unyamwezi, Sohari, taken in Ugogo, etc., etc. These were deemed amply sufficient for the subsistence of one hundred men for twelve months. Two years at this rate would require 16,000 yards of American sheeting, 8,000 yards of Kaniki, and 5,200 yards of colored cloths. Second in importance to the amount of cloth required was the quantity and quality of the beads necessary. Beads, he was told, took the place of cloth currency among some tribes of the interior. One tribe preferred white to black beads, brown to yellow, red to green, green to white, and so on. Such being the case, he was obliged to study closely, and calculate the probable stay of the expedition in the several countries, so as to be sure to provide a sufficiency of each kind, and guard against any great overplus,

STANLEY AND HIS FAITHFUL NATIVES.

After the beads, came the wire question. He discovered, after considerable trouble, that Nos. 5 and 6—almost of the thickness of telegraph wire—were considered the best numbers for trading purposes. While beads stand for copper coins in Africa, cloth measures for silver; wire is reckoned as gold in the countries beyond the Tanganyika. Ten frasilah, or 350 lbs. of brass wire, his Arab adviser thought, would be ample.

Having purchased the cloth, the beads and the wire, it was with no little pride that he surveyed the comely bales and packages lying piled up, row above row, in Capt. Webb's capacious store-room. Yet his work was not ended; it was but beginning. There were provisions, cooking-utensils, boats, rope, twine, tents, donkeys, saddles, bagging, canvas, tar, needles, tools, ammunition, guns, equipments, hatchets, medicines, bedding, presents for chiefs—in short, a thousand things not yet purchased. The ordeal of chaffering and haggling with Banyans, Hindis, Arabs, and half-castes was most trying. For instance, he purchased twenty-two donkeys at Zanzibar. Forty and fifty dollars were asked, which he had to reduce to fifteen and twenty dollars by an infinite amount of argument worthy (as he thought) of a better cause.

Two white men, Farquhar and Shaw, were the first engaged. The explorer then engaged upon enlisting, arming and equipping a faithful escort of twenty men for the road. The chief dragoman of the American Consulate informed him that he knew where several of Speke's Faithfuls were to be found. The idea had struck him before, that if he could obtain the services of a few men acquainted with the ways of white men, and who could induce other good men to join the expedition, it would be a most fortunate thing. More especially had he thought of Bombay, considered to be the "faithfulest" of the Faithfuls.

With the aid of the dragoman, he secured in a few hours the services of five of the Faithfuls, Ulimengo, Baruti, Ambari, Mabruki, and Uledi. When he asked them if they were willing to join another white man's expedition to Ujiji, they replied very readily that they were willing to join any brother of "Speke's." Dr. Kirk, who was present, told them that though Mr. Stanley was no brother of Speke's, he spoke his language. This distinction mattered but little to them; and he heard them, with great delight, declare their readiness to go anywhere with him, or do anything he wished.

Bombay, his captain of escort, succeeded in getting eighteen more freemen to volunteer as "askari" (soldiers), men who he knew would not desert, and for whom he declared himself responsible. They were an exceedingly fine-looking body of men, far more intelligent in appearance than their employer had ever believed African barbarians could be. Their wages were set down at $36 each man per annum, or $3 each per month. Each soldier was provided with a flint-lock musket, powder-horn, bullet-pouch, knife, and hatchet, besides enough powder and ball for two hundred rounds.

Bombay, in consideration of his rank, was engaged at $80 a year, half that sum in advance; a good muzzle-loading rifle, besides a pistol, knife and hatchet were given to him; while the five other Faithfuls were engaged at $40 a year, with proper equipments as soldiers.

In order that he might not be delayed if the caprice of a native chief refused him the means of crossing a river or lake, Stanley determined to carry his own boats. He accordingly procured one large boat, capable of carrying twenty persons, and a smaller one, which would hold six men, with suitable stores. He did not intend to carry the boats whole or bodily, but to strip them of their boards, and carry the timbers and thwarts only. As a substitute for the boards, he proposed to cover each boat with a double canvass skin well tarred.

An insuperable obstacle to rapid transit in Africa is the want of carriers; and as speed was the main object of the expedition under his command, his duty was to lessen this difficulty as much as possible. His carriers could only be engaged after arriving at Bagamoyo, on the main land. He had over twenty good donkeys ready, and he thought a cart adapted for the goat-paths of Africa might prove an advantage. Accordingly, he had one constructed, eighteen inches wide and five feet long, supplied with two fore-wheels of a light American wagon, more for the purpose of conveying the narrow ammunition-boxes. He estimated that if a donkey could carry to Unyanyembe a load of four frasilahs, or one hundred and forty pounds, he ought to be able to draw eight frasilahs on such a cart, which would be equal to the carrying capacities of four stout pagazis.

When his purchases were completed, and he beheld them piled up, tier after tier, and row upon row, he was rather abashed at his own temerity. Here were nearly six tons of material; and as a man's maximum load does not exceed seventy pounds, his eleven thousand pounds would require about one hundred and sixty men.

Shortly before their departure from Zanzibar, Mr. Stanley was presented to the sultan, who gave him letters to his officers at Bagamoyo and Kaole, and a general introductory letter to all Arab merchants whom he might meet on the road; and concluded his remarks to the traveler with the expressed hope that, on whatever mission he was bound, he would be perfectly successful.

By the fourth of February, all his preparations were completed; and on the fifth, the New York *Herald* expedition sailed from Zanzibar to the mainland. This space has been devoted to the fitting out of the expedition, because only a fairly detailed account can give any idea of the difficulties which an experienced traveler, of more than ordinary intelligence and energy (to put it mildly) encounters in organizing an expedition to Central Africa, even with unlimited means at his command.

There were two good and sufficient reasons why Mr. Stanley was to devote all his energy to leading the expedition as quickly as possible from Bagamoyo. First he wished to reach Ujiji before the news reached Livingstone that any one was in search of him; for his impression of the great missionary was that he was a man who would try to put as much distance as possible between them, rather than make an effort to shorten it, and he would have his long journey for nothing. Second, the Masika, or rainy season, would soon be upon them, which, if it caught him at Bagamoyo, would prevent his departure until it was over, which meant a delay of forty days.

On the 25th of March, exactly seventy-three days after his arrival at Zanzibar, Stanley's fifth caravan, led by himself, left the town of Bagamoyo for the first journey westward. The other caravans had preceded him, some by as much as a month. They left Bagamoyo, the attraction of all the curious, with much eclat; and defiled up a narrow lane shaded almost to twilight by the dense umbrage of two parallel rows of mimosas. They were all in the highest spirits. The first camp, Shamba Gonera, they arrived at in one hour and thirty minutes, equal to three and one-fourth miles. The first or "little journey," was performed very well, "considering," as the Irishman says. The boy Selim upset the cart not more than three times; Zaidi, the soldier, only once let his donkey, which carried his master's box of ammunition and one bag of his clothes, lie in a puddle of black water. The clothes had to be re-washed; the ammunition-box, thanks to its owner's prevision, was waterproof. Kamna perhaps knew the art of donkey-driving, but

THE EXPLORING EXPEDITION EN ROUTE.

had sung himself into oblivion of the difficulties with which an animal of the pure asinine breed has to contend, such as not knowing the road, and inability to resist the temptation of straying into a manioc-field; and the donkey, misunderstanding the direction in which he was required to go, ran off at full speed along an opposite road, until his pack got unbalanced, and he was fain to come to the earth. But these incidents were trivial, of no importance, and natural to the first "little journey" in Africa.

The road was a mere foot-path, and led over a soil which, though sandy, was of surprising fertility, producing grain and vegetables a hundred fold, the sowing and planting of which was done in the most unskilful manner. In their fields, at heedless labor, were men and women in the scantiest costumes, compared with which Adam and Eve, in their fig-leaf apparel, must have been modesty indeed.

They were detained for three days at this first stopping-place; but shortly after leaving it reached the turbid Kingani, famous for its hippopotami. They began to thread the jungle along its right bank until they were halted point-blank by a narrow sluice having an immeasurable depth of black mud. The difficulty presented by this was very grave, although its breadth was barely eight feet; the donkeys, and least of all the horses, could not be made to traverse two poles like the biped carriers, neither could they be driven into the sluice, where they would quickly founder. The only available way of crossing it in safety was by means of a bridge, to endure in this conservative land for generations as the handiwork of the Wasungu. So they set to work, there being no help for it, with American axes, to build a bridgo. It was composed of six stout trees thrown across; over these were laid crosswise fifteen pack saddles, these covered again with a thick layer of grass. All the animals crossed it safely; and then for the third time that morning the process of wading was performed.

A half-mile to the north, and they reached the ferry; while the work of unloading the donkeys was going forward, Stanley sat down on a condemned canoe to amuse himself with the hippopotami by peppering their thick skulls with his No. 12 smooth-bore. One old fellow, with the look of a sage, was tapped close to the right ear by one of his smaller bullets; instead of submerging himself as others had done, he coolly turned round his head as if to ask:

"Why this waste of valuable cartridges on us?"

The response to this mute inquiry of his sageship was an

ounce and a quarter bullet from the smoothbore, which made him bellow with pain, and in a few moments he rose again, tumbling in his death agonies. As his groans were so piteous, the sportsman refrained from a useless sacrifice of life, and left the amphibious horde in peace.

Mr. Stanley was anxious to try what a good watch-dog might do to protect him from the unmannerly Wagogo, of whom he had heard much from the Arabs; and had accordingly brought one with him. He found it of very great use, in keeping out of his tent these ruffians of the wilderness. Shortly after crossing the above-named river, the fifth caravan became the fourth, by reason of delays which sickness imposed upon that which had started the earlier.

They pushed on toward Kingaru, the rainy season having now begun, and made travel very difficult. The natives poured into camp from the villages in the woods with their vendibles. Foremost among these, as in duty bound, came the chief, bearing three measures of matama and a half-measure of rice, of which he begged, with paternal smiles, the traveler's acceptance. But under the smiling mask, bleared eyes, and wrinkled front of him was visible the soul of trickery, which was of the cunningest kind. Responding under the same mask adopted by this knavish elder, Stanley said:

"The chief of Kingaru has called me a rich sultan. If I am a rich sultan why comes not the chief with a rich present to me that he might get a rich return?"

Said he, with another leer of his wrinkled visage:

"Kingaru is poor, there is no matama in the village."

To this appeal, Mr. Stanley replied that since there was no matama in the village, he would pay the chief half a shukka, or a yard of cloth, which would be exactly equivalent to his present; that if the chief preferred to call his small basketful a present, the white man would be content to call his yard of cloth a present. With this logic the chief had to be satisfied.

One of the two horses brought from Zanzibar died the next day, and by the orders of the leader, was buried, in order that the decaying flesh might not affect the health of the people of Kingaru. This consideration, however, was but poorly repaid; for the chief demanded that the white man should pay a fine of two doti of Merikani for his presumption in burying the horse within his domain. To this Stanley replied by demanding how many soldiers he had. The question was repeated before the answer was given that he had none, only a few young men. To this the white man retorted:

"Oh, I thought you might have a thousand men with you, by your going to fine a strong white man, who has plenty of guns and soldiers, two doti for burying a dead horse."

The chief was staggered but not convinced; whereupon Stanley, after explaining the sanitary reasons for burying the animal, generously offered to repair his error at once:

"This minute my soldiers shall dig him out again, and cover up the soil as it was before; and the horse shall be left where he died. Ho! Bombay, take soldiers with jembes to dig my horse out of the ground, drag him to where he died, and make everything ready for a march to-morrow morning."

Kingaru, his voice considerably higher, and his head moving to and fro with emotion, cries out:

"No, no, master! Let not the white man get angry. The horse is dead, and now lies buried; let him remain so, since he is already there; and let us be friends again."

The second horse died that night. Other misfortunes came. Out of a force of twenty-five men, one deserted, and ten were on the sick-list. They left Kingaru April 6; but the long stay there had completely demoralized soldiers and pagazis. Only a few of them had strength to reach Imbiki before night; the others, attending the laden donkeys, put in an appearance next morning, in a lamentable state of mind and body.

At Muhalleh, which they reached a little after the middle of April, they met Selim bin Bashid, bound eastward, with a huge caravan carrying three hundred ivory tusks. This good Arab, besides welcoming the newcomer with a present of rice, gave him news of Livingstone. He had met the old traveler at Ujiji, had lived in the next hut to him for three weeks, described him as looking old, with long gray mustaches and beard, just recovered from severe illness, looking very wan; when fully recovered Livingstone intended to visit a country called Manyuema by way of Marungu.

We need not recount the many incidents of the journey for some time to come; choice must be made between them. The first of May found them struggling through the mire and water of the Makata with a caravan bodily sick, from the exertion and fatigue of crossing so many rivers and wading through marshes. For thirty miles from their camp was the Makata plain, an extensive swamp. The water was on an average a foot in depth; in some places they plunged into holes three, four, and even five feet deep. Plash, splash, plash, splash, were the only sounds they heard from the commencement of the march until they found the bomas occupy-

STANLEY CROSSING THE GREAT MAKATA SWAMP.

ing the only dry spots along the line of march. This kind of work continued for two days, until they came in sight of the Rudewa River, another powerful stream with banks brimful of rushing rainwater. The acme of discomfort and vexation was realized on the five-mile march from the Rudewa branch. After three hours of splashing through four feet of water, they reached dry land, and had traversed the swamp of Makata. But not without the swamp and its horrors having left a durable impression upon our minds; no one was disposed to forget its fatigues, nor the nausea of travel which it almost engendered. Subsequently, they had to remember its passage still more vividly, and to regret that they had undertaken the journey during the Masika season. When the animals died from this date by twos and threes, almost every day, until but five sickly, worn-out beasts remained; when the Wanguana, soldiers and pagazis sickened of diseases innumerable; and when Stanley himself was brought to the very brink of the grave by illness.

But illness was not the only danger with which he had to contend. Of the two white men hired at Zanzibar, Farquhar had shown himself to be inexcusably extravagant in the expenditure of the stores committed to his care. He was continually crying out like a sick baby for half a dozen people to wait upon him, and if they did not happen to understand the English language in which he addressed them, he poured out a volley of the most profane abuse that ever offended the ears of a Christian gentleman. The soldiers were in such dread of his insane violence that they feared to go near him. He was ill with a disease of which Stanley could secure no definite description of the symptoms; and by his weight and see-sawing method of riding killed every donkey that he rode.

But Shaw was even worse to deal with than Farquhar; and since he had been with the caravan which Stanley led in person, the leader's patience, so far as he was concerned, was about exhausted, when on May 15, the crisis came. It was at breakfast time; the meal had just been served, and Stanley had asked Shaw to carve.

"What dog's meat is this?" he asked, in the most insolent way imaginable.

"What do you mean?" asked Stanley.

Then ensued a volley of abuse, tempered with profanity; to which the indignant chief replied by a recapitulation of what they had brought upon him; closing with an expostulation at being sworn at at his own table, and reminding Shaw that he was his (Stanley's) servant. An oath was the rejoinder; but before Mr. Shaw could say more, he had measured his length on the ground.

He thereupon demanded his discharge; to which Stanley most willingly agreed; giving orders at once that Shaw's tent should be struck, and that he and his baggage should be escorted two hundred yards outside the camp. After breakfast was over, Stanley explained to Farquhar how necessary it was for him to be able to proceed; that as Farquhar was sick, and would probably be unable to march for a time, it would be better that he should be left in some quiet place, under the care of a good chief, who would, for a consideration, look after him until he got well. To this Farquhar had agreed.

Stanley had barely finished speaking before Bombay came to the door and informed him that Mr. Shaw would like to speak to him. He went out to the gate of the camp, and there met Shaw, looking extremely penitent and ashamed. He commenced to ask pardon, and began imploring Stanley to take him back again; promising that he should never find fault with him again. Stanley held out his hand to him, saying:

"Don't mention it, my dear fellow. Quarrels occur in the best of families. Since you apologize, there is an end of it."

That night as Stanley was falling asleep, he heard a shot, and a bullet tore through his tent, a few inches above his body. He snatched his revolvers and rushed out of his tent, and asked the men about the watchfires, "Who shot?" They had all jumped up, rather startled at the sudden report.

"Who fired that gun?"

"Bana Mdogo," said one, (the little master, *i. e.*, Shaw).

Stanley lit a candle, and walked with it to Shaw's tent.

"Shaw, did you fire?"

There was no answer. He seemed to be asleep, he was breathing so hard.

"Shaw! Shaw! did you fire that shot?"

"Eh—eh?" said he, suddenly awaking—"me?—me fire? I have been asleep."

Stanley's eye caught sight of his gun lying near him. He seized it, felt it, put his little finger down the barrel. The gun was warm, his finger was black from the burnt gunpowder.

"What is this?" he asked, holding his finger up; "the gun is warm. The men tell me you fired."

"Ah, yes," replied Shaw; "I remember it. I dreamed I saw a thief pass my door, and I fired. Ah—yes—I forgot. I did fire. Why, what is the matter?"

"Oh, nothing," said Stanley. "But I would advise you in future, in order to avoid all suspicion, not to fire into my tent, or at least so near me. I might get hurt, you know, in which case ugly reports would get about, and this perhaps would be disagreeable, as you are probably aware. Good night."

But what a clumsy way to murder! Surely, had he done so, Stanley's own men would have punished him as the crime deserved. A thousand better opportunities than this would be presented in a month's march. Stanley could only account for it by supposing he was momentarily insane.

The next thing which must be done was to provide a home for Farquhar until he should be able to return to the coast. Leucole, the chief of the village, with whom Stanley made arrangements for Farquhar's protection and comfort, suggested that he should appoint some man in his employ to wait on him, and interpret his wishes to Leucole's people. Making inquiry, Stanley was assured by Bombay that any soldier whom he might appoint for this purpose would obey him until he was gone, and then run away. Despite Bombay's assertion, the leader inquired of each man personally whether he would be willing to stay behind, and wait on the sick Musungu (white man). From each man he received an answer in the negative; they were afraid of him, he damned them so; and Ulimengo mimicked him so faithfully, yet so ludicrously, that it was almost impossible to abstain from laughing. As, however, the sick man absolutely needed some one to attend him, Stanley was compelled to use his authority; and Jako, who could speak English, was, despite his protestations and prayers, appointed. Six months provisions of white beads, besides a present for Leucole, a carbine, ammunition and tea were set aside for Farquhar's wants.

This took place in the neighborhood of the Mpwapwa range of mountains, a country memorable to the traveler by reason of its plentiful and excellent milk, and its equally plentiful earwigs, for which he did not feel quite so grateful as for the milk. Second to the earwigs in importance and numbers he found the white ants, whose powers of destructiveness were simply awful. Mats, cloth, portmanteaus, clothes, in short, every article he possessed, seemed to be on the verge of destruction; and as he witnessed their voracity, he felt anxious lest his tent should be devoured while he slept.

Marenga Mkali, over thirty miles across, was at last before them. This distance had to be traversed within thirty-six hours, so that the fatigue of the ordinary march would be more than doubled by this. From Chunyo to Ugogo not one drop of water was to be found. As a large caravan, say over two hundred souls, seldom travels over one and three-quarter miles an hour, a march of thirty miles would require seventeen hours of endurance, without water and with but little rest. East Africa generally possessing unlimited quantities of water, caravans have not been compelled, for lack of that element, to have recourse to the mushok of India and the khirbeh of Egypt. Being able to cross the waterless districts by a couple of long marches, they content themselves at the time with a small gourdful, and with keeping their imaginations dwelling upon the copious quantities they will drink upon arriving at the watering-place.

The march through this waterless district was most monotonous, and a dangerous fever attacked Stanley, which seemed to eat into his very vitals. The wonders of Africa that bodied themselves forth in the shape of flocks of zebras, giraffes, elands, or antelopes, galloping over the jungleless plain, had no charm for him; nor could they serve to draw his attention from the severe fit of illness which depressed him. Toward the end of the first march he was not able to sit upon the donkey's back; nor would it do, when, but a third of the way across the wilderness, to halt until the next day; soldiers were therefore detailed to carry him in a hammock, and when the terekeza, or afternoon march, was performed, he lay in a lethargic state, unconscious of all things. With the night passed the fever, and at three o'clock in the morning, when the march was resumed, he was booted and spurred, and the recognized mtongi of his caravan once more. At eight A. M. they had performed the thirty-two miles. The wilderness of Marenga Mkali had been passed, and they had entered Ugogo.

From their entrance into Ugogo until they quitted it, they were assailed by the most shameless demands from the chiefs for presents. If a sheep was "given" the traveler, twice its value in cloth was demanded. This was in consequence of the subservience of the Arabs, who had always been afraid to resist such extortions. But Stanley was of different mettle; and by dint of resolution, and displaying his Winchesters to good advantage, he succeeded in getting provisions at not much more than the price which should have been asked for them.

June 9, they arrived at the limits of Ugogo; and the 13th brought them to the last village of Magunda Mkali. Here Stanley, as a reward to his faithful soldiers and pagazis, purchased a bullock and had it slaughtered, and gave each a khete of red beads to indulge his appetite for whatever little luxury the country afforded. On the morning of the 17th, they reached Eastern Tura, the frontier village of Unyamwezi. Five

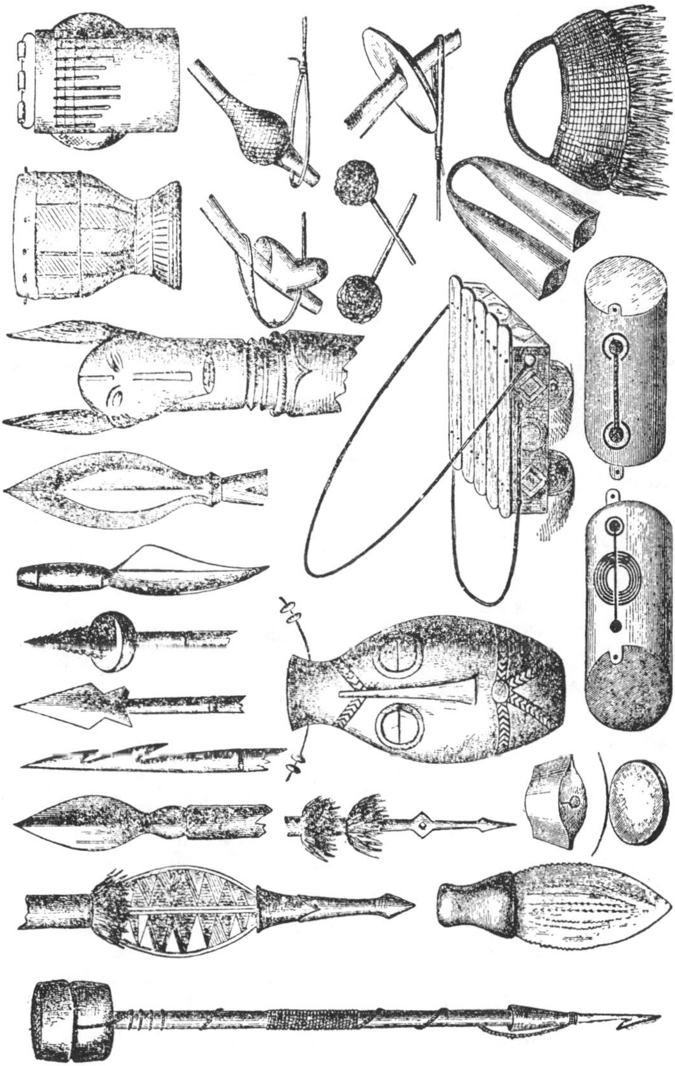

African Musical Instruments, Weapons, Etc.

days later, they were on the borders of Unyanyembe. Here Stanley again slaughtered a bullock for the benefit of the men who had made such good time. No one slept much that night.

Long before dawn the fires were lit, and great steaks were broiling, that their stomachs might rejoice before parting with the Musungu, whose bounty they had so often tasted. Six rounds of powder were served to each soldier and pagazi who owned a gun, to fire away when they should be near the Arab houses. The meanest pagazi had his best cloth about his loins, and some were exceedingly gorgeous in Ulyah "Combeesa Poonga" and crimson "Jawah," the glossy "Rehani," and the neat "Dabwani." The soldiers were mustered in new tarbooshes, and the long white shirts of the Mrima and the island. For this was the great and happy day which had been on their tongues ever since quitting the coast, for which they had made those noted marches latterly—one hundred and seventy-eight and a half miles in sixteen days, including pauses—something over eleven miles a day!

The signal sounded, and the caravan was joyfully off with banners flying, and trumpets and horns blaring. A short two hours and a half's march brought them within sight of Kwikuru, which is about two miles south of Tabora, the main Arab town; on the outside of which they saw a long line of men in clean shirts, whereat they opened their charged batteries, and fired a volley of small arms such as Kwikuru seldom heard before. The pagazis closed up and adopted the swagger of veterans; the soldiers blazed away uninterruptedly; while Stanley, seeing that the Arabs were advancing toward him, left the ranks, and held out his hand, which was immediately grasped by Sheikh Sayd bin Salim, and then by about two dozen people. And thus their entree into Unyanyembe was effected.

The traveler received a noiseless ovation as he walked by the side of the governor, toward his tembe in Kwikuru, or the capital. The Wanyamwezi pagazis were out by hundreds, the warriors of Mkasiwa, the sultan, hovered around their chief; the children—naked dusky cherubs—were seen between the legs of their parents, even infants a few months old slung over their mothers' backs, all paid the tribute due to his color, with one grand concentrated stare.

As he approached the tembe of Sayd bin Salim, Sheikh bin Nasib and other great Arabs joined them. Before the great door of the tembe the men had stacked the bales, and piled the boxes, and were using their tongues at a furious rate, relating to the chiefs and soldiers of the first, second and fourth caravans the many events which had befallen them, and which seemed to them the only things worth relating. It must be borne in mind that the third caravan, under the leadership of Farquhar, had long since been consolidated with that led by Stanley in person.

Outside of their own limited circles the men evidently cared for nothing. Then the several chiefs of the other caravans had in turn to relate their experiences of the road; and the noise of tongues was loud and furious. But as Stanley and the sheikhs approached, all this loud-sounding gabble ceased, and his caravan chiefs and guides rushed to him to hail him as "master," and to salute him as their friend. One fellow, faithful Baruti, threw himself at his feet; the others fired their guns and acted like madmen suddenly become frenzied; and a general cry of welcome was heard on all sides.

"Walk in, master; this is your house now; here are your men's quarters; here you will receive the great Arabs; here is the cook-house; here is the store-house; here is the prison for the refractory; here are your white man's apartments; and these are your own; here is the bed-room, here is the gun-room, bath-room, etc.;" so spoke Sheikh Sayd as he showed the several places.

Bombay was ordered to unlock the strong store-room, to pile the bales in regular tiers, the beads in rows one above another, and the wire in a separate place. The boats, canvas, etc., were to be placed high above the reach of white ants, and the boxes of ammunition and the powder-kegs were to be stored in the gun-room, out of the reach of danger. Then a bale of cloth was opened, and each carrier was rewarded according to his merits, that each of them might proceed home to his friends and neighbors, and tell them how much better the white man had behaved than the Arabs.

The reports of the leaders of the first, second and fourth caravans were then received, their separate stores inspected, and the details and events of their marches heard. Each leader was then and there rewarded with a handsome cloth, and five doti of Merikani. The number of Stanley's followers was now reduced to twenty-five.

But the road to Ujiji was closed by Mirambo, chief of Uyoweh; what was to be done? Stanley found himself in the midst of preparations for war on the part of the Arabs of Unyanyembe.

This Mirambo of Uyoweh, it seems, for the past few years had been in a state of chronic discontent with the policies of the neighboring chiefs. Formerly a pagazi for an Arab, he had now assumed regal power, with the usual knack of unconscion-

A WEDDING DANCE IN AFRICA.

able rascals who care not by what means they step into power. When the chief of Uyoweh died, Mirambo, who was head of a gang of robbers infesting the forests of Wilyankuru, suddenly entered Uyoweh, and constituted himself lord paramount by force. Some feats of enterprise, which he performed to the enrichment of all those who recognized his authority, established him firmly in his position. This was but a beginning; he carried war through Ugara to Ukonongo, through Usagozi to the borders of Uvinza, and after destroying the population over three degrees of latitude, he conceived a grievance against Mkasiwa, and against the Arabs, because they would not sustain him in his ambitious projects against their ally and friend with whom they were living in peace.

The first outrage which this audacious man committed against the Arabs was the halting of an Ujiji-bound caravan, and the demand for five kegs of gunpowder, five guns, and five bales of cloth. This extraordinary demand, after expending more than a day in fierce controversy, was paid; but the Arabs, if they were surprised at the exorbitant blackmail demanded of them, were more than ever surprised when told to return the way that they came; and that no Arab caravan should pass to Ujiji except over his dead body.

On the return of the unfortunate Arabs to Unyanyembe, they reported the facts to Sheikh Sayd bin Salim, the chief of the Arab colony. This old man being averse to war, of course tried every means to induce Mirambo as of old to be satisfied with presents, but Mirambo this time was obdurate, and sternly determined on war unless the Arabs aided him in the warfare he was about to wage against old Mkasiwa, sultan of the Wanyamwezi of Unyanyembe.

Stanley was invited to attend the council of war, which was held a few days after his arrival in Unyanyembe, the dispute with Mirambo having begun but a short time before he reached that place. Two speeches delivered on that occasion have been preserved, and shall here be reproduced. The first speaker was Khamis bin Abdullah, a bold and brave man, ever ready to stand up for the privileges of the Arabs, and their right to pass through any country for legitimate trade. He was the man, who, in Speke's journal, is reported to have shot Maula, an old chief who sided with Manwa Sera during the wars of 1860.

"This is the status of affairs: Mirambo says that for years he has been engaged in war against the neighboring Washensi and has come out of it victorious; he says that this is a great year with him; that he is going to fight the Arabs and the Wanyamwezi of Unyanyembe, and that he shall not stop until every Arab is driven from Unyanyembe, and he rules over this country in place of Mkasiwa. Children of Oman, shall it be so? Speak, Salim, son of Sayf, shall we go to meet this Mshensi [pagan] or shall we return to our island?"

A murmur of approbation followed the speech of Khamis bin Abdullah, the majority of those present being young men eager to punish the audacious Mirambo. Salim, the son of Sayf, an old patriarch, slow of speech, tried to appease the passions of the young men; but Khamis' bold words had made too deep an impression on their minds. Then Soud spoke:

"My father used to tell me that he remembered the days when Arabs could go through the country from Bagamoyo to Ujiji, and from Kilwa to Lunda, and from Usenda to Uganda armed with canes. Those days are gone by. We have stood the insolence of the Wagogo long enough. Swaruru of Usui just takes from us whatever he wants; and now, here is Mirambo, who says, after taking more than five bales of cloth as tribute from one man, that no Arab caravan shall go to Ujiji, but over his body. Are we prepared to give up the ivory of Ujiji, of Urundi, of Karagwah, of Uganda, because of this one man? I say war—war until we have got his beard under our feet—war until the whole of Uyoweh and Wilyankuru is destroyed—war until we can again travel through any part of the country with only our walking-canes in our hands!"

The universal assent that followed Soud's speech showed that there was to be a war. Stanley thought of Livingstone—what if he were marching to Unyanyembe directly through the war country?

Having found from the Arabs that they intended to finish the war quickly—at most within fifteen days, as Uyoweh was only four days' march distant—the traveler volunteered to accompany them, take his loaded caravan with him as far as Mfuto, and there leave it in charge of a few guards, and with the rest march on with the Arab army. His hope was, that it might be possible, after the defeat of Mirambo, and his forest banditti, the Ruga-Ruga, to take his expedition direct to Ujiji by the road now closed. The Arabs were sanguine of victory; and the white man partook of their enthusiasm.

In Unyanyembe Stanley found the Livingstone caravan, which had been ready at Bagamoyo before his own was prepared to start. He found that the chief of the caravan had in his possession a packet of letters addressed to Dr. Livingstone, which had been sealed up at Zanzibar November 1, 1870.

The fever attacked the expedition in Unyanyembe while the Arabs were making their warlike preparations; first, the leader was prostrated, and was unconscious for a week. On the tenth day after his attack, Shaw was taken down; next, Selim, the Christian Arab boy who acted as interpreter, was attacked; but by July 28, all were recovered; and on the next morning Stanley had fifty men loaded with bales, beads and wire for Ujiji. The fourth day after leaving Unyanyembe, they reached Mfuto, the rendezvous of the Arab army. A halt was ordered for the next day, in order to make themselves strong by eating the beeves, which they freely slaughtered.

This army numbered something like two thousand five hundred men; of whom, however, twelve hundred and fifty-five were slaves, and three hundred consisted of independent chiefs and their followers. Of these men fifteen hundred were armed with guns, flint-lock muskets, German and French double-barrels, some English Enfields, and American Springfields. Besides these muskets, they were mostly armed with spears and long knives, for the purpose of decapitating and inflicting vengeful gashes in the dead bodies. Powder and ball were plentiful; some men were served a hundred rounds each; Stanley's people received each man sixty rounds.

The date of their leaving Mfuto for battle was August 3. All the searcher's goods were stored in Mfuto, ready for the march to Ujiji, should they be victorious over the African chief, but at least for safety, whatever befell them.

Before they left Umanda, six hours distant from Mfuto, the army was thoroughly aroused by a speech from an Arab orator. A loud, wild shout followed his bold harangue, the gates of the village were thrown open, and blue, red, and white-robed soldiers were bounding upward like so many gymnasts, firing their guns incessantly, in order to encourage themselves with noise, or to strike terror among those who awaited them within the strong enclosure of Zimbizo. As Zimbizo was distant only five hours from Umanda, at 11 A. M. they came in view of it. They halted on the verge of a cultivated area surrounding it and its neighbors, within the shadow of the forest. Strict orders had been given by the several chiefs that their respective commands were not to fire, until they were within shooting distance of the boma.

Khamis bin Abdullah crept through the forest to the west of the village. The Wanyamwezi took their position before the

THE ATTACK ON ZIMBIZO.

main gateway, aided by the forces of Soud, the son of Sayd on the right, and the son of Habib on the left; Abdullah, Mussoud, Stanley and others made ready to attack the eastern gates, which arrangement effectually shut them in, with the exception of the northern side.

Suddenly, a volley opened upon them, as they emerged from the forest along the Unyanyembe road, in the direction they had been anticipating the sight of an enemy, and immediately the attacking forces began their firing in most splendid style. There were some ludicrous scenes of men pretending to fire, then jumping off to one side, then forward, then backward, with the agility of hopping frogs, but the battle was none the less in earnest. Then there was a lull in the firing, and the assailants were rushing into the village from the west, the south, the north, through the gates and over the tall palings that surrounded the village, like so many merry Andrews; and the poor villagers were flying from the enclosure toward the mountains, through the northern gate, pursued by the fleetest runners of the attacking force, and pelted in the back by bullets from breech-loaders and shot-guns.

The village was strongly defended, and not more than twenty dead bodies were found in it, the strong, thick wooden paling having afforded excellent protection against the bullets.

From Zimbizo, after having left a sufficient force to defend it, they sallied out, and in an hour had cleared the neighborhood of the enemy, having captured two other villages, which they committed to the flames, after gutting them of all valuables. A few tusks of ivory, and about fifty slaves, besides an abundance of grain, composed the "loot" which fell to the portion of the Arabs.

On the next day, a detachment of Arabs and slaves, seven hundred strong, scoured the surrounding country, and carried fire and devastation up to the boma of Wilyankuru. On the succeeding day, the 6th, Soud bin Sayd and about twenty other young Arabs led a force of five hundred men against Wilyankuru itself, where it was supposed that Mirambo was living. Another party went out toward the low wooded hills, a short distance north of Zimbizo, near which place they surprised a youthful forest thief asleep, whose head they stretched backward, and cut it off as though he were a goat or a sheep. Another party sallied out southward, and defeated a party of Mirambo's "bushwhackers," news of which reached the main body at noon.

In the morning, Stanley had gone to Sayd bin Salim's tembe, to represent to him how necessary it was to burn the long grass in the forest of Zimbizo, lest it might hide any of the enemy; but soon afterward, he had been struck down with another attack of intermittent fever, and was obliged to turn in and cover himself with blankets to produce perspiration; but not, however, until he had ordered Bombay and Shaw not to permit any of his men to leave the camp. He was told soon afterward by Selim that more than one-half had gone to the attack on Wilyankuru, with Soud bin Sayd.

About six P. M. the entire camp of Zimbizo was electrified with the news that all the Arabs who had accompanied Soud bin Sayd had been killed; and that more than one-half of his party had been slain. Some of Stanley's men had returned, and from them he learned that five of their number had been killed. He learned also that they had succeeded in capturing Wilyankuru in a very short time; that Mirambo and his son were there; that as they succeeded in effecting an entrance, Mirambo had collected his men, and after leaving the village, had formed an ambush in the grass, on each side of the road, between Wilyankuru and Zimbizo, and that as the attacking party was returning home laden with over a hundred tusks of ivory, and sixty bales of cloth, and two or three hundred slaves, Mirambo's men suddenly rose up on both sides of them, and stabbed them with their spears. The brave Soud had fired his double-barreled gun and killed two men, and was in the act of loading again when a spear was launched, which penetrated through and through him; all the other Arabs shared the same fate. This sudden attack from an enemy they believed to be conquered, so demoralized the party that, dropping their spoil, each man took to his heels, and after making a wide detour through the woods, returned to Zimbizo to repeat the dolorous tale.

The effect of this defeat is indescribable. It was impossible to sleep, from the shrieks of the women whose husbands had fallen. All night they howled their lamentations, and sometimes might be heard the groans of the wounded who had contrived to crawl through the grass unperceived by the enemy. Fugitives were continually coming in through the night, but none of Stanley's men who were reported to be dead were ever heard of again.

The 7th was a day of distrust, sorrow, and retreat; the Arabs accused one another for urging war without expending all peaceful means first. There were stormy councils of war held, wherein some proposed to return at once to Unyanyembe, and keep within their own houses; and Khamis bin Abdullah raved like an insulted monarch against the abject cowardice of his compatriots. These stormy meetings and propositions to retreat were soon known throughout the camp, and assisted more than anything else to demoralize completely the combined forces of Wanyamwezi and slaves. Stanley sent Bombay to Sayd bin Salim to advise him not to think of retreat, as it would only be inviting Mirambo to carry the war to Unyanyembe.

After dispatching Bombay with this message, he fell asleep; but about half-past one was awakened by Selim saying:

"Master, get up, they are all running away, and Khamis bin Abdullah himself is going."

With the aid of Selim, the sick man dressed himself and staggered toward the door. His first sight was of Thani bin Abdullah being dragged away, who, when he caught sight of Stanley, shouted out:

"Bana—quick—Mirambo is coming!"

He was then turning to run, and putting on his jacket, with his eyes almost starting out of their sockets with terror. Khamis bin Abdullah was also about departing, he being the last Arab to leave. Two of Stanley's men were following him; these Selim was ordered to force back with a revolver. Shaw was saddling his own donkey with his master's saddle, preparatory to giving him the slip and leaving him in the lurch to the tender mercies of Mirambo. There were only Bombay, Mabruki Speke, Chanda (who was coolly eating his dinner), Mabruki Unyanyembe, Mtamani, Juma, and Sarmean—only seven out of fifty. All the others had deserted, and were by this time far away, except Uledi and Zaidi, whom Selim brought back at the point of a loaded revolver. Selim was then told to saddle his master's donkey and Bombay to assist Shaw to saddle his own. In a few moments they were on the road, the men ever looking back for the coming enemy; they belabored the donkeys to some purpose, for they went at a hard trot, which gave the sick man intense pain. He would gladly have lain down to die, but life was sweet, and he had not yet given up all hope of being able to preserve it to the full and final accomplishment of his mission. His mind was actively at work contriving and planning during the long, lonely hours of night which they employed to reach Mfuto, whither he found the Arabs had retreated. In the night Shaw tumbled off his donkey, and would not rise, though implored to do so. As Stanley did not despair himself, so he did not intend that Shaw should despair. He was lifted on his animal, and a man was placed on each side of him to assist him; thus they rode through the darkness. At midnight they reached Mfuto safely, and were at once admitted into the village, from which they had issued so valiantly, to which they returned so ignominiously.

Stanley found that all his men had arrived here before dark. Ulimengo, who had distinguished himself by a song boasting of weapons and numbers on starting out, and was so sanguine of victory, had performed the eleven hours' march in six hours; sturdy Chowpereh, whom he regarded as the faithfulest of his people, had arrived only half an hour later than Ulimengo; and frisky Khamisi, the dany, the orator, the rampant demagogue—yes, he had come third; and Speke's "Faithfuls" had proved as cowardly as any poor "nigger" of them all. Only Selim, the Arab boy from Jerusalem, had proved brave and faithful. Shaw, though an European born, proved that he possessed a soul as mean and base as, if not meaner than, that of the negroes.

"Why did you not also run away," Stanley asked of Selim," and leave your master to die?"

"Oh, sir," said the Arab boy, naively, "I was afraid you would whip me."

It never occurred to the Arab magnates that Stanley had cause of complaint against them, it never occurred to them that he had a right to feel aggrieved at their conduct, for the base desertion of an ally who had, as a duty to friendship, taken up arms for their sake. Their "salaams" the next morning after the retreat was given as if nothing had transpired to mar the good feeling that had existed between him and them. They were hardly seated, however, before he began to inform them that as the war was only between them and Mirambo, and that as he was afraid, if they began to run away after every little check, that the war might last a much longer time than he cared to lose, and that as they had deserted their wounded on the field, and left their sick friends to take care of themselves, they must not consider him in the light of an ally any more. The Arabs protested that they had not intended to leave him, but that the Wanyamwezi had raised the cry that the Musungu was gone, and the cry had caused a panic among their people, which it was impossible to allay. Later that day, they continued their retreat to Tabora, twenty-two miles distant from Mfuto. Stanley determined to proceed more leisurely, and on the second day after the flight from Zimbizo, his expedition, with all the stores and baggage, marched back to Masangi, and on the third day to Kwihara.

One road to Ujiji had been tried, and had been found impassable. The southern route was not well known to those about him; and they vaguely hinted of want of water and robber Wazavira as obstacles in the way.

But before he could venture on this new route, he had to employ a new set of men, as those whom he took to Mfuto considered their engagement at an end, and the fact of five of their number being killed rather damped their ardor for traveling. It was useless to hope that Wanyamwezi could be engaged, because it was against their custom to go with caravans, as carriers, during war-times. His position was most serious; but although he had a good excuse for returning to the coast, he felt that he must die sooner than return.

While Stanley was still uncertain what to do, or how to procure a sufficient number of pagazis, firing was heard from the direction of Tabora, where the Arabs were still encamped. Some of the men who were sent out to ascertain the cause came running back with the information that Mirambo had attacked Tabora with over two thousand men, and that a force of over one thousand Matuta, who had allied themselves with him for the sake of plunder, had come suddenly upon Tabora, attacking from opposite directions. Later in the day, or about noon, the way was crowed with fugitives from Tabora, who were rushing to Kwihara for protection. From these people, Stanley received the sad information that the noble Khamis bin Abdullah, with many of his adherents, had been slain. Perceiving that his people were ready to stand by him, Stanley made preparations for defence by boring loop-holes for muskets into the stout clay walls of his tembe. They were made so quickly, and seemed so admirably adapted for the efficient defence of the tembe that his men got quite brave; and Wangwana refugees with guns in their hands, driven out of Tabora, asked to be admitted to this tembe to assist in its defence. Livingstone's men were also collected, and invited to help defend their master's goods against Mirambo's supposed attack. By night, Stanley had one hundred and fifty armed men in his courtyard, stationed at every possible point where an attack was to be expected. The next day, Mirambo had threatened, he would come to Kwihara; Stanley hoped that he would come, and was resolved that if he came within range of an American rifle, it should be seen what virtue lies in American lead.

STANLEY AND HIS RETINUE IN AFRICA.

The tembe was fortified so strongly that Stanley expressed it as his firm conviction that ten thousand Africans could not take it; four or five hundred Europeans without cannon, or fifty with its aid, he adds, might take it. But having expended all this care, and waited so anxiously to give Mirambo a taste of American lead, that gentleman chose to avoid the place where such a reception had been prepared for him, and turned his attention to Mfuto.

While he was anxiously gathering up a sufficient number of men to transport his necessary baggage to Ujiji, Stanley received a present. This was nothing less than a little boy slave, named Ndugu M'hali. The name did not suit his fancy, and he called the chiefs of his caravan together and asked them to choose a better one. Various names were suggested, but Ulimengo, after looking at his quick eyes, and noting his celerity of movement, pronounced the name "Ka-lu-lu" best for him, "Because," said he, "just look at his eyes! So bright! Look at his form! So slim! Watch his movements! So quick!"

"Yes, bana," said the others, "let it be Kalulu."

Kalulu is a Kisawahili term for the young of the blue-buck antelope.

"Well, then," said Stanley, water being brought in a huge tin pan, Selim, who was willing to stand god-father, holding him over the water, "let his name henceforth be Kalulu, and let no man take it from him."

The next day, (Sept. 8) word was received that Mirambo had attacked Mfuto; the result of the engagement was not told until the next day, when the welcome news was received that Mirambo had been repulsed with severe loss. From this point forward, Mirambo had but little terror for the people at Kwihara, and Stanley was able to carry on his work of getting ready for the journy to Ujiji, unhindered by any circumstance except the sickness of Shaw and Selim.

A farewell banquet was given on the 17th; two bullocks were barbecued; three sheep, two goats, and fifteen chickens, one hundred and twenty pounds of rice, twenty large loaves made of Indian corn flour, one hundred eggs, ten pounds of butter, and five gallons of sweet milk were the contents of which the banquet was formed.

But an attack of fever compelled Stanley to postpone his departure. The solitude of his sick-chamber was cheered by an inquiry from Shaw, as to whom he should write in case Stanley should die. Shaw had already told Selim that Stanley would die like a donkey; that he would then take charge

A GIRAFFE HUNT.

of his journals and trunks and proceed to the coast immediately. Later on, he appears to have changed this plan, for he announced his intention to stock the yard of the tembe full of chickens, in order to be able to get fresh eggs every day, and buy a cow, so that he might have plenty of milk. Unfortunately for Mr. Shaw's castles in the air, Mr. Stanley did not die.

The 20th of September arrived. Stanley was still very weak from the fever of the day before, and it was a most injudicious act to commence a march under such circumstances. But he had boasted to Sheikh bin Nasib that a white man never breaks his word, and his reputation as a white man would have been ruined if he had stayed behind or postponed the march, in consequence of feebleness.

His caravan numbered fifty-four souls besides himself. The goods with which he had burdened them consisted of four thousand yards of cloth, six bags of beads, four loads of ammunition, one tent, one bed and clothes, one box of medicine, sextant and books, two loads of tea, coffee, and sugar, one load of flower and candles, one load of canned meats, sardines, and miscellaneous necessaries, and one load of cooking utensils.

A parting salute was fired; the flags were raised by the guides, each pagazi rushed for his load, and in a short time, with songs and shouts, the head of the expedition had filed round the western end of the tembe along the road to Ugunda.

Considerable difficulty was experienced with Shaw, who much preferred to stay where he was; and after several days' journey he was sent back. The traveler also had trouble, during the early part of his march, to keep his men together, several attempting to desert.

The march was without other incidents for several days. It was Oct. 2 that they caught sight of a herd of giraffes, whose long necks were seen towering above a bush they had been nibbling at. This sight was greeted with a shout, for they now knew that they had entered the game country, and that near the Gombe, where they intended to halt, they would find plenty of these animals.

Three hours brought them to Manyara. Arriving before the village-gate, they were forbidden to enter, as the country was throughout in a state of war, and the villagers did not wish to be compromised. The travelers were directed to ruined huts outside the town, near a pool of clear water. After they had built their camp, the guide was sent to buy food; he was informed that the chief had forbidden his people to sell any grain whatever. Two royal cloths were selected, and sent by Bombay to propitiate the chief; but proved useless; and all the caravan went supperless to bed.

The bale of choice cloths was opened again the next morning and four royal cloths were this time selected, and two dotis of Merikani, and Bombay was again dispatched, burdened with compliments and polite words. It was necessary to be very politic with a man who was so surly, and too powerful to make an enemy of. What if he made up his mind to imitate the redoubtable Mirambo, king of Uyoweh! The effect of Stanley's munificent liberality was soon seen in the abundance of provender which came into the camp. Before an hour went by, there came boxes full of choroko, beans, rice, matama or dourra, and Indian corn, carried on the heads of a dozen villagers; and shortly afterward the Mtemi himself came, followed by about thirty musketeers and twenty spearmen, to visit the first white man ever seen on this road. Behind these warriors came a liberal gift, fully equal in value to that sent to him, of several large gourds of honey, fowls, goats, and enough vetches and beans to supply the caravan with four days' food.

Stanley met the chief at the gate of his camp, and, bowing profoundly, invited him to his tent, which he had arranged as well as his circumstances would permit, for this reception. His Persian carpet and bear skin were spread out, and a broad piece of bran-new crimson cloth covered his kitanda, or bedstead.

The chief, a tall, robust man, and his chieftains were invited to seat themselves. They cast a look of such gratified surprise at their host, his face, his clothes, and guns, as it is impossible to describe. They looked at him intently for a few seconds, and then at each other, which ended in an uncontrollable burst of laughter, and repeated snappings of the fingers. After a short period expended in exchanging compliments, the chief desired Stanley to show him his guns. The Winchester rifle elicited a thousand flattering observations from the excited man; and the tiny deadly revolvers, whose beauty and workmanship they thought were superhuman, evoked such gratified eloquence that the American was glad to try something else. The double-barreled guns fired with heavy charges of powder caused them to jump up in affected alarm, and then to subside to their seats convulsed with laughter. As the enthusiasm of the guests increased, they seized each other's index fingers, screwed them and pulled at them until the host feared they would end in their dislocation. After having explained to them the difference between white men and Arabs, Stanley pulled out his medicine chest, which evoked another burst of rapturous sighs at the cunning neatness of the array of vials. He asked what they meant.

"*Dowa*," replied Stanley, sententiously; a word which may be interpreted, medicine.

"Oh-h, oh-h," they murmured, admiringly. The white man succeeded, ere long, in winning unqualified admiration; and his superiority, compared with the best of the Arabs they had seen, was but too evident. "*Dowa, dowa*," they added.

"Here," said Stanley, uncorking a vial of medicinal brandy, "is the Kisungu pombe (white man's beer); take a spoonful and try it," at the same time handing it.

"*Hacht, hacht*, oh, *hacht!* What! Eh! What strong beer the white men have! Oh, how my throat burns!"

"Ah, but it is good," said Stanley; "a little of it makes men feel strong and good; but too much of it makes men bad, and they die."

"Let me have some," said one of the chiefs; and the request was echoed until all had asked.

The exhibitor next produced a bottle of concentrated ammonia, which he explained was for snake-bites, and headaches; the sultan immediately complained he had a headache, and must have a little. Telling him to close his eyes, Stanley suddenly uncorked the bottle, and presented it to his majesty's nose. The effect was magical, for he fell back as if shot, and such contortions as his features underwent are indescribable. His chiefs roared with laughter, and clapped their hands, pinched each other, snapped their fingers, and did many other ludicrous things. Finally the sultan recovered himself, great tears rolling down his cheeks, and his features quivering with laughter; then he suddenly uttered the word "*Kali*," strong, quick, or ardent medicine. He required no more; but the other chiefs pushed forward to get one wee sniff, which they no sooner had than all went into paroxysms of uncontrollable laughter. The entire morning was passed in this state visit, to the satisfaction of all concerned.

"Oh," said the sultan at parting, "these white men know everything! The Arabs are dirt compared to them."

October 4. they left their camp here, and traveled toward Gombe, which is four hours and a quarter from Manyara. Here, at last, was the hunter's paradise. Hunters were now

TRYING WHITE MAN'S MEDICINE.

directed to proceed east and north to procure meat, because in each caravan it generally happens that there are fundi, whose special trade is to hunt for meat for the camp. Some of these are experts in stalking, but often find themselves in dangerous positions, owing to the near approach necessary before they can fire their most inaccurate weapons with any degree of certainty.

We have not space here to detail Stanley's prowess in hunting, since it brought nothing of special adventure; we must pass on to a more dangerous incident.

The caravan remained two days at this camping-place, the hunters procuring plenty of meat, which the others cut and sliced so that it might be dried for future use; and even then the meat-loving, lazy Wangwana did not wish to go. They delegated Bombay early in the morning of the 7th to speak to Stanley, and entreat him to stop one day longer. Bombay was well scolded for bearing any such request after two days' rest; and Bombay was by no means in the best of humors; flesh-pots full of meat were more to his taste than a constant tramping, and its consequent fatigues. Stanley saw his face settle into sulky ugliness, and his great nether lip hanging down limp, which means, as if expressed in so many words:

"Well, get them to move yourself, you wicked, hard man! I shall not help you."

An ominous silence followed Stanley's order to the kirangozi to sound the horn, and the usual singing and chanting were not heard. The men turned sullenly to their bales, and Asmani, the gigantic guide, was heard to say grumblingly that he was sorry he had engaged to guide the Musungu to the Tanganyika. However, they started, though reluctantly. Stanley stayed behind with the gun-bearers, to drive the stragglers on. In about half an hour he sighted the caravan at a dead stop, with the bales thrown on the ground, and the men standing in groups talking angrily and excitedly.

Taking his double-barreled gun from Selim's shoulder, he selected a dozen charges of buckshot, and slipping two of them into the barrels, and adjusting his revolvers in order for handy work, he walked on toward them. He noticed that the men seized their guns as he advanced. When within thirty yards of the groups, he discovered the heads of two men appear above an ant-hill on his left, with the barrels of their guns carelessly pointed toward the road.

He halted, threw the barrel of his gun into the hollow of the left hand, and then, taking a deliberate aim at them, threat-

QUELLING A MUTINY.

ened to blow their heads off if they did not come forward to talk to him. These two men were gigantic Asmani, and his sworn companion Mabruki, the guides of Sheikh bin Nasib. As it was dangerous not to comply with such an order, they presently came; but keeping his eye on Asmani, Stanley saw him move his fingers to the trigger of his gun, and bring his gun to a "ready." Again the white man lifted his gun, and threatened him with instant death, if he did not drop his musket.

Asmani came on in a sidelong way, with a smirking smile on his face, but in his eyes shone the lurid light of murder as plainly as it ever shone in a villain's eyes. Mabruki sneaked to Stanley's rear, deliberately putting powder in the pan of his musket; but sweeping the gun sharply around, the Musungu planted the muzzle of it about two feet from his wicked-looking face, and ordered him to drop his gun instantly. He let it fall from his hand quickly; and, giving him a vigorous poke in the stomach with the double-barrel, which sent him reeling a few feet, Stanley turned to Asmani, and ordered him to put his gun down; accompanying the order with a nervous movement of his own weapon, pressing gently on the trigger at the same time. Never was a man nearer his death than was Asmani during those few moments. The white man was reluctant to shed his blood, and he was willing to try all possible means to avoid doing so; but if he did not succeed in cowing this ruffian, authority was at an end. The truth was, they feared to proceed farther on the road, and the only possible way of inducing them to move was by an overpowering force and exercise of his power and will in this instance, even though he might pay the penalty of his disobedience with death. As Stanley was beginning to feel that Asmani had passed his last moment on earth, as he was lifting his gun to his shoulder, a form came up behind him, and Mabruki Speke cried in horror-struck accents:

"Man, how dare you point your gun at the master?"

Mabruki then threw himself at Stanley's feet, and endeavored to kiss them, and entreated him not to punish him:

"It is all over now," he said, "there will be no more quarreling; we will all go to the Tanganyika, without any more noise; and *Inshallah*! we shall find the old Musungu at Ujiji! Speak, men, freedmen, shall we not? Shall we not go to the Tanganyika without any more trouble? Tell the master with one voice."

"*Ay Wallah! Ay Wallah! Bana yango! Hamuna man-*

neno mgini!" which, being literally translated, means:

"Yes, by God! Yes, by God! my master! There are no other words."

"Ask the master's pardon, man, or go thy way," said Mabruki, peremptorily, to Asmani; which Asmani did, to the gratification of them all. It only remained for Stanley to extend a general pardon to all, except to Bombay and Ambari, the instigators of the mutiny, which was now happily quelled. For Bombay could by a word, as the captain, have nipped all manifestation of bad temper at the outset, had he been so disposed. But no, Bombay was more averse to marching than the cowardliest of his fellows, not because he was cowardly, but because he loved indolence, and made a god of his belly. So, snatching up a spear, Stanley laid its staff vigorously on Bombay's shoulders, and then sprang upon Ambari, whose mocking face soon underwent a remarkable transformation; and then clapped them both in chains, with a threat that they would be kept chained until they knew how to ask their master's pardon. Asmani and Mabruki were told to be cautious not to exhibit their ugly tempers any more, lest they might taste the death they had so fortunately escaped.

Again the word was given to march, and each man, with astonishing alacrity, seized his load, and filed off quickly out of sight; Bombay and Ambari in the rear in chains, with Kingaru and Asmani, the deserters, weighted with the heaviest loads. They had barely traveled an hour from the Gombe before Bombay and Ambari in trembling accents implored their master's pardon; he permitted them to continue for half an hour longer, when he finally relented, releasing them both from their chains, and restoring Bombay to his full honors as captain.

They traveled fourteen days in a southwesterly direction, and Stanley intended to have gone still further south; but rumors of war on the path before them induced him to change this plan. After consulting with Asmani, the guide, he decided to strike across toward the Tanganyika, on a west-by-north course through the forest, traveling, when it was advantageous, along elephant tracks and local paths.

All were firm friends now; all squabbling had long ceased. Bombay and his master had forgotten their quarrel; the *kirangozi* and Stanley were ready to embrace. Confidence returned to all hearts; for now, as Mabruki Unyanyembe said: "They could smell the fish of the Tanganyika."

They were now in a country where the most dangerous animals were to be found; Stanley had already seen the first herd of elephants in their native wilds; and their camp on the Mtambu proved to be near the lairs of leopards and of lions. As some of the men were taking the two donkeys to water from this camp, a leopard sprang upon one of the animals, and fastened its claws in his throat. The frightened donkey began to bray so loudly, and was so warmly assisted by its companions, that the leopard bounded away through the brake, as if in sheer dismay at the noisy cries which the attack had provoked. The donkey's neck exhibited some frightful wounds, but the animal was not dangerously hurt.

Stanley, thinking that possibly he might meet with an adventure with a lion or leopard in that dark belt of tall trees, took a stroll along that awesome place with the gun-bearer, Kalulu, carrying an extra supply of ammunition and an additional gun. But after an hour's search for adventure he had encountered nothing, and strolled further in search of something to shoot. Presently he saw a huge wild boar feeding quietly at some distance from him. He got two shots at this animal, but his bullets were not heavy enough to penetrate his thick hide and do any material damage, so that the boar escaped. As it was now getting late, and the camp was three miles away, they were obliged to return without the meat. On their way to camp they were accompanied by a large animal which persistently followed them on their left. It was too dark to see plainly, but a large form was visible, if not very clearly defined. It must have been a lion.

About eleven that night, they were startled by the roar of a lion very near the camp; soon it was joined by another and another, and the novelty of the thing kept the white man awake. He endeavored to sight a rifle; but the cartridges might as well have been filled with sawdust for all the benefit which he derived from them. Disgusted with the miserable ammunition, he left the lions alone, and turned in, with their roar as a lullaby.

November 3, being then in Uvinza, they saw a caravan which came from the direction of Ujiji, consisting of about eighty Waguhha. They asked the news, and were told that a white man had just arrived at Ujiji from Manyuema. This news startled them all.

"A white man?" Stanley asked.

"Yes, a white man," was the reply.

"How is he dressed?"

"Like the master," they said, referring to Stanley.

AN UNWELCOME VISITOR.

"Is he young or old?"

"He is old. He has white hair on his face, and he is sick."

"Where has he come from?"

"From a very far country away beyond Uguhha, called Manyuema."

"Indeed! And is he stopping at Ujiji now?"

"Yes, we saw him about eight days ago."

"Do you think he will stop there until we see him?"

"*Sigue*" (don't know).

"Was he ever at Ujiji before?

"Yes, he went away a long time ago."

It must be Livingstone. It can be no other; but still—he may be some one else—some one from the west coast—or perhaps he is Baker. No, Baker has no white hairs on his face. But they must now march quickly, lest he hears that they are coming, and runs away. Stanley addressed his men, and asked them if they were willing to march to Ujiji without a single halt: and then promised them, if they acceded to his wishes, two doti for each man. All answered in the affirmative, almost as much rejoiced as he was himself. But he was madly rejoiced, intensely eager to solve the burning question: "Is it Dr. Livingstone?" He did wish there was a railroad, or at least horses in this country; with a horse he could reach Ujiji in about twelve hours.

But the time necessary was much longer than this. They must pass through Uhha, and there they were subject to many delays. The messenger of the king demanded *honga*, or tribute, to an enormous extent. After considerable haggling, this was paid; a few miles further on, the king himself demanded *honga*, and denied all knowledge of his supposed agent. This, too, had to be paid. Yet farther, the king's brother required *honga*, for he was almost as powerful as the king.

Upon consultation with his chief men, Stanley decided that the only way to escape absolute penury as the result of a journey through Uhha, was to keep away from the villages and roads, and, trusting only to the compass, plunge boldly into the forests and make their way, by a hitherto untrodden path, out of the country. Provisions sufficient to last six days were purchased, the guides were given an extra *douceur*, orders for the strictest silence throughout the march were issued, and the caravan marched.

They stole out of their camp near a village at 3 A. M.; and by 8 had reached the Rusugi, where they camped in a clump of jungle near its banks. An hour after they had rested, some natives, carrying salt from the Malagarazi, were seen coming up the right bank of the river. When abreast of the hiding-place they detected the strangers, and dropping their salt-bags, they ran to give the alarm to the neighboring villages, four miles away. The men were immediately ordered to take up their loads, and in a few minutes they had crossed the Rusugi, and were making direct for a bamboo jungle which appeared in their front. Almost as soon as they entered, a weak-brained woman raised a series of piercing yells. The men were appalled at this noisy demonstration, which would call down upon their heads the vengeance of the Wahha for evading the tribute to which they thought themselves entitled. In half an hour they would have hundreds of howling savages about them in the jungle, and probably a general massacre would ensue. The woman screamed fearfully, again and again, for no cause whatever. Some of the men with the instinct of self-preservation, at once dropped their bales and their loads, and vanished into the jungle. The guide came rushing back to Stanley, imploring him to stop her noise. The woman's husband, livid with rage and fear, drew his sword, and asked his master's permission to cut off her head at once. Had Stanley given the least signal, the woman had paid for her folly with her life. He attempted to hush her cries by putting his hand over her mouth, but she violently wrestled with him, and continued her cries worse than ever. There remained nothing else for him to do but to try the virtues of his whip over her shoulders. He asked her to desist after the first blow. No! She continued her insane cries with increased force and volume. Again his whip descended upon her shoulders. "No, no, no!" Another blow. Will you hush?" "No, no, no!" Louder and faster she cried, and faster and faster he showered the blows for the taming of this shrew. However, seeing he was as determined to flog as she was to cry, she desisted before the tenth blow, and was silent. A cloth was folded over her mouth, and her arms were tied behind her; and in a few moments, the runaways having returned to their duties, the expedition moved forward again with redoubled pace.

Still keeping silence, they at last passed through Guhha, and were out of danger of extortion. They arrived at a point whence the Tanganyika could be seen, November 10. It was the fifty-first day after leaving Unyanyembe, and the two hundred and thirty-sixth after leaving Bagamoyo. They now pushed on rapidly, lest the news of their coming might reach the people of Bunder Ujiji before they came in sight and were ready for them. They halt at a little brook, then ascend the long slope of a naked ridge, the very last of the myriads they have crossed. They arrive at the summit, travel across and arrive at its western rim, and the port of Ujiji is below them, embowered in the palms, only five hundred yards from them. Their hearts and feelings are with their eyes, as they peer into the palms and try to make out in which hut or house lives the white man with the gray beard they heard about on the Malagarazi.

"Unfurl the flags, and load your guns!"

"*Ay Wallah, Ay Wallah, bana!*" respond the men, eagerly.

"One—two—three—fire!"

A volley from nearly fifty guns roars like a salute from a battery of artillery; we shall note its effect presently on the peaceful-looking village below.

"Now, *kirangozi*, hold the white man's flag up high, and let the Zanzibar flag bring up the rear. And you men keep close together and keep firing until we halt in the market-place, or before the white man's house. You have said to me often that you could smell the fish of the Tanganyika—I can smell the fish of the Tanganyika now. There are fish, and beer, and a long rest waiting for you. MARCH."

Before they had gone a hundred yards their repeated volleys had had the effect desired. They had awakened Ujiji to the knowledge that a caravan was coming, and the people were witnessed rushing up in hundreds to meet them. The mere sight of the flags informed every one at once that they were a caravan, but the American flag born aloft by gigantic Asmani, whose face was one vast smile on this day, rather staggered them at first. However, many of the people who now approached them remembered the flag. They had seen it float over the American consulate and from the mast of many a ship in the harbor of Zanzibar; and they were soon welcoming the beautiful flag with cries of "*Bindera Kisuggu!*—a white man's flag! *Bindera Merikani*—the American flag!"

Then the newcomers were surrounded by them; by Wajiji, Wanyamwezi, Wangwana, Warundi, Waguhha, Wamanyuema and Arabs, and were almost deafened with shouts of "*Yambo, yambo, bana! Yambo, bana! Yambo bana!* To all and each of Stanley's men the welcome was given.

They were now about three hundred yards from the village of Ujiji, and the crowds were dense about them. Suddenly Stanley heard a voice on his right say:

"Good morning, sir."

Startled at hearing this greeting in the midst of such a crowd of black people, he turns sharply around in search of the man, and sees him at his side, with the blackest of faces, but animated and joyous—a man dressed in a long white shirt, with a turban of American sheeting around his woolly head; and he asks:

"Who the mischief are you?"

"I am Susi, the servant of Dr. Livingstone," said he, smiling and showing a gleaming row of teeth.

"What! Is Dr. Livingstone here?"

"Yes, sir."

"In this village?"

"Yes, sir."

"Are you sure?"

"Sure, sure, sir. Why, I leave him just now."

"Good morning, sir," said another voice.

"Hallo," said Stanley. "Is this another one?"

"Yes, sir."

"Well, what is your name?"

"My name is Chuma, sir."

"What, are you Chuma, the friend of Wekotani?"

"Yes, sir."

"And is the doctor well?"

"Not very well, sir."

"Where has he been so long?"

"In Manyuema."

"Now you, Susi, run and tell the doctor I am coming."

"Yes, sir;" and off he darted like a madman.

But by this time they were within two hundred yards of the village, and the multitude was getting denser, and almost preventing their march. Flags and streamers were out; Arabs and Wangwana were pushing their way through the natives in order to greet the new-comers; for according to their account, the strangers belonged to them. But the great wonder of all was:

"How did you come from Unyanyembe?"

Soon Susi came running back, and asked Stanley his name; he had told the doctor that a white man was coming, but the doctor was too surprised to believe him; and when asked the white man's name, Susi was rather staggered. But during Susi's absence, the news had been conveyed to the doctor that it was surely a white man that was coming, whose guns were firing and whose flag could be seen; and the great Arab magnates of

Ujiji had gathered together before the doctor's house, and the doctor had come out from his veranda to discuss the matter and await his arrival.

In the meantime, the head of the expedition had halted, and the *kirangozi* was out of the ranks, holding his flag aloft; and Selim said to his master:

"I see the doctor, sir. Oh, what an old man! He has got a white beard."

And Stanley—what would he not have given for a bit of friendly wilderness, where he might vent his joy in some mad freak, such as idiotically biting his hand, turning a somersault, or slashing at trees, in order to allay those exciting feelings that were well nigh incontrollable. His heart beats fast, but he must not let his face betray his emotions, lest it shall detract from the dignity of a white man appearing under such extraordinary circumstances.

So he did that which he thought was most dignified. He pushed back the crowds, and passing from the rear, walked down a living avenue of people, until he came in front of the semi-circle of Arabs, in the front of which stood the white man with the gray beard. As he advanced slowly toward him, he noticed that the great explorer was pale, looked wearied, had a gray beard, wore a bluish cap with a faded gold band round it, had on a red-sleeved waistcoat, and a pair of gray tweed trousers. Stanley would have run to him, only he says, "I was a coward in the presence of such a mob—would have embraced him, only, he being an Englishman, I did not know how he would receive me; so I did what cowardice and false pride suggested was the best thing—walked deliberately to him, took off my hat, and said:

"'Dr. Livingstone, I presume?'"

"Yes," said he, with a kind smile, lifting his cap slightly.

Stanley replaced his hat on his head, and Livingstone put on his cap; and they both grasped hands; and Stanley then said aloud:

"I thank God, Doctor, that I have been permitted to see you."

"I feel thankful, replied Livingstone, "that I am here to welcome you."

Stanley turned to the Arabs, took off his hat to them in response to the saluting chorus of "*Yambos*" he received, and the doctor introduced them to him by name. Then oblivious of the crowds, oblivious of the men who had shared dangers with him, Livingstone and Stanley turned their faces toward the

MEETING OF STANLEY AND LIVINGSTONE IN THE HEART OF AFRICA.

elder man's tembe. They are seated with their backs to the wall. The Arabs take seats on their left. More than a thousand natives are in front of them, filling the whole square densely, indulging their curiosity, and discussing the fact of two white men meeting at Ujiji—one just come from Manyuema, in the west, and one from Unyanyembe in the east.

Conversation began; questions innumerable, yet of the simplest kind; then Livingstone began to tell the story of his travels, while Stanley listened entranced. The Arabs rose with a delicacy of which the white men approved, as if they intuitively knew that they ought to be left to themselves. Stanley sent Bombay with them, to give them the news they also wanted so much to know about the affairs at Unyanyembe; they all had friends there, and it was but natural that they should be anxious to hear of what concerned them.

Presently Stanley called to him the man who had charge of Dr. Livingstone's letter bag, and bade him deliver it to the master. The doctor kept the letter-bag on his knee, then, presently, opened it, looked at the letters contained there, and read one or two of his children's letters, his face in the meanwhile lighting up. He asked Stanley to tell him the news.

"No, doctor," was the reply, "read your letters first, which I am sure you must be impatient to read."

"Ah," said he, "I have waited years for letters, and I have been taught patience. I can surely afford to wait a few hours longer. No, tell me the general news: how is the world getting along?"

"You probably know much already. Do you know that the Suez canal is a fact—is opened, and a regular trade carried on between Europe and India through it?"

"I did not hear about the opening of it. Well, that is grand news! What else?"

Shortly, Stanley found himself acting the part of an annual periodical to him. There was no need of any exaggeration—of any penny-a-line news, or of any sensationalism. The world had witnessed and experienced much during the past few years. The Pacific railroad had been completed; Grant had been elected President of the United States; Egypt had been flooded with savans; the Cretan Rebellion had been terminated; a Spanish Revolution had driven Isabella from the throne of Spain, and a regent had been appointed; General Prim was assassinated; a Castelar had electrified Europe with his advanced ideas upon the liberty of worship; Prussia had humbled Denmark, and annexed Schleswig-Holstein, and her armies were now around Paris; the "Man of Destiny" was a prisoner at Wilhelmshohe; the Queen of Fashion and the Empress of the French was a fugitive; and the child born in the purple had lost forever the imperial crown intended for his head; the Napoleon dynasty was extinguished by the Prussians, Bismarck and Von Moltke; and France, the proud empire, was humbled to the dust. What could a man have exaggerated of these facts? What a budget of news it was to one who had emerged from the depths of the primeval forests of Manyuema!

Not long after the Arabs had left them, a dish of hot hashed meat-cakes was sent by Sayd bin Majid, and a curried chicken was received from Mahammed bin Sali, and Moeni Kheri sent a dishful of stewed goat-meat and rice; and thus presents of food came in succession, and as fast as they were brought the recipients set to. Stanley had a healthy, stubborn digestion—the exercise he had taken had put it into prime order; but Livingstone—he had been complaining that he had no appetite, that his stomach refused everything except a cup of tea now and then—he ate also; ate like a vigorous, hungry man; and as he vied with his guest in demolishing the pancakes, he kept repeating:

"You have brought me new life. You have brought me new life."

"Oh, by George!" said Stanley; "I have forgotten something. Hasten, Selim, and bring that bottle; you know which; and bring me the silver goblets. I brought that bottle on purpose for this event, which I hoped would come to pass, though often it seemed useless to expect it.

Selim knew where the bottle was, and he soon returned with it—a bottle of Sillery champagne; and handing the doctor a goblet brimful of the exhilarating wine, and pouring a small quantity into his own, the young man said:

"Dr. Livingstone, to your very good health, sir."

"And to yours," he responded.

But they kept on talking, and talking, and prepared food was being brought to them all that afternoon; and they kept on eating every time it was brought, until even Stanley had eaten to repletion, and Livingstone was obliged to confess that he had eaten enough. Halimah, the female cook of the doctor's establishment, was in a state of the greatest excitement. She had been protruding her head out of the cook-house to make sure that there were really two white men sitting down in the veranda, where there used to be only one, who would not because he could not eat anything; and she had been considerably exercised in her mind about this fact. She was afraid the doctor did not properly appreciate her culinary abilities; but now she was in a state of amazement at the extraordinary quantities of food eaten. Poor faithful soul! The doctor told his guest of the terrible anxiety she evinced when the guns first announced the arrival of another white man in Ujiji; how she was in despair at the scantiness of the larder, how she was anxious to make up for their poverty by a grand appearance—to make up a sort of Barmecide feast to welcome the white man.

"Why," said she, "is he not one of us? Does he not bring plenty of cloth and beads? Talk about the Arabs! Who are they that they should be compared to white men? Arabs, indeed!"

As yet, Dr. Livingstone was not aware of the reason why Stanley had come to the heart of Africa. He had thought, when it was first told him that a white man was approaching, that it might be the successor of Lieut. Le Saint, an emissary of the French government who had died near Gondokoro; and the thought that he could not speak French, and that possibly the new-comer could not speak English, had troubled him not a little. They would have been a pretty pair of white men in Ujiji! It was not until the day after his arrival, that Stanley told the whole story—how he had been sent by Bennett especially to FIND LIVINGSTONE.

A comparison of notes made the younger traveler extremely thankful that he had made so long a detour before beginning his African journey. Supposing that he had gone direct from Paris to Zanzibar, seven or eight months afterward, perhaps, he would have found himself at Ujiji. But Livingstone would not have been found there then; he would have been on the Lualaba; and Stanley would have had to follow him on his devious tracks through the primeval forests of Manyuema, and up along the crooked course of the Lualaba for hundreds of miles. The time taken by Stanley in traveling up the Nile, back to Jerusalem, then to Constantinople, Southern Russia, the Caucasus, and Persia, was employed by Livingstone in fruitful discoveries west of the Tanganyika. Again, consider that Stanley arrived at Unyanyembe in the latter part of June, and that owing to a war he was delayed three months in Unyanyembe, leading a fretful, peevish, and impatient life. But while he was thus fretting himself and being delayed by a series of accidents, Livingstone was being forced back to

Ujiji in the same month. It took him from June to October to march to Ujiji. Now, in September, Stanley broke loose from the thraldom which accident had imposed upon him, and hurried southward to Ukonongo, then westward to Kawendi, then northward to Uvinza, then westward to Ujiji, only about three weeks after the doctor's arrival, to find him resting on the veranda of his house with his face turned eastward, the direction from which his seeker was to come.

The days came and went peacefully and happily under the palms of Ujiji. The missionary was improving in health and spirits. Life had been brought back to him; his fading vitality was restored, his enthusiasm for his work was growing up again into a desire that was compelling him to be again up and doing. But what could he do, with five men and fifteen or twenty cloths?

"Have you seen the northern head of the Tanganyika, doctor?" Stanley asked one day.

"No: I did try to go there, but the Wajiji tried their best to fleece me, as they did both Burton and Speke, and I had not a great deal of cloth. If I had gone to the head of the Tanganyika, I could not have gone to the Manyuema. The central line of drainage is most important, and that is the Lualaba. Before this line the question whether there is a connection between the Tanganyika and the Albert Nyanza sinks into insignificance. The great line of drainage is the river flowing from latitude eleven degrees south, which I have followed for over seven degrees northward. The Chambezi, the name given to its most southern extremity, drains a large tract of country south of the southermost source of the Tanganyika; it must, therefore, be the most important. I have not the least doubt, myself, but that this lake is the Upper Tanganyika, and the Albert Nyanza of Baker is the Lower Tanganyika, which are connected by a river flowing from the upper to the lower. This is my belief, based upon reports of the Arabs, and a test I made of the flow with fresh-water plants. But I really never gave it much thought."

"Well, if I were you, doctor, before leaving Ujiji, I should explore it, and resolve the doubts upon the subject; lest, after you leave here, you should not return by this way. The Royal Geographical Society attach much importance to this supposed connection, and declare you are the only man who can settle it. If I can be of any service to you, you may command me. Though I did not come to Africa as an explorer, I have a good deal of curiosity upon the subject, and should be willing to accompany you. I have with me about twenty strong men who understand rowing; we have plenty of cloth, guns, and beads; and if we can get a canoe from the Arabs we can manage the thing easily."

"Oh, we can get a canoe from Sayd bin Majid. This man has been very kind to me, and if ever there was an Arab gentleman, he is one."

"Then it is settled, is it, that we go?"

"I am ready, whenever you are."

"I am at your command. Don't you hear my men call you the Great Master and me the Little Master? It would never do for the Little Master to command."

Thus it was arranged that they should explore the Tanganyika to its northern head. It should be noted that this conversation represents Livingstone as expressing the belief that this lake was one of the sources of the Nile. A reference to the last chapter, a condensation of Livingstone's Last Journal, will show that he always believed that this was the case; and that up to the time that he died, he was by no means assured that the Lualaba was not a tributary of the Nile. The idea had suggested itself to his mind that this river might be a feeder of the Congo, but it was a contradiction of his darling theory, and was only reluctantly entertained.

During the stay at Ujiji, Stanley studied his host thoroughly, and learned how erroneous had been the estimate formed from Dr. Kirk's account of him. He saw for himself that the statement that he took no notes or kept no journal was false; and he learned to despise the insinuation that Livingstone was so crabbed and cross-grained that it required a very patient man (like Dr. Kirk) to avoid quarreling with him. Stanley's own servants noted the difference between the two men; and since Stanley himself has recorded the observation, there can be no unkindliness to the younger explorer in here repeating it.

"Your master," said Stanley's servants to Livingstone's, "is a good man, a very good man; he does not beat you, for he has a kind heart; but ours—oh, he is sharp!—hot as fire!"

Upon application to Sayd bin Majid, he at once generously permitted them to use his canoe for whatever purpose they might require it. After engaging two Wajiji guides, they prepared to sail from the port of Ujiji, a week or so after Stanley had reached that point. Sayd bin Majid had stated that his canoe would carry twenty-five men, and three thousand five hundred pounds of ivory; but experiment showed that it would

STANLEY AND LIVINGSTONE ON THE RUSIZI.

not carry quite so great a load. Besides the two white men, there were sixteen rowers, Selim, Ferajji, and the two guides.

The explorer had been told by many Arabs and natives that a river near the head of the lake flowed out of it—the Rusizi; and this it was that they proposed to explore. The information was confirmed several times during their voyage, but as they drew near the northern end of Tanganyika, a very intelligent chief told them that the river flowed into the lake, and not out of it. This contradiction of the statement which Livingstone wished to believe was verified by their own experience; for although the current was very sluggish, its direction was undeniable.

The question "Is the Rusizi an effluent or an influent?" was answered forever. There was now no doubt on that point. In size, it was not to be compared with the Malagarazi river, neither is it, nor can it be, navigable for anything but the smallest canoes. The only thing remarkable about it is that it abounds in crocodiles, but not one hippopotamus was seen; which may be taken as another evidence of its shallowness.

December 8, they landed at a group of islets, three in number, all very steep and rocky; the largest about three hundred feet in length at the base, and about two hundred feet in breadth. As these islands were with difficulty pronounced by Stanley as Kavunvweh, the doctor, seeing that they were the only objects they were likely to discover, named them "The New York *Herald* Islands;" and in confirmation of the new designation given them, shook hands with the representative of that journal upon it. They arrived at Ujiji four days later, having traversed over three hundred miles of water during their voyage of twenty-eight days.

December 27, Stanley having persuaded Livingstone that it would be best for him to go to Unyanyembe and there obtain a new supply of goods, since the veteran explorer refused to return home for a rest until the sources of the Nile should have been discovered, the caravan left Ujiji. It was their intention for a part of their number, including the two leaders, to coast along the shore of the lake as far south as Cape Tongwe, while the remainder of the force followed by a nearly parallel course on land. From this point they would strike across the country; and by providing themselves with a stock of food on starting, and occasionally doing a little hunting on the way, they could make their way across to Unyanyembe without drawing near to a single village, and hence, without having to pay a single cloth for provisions and shelter. This

BAGGING A MAN-EATING CROCODILE WITH BAIT WARRANTED TO ATTRACT.

route was marked out by Stanley, who had prepared, from his own observations, a chart of the country between the two places.

Their voyage was not remarkable, save for the number of crocodiles that they saw along the banks, and for the herd of zebras which Stanley stalked, one of which fell with a bullet through his heart, while the others, alarmed, galloped off to a place of safety. The same hand, a little later, brought down a fine buffalo cow. This country abounded in game of every kind, and although Stanley did not hire from mercenary parents the pickaninny bait warranted to attract of which other hunters have not scrupled to avail themselves, sport was plentiful on all hands.

On a hunting expedition shortly afterward, in which he was armed only with his Winchester, Stanley came full upon an immense bull-elephant. Recovering from his astonishment, he thought it prudent to retire; and this appears to be his nearest approach to elephant-hunting on this journey. But then, it must be recollected that he does not narrate his adventures as a hunter, but rather those of a seeker for another man. If we may be permitted to paraphrase a famous expression, he was a hunter of men, as St. Peter was a fisher of men. It is for this reason, because he had something better to do, that we find few hunting stories told; and if he narrates no mavelous stories of being chased by buffalo or elephants, he usually bagged the game for which he went prepared.

It was some days after this, and as they traveled, the sportsman had several times shot fine animals, that they came to their old quarters on the Gombe, a district which Stanley had already described as the hunter's paradise. The rain had scattered the greater number of the herds, but there was plenty of game in the vicinity. Soon after breakfast he took Khamisi and Kalulu with him for a hunt. After a long walk they arrived near a thin jungle, where he discovered the tracks of several animals—boar, antelope, elephant, rhinoceros, hippopotamus, and an unusual number of imprints of the lion's paw. Suddenly he heard Khamisi say:

"Master! Master! Here is a *simba* (lion)!"

He came up to his master trembling with excitement and fear—for the young fellow was an arrant coward—to point out the head of a beast, which could just be seen across the tall grass, looking steadily at them. It immediately afterward bounded from side to side, but the grass was so high that it was impossible to tell exactly where it was. Taking advantage

STANLEY AND LIVINGSTONE RECEIVING "WHITE MAN'S NEWS" IN THE HEART OF AFRICA.

of a tree in front, Stanley crept quietly onward, intending to rest the heavy rifle against it, as he was so weak from the effects of several fevers that he felt himself utterly incapable of supporting the piece for a steady aim. But his surprise was great when he cautiously laid it against the tree, and then directed its muzzle to the spot where he had seen the lion stand. Looking further away, to where the grass was thin and scant, he saw the animal bound away at a great rate, and it was a lion; the noble monarch of the forest was in full flight! From that moment the hunter ceased to regard him as "the mightiest among the brutes," or his roar as anything more fearful in broad daylight than a sucking dove's.

February 14, they arrived at Uganda, where they found no less than seven packets of letters and newspapers for Stanley, one containing some letters for Livingstone. The letters were of course read with much interest, but the papers were skimmed over, and those which contained merely news were laid aside for—*Punch*.

While they were thus engaged, their doors were crowded with curious natives, who looked with indescribable wonder at the great sheets. Stanley heard them often repeat the words, "*Khabari, Kisungu*,"—white man's news—and heard them discussing the nature of such a quantity of news, and expressing their belief that the *Wasungu* were very "*mbyah sana*," and "*mkali*," by which they meant to say that the white men were very wicked, and very smart and clever; though the term wicked is often used to express high admiration.

Stanley bade farewell to Livingstone March 14, 1872; it was with much regret that he did so, for although their acquaintance had been but four months in duration, it had been so intimate, and he had learned so to revere and love the elder man that it was as if he were leaving the tried friend of many years.

Livingstone committed to Stanley's care his journal, properly sealed, and many papers and letters. The box containing these precious documents was of course most jealously guarded; but on one occasion it was run into danger. The caravan had arrived at the banks of the Mukondokwa River. It had rained the whole night, and the morning brought no cessation. Mile after mile they traversed, over fields covered by the inundation, until they came to a branch river-side once again, where the river was narrow, and too deep to ford in the middle. They proceeded to cut a tree down, and so contrived that it should fall right across the stream. Over this fallen tree,

"YOU DROP THAT BOX—I'LL SHOOT."

the men, bestriding it, cautiously moved before them their bales and boxes; but one young fellow, Rojab, through over-zeal, or in sheer madness, took up the doctor's box which contained his letters and Journal of his discoveries on his head, and started into the river. Stanley had been the first to arrive on the opposite bank, in order to superintend the crossing, when he caught sight of this man walking in the river with the most precious box of all upon his head. Suddenly he fell into a deep hole, and the man and box went almost out of sight, while the white man was in an agony at the fate that threatened the dispatches. Fortunately, he recovered himself and stood up, while Stanley shouted to him, with a loaded revolver pointed at his head:

"Look out! Drop that box and I'll shoot you!"

All the men halted in their work while they gazed at their comrade who was thus imperiled by bullet and flood. The man seemed himself to regard the pistol with the greatest awe, and after a few desperate efforts succeeded in getting the box safely ashore. As the articles within were not damaged, Rojab escaped punishment, with a caution not to touch the box again on any account; and it was transferred to the keeping of the sure-footed and perfect pagazi, Maganga.

From this stream, in about an hour, they came to the main river, but one look at its wild waters was enough. They worked hard to construct a raft, but after cutting down four trees and lashing the green logs together, and pushing them into the whirling current, they saw them sink like lead. They then tied together all the strong rope in their possession, and made a line one hundred and eighty feet long, with one end of which tied round his body, Chowpereh was sent across to lash it to a tree. He was carried far down the stream, but being an excellent swimmer he succeeded in his attempt. The bales were lashed around the middle, and, heaved into the stream, were dragged through the river to the opposite bank, as well as the tent, and such things as could not be injured much by the water. Several of the men, as well as the leader, were also dragged through the water, each of the boys being attended by the best swimmers; but when they came to the letter boxes and valuables, they could suggest no means to take them over. Two camps were accordingly made, one on each side of the stream; the one on the bank from which the crossing was made occupying an ant-hill of considerable height, while the party that had crossed was obliged to content itself with a flat, miry marsh. An embankment of soil, nearly a foot high, was thrown up in a circle nearly thirty feet in diameter, in the center of which the leader's tent was pitched and around it booths were erected.

It was an extraordinary and novel position in which they found themselves; within twenty feet of their camp was a rising river, with low, flat banks; above them was a gloomy, weeping sky; surrounding them on three sides was an immense forest, on whose branches they heard the constant, pattering rain; beneath their feet was a great depth of mud, black and loathesome; add to these the thought that the river might overflow, and sweep them to utter destruction.

In the morning the river was still rising; and an inevitable doom seemed to hang over them. There was yet time to act, to bring over the people, with the most valuable effects of the expedition, as its leader considered Dr. Livingstone's Journal and letters and his own papers. While looking at the awful river an idea struck him that he might possibly carry the boxes across, one at a time, by cutting two slender poles, and tying cross-sticks to them, making a kind of hand-barrow, on which a box might rest when lashed to it. Two men swimming across, at the same time holding on to the rope, with the ends of the poles resting on their shoulders, he thought, would be enabled to convey over a seventy-pound box with ease. In a short time one of these was made, and six couples of the strongest swimmers were prepared, and stimulated with a rousing glass of grog for each man, with a promise of cloth also to each if they succeeded in getting everything ashore undamaged by the water. When he saw with what ease they dragged themselves across, the barrow on their shoulders, he wondered that they had not thought of the plan before. Within an hour after the first couple had gone over, the entire expedition was safe on the eastern bank; and at once breaking camp they marched north through the swampy forest, which in some places were covered with four feet of water. Seven hours constant splashing brought them to Rehenneko. On a hill near this point, they encamped for ten days or until April 25; when, the rain having entirely ceased, they resolved to attempt the crossing of the Makata. But they should have waited a month longer, for the inundation had not abated four inches. However, after they had once struggled up to their necks in water, it was useless to turn back. For two marches of eight hours each they plunged through slush, mire, deep sloughs, water up to their necks, and muddy cataclysms, swam across nullahs, waded across gullies, and near sunset of the second day arrived at the banks of the Makata River. They were not likely to forget that night; not one of them was able to sleep until long past midnight, because of the clouds of mosquitoes, which threatened to eat them all up; and when the horn sounded for the march of another day, there was not one dissentient among them.

It was 5 A. M. when they began the crossing of the Makata River; but beyond it for six miles stretched one long lake, the waters of which flowed gently toward the Wami. This was the confluence of the streams; four rivers were here gathered into one. The natives of Kigongo warned them not to attempt it, as the water was over their heads; but the leader had only to give a hint to his men, and they set out on their way. They were soon up to their arm-pits; then the water shallowed to the knee; then they stepped up to the neck, supporting the children above the water. The same experiences occurred as those which they had suffered the day before, until they were halted on the edge of the Little Makata, which raced along at the rate of eight knots an hour; but it was only fifty yards wide, and beyond it rose a high bank and dry park lands which extend as far as Simbo. They had no other option than to swim it; but it was a slow operation, the current was so swift and strong. Activity and zeal, high rewards, presents of money, backed by the lively feeling that they were nearing home, worked wonders, and in a couple of hours they were beyond the Makata.

Cheery and hopeful, they sped along the smooth, dry path that now lay before them, with the ardor and vivacity of heroes, and the ease and power of veterans. They rolled three ordinary marches into one that day, and long before night arrived at Simbo.

But it is not our province to attend the traveler when his journey is rapid and prosperously uneventful; we therefore omit details of the length of marches, etc., and merely note the end. At sunset on the 6th of May they entered Bagamoyo. Here Mr. Stanley found Lieut. Henn and Mr. Oswald Livingstone, who were in charge of the Livingstone Search and Relief Expedition. The first head of that expedition, Lieut. Dawson, had hurried off to Zanzibar and resigned the command of it as soon as he heard that Stanley had found Livingstone. The traveler was warmly congratulated by these two gentlemen, and his advice asked as to what remained for them to do. He assured them that Dr. Livingstone wanted only for a few things, which he had promised to send by an escort of fifty trusty men as soon as he reached Zanzibar; but advised that Mr. Livingstone should go to his father.

But the son was not possessed of the father's iron constitution; and his health at this time was such that Dr. Kirk strongly advised him not to attempt the trip. He therefore decided not to go; and Stanley followed his original plan of sending a caravan with the needed supplies under the guidance of Arabs.

The New York *Herald* Expedition to Africa had originally consisted of one man; later on, there were three white men, two of whom, however, died in Africa; the discharge of the black servitors reduced it to its original strength again; and the expedition may be considered to have been disbanded when Stanley sailed for England. He arrived there late in July, 1872, in company with Mr. Livingstone and Lieut. Henn, who had definitely given up the idea of heading the Royal Geographical Society's Search and Relief Expedition.

Stanley's reception in England would be of no interest at this time, were it not for the purpose of comparing it with future receptions in the same country. An intense jealousy of the American Expedition existed; so certain were the English that it could not succeed, that the leader of the English Expedition had actually received no instructions as to his course in case Stanley should have found and relieved Livingstone. The newspapers reflected the popular sentiment at the time when they said that Stanley had not found Livingstone so much as Livingstone had found Stanley.

This state of affairs, however, continued but a short time; and although the Geographical Society was a little stubborn about acknowledging the results of the trip, the government was less dilatory. The Queen's appreciation of his services was expressed by a suitable letter from the Minister for Foreign Affairs, and a gift of a beautiful gold snuff-box set with brilliants.

Of the appreciation with which his services met by his employer and that employer's master, the great American people and the other readers of the newspapers, it is not necessary to speak. His name had become known, before the beginning of his second African trip, in every household throughout the length and breadth of the land; and this, as things go now, is fame. What more could an adventurous man ask, even as a reward for finding Livingstone?

CHAPTER XVIII.

THE CAMERON-LIVINGSTONE SEARCH EXPEDITION.

AS we have seen from the conclusion of Stanley's narrative regarding the finding of Livingstone, the Royal Geographical Society had sent out, some time after the Herald's representative started, an expedition to find and relieve the great explorer who was acting under the instructions of this association. We have seen that this expedition was unnecessary, and that division among those composing it quickly put an end to its attempts to reach Livingstone.

Lieutenant Verney Lovett Cameron, of the British Navy, had volunteered his services for this expedition, but they were not accepted, for some reason or other. When, however, Dawson's expedition was reported to have broken up, he again volunteered to proceed to join Dr. Livingstone, taking with him such instruments and stores as the discoverer might require, and placing his services unreservedly at the doctor's disposal. There was then, apparently, no idea of sending out another expedition. Cameron next drew up a scheme for the exploration of the route to Victoria Nyanza via Mounts Kilima Njaro and Kenia, and the volcano reported to lie north of them—thus passing close to the water-shed between the coast rivers and the feeders of the Victoria Nyanza—and after surveying that lake, to work his way to the Albert Nyanza or Mwuta Nzige, and thence through Ulegga to Nyangwe and down the Congo to the west coast. The Council of the Royal Geographical Society were, however, of the opinion that this scheme could not be carried out with the funds at its disposal. But it was afterward decided to use the surplus remaining from the subscriptions for the first Livingstone Search Expedition in fitting out another; and of this Lieut. Cameron was chosen the leader. Mr. W. E. Dillon, a surgeon, was chosen as his companion; and after they reached Aden, Lieut. Cecil Murphy, R. A., volunteered to accompany them.

Arriving at Zanzibar, Lieut. Cameron esteemed himself fortunate in securing the services of Bombay, of whom mention has been made in connection with the explorations of Speke and Grant, and the first trip of Stanley. Bombay, however, was not the acquisition that they thought him; he was inclined to trade upon his reputation; and when appointed to hunt out good men for their service, he picked them up whereever he could find them, no matter what they might have been.

The expedition arrived at Bagamoyo, February 2, 1873. There was the usual difficulty about obtaining a sufficient number of pagazis for the trip; and after they started from Bagamoyo, something over a month after they reached the place, there was much the same trouble about deserters that every African traveler experiences. Nor had they gone many miles before they found out how hard it is to get food when those who have it persist that they do not wish to sell.

About the end of the first week in April, they heard that a village was close in front, and sent messengers to acquaint the chief of their approach. Astounding rumors were brought back, to the effect that the chief would not allow them to pass. They did not quite trust this, for each messenger told a different story; but camped where they were for one day until they should receive a definite answer. The hoped-for answer not having arrived on the 7th of April, they started on, and about noon arrived at the outskirts of a village. They found that the chief would not forbid their passing his village, provided they paid him mhongo, or tribute, to the extent of thirty doti. This chief of Msuwah had entered into a treaty with the people of Whinde, to pay them a certain number of slaves, in return for the privilege of taxing all the caravans passing through his country, except those who came from Whinde. Cameron cites this as an instance of how little the sultan of Zanzibar can do to put down the slave-trade.

After various delays at points not far from the coast, they were joined by three caravans bound for the interior, so that when they marched from the Mukondokwa, June 11, they were over five hundred strong—powerful enough to defy the hostile natives if they should come in contact with any such. Ugogo was entered June 21, a country of which they had heard such stories that they anticipated some difficulty in passing through. The Wagogo are reputed to be great thieves, and so overbearing that any insult they inflict, Cameron was told, he must bear without resistance. Should a Wagogo be struck, or receive any injury, however imaginary, a fine was exacted; and if this were not immediately paid, they would attack and plunder the caravan. Such was the character which the travelers received; but although they found that the Wagogo were disposed to be insolent enough, they found also that they were the veriest cowards and poltroons it is possible to conceive.

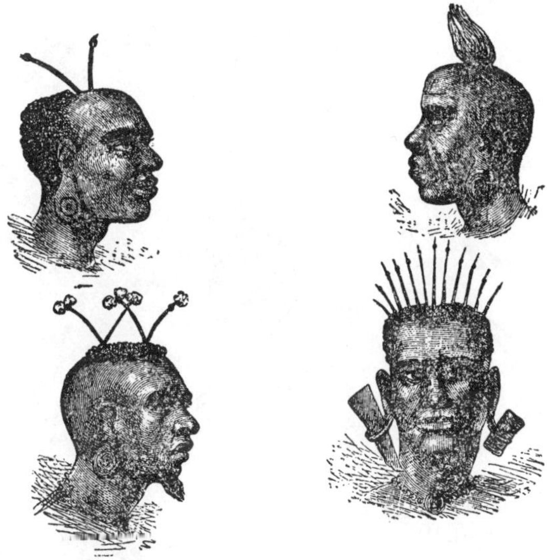

Wagogo Heads.

Their neighbors to the northward, however, are more courageous. These are the Wahumba, a branch of the great Masai nation, who possess large herds, but do not cultivate the grounds or maintain permanent habitations. Their diet consists entirely of milk mixed with blood and meat, which they devour almost raw. They move from place to place in search of pasture, sheltering themselves at night under a frame-work of small branches covered with one or two dressed hides. Their arms are short, heavy spears unfit for throwing, and double-edged swords; they also carry a huge shield.

The Wagogo complain much of the ravages of these neighbors, who are much braver than they are; and since the Masai do not recognize the right of other tribes to own cattle, they help themselves to these animals whenever they find a herd handy.

A MASAI WARRIOR.

Arriving at Unyanyembe in August, after a journey the details of which need not here be repeated, since it was over the same route as that traversed by the *Herald* Expedition, and was marked by no events of special importance, they were well received by the Arabs of the place, and lodged in the

Lieut. V. L. Cameron.

house which Livingstone had occupied, with Stanley as his guest. While they were here, a caravan arrived from Mtesa, the great chief of the Waganda, bringing a letter from Sir Samuel Baker addressed to Dr. Livingstone. Lieut. Cameron thought it advisable to open this letter, as it might contain some clue to Livingstone's movements; and sent in reply to it a letter to Sir Samuel, and one, written both in English and Arabic, to Mtesa.

For weeks they remained in Unyanyembe, unable to leave because they could not secure sufficient pagazis to carry their baggage. Nor could they have gone on if they had had the necessary help; for all three white men were frequently prostrated by fever, and their eyes were so affected that now one and now another would be completely blind. It was October 20, when Cameron lay on his bed, listless and enfeebled from repeated attacks of fever, his mind dazed and confused with whirling thoughts and fancies of home, that his servant came running into the tent with a letter in his hand. Cameron snatched it from him, and demanded to know where it came from.

"Some man bring him," was the only reply.

It was that letter which Jacob Wainwright had written, announcing his master's death to the leader of the Relief Expedition, who, it was supposed, must be Mr. Oswald Livingstone. Being half blind, it was with some difficulty that Cameron deciphered the writing, and then, failing to attach any definite meaning to it, he went to Dillon. His brain was in much the same state of confusion from the fever, and they read it again together, each having the same vague idea: "Could it be my own father who is dead?"

But when they knew that it was Chuma who had brought the letter, they understood what they had been reading. Supplies were at once sent for the caravan, and a messenger was dispatched to the coast to announce Dr. Livingstone's death.

What was now to be done? Obviously, the Livingstone Search and Relief Expedition was at an end. Dillon and Murphy decided to return to the coast, the health of both being seriously affected by the fever; while Cameron, more indomitable, persisted in advancing, with the intention of following up, if possible, the discoveries of Livingstone. Nov. 9, both caravans started; one for the eastern coast, comprising Livingstone's attendants bearing his body, Murphy and Dillon; while Cameron set out for the West. His expedition now consisted of himself, Bombay, Asmani and Mabruki, who had been with Stanley, four others as servants, cooks, etc., and about a hundred pagazis and askaris, the number varying from day to day, as some deserted and more enlisted.

The Sindi was crossed by means of one of the floating islands of vegetation which are common to this river; and the Malagarazi by means of the canoes of native ferrymen. It was Feb. 18, 1874, when they first came within sight of Tanganyika. The first sight was disappointing; lying at the bottom of a steep descent was a bright blue patch about a mile long, then some trees, and beyond them a great gray expanse, having the appearance of a sky with floating clouds. It was not until his men had persisted that this was the lake, that it dawned upon Cameron that the vast gray expanse was Tanganyika, and that the "clouds" were the distant mountains of Ugoma, while the blue patch was an inlet lighted up by a passing ray of the sun.

Hurrying down the descent and across the flat at the bottom, they reached the shore, and embarked in two canoes which the Arabs had sent from Ujiji. After an hour's pull they reached Kawele. Here he endeavored to get a boat for a sail on Tanganyika; but the owner demanded ivory in payment, of which commodity he had none. He learned that Mohammed bin Salib had ivory to sell for cloth; but as Cameron had no cloth, this did not help matters any. Further investigation revealed that Mohammed bin Gharib had cloth, and wanted wire, of which Cameron had a supply. Accordingly, the wire was traded for the cloth, the cloth was traded for the ivory, and the ivory was traded for the use of the boat, and he set out on his voyage.

It was March 13 when he began this trip about the lake; for ten days he traversed the same part of it that had been gone over by Livingstone and Stanley; on the 23d he rounded Ras Kungwe, and entered upon that part of the lake which had hitherto been unexplored, and indeed unseen by any white man. Ras Kungwe is situated near the narrowest part of the lake, where it is not more than fifteen miles across. But they did not go far beyond this point. A single day's sail, and they turned back toward the starting-point.

They landed at several villages on their voyage, for the purpose of obtaining food; and usually camped on shore, although not always near a village. Wherever in contact with the people, Lieut. Cameron noted with a keen eye the evidences of their manufactures, habits, and other particulars. A single paragraph will show how concisely he gives his impressions of their appearance:

"No imported cloth was to be seen at the village of Kitata, the people wearing skins, bark-cloth, or cotton of their own manufacture. The natives suspend their clothing around the waist by rope as thick as the little finger, bound neatly with

VILLAGE OF KITATA, TANGANYIKA LAKE.

brass wire. Their wool is sometimes anointed with oil in which red earth has been mixed, giving them the appearance of having dipped their heads in blood."

Reaching Kasongalowa, he determined to cross the lake and work northward along the opposite shore. It was his great desire to find what Livingstone and Stanley had sought, the outlet of Tanganyika. In order to do so, he had scrupulously investigated the direction of every river to which they came, until his men became a little particular as to whether a river about which he asked information flowed into the lake or out of it; many Africans will give the answer which they think is desired, and while this is pleasant enough at the time, it does not afford much satisfaction when the traveler has disproved the assertion.

On the 3d of May, he arrived at the Lukuga, which he had previously been assured flowed outward. A chief had told him very positively, in addition to the less detailed statements that he obtained from his own men, that the river was well-known to his people, who often traveled for more than a month along its banks, until it fell into a larger river, the Lualaba, and that in its course it received the Lulumbiji and many small streams.

Cameron went four or five miles down this stream, but found it blocked with vegetable obstructions. He hired natives, however, to cut a passage through these masses of plants, and determined to follow its course. Further consideration, however, told him that he had not sufficient means to justify him in cutting the channel through the grass and buying canoes; and accordingly the project was given up, and the traveler returned to Ujiji.

During this second stay at Ujiji, he had many talks with the Arabs who were familiar with the country, and learned from them that in their opinion the Lualaba was the same as the Congo. "Whence they got this idea," he says, "I could not ascertain." This is the first hint, we believe, in any published book, that the Lualaba is the Congo, or a tributary of it; and it should be remembered that this was said to him by the Arabs before Livingstone's Last Journal, suggesting that it might be so (although he did not wish to believe that the Lualaba was not a tributary of the Nile system), was published.

Having determined upon traveling by land, at least until the obstructions in the river should be passed, Cameron left Ujiji May 31. Marching through the heat (the thermometer

PLENTY OF COMPANY, YET LONELY IN THE HEART OF AFRICA.

registered one hundred and thirty-one degrees in partial shade), they forded the Lugumba at noon the next day. That same afternoon, they crossed the water-shed between the Lugumba and the Lukuga. The former of these two streams must not be confused with the Ruhumba, as is often done; this river was crossed several days later, the current being so swift that they were obliged to throw across it a rope made of the wild creepers for the men to hold to, that they might not be swept away.

It is to be noted that here to the west of Tanganyika Cameron found a custom prevalent among the tribes east of it, noted by Livingstone; but whereas in the eastern country it was followed by all classes, in the western only the lower classes disfigured their women in this way; leading Cameron to believe that these were the aborigines, who had retained one of their customs which their conquerors disdained to observe. The custom is that of wearing the lip-ring, which obtains only among the women as a rule, although some cases have been noted of men wearing it. The upper lip of a small girl is perforated, and a piece of stone, wood, or metal, inserted to prevent the wound growing up. Gradually the orifice is enlarged by substituting a larger piece of material for that previously used; and in some cases the lip protrudes an inch and a half or two inches. The lip-ring cannot be said to add to a lady's beauty, but it is the fashion in Ubudjua and some other countries, and is most cheerfully and even proudly worn.

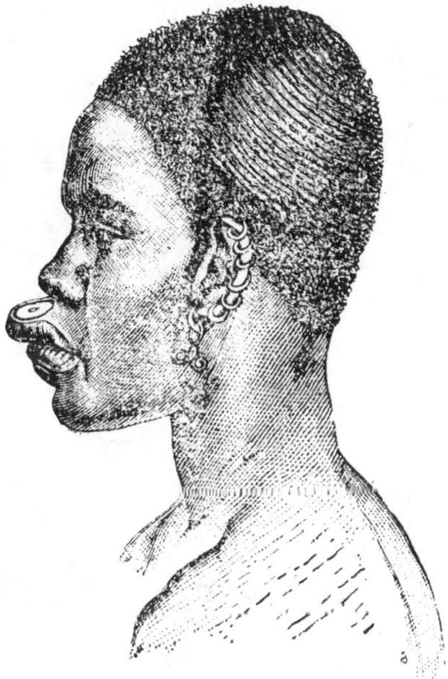

The Pelele or Lip-Ring.

At Pakundi, they fell in with a caravan of about two hundred and fifty, with whom, for mutual protection, they continued their journey through Manyuema. The caravan was in reality composed of several, and some of the leaders were slave-traders. Cameron thus had an opportunity of witnessing

VILLAGE IN MANYUEMA.

for himself something of the system of buying slaves; and gives it as his opinion that the slaves are much better treated by the traders than while they remained in the hands of their native owners. They were mostly captives, surprised when in the woods a short way from their own villages, and had, of course, to be kept in chains to prevent their escaping; otherwise they were not really badly used, being fairly fed and not overloaded. In the few cases of bad treatment which came under his notice, the owners were either slaves themselves, or freedmen who, on beginning to taste the delights of freedom, seemed anxious to prevent any one lower in the scale from rising to a like state of happiness. This is one man's observation of the slave-trade; Livingstone saw the other side of the question when he described the bodies that he had seen, the victims of their master's rage because their strength had failed them.

As usual, Cameron closely observed the clothing, household arrangements, and customs of the people. His descriptions of musical instruments used in Manyuema are especially interesting, as enabling the reader to see clearly the original form of the complicated instruments in use among civilized peoples. For instance, the *marimba* evidences a musical genius which, among more cultured surroundings, might have produced a Beethoven. It is formed of two rows of gourds fitted into a framework; and over each pair of gourds a clef of hard wood is placed; when struck with sticks having india-rubber heads, this gives out a metallic sound. The gourds are of course varied in size to produce the different notes; and there were different sizes of the sticks, the player dexterously changing one for another, as a sharper or duller sound was required. Bells, drums, gongs and rattles were also used by the native band by which he was on one occasion serenaded.

The Lulindi was crossed July 18. This stream was rendered remarkable to the Englishman by a bridge which had been made across it, since it is unfordable in time of flood. At a height of twenty feet above the water, four large cables of creepers were fastened to the trunks of trees, one pair about four feet higher than the other; and to these cables were secured other creepers from the tops of the loftiest trees on each side of the stream, while horizontal guys prevented the bridge from swaying about. Across the lower pair of cables sticks were laid to form a roadway. These were lashed to their places and wattled in with creepers, while a large network of the same connected the upper and lower cables on the same side of the bridge. Altogether it was a very ingenious and effective structure, and rather astonished the officer, as he had never seen any similar construction in Africa and never afterward met with such another.

Native Suspension Bridge Across the Lulindi.

They came in sight of the Lualaba August 3—a strong and sweeping current of turbid yellow water fully a mile wide, and flowing at the rate of three or four knots an hour. There were enormous herds of hippopotami blowing and snorting, and here and there the long scaly back of a crocodile floating almost flush with the water. The passage down the river was rapid and pleasant, owing to the swift current and the beauty of the scenery; and they arrived at Nyangwe late that afternoon.

But at Nyangwe it was impossible to get canoes to continue the journey; those who owned them, and were willing to sell, refused to accept anything but slaves in payment; and Cameron explained, again and again, that a British subject could not deal in slaves. His party was too small to travel by land with any safety, and his cowardly black companions flatly told him that they would not attempt it; he was therefore very glad when Tipo-Tipo, whose camp was about ten marches off, came to Nyangwe to act as arbitrator between the people of that place and the chief Rossuna; and permitted the Englishman to travel under his escort.

The time at Nyangwe was not wasted, but spent in collecting geographical information. Here it was that Cameron definitely discovered that the Lualaba could not be a tributary of the Nile, since it is lower at Nyangwe than the Nile at Gondokoro, below the point at which it has received all its affluents. He learned from the natives that the Lualaba flowed into a great lake, which he supposed to be that which Livingstone had named Lake Lincoln.

They reached the Rovubu shortly after setting out, and crossed it by means of a native bridge, displaying great pains, but scarcely as much engineering skill as that made of the creepers. They arrived at Rossuna's village August 29, and halted there for two days. During this time, the chief frequently visited Cameron, bringing a different wife with him each time. Finally the women visited him in a body, and became very inquisitive, turning back the legs and sleeves of his clothes to see if it was his face alone that was white. They became so inquisitive that he began to fear they would undress him altogether, and threw some beads and cowries among them, to scramble for; and thus escaped their attentions.

Before making preparations for crossing the Lomami, they had to receive a visit from Kasongo, the chief of the district. They arrayed themselves in their best, and assembled in an open shed, which was the general meeting-place of the settlement during the day, and often far into the night. The chief's master of ceremonies first arrived, carrying a long carved walking-stick as a badge of office; after him, different sub-chiefs and shield-bearers came, a few of the more important being followed also by drummers. After some time, drumming and shouting announced the approach of the great man himself, who came in grand procession. With him Cameron had a long conversation, acquainting Kasongo with his wish to cross the river and proceed to Lake Sankorra. The chief graciously promised to secure permission for the white man to pass through the territories of the chief across the river; and took his departure in the state in which he had come. The visit was returned two days afterward; and Cameron learned that permission to travel through the neighboring chief's country would not be given.

His direct road to the lake being thus closed, he tried to find some more circuitous route; and decided to make his way to the country of the Warua, and then work backward to Sankorra. Nearing the Lukazi River, he found that the natives were not friendly, as his men had predicted. While he was in front looking for the road, he was unpleasantly surprised by some arrows being shot at them from a narrow strip of jungle. One of them glanced off his own shoulder; and catching sight of the fellow who shot at him lurking behind a tree, he dropped his rifle and started in chase. Fortune favored the white man, for his enemy tripped and fell; and before he could regain his feet, the pursuer was down upon him, and after giving him as sound a thrashing as he ever had in his life, smashed his bow and arrows. This finished, the white man pointed to some of the black man's friends who were now in view, and considerably assisted him in joining them by means of stern propulsion, the kick being a hearty one.

Passing through some villages near this point, they met with anything but a cordial reception; a number of arrows being discharged at them as soon as they came in sight. The key to this behavior on the part of the natives is to be found in the fact that several caravans of slave-traders had recently passed through that country, and Cameron was taken for one of that ilk.

Rumors reached them continually of traders who were "Wasungu," or white men; and Cameron learned, some time in October, that he was to receive a visit from one of these, Jose Antonio Alvez. Great was his disappointment when an old and ugly negro turned out of the hammock in which he had come in state. Alvez insisted that he was thoroughly civilized, and the same as an Englishman or any other white man; and insisted that his word was as good as his bond, that he never lied, that he was altogether the most honest man on the face of the earth.

Cameron received promises of protection from Alvez, if the Englishman would agree to pay him a certain amount when they reached the coast in safety; and arrangements were accordingly made for traveling with him. But since he did not propose to start for about a month, the Englishman decided to explore Lake Mohrya in the meantime.

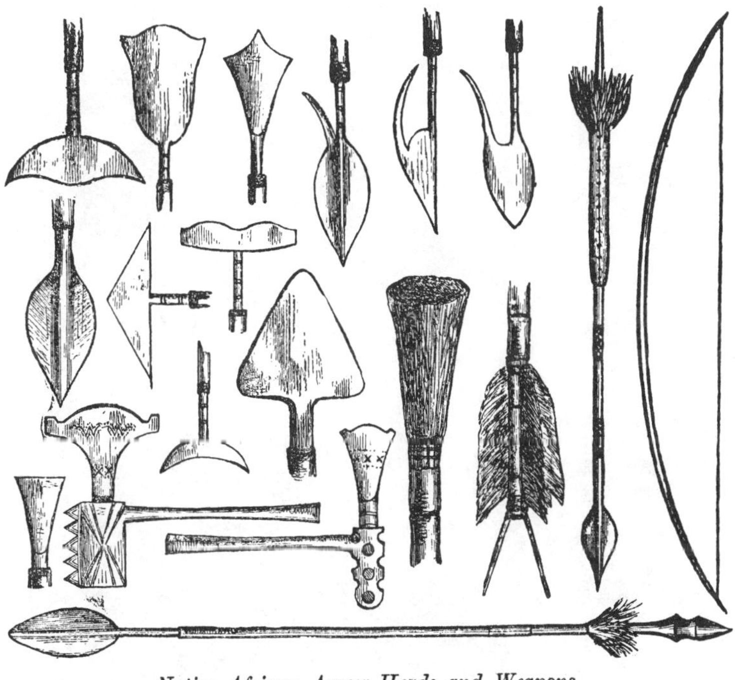

Native African Arrow-Heads and Weapons.

It was his special desire to visit the lake-dwellers of Mohrya, but he found it impossible to procure canoes when he had arrived at the shores of the lake. He was therefore obliged to content himself with sketches made from the shore; and on his way back to the camp of Alvez busied himself with details of the customs of the Warua, their manners, religion, and dress.

Lake Kassali, or Kikonja, was also attempted; but the white man was not permitted to reach it.

KASONGO AND HIS COURT.

Alvez had professed that he was waiting for Kasongo to return from an extensive raid, in order to secure that chief's permission to depart and travel through his territories; and Cameron thought that when the chief returned to the capital, he would soon be off for the coast. But if Alvez's word was as good as his bond, the bond was utterly worthless; for Cameron found him to be a most accomplished liar. It is true that shortly after Kasongo's return, the latter held an imposing ceremony, which was intended to give Cameron to understand that he and Alvez were now free to leave the village; threatening Alvez with his vengeance if Cameron did not reach the coast in safety. A short description of the scene will not be out of place:

"Alvez and his men, all of whom carried guns, were formed in line along one side of the open space toward the entrance to the mussumba, and Jumah Merikani and myself, with our followers, sat opposite. Midway between these two lines, and towards one end, stood Kasongo. Facing him was a man supporting a curiously shaped axe, and immediately behind him were four women, one of whom also carried an axe similar in form to that in front. Then followed two Waganga, and women bearing Kasongo's shields, and behind them a party of men with all Kasongo's guns, standing in line, and flanked on either side by executioners and other officials. In rear of all were his wives and children. Opposite to Kasongo, and close to the entrance of the mussumba, were the chiefs who had been summoned to attend with their followers, all arrayed in their best."

Upon one pretext after another, Alvez delayed their departure; and it was not until February 25 that they actually set out. The whole caravan numbered about seven hundred; and before leaving Urua, they had collected about fifteen hundred slaves, chiefly by force and robbery. Cameron found that the Portuguese were by far the most inhuman of those who had to do with slaves; and had he not seen the treatment to which these unfortunate beings were subjected, be could scarcely have believed that any men could be so wantonly and brutally cruel.

March and April passed without making any real progress; for in February they had only advanced as far as another settlement of Kasongo's. After every other excuse had been exhausted, an unfortunate fire occurred. One of Cameron's men had smoked himself stupid with *bhang*, and the lighted fire inside his hut, unwatched, reached the hut itself, which was to windward of the camp. It spread rapidly, and Cameron's journals and other books were only saved by the exertions of two of his men, who left their own property to burn while they assisted their master. Cameron, of course, had to pay for the property that was destroyed; and was convinced that he paid for many things which had never been in the huts that were burned.

Alvez proved so dilatory that Cameron at last became impatient; and when they halted for an indefinite time upon the road, declared that he would go on alone. A considerable party traveling with Alvez for the sake of the security which numbers give promised to follow him; and the smaller party accordingly started onward.

Slave-Driver and Slave.

The next morning Cameron received an impertinent message from Alvez which made him determine to visit that worthy; and the result was that they again joined forces. One of Alvez' subordinates had been on a slave-hunt during this halt, and had returned with fifty-two women, tied together in lots of seventeen or eighteen, all laden with huge bundles of grass-cloth and other plunder. Cameron calculates that to obtain this number, at least ten villages had been destroyed, each having a population of from one to two hundred souls or about fifteen hundred in all. Some may, perchance, have escaped to neighboring villages, but the greater portion were undoubtedly burned when their village was surprised, shot while attempting to save their wives and families, or doomed to die of starvation in the jungle unless some wild beast put a more speedy end to their miseries. These poor, weary and footsore creatures who accompanied the caravan were covered with weals and scars, showing how unmercifully cruel had been the treatment of the savage who called himself their owner.

Toward the end of August, they arrived at the village of of Katende, the principal chief of a large portion of Lovale, which now consists of two or three divisions, although it was formerly under one ruler. Alvez and Cameron paid a visit to this chief in company, and found him sitting in state under a large tree, surrounded by his councilors. On either side was a fetich hut; one containing two nondescript figures of animals, and the other, caricatures of the human form divine; while from the branch of a tree a goat's horn was suspended from a rope of creepers as a charm, and dangled within a few feet of the sable potentate's nose.

He was dressed for the occasion in a colored shirt, felt hat, and a long petticoat made of colored pocket-handkerchiefs. He smoked unremittingly the whole time, for he was an ardent lover of the soothing weed. As it happened that his stock of tobacco was nearly exhausted, Cameron gained his esteem by making him a present of a little, in return for which he received a fowl and some eggs. To the Englishman's questions about Livingstone, the chief replied that he remembered him as having passed by his village; but there was very little information to be obtained respecting the great traveler, except that he rode an ox, a circumstance which seemed to have impressed itself indelibly upon Katende's memory.

Detained for several days at the village of Sha Kalembe, chief of the last district in Lovale, Cameron met with an experience which he considered decidedly unique. One of Alvez' men, learning that Cameron possessed some viongwa, planned to steal them; and hired one of Cameron's own men, for the consideration of a certain quantity of beads, to commit the actual theft. Fortunately, the Englishman's body servant, Jumah, knowing the value of the viongwa, had locked them securely up; so that the thief, not being provided with a "jimmy," could not get them. It appears that the beads were paid in advance, and expended before the uselessness of the effort was discovered; for when they found that it would not work, the directors of the scheme brought a claim against Cameron for the value of the beads with which they had bribed his man

RECEPTION OF CAMERON BY KATENDE.

to rob him, and for the value of the fish for which they intended to have traded the viongwa. Naturally enough, Cameron declined to pay this claim; whereupon the assertors of it threatened to seize as a slave the man who had received the beads. Although the fellow had proven himself thievish, his master recognized that he was possessed of some sterling qualities, and perceiving that the conspirators meant what they said, he decided that it would be wisest to satisfy their demand, preposterous as it was.

One of the most singular sights that he saw during his journey, was a figure which he was told was a "sham devil," a man dressed in a net-work of beads, wearing a painted mask, and completing his costume by a kilt of grass and a strip of fur down the back. Upon inquiring what a sham devil was, he learned that these men went to places supposed to be frequented by real devils, who, on seeing their prototypes, were scared away. He afterward saw several men, at different times, gotten up in this style, with slight variations.

Reaching Bihe early in October, he was at last rid of Alvez, who had plundered him most unmercifully upon all occasions. Thence he went to the coast with only his own party, the road being safe and comparatively well known. But when they reached a point a hundred and twenty-six miles from their destination, the party appeared so broken down by disease that Lieut. Cameron decided to take those who were strongest and most willing and push on by forced marches, sending assistance to the others. Five of his men volunteered to accompany him; and there were some others in the settlement whence they set out that expressed their willingness to keep up with him at any pace that he might use. His walking was a little too rapid for them, however, and they fell back. On the fourth day, a line appeared upon the horizon—a line that was clearly unmistakable as they looked more intently. It was the sea.

They were not only tired, but hungry, having but little food to start with, and having marched too rapidly to obtain much on the road. Eating their last morsel, they rested for the night; and early the next morning were again on the way. A messenger had been sent ahead, asking any charitably disposed person to send a little food to meet them on the way; and this morning, a messenger met them, carrying a basket containing wine, bread, tins of sardines, and a sausage. A trader at Katombela had sent them; and as they approached the town, they saw a couple of hammocks coming, followed by three men carrying baskets; another good Samaritan had come to meet the white man who had crossed Africa from the eastern to the western coast.

Having thus followed Lieut. Cameron's footsteps to the limits of civilization, here we leave him; for once arrived at settlements of white men, however rude they may be, and largely populated by the natives of Africa, we pursue his adventures no longer.

Native Women Carrying Their Children on the March.

What had been accomplished by his journey? We shall see later on how Stanley esteemed his discovery that the Lukuga was the outlet of Tanganyika; but there was one fact which he had indubitably ascertained—that the Lualaba was not a tributary of the Nile. Livingstone had unwillingly admitted that it might be a confluent of the Congo; Cameron found that this was most probably true; it remained for Stanley to prove, by the best of all evidence, that this great river of Central Africa reaches the sea by the estuary so long known to the civilized world, but never thoroughly explored until within the ninth decade of the nineteenth century.

CHAPTER XIX.

STANLEY CROSSES THE DARK CONTINENT FROM OCEAN TO OCEAN.

IN 1873, in consequence of the cession of some Dutch forts on the African coast to Great Britain, the latter country found itself involved in a war with Ashantee. This contest, in which Sir Garnet Wolseley, then but a young man won many laurels, interests us only because Henry M. Stanley was correspondent of the New York *Herald* from the seat of war; and followed the army through its perilous marches and into the battles which were fought. The first half of his volume entitled "Coomassie and Magdala" is based upon his experiences there, being largely composed of information furnished the readers of the newspaper which he represented. He returned to England in April, 1874, peace having been concluded, and devoted himself assiduously to the preparation of this volume for publication.

After the completion of this task, he was free from demands upon his time; and strolling about London, began to accumulate books upon African geography, geology, botany and ethnology. He knew what had been accomplished by African explorers, and how much remained to be done; and with the zeal of one who has a living interest in the subject, sat "inventing and planning, sketching out routes and laying out lines of possible explorations, noting many suggestions which the continued study of my project created. I also drew up lists of instruments and other paraphernalia that would be required to map, lay out, and describe the new regions to be traversed.

"I had strolled over to the office of the *Daily Telegraph* one day, full of the subject. While I was discussing journalistic enterprise in general with one of the staff, the editor entered. We spoke of Livingstone and the unfinished task remaining behind him. In reply to an eager remark which I made, he asked:

"'Could you, and would you complete the work? And what is there to do?'

"I answered:

"'The outlet of Lake Tanganyika is yet undiscovered. We know nothing, scarcely,—except what Speke has sketched out —of Lake Victoria; we do not even know whether it consists of one or many lakes; and therefore the sources of the Nile are still unknown. Moreover, the western half of the African continent is still a white blank.'

"'Do you think you can settle all this, if we commission you?'

"'While I live, there will be something done. If I survive the time required to perform all the work, all shall be done.'"

Thus was the matter begun; and this was the work marked out. But arrangements could not be at once concluded, because the New York *Herald* had prior claims on him. A cablegram was accordingly dispatched asking if Mr. Bennett would join the *Daily Telegraph* in sending Stanley to Africa, to complete the discoveries of Speke, Burton and Livingstone; to which was received the laconic reply: "Yes; Bennett."

Preparations were at once begun. Equipments—guns, ammunition, ropes, saddles, medical stores, provisions, gifts for native chiefs, scientific instruments, stationery, etc., were purchased; orders were given for the pontoons and boats which would be needed; and by the middle of August everything was prepared.

The most important single article of the outfit was a barge, the invention of Mr. Stanley himself. This was made of Spanish cedar, 3-8 of an inch thick, forty feet long, six feet beam, and thirty inches deep. It was built in sections, each eight feet long; and if these sections should prove too heavy for portage, they could again be divided into halves. A yawl and a gig were also provided, besides the pontoons; the latter of which proved unnecessary, the barge doing the work so well.

His companions were three in number; Frederick Barker, a clerk at the Langham Hotel; and two young Thames watermen, Francis John Pocock and his brother Edward. Mr. Edwin Arnold suggested that young English boatmen of good character would be of service to him by their river knowledge; and secured these stalwart and trustworthy young men.

Two magnificent mastiffs, a retriever, a bull-dog and a bull-terrier accompanied them. They sailed for Zanzibar August 15, 1874, and arrived there September 21. Several short excursions were made along the coast, in the intervals of the work of obtaining porters, etc., the most important of these being the exploration of the Rufiji River; a number of those connected with the former expedition, or who had been dispatched to Livingstone's relief after Stanley's return to the coast, were engaged; and November 12, 1874, they set sail from Zanzibar, and reached the mainland.

November 17, they left Bagamoyo, a party three hundred and fifty-six in number, including thirty-six women and ten boys, the line being nearly half a mile in length. The road which they chose lay some thirty miles to the north of that which has been adopted by most travelers. Their march through Ugogo was apparently a progress in a country of starvation; for the improvident natives had not saved enough grain for themselves from the last harvest, and this was the month (December) for planting. As they advanced, it became worse; and on one occasion they were reduced to two cupfuls of oatmeal gruel for each person, no native stores being attainable.

Reaching Sun January 12, they were much troubled by sickness among the caravan; and Edward Pocock was dangerously ill. But the discontent of the people at the difficulty of obtaining food was such that Stanley judged it best to keep moving, if only two or three miles a day. Accordingly, those who were in the worst condition were carried in hammocks, and they proceeded by easy stages. They reached Chiwyu January 18, and had just begun to erect grass huts, when the sick European died from typhus fever. Here they buried him at the foot of a hoary acacia with wide-spreading branches, and the lessened group of Europeans, with their army of black attendants, took up their journey westward the next day. This was by no means the first death in the expedition, although it was the first white man. Since leaving Bagamoyo, twenty had died, and no less than eighty-nine had deserted.

Hitherto, in the case of all explorers, the story has rather been one of difficulties resulting from the nature of the country than from the hostility of the natives. Mungo Park alone, of the great African explorers, met with his death at the hands of Africans. But the story of Stanley's journey across the continent is, throughout, a story of battle, he had learned forbearance, he tells us, from Livingstone; but this is a virtue which savage adversaries seldom appreciate, mistaking it for weakness and cowardice.

While encamped at Vinyata, a few days after Pocock's death, they received a visit from a great magic doctor, who brought

BURIAL OF EDWARD POCOCK.

them the welcome present of a fine fat ox. Repaid about four-fold for it, he came again the next day, bringing some milk, and again received a present. Stanley continues:

"Half an hour after the departure of the magic doctor, while many of the Wangwana were absent purchasing grain, and and others were in the forest collecting fagots, we heard war-cries. Imagining that they were the muster-call to resist their neigbors of Izanjeh, or of some tribe to the east, we did not pay much attention to them. However, as these peculiar war-cries, which may be phonetically rendered '*Hehua hehu*,' appeared to draw nearer, we mustered a small party on the highest ground of the camp, in an attitude of doubt and inquiry, and presently saw a large body of natives, armed with spears,

Curious African Head Dress.

bows and arrows, and shields, appear within a hundred yards on a similar high ground outside the camp. The sight suggested to us that they had mustered against us, yet I could divine no cause of grievance or subject of complaint to call forth a warlike demonstration.

"I dispatched two unarmed messengers to them to ask them what their intentions were, and to ascertain the object of this apparently hostile mob. The messengers halted midway between the camp and the crowd, and sitting down, invited two of the natives to advance to them for a '*shauri*' [palaver or conference].

"We soon discovered upon the return of the messengers that one of the Wangwana had stolen some milk, and that the natives had been aroused to make war on us because of the

SIGNS OF TROUBLE.

theft. They were sent back to inform the natives that war was wicked and unjust for such a small crime, and to suggest that they should fix a price upon the milk, and permit us to atone for the wrong by a handsome gift. After some deliberation the proposition was agreed to. A liberal present of cloth was made, and the affair had apparently terminated.

"But as this mob was about to retire peacefully, another large force appeared from the north. A consultation ensued, at first quietly enough, but there were one or two prominent figures there, who raised their voices, the loud, sharp and peremptory tones of which instinctively warned me that their owners would carry the day. There was a bellicose activity about their movements, an emphasis in their gestures, and a determined wrathful fury about the motion of head and pose of body that were unmistakable. They appeared to be quarreling doggedly with those who had received cloth for the milk, and were evidently ready to fight with them if they persisted in retiring without bloodshed.

"In the midst of this, Soudi, a youth of Zanzibar, came hastily upon the scene. He had a javelin gash near the right elbow joint, and a slight cut as though from a flying spear was visible on his left side, while a ghastly wound from a whirling knob-stick had laid open his temples. He reported his brother Suliman as lying dead near the forest, to the west of the camp.

"We decided, nevertheless, to do nothing. We were strong disciples of the doctrine of forbearance, for it seemed to me then as if Livingstone had taught it to me only the day before. 'Keep silence,' I said; 'even for this last murder I shall not fight; when they attack the camp, then it will be time enough.' To Frank I simply said that he might distribute twenty rounds of ammunition without noise to each man, and dispose our party on either side the gate, ready for a charge should the natives determine upon attacking us.

"The loudly arguing mob had not yet settled conclusively what they should do, and possibly hostilites might have been averted, had not the murderers of young Suliman, advancing red-handed and triumphant, extorted from all the unanimous opinion that it would be better after all to fight 'the cowardly Wangwana and the white men who were evidently only women.'

"They quickly disposed themselves, delivered loud whoops of triumph, prepared their bows, and shot their first arrows. The Wangwana became restless, but I restrained them. Perceiving no sign of life in our camp, the Wanyaturu judged, doubtless, that we were half dead with fright, and advanced boldly to within thirty yards, when the word was given to the Wangwana and the Wanyamwezi, who rushed outside, and by the very momentum of the rush drove the savages to a distance of two hundred yards. The Wangwana were then ordered to halt, and deployed as skirmishers.

"We still waited without firing. The savages, not comprehending this extraordinary forbearance, advanced once more. The interpreters were requested to warn them that we should delay no longer. They replied: 'Ye are women, ye are women: go, ask Mirambo how he fared in Ituru,' saying which they twanged their bows. It was only then, perceiving that they were too savage to understand the principles of forbearance, that the final word to fight was given. A brisk encounter was sustained for an hour, and then, having driven the savages away, the Wangwana were recalled to camp.

"Meanwhile Frank was busy with sixty men armed with axes in constructing a strong stockade, and on the return of the Wangwana they were employed in building marksmen's nests at each corner of the camp. We also cleared the ground to the space of two hundred yards around the camp. By night our camp was secure and perfectly defensible."

The 24th dawned, but Stanley and his men were in no mood for attacking. They were so hungry, exhausted and wretched as to be thankful if only their barbarian enemies would but let them alone. The camp seemed filled with invalids, frightened porters, donkey-boys, women and children instead of fighters. There were but seventy effective men ready for the struggle, and these were so dispirited by the circumstances as to desire nothing so much as immunity from further attack by the ruthless savages. But in the forenoon the hostile natives gathered again in their front larger than before in numbers and still fiercer for the fight; the whole neighboring country seemed to have been roused. The prospect seemed darker than ever, and danger of starvation or gradual extinction as one after another defender fell, seemed the only end in view. The situation was growing more desperate every hour. As Mr. Stanley adds in his intensely interesting account of the present perilous situation of his command:

"Our position, as strangers in a hostile country, is such that we cannot exist as a corporate expedition, unless we resist with all our might and skill, in order to terminate hostilities and secure access to the western country. We therefore wait until they advance upon our camp, and drive them back from its vicinity as we did the day before. In half an hour our people are back, and organized into four detachments of ten men each under their respective chiefs, two more detachments of ten men each are held in reserve, and one other, of ten also, detailed for the defense of the camp. They are instructed to proceed in skirmishing order in different directions through the hostile country, and to drive the inhabitants out wherever they find them lodged, to a distance of five miles east and north, certain rocky hills, the rendezvous of the foe, being pointed out as the place where they must converge. Messengers are sent with each detachment to bring me back information.

"The left detachment, under Chief Farjalli Christie, was thrown into disorder, and were killed to a man, except the messenger who brought us the news, imploring for the reserve, as the enemy were now concentrated on the second detachment. Manwa Sera was dispatched with fifteen men, and arrived at the scene only in time to save eight out of the second detachment. The third plunged boldly on, but lost six of its number; the fourth, under Chief Safeni, behaved prudently and well, and as fast as each inclosed village was taken set it on fire. But ten other men dispatched to the scene retrieved what the third had lost, and strengthened Safeni.

"About 4 P. M., the Wangwana returned, bringing with them oxen, goats and grain for food. Our losses in this day's proceedings were twenty-one soldiers and one messenger killed, and three wounded.

"On the morning of the 25th we waited until 9 A. M., again hoping that the Wanyaturu would see the impolicy of renewing the fight; but we were disappointed, for they appeared again, and apparently as numerous as ever. After some severe volleys we drove them off again on the the third day, but upon the return of the Wangwana, instead of dividing them into detachments, I instructed them to proceed in a compact body. Some of the porters volunteered to take the place of the soldiers who perished the previous day, and we were therefore able to show still a formidable front. All the villages in our neighborhood being first consumed, they continued their march, and finally attacked the rocky hill, which the Wanyaturu had adopted as a stronghold, and drove them flying precipitately into the neighboring country, where they did not follow them.

"We knew now that we should not be disturbed. * * * Our losses in Ituru were twenty-four killed and four wounded, and as we had twenty-five men on the sick-list, it may be imagined that to replace these fifty-three men great sacrifices were necessary, and much ingenuity had to be exercised. Twelve loads were accordingly placed on the asses, and ten chiefs were detailed to carry baggage until we should arrive in Usukuma. Much miscellaneous property was burned, and on the morning of the 26th, just before day-break, we resumed our interrupted journey."

Usiha proved much more hospitable, and they were not only kindly welcomed, but were able to procure the food which they needed so badly. Here, however, they were once in danger from the braying of an ass.

"When in sight of their conical cotes, we dispatched one of our native guides to warn the natives that a caravan of Wangwana was approaching, and to bear messages of peace and good will. But in his absence, one of the Kinyamwezi asses set up a terrific braying, which nearly created serious trouble. It appears that on one of his former raids the terrible Mirambo possessed a Kinyamwezi ass which also brayed, and like the geese of the Roman Capitol, betrayed the foe. Hence the natives insisted, despite the energetic denial of our guide, that this ass must also belong to Mirambo, and for a short period he was in a perilous state. They seized and bound him, and would probably have dispatched him had not the village scouts returned laughing heartily at the fright the vicious ass had caused."

Feb. 27, they reached the shores of the Victoria Nyanza. "The first quick view revealed to us a long, broad arm of water, which a dazzling sun transformed into silver, some six hundred feet below us, at a distance of three miles. A more careful and detailed view of the scene showed us that the hill on which we stood sloped gradually to the broad bay or gulf edged by a line of green wavy reeds and thin groves of umbrageous trees scattered along the shore, on which stood several small villages of conical huts. Beyond these, the lake stretched like a silvery plain far to the eastward, and away across to a boundary of dark blue hills and mountains, while several gray rocky islets mocked us at first with an illusion of Arab dhows with white sails."

The inhabitants of the nearest village, supposing that they were a force of Mirambo's men, hastily assembled in warlike array; but discovering their mistake, gave them a military reception. This village, Kagehyi, was to be their resting-place for some time; and Stanley's people began at once to make arrangements for building grass-huts in which to spend the time of rest.

Stanley soon found that it would be impossible to secure volunteers for the exploration of the great lake. He was informed that it was so large that it would take years to trace its shores; and who then would be alive? There were a people dwelling on its shores who were gifted with tails; another who trained enormous and fierce dogs for war; another a tribe of cannibals, who preferred human flesh to all kinds of meat. Its opposite shores, from their very vagueness of outline, and its people, from the distorting fogs of misrepresentation through which they were seen, only heightened the fears of Stanley's men as to the dangers which filled the prospect.

Within seven days the boat was ready, and strengthened for a rough sea life. Provisions of flour and dried fish, bales of cloth and beads of various kinds, odds and ends of all possible necessaries were boxed, and she was declared, at last, to be only waiting for her crew. Stanley called for volunteers from among his own men; not one offered to go. Rewards and extra pay were offered; still there was silence. At last, Manwa Sera said:

"Master, have done with these questions. Command your party. All your people are your children, and they will not disobey you. While you ask them as a friend, no one will offer his services. Command them, and they will all go."

After a little more delay, Stanley selected ten men and a steersman, and with this crew, set sail in the Lady Alice March 8, 1875, upon the waters of Speke Gulf of Victoria Nyanza. Kagehyi is situated near the entrance to Speke Gulf; their course was therefore westward until they should reach the head of this indentation. They reached its eastern point March 12, after a tempestuous voyage of three days, during which time the Lady Alice "bounded forward like a wild courser." The next day they visited the island of Ukerewe, which is separated from the mainland by a channel only six feet wide.

Coasting along Ururi, the country to the northeast of this island, they received the remarkable information that it would require eight years to circumnavigate the lake. Farther along, the natives expressed the most unqualified contempt of the method used for propelling the Lady Alice, but fled in terror when the sail was hoisted.

March 24, they reached the northeastern part of the lake, and their voyage along the northern shore began. Taking

ATTACKED BY GREAT WAR CANOE.

shelter from a furious northwester the next day near Ngevi Island, they saw a small canoe containing two men advancing toward them. Nothing could induce these men to come within one hundred yards; but presently, as if this had been a reconnoissance, a large canoe, propelled by forty paddlers, came towards them. Half of this number, who were seated forward, sprang up when they came within fifty yards, and seizing long tufted lances and shields, began to sway them menacingly. * * * After trial of several languages, a conversation in Kiganda was begun.

"They edged toward us a little nearer, and ended by ranging their long canoe alongside of our boat. Our tame, mild manners were in striking contrast to their bullying, overbearing and insolent demeanor. The paddlers, half of whom were intoxicated, laid their hands with familiar freedom upon everything. We still smiled, and were as mild and placable as though anger and resentment could never enter our hearts. We were so courteous, indeed, that we permitted them to handle our persons with a degree of freedom which appeared to them unaccountable—unless we were so timid that we feared to give offense. If we had been so many sheep, we could not have borne a milder or more innocent aspect. Our bold friends, reeling and jostling one another in their eagerness to offend, seized their spears and shields, and began to chant in bacchanalian tones a song that was tipsily discordant. Some seized their slings and flung stones to a great distance, which we applauded. Then one of them, under the influence of wine, and spirits elated by the chant, waxed bolder, and looked as though he would aim at myself, seated observant but mute in the stern of my boat. I made a motion with my hand as though deprecating such an action. The sooty villain seemed to become at once animated by an hysteric passion, and whirled his stone over my head, a loud drunken cheer applauding his boldness.

"Perceiving that they were becoming wanton through our apparently mild demeanor, I seized my revolver and fired rapidly into the water, in the direction the stone had been flung, and the effect was painfully ludicrous. The bold, insolent bacchanals had at the first shot sprung overboard, and were swimming for dear life to Ngevi, leaving their canoe in our hands. 'Friends, come back, come back; why this fear?' cried out our interpreter; 'we simply wished to show you that we had weapons as well as yourselves. Come, take your canoe; see, we push it away for you to seize it.' We eventually won them back with smiles. We spoke to them as sweetly

PURSUED BY A FLEET OF WAR-CANOES.

as before. The natives were more respectful in their demeanor. They laughed, cried out admiringly; imitated the pistol shots; 'Boom, boom, boom,' they shouted. They then presented me with a bunch of bananas. We became enthusiastic admirers of each other."

Encamping upon the shore of the Munulu River for a stormy night, they were actually attacked by the natives as they sheered off the next morning; and the steersman was wounded. Stanley discharged his revolver at them, and one fell, wounded; the others took the hint and retreated.

Coasting along the country of Uvuma, they found suddenly thirteen native canoes emerging from a small inlet. Not one had any articles on board but the first, which offered twenty potatoes for sale. The explorer offered various kinds of beads in return for the yams, but all were indignantly rejected; and the white man became convinced that they had not come to trade with him.

"They waxed noisy, then insolent, and finally aggressive. They seized one thing after another with a cunning dexterity, which required all our attention to divine their purposes; and while we were occupied with the truculent rabble in our front, a movement of which we were unaware was being made successfully at the stern; but the guide, Saramba, catching sight of a thief, warned me to cast my eyes behind, and I detected him in the act of robbery. Becoming assured by this time that the Wavuma had arrived in such numbers for the sole purpose of capturing what appeared to them an apparently easy prey, and that their maneuvers were evidently intended to embarrass us and distract our attention, I motioned them to depart with my hand, giving orders to the boat's crew at the same time to make ready their oars. This movement, of necessity, caused them to disclose their purposes, and they manifested them by audaciously laying their hands on the oars, and arresting the attempts of the boat's crew to row. Either we were free or we were not. If yet free men, with the power to defend our freedom, we must be permitted to continue our voyage on the sea without let or hindrance. If not free men, we had first to be disarmed. I seized my gun, and motioned them again to depart. With a loud, scornful cry, they caught up their spears and shields, and prepared to launch their weapons. To be saved, we must act quickly; and I fired over their heads; and as they fell back into the boats, I bade my men pull away. Forming a line on each side of us, about thirty yards off, they flung their spears, which the boat's crew avoided by dropping into the bottom of the boat. The canoes astern clapped their hands gleefully, showing me a large bunch of Matunda beads which had been surreptitiously abstracted from the stern of the boat. I seized my repeating rifle and fired in earnest, to right and to left. The fellow with the beads was doubled up, and the boldest of those nearest to me was disabled. The big rifle, aimed at the water-line of two or three of the canoes, perforated them through and through, which compelled the crews to pay attention to their sinking crafts, and permitted us to continue our voyage."

More friendly natives were found as they proceeded; and they were most hospitably entertained by the chief of Buka. He dispatched a messenger instantly upon their arrival to the Kabaka Mtesa to announce the coming of a stranger in the land; declaring, at the same time, his intention not to abandon the travelers until he had brought them face to face with the great monarch of Equatorial Africa. He smilingly assured them that in Mtesa they would find a friend, and that they might sleep secure under his protection.

April 2, under the escort of this chief, they proceeded on their way, purposely making their voyages short, in order that the Kabaka might be informed in time of their coming. Just as they were about to depart the next morning, they saw six beautiful canoes, crowded with men, coming round a point; and for a short period were under the impression that they were a piratical fleet on its way to intercept them. On surveying them with his glass, Stanley saw that they were dressed in in white, like the Wangwana; and received the information from his guides that these were the Kabaka's people. As they approached, the commander was seen arraying himself for the occasion. He donned a bead-work head-dress, over which long white cock's feathers waved; and a snowy white and long-haired goat-skin, while a crimson robe, depending from his shoulders, completed the full dress.

In the middle of the Bay of Kadzi, they encountered, and a most ceremonious greeting took place. This was the message which was brought, as it has been recorded by Stanley:

"The Kabaka sends me with many salaams to you. He is in great hopes that you will visit him, and has encamped at Usavara, that he may be near the lake when you come. He does not know from what land you have come, but I have a swift messenger with a canoe who will not stop until he gives all the news to the Kabaka. His mother dreamed a dream a few nights ago, and in her dream she saw a white man on this lake in a boat coming this way, and the next morning she told the Kabaka, and lo! you have come. Give me your answer, that I may send the messenger. *Twiyanzi-yanzi-yanzi!*" [Thanks, thanks, thanks.]

The embassador persuaded the traveler to rest at the village of Kadzi for a day, that he might see the hospitality of the country. The only difficulty with which Stanley met here, was in restraining the excessive extortions of Magassa, the envoy of Mtesa. Uganda was new to the explorer then; he was not aware how supreme the Kabaka's authority was; he suspected that the vast country which recognized his power was greatly abused, and grieved that these new acts of tyranny were inflicted for his sake.

April 5, they approached Usavara, the hunting village of the Kabaka; but Stanley must himself tell of his reception:

"When about two miles from Usavara, we saw what we estimated to be thousands of people arranging themselves in order on gently rising ground. When about a mile from the shore, Magassa gave the order to signal our advance with fire-arms, and was at once obeyed by his dozen musketeers. Half a mile off I saw that the people on the shore had formed themselves into two dense lines, at the ends of which stood several finely dressed men, arrayed in crimson and black and snowy white. As we neared the beach, volleys of musketry burst out from the long lines. Magassa's canoes steered outward to right and left, while two or three hundred heavily loaded guns announced to all around that the white man, of whom Mtesa's mother had dreamed, had landed. Numerous kettles and bass drums sounded a noisy welcome, and flags, banners and bannerets waved, and the people gave a great shout. Very much amazed at all this ceremonious and pompous greeting, I strode up toward the great standard, near which stood a short young man, dressed in a crimson robe which covered an immaculately white dress of bleached cotton, before whom Magassa, who had hurried ashore, kneeled reverently, and turning to me begged me to understand that this short young man was the Katekiro. Not knowing very well who the Katekiro was, I only bowed, which, strange to say, was imitated by him, only that his bow was far more profound and stately than mine. I was perplexed, confused, embarrassed, and I believe I blushed inwardly at all this regal reception, though I hope I did not betray my embarrassment.

"A dozen well-dressed people now came forward, and grasping my hand declared in the Swahili language that I was

RECEPTION OF STANLEY BY MTESA'S BODY-GUARD.

welcome to Uganda. The Katekiro motioned with his head, and amid a perfect concourse of beaten drums, which drowned all conversation, we walked side by side, and followed by curious thousands, to a court-yard, and a circle of grass-thatched huts surrounding a larger house, which I was told were my quarters.

"The Katekiro and several of the chiefs accompanied me to my new hut, and a very sociable conversation took place. There was present a native of Zanzibar, named Tori, whom I shortly discovered to be chief drummer, engineer, and general jack-of-all-trades for the Kabaka. From this clever, ingenious man I obtained the information that the Katekiro was the prime minister, or the Kabaka's deputy. * * * * Waganda, as I found subsequently, were not in the habit of remaining incurious before a stranger. Hosts of questions were fired off at me about my health, my journey and its aim, Zanzibar, Europe and its peoples, the seas and the heavens, sun, moon and stars, angels and devils, doctors, priests, and craftsmen in general; in fact, as the representative of nations who 'know everything,' I was subjected to a most searching examination, and in one hour and ten minutes it was declared unanimously that I had 'passed.' Forthwith after the acclamation, the stately bearing became merged into a more friendly one, and long, thin, nervous black hands were pushed into mine enthusiastically, from which I gathered that they applauded me as if I had won the honors of a senior wrangler. Some proceeded direct to the Kabaka and imformed him that the white man was a genius, knew everything, and was remarkably polite and sociable; and the Kabaka was said to have 'rubbed his hands as though he had just come into possession of a treasure.'"

After this searching examination was concluded, and reported to Mtesa, that chief dispatched refreshments for his guest. "These few things," as they were styled in the message accompanying them, were fourteen fat oxen, sixteen goats and sheep, a hundred bunches of bananas, three dozen fowls, four wooden jars of milk, four baskets of sweet potatoes, fifty ears of green Indian corn, a basket of rice, twenty fresh eggs, and ten pots of maramba wine. When the traveler had eaten and was satisfied, the Kabaka would send for him.

Promptly at the appointed hour, two pages came to summon the traveler to the presence of the foremost man of Central Africa.

"Forthwith we issued from our courtyard, five of the boat's

MTESA EXECUTES A FEW SUBJECTS IN HONOR OF A VISITOR.

crew on each side of me armed with Snider rifles. We reach a short broad street, at the end of which is a hut. Here the Kabaka is seated with a number of chiefs, *Wakungu* [generals] and *Watóngeleh* [colonels] ranked from the throne in two opposing kneeling or seated lines, the ends being closed in by drummers, guards, executioners, pages, etc., etc. As we approached the nearest group, it opened, and the drummers beat mighty sounds, Tori's drumming being conspicuous from its sharper beat. The foremost man of Equatorial Africa rises and advances, and all the kneeling and seated lines rise—generals, colonels, chiefs, cooks, butlers, pages, executioners, etc., etc.

The Kabaka, a tall, clean-faced, large-eyed, nervous-looking, thin man, clad in a tarbush, black robe, with a white shirt belted with gold, shook my hands warmly and impressively, and bowing not ungracefully, invited me to be seated on an iron stool. I waited for him to show the example, and then I and all the others seated ourselves.

"He first took a deliberate survey of me, which I returned with interest, for he was as interesting to me as I was to him. His impression of me was that I was younger than Speke, not so tall, but better dressed. This I gathered from his criticisms as confided to his chiefs and favorites.

"My impression of him was that he and I would become better acquainted, that I should make a convert of him, and make him useful to Africa."

It will be remembered that Speke's description of this potentate was not a very favorable one—vain and heartless, a wholesale tyrant and murderer, delighting in fat women. It had been his custom, in receiving a visitor with honors, to have his executioners strike off the heads of several slaves or subjects on the spot. Stanley found him intelligent, and well worthy the heartiest sympathies that Europe had to give him. What was the reason for this change? Stanley answers in his journal, in the entry written at this very time:

"I see that Mtesa is a powerful emperor, with great influence over his neighbors. * * * * I have witnessed with astonishment such order and law as is obtainable in semi-civilized countries. All this is the result of a poor Muslim's labor; his name is Muley bin Salim. He it was who first began teaching here the doctrines of Islam. False and contemptible as these doctrines are, they are preferable to the ruthless instincts of a savage despot, whom Speke and Grant left wallowing in the blood of women, and I honor the memory of Muley bin Salim

— Muslím and slave trader though he be—the poor priest who had wrought this happy change. With a strong desire to improve still more the character of Mtesa, I shall begin building on the foundation stones laid by Muley bin Salim. I shall destroy his belief in Islam, and teach the doctrines of Jesus of Nazareth."

Two days after his arrival at Usavara, Mtesa distinguished "Stamlee" by holding what he termed a review of his fleet, forty canoes, holding some twelve hundred men. "The captain of each canoe was dressed in a white cotton shirt and a cloth head-cover, neatly folded turban fashion, while the admiral wore over his shirt a crimson jacket profusely decorated with gold braid, and on his head the red fez of Zanzibar. Each captain, as he passed us, seized shield and spear, and with the bravado of a matador addressing the Judge of the Plaza to behold his prowess, went through the performance of defense and

A Waganda Band.

attack by water. The admiral won the greatest applause, for he was the Hector of the fleet, and his actions, though not remarkably graceful, were certainly remarkably extravagant. The naval review over, Mtesa commanded one of the captains of the canoes to try and discover a crocodile or hippopotamus. After fifteen minutes he returned with the report that there was a young crocodile asleep on a rock about two hundred yards away.

"'Now, Stamlee,' said Mtesa, 'show my women how white men can shoot.'

"[For the great chief was attended by a considerable number of the women composing his harem.] To represent all the sons of Japhet on this occasion was a great responsibility, but I am happy to say that—whether owing to the gracious influense of some unseen divinity who has the guardianship of their interests or whether from mere luck—I nearly severed the head of the young crocodile from its body at the distance of one hundred yards with a three-ounce ball, an act which was accepted as proof that all white men are dead shots."

Three days later, the court broke up its hunting-lodge and returned to the capital, Stanley following at a later hour, since it was necessary to house his boat from the sun. The road was eight feet wide, through jungle and garden and forest and field. We need not linger over the description of the beautiful scenery enjoyed during the three hours' march before they came in sight of a large cluster of tall, conical grass huts, in the center of which rose a spacious, lofty barn-like structure. The large building, they were told, was the palace, the hill, Rubaga, and the cluster of huts, the imperial capital!

A surprise awaited Stanley here. Received by Mtesa shortly after his arrival, he was informed that he would meet a white man at the palace the next day.

"A white man, or a Turk?"

"A white man, like yourself," repeated Mtesa.

"No; impossible!"

"Yes, you will see; he come from *Masr* (Cairo), from Gordoom (Gordon) Pasha."

"The white man, reported to be coming the next day, arrived at noon with great eclat and flourishes of trumpets, the sounds of which could be heard all over the capital. Mtesa hurried off a page to invite me to his burzah. I hastened up by a private entrance. Mtesa and all his chiefs, guards, pages, executioners, claimants, guests, drummers and fifers were already there, *en grande tenue.*

APPROACH TO MTESA'S PALACE AND CAPITAL.

Mtesa was in a fever, as I could see by the paling of the color under his eyes and his glowing eye-balls. The chiefs shared their master's excitement.

"'What shall we do,' he asked, 'to welcome him?'

"'Oh, form your troops in line from the entrance to the burzah down to the gates of the outer court, and present arms, and as he comes within the gate, let your drums and fifes sound a loud welcome.'

"'Beautiful!' said Mtesa. 'Hurry, Tori, Chambarango, Sekebobo; form them in two lines just as Stamlee says. Oh, that is beautiful! And shall we fire guns, Stamlee?"

"'No, not until you shake hands with him; and as he is a soldier, let the guards fire; then they will not injûre any one."

"Mtesa's flutter of excitement on this occasion made me think that there must have been a somewhat similar scene before my landing at Usavara, and that Tori must have been consulted frequently upon the form of ceremony to be adopted."

The stranger was M. Linant de Bellefonds, a member of the Gordon Pasha Expedition; and he and Mr. Stanley became excellent friends at once after this unexpected meeting in the heart of Africa. The coming of the Frenchman advanced one of Stanley's objects considerably. The envoy of the two great newspapers had, as we have already heard from his own lips, determined to make an effort to convert Mtesa to Christianity. It was his first missionary work; for up to the period of his first journey into the interior of Africa at least, he had "cared for none of these things." The four months' intercourse with Livingstone, however, close and constant as it was, had wrought a change; it was owing to no set effort of the elder man; but the influence of his life and character taught Stanley the worth of the religion which he professed. On the evening of the day that the traveler had his first interview with Mtesa, he wrote in his diary:

"In this man I see the possible fruition of Livingstone's hopes, for with his aid the civilization of Equatorial Africa becomes feasible. I remember the ardor and love which animated Livingstone when he spoke of Sekeletu; had he seen Mtesa, his ardor and love for him had been tenfold, and his pen and tongue would have been employed in calling all good men to assist him."

At every interview between them, the white man had made some effort to turn the conversation to the subject of religion; and not in vain. Mtesa and his principal chiefs soon became so absorbingly interested in the story of the Gospel as Stanley gave it to them that little of other business was done. Of course only the bare outlines were touched upon—those essential points which are accepted by all, and which are as intelligible to the savage and the child as to the doctor of divinity.

"I showed the difference in character between Him whom white men love and adore, and Mohammed, whom the Arabs revere; how Jesus endeavored to teach all mankind that we should love all men, excepting none; while Mohammed taught his followers that the slaying of the pagan and unbeliever was an act that merited Paradise. I left it to Mtesa and his chiefs to decide which was the worthier character. I also sketched in brief the history of religious belief from Adam to Mohammed. I had also begun to translate to him the Ten Commandments, and Idi, the emperor's writer, transcribed in Kiganda the words of the Law as given to him in choice Swahili by Robert Feruzi, one of my boat's crew, and a pupil of the Universities' Mission at Zanzibar."

M. Linant was a devout French Protestant. To him, shortly after his arrival, Mtesa directed certain inquiries regarding things which "Stamlee" had told him. To the astonishment of the king, the newcomer employed nearly the same words that had been used by his first instructor. "The remarkable fact that two white men, who had never met before, one having arrived from the southeast, the other from the north, should nevertheless both know the same things, and respond in the same words, charmed the popular mind without the burzah as a wonder, and was treasured in Mtesa's memory as being miraculous."

But Stanley must be looking after the men whom he had left at Kagehyi, leaving the completion of his missionary work for the present. Mtesa gave him permission to depart, and ordered Magassa to have ready thirty canoes to serve as escort. M. Linant remained at the capital, intending to stay there until Stanley's return, which was fixed for a month from the date of departure, if not earlier. It may be incidentally mentioned here that he waited for six weeks; but Stanley having been detained beyond that time, was obliged to go on his way. *En route* to Ismalia, he was attacked by several thousand Wanyoro, the fight lasting for fourteen hours. Escaping these, and reaching Gen. Gordon's headquarters in safety, he was sent on another mission, and being attacked by a party of Bari near Labore, he and his thirty-six soldiers were massacred.

Escorted by Magassa, who had not been able to procure the thirty canoes which Mtesa had commanded, Stanley set out upon his journey April 17, 1875. The return voyage was along the western coast of the lake. No attempt was made to ascend the Katonga, with its almost imperceptible current; but Stanley resolved to learn something of the Alexandra Nile, or Kagera. The current of this river, however, proved so strong that they made but little headway against it; and after ascending it for three miles, gave up the project. This stream is called by the natives "the mother of the river at Jinja," *i. e.*, Ripon Falls, in the Victoria Nile.

Magassa had returned with the few canoes that he had been able to prepare, to see if others could not be obtained. From two days after the start, then, the Lady Alice and her crew were alone on the journey. Her commander fully expected Magassa to overtake him on the 27th of April, and for that reason steered to Alice Island, where some food was purchased. That same night they reached Barker's Island, in the Bumbireh group; and here they spent a most miserable night, in a pouring rain, with nothing to eat; for the provisions obtainable at Alice Island had been barely sufficient for one meal. The next morning dawned bright and clear, and they set sail for Bumbireh itself, about two miles away; and ran down the coast in search of a haven for their boat while they should be bartering their beads for edibles.

"As soon as we had sailed a little distance along the coast, we caught sight of a few figures which broke the even and smooth outline of the grassy summit, and heard the well-known melodious war-cries employed by most of the Central African tribes: '*Hehu-a hehu u-u-u!*' loud, long-drawn, and ringing.

"The figures increased in number, and fresh voices joined in the defiant and alarming note. Still, hungry wretches as we were, environed by difficulties of all kinds, just beginning to feel warm after the cold and wet of the night before, with famine gnawing at our vitals, leagues upon leagues of sea between us and our friends at Usukuma, and nothing eatable in our boat, we were obliged to risk something reminding ourselves that 'there are no circumstances so desperate which Providence may not relieve.'

"At 9 A. M. we discovered a cove near the southeast end of the long island, and pulled slowly into it. Immediately the natives rushed down the slopes, shouting war-cries and uttering fierce ejaculations. When about fifty yards from the shore, I bade the men cease rowing; but Safeni and Baraka said:

HOSTILE RECEPTION AT BUMBIREH ISLAND.

" 'It is almost always the case, master, with savages. They cry out, and threaten, and look big, but you will see that all *that* noise will cease as soon as they hear us speak. Besides, if we leave here without food, where shall we obtain it?' "

To this argument even Stanley could find no immediate answer: and while he was considering the difficult question, four of his men resumed their oars, and impelled the boat slowly onward; while Safeni and Baraka prepared themselves to explain to the natives who came rushing down to the water's edge. Some of these made ready stones and other weapons.

"We were now about ten yards from the beach, and Safeni and Baraka spoke, earnestly pointing to their mouths, and by gestures explaining that their bellies were empty. They smiled with insinuating faces; uttered the words 'brothers,' 'friends,' 'good fellows,' most volubly; cunningly interpolated the words Mtesa, the Kabaka, Uganda, and Antari, king of Ihangiro, to which Bumbireh belongs. Safeni and Baraka's pleasant volubility seemed to have produced a good effect, for the stones were dropped, the bows were unstrung, and the lifted spears lowered, to assist the steady, slow-walking pace with which they now advanced. Safeni and Baraka turned to me triumphantly and asked:

" 'What did we say, master?'

"And then, with engaging frankness, invited the natives, who were now about two hundred in number, to come closer. The natives consulted a little while, and several—now smiling pleasantly themselves, advanced leisurely into the water until they touched the boat's prow. They stood a few seconds talking sweetly, when suddenly with a rush they ran the boat ashore, and then all the others, seizing hawser and gunwale, dragged her about twenty yards over the rocky beach high and dry, leaving us almost stupefied with astonishment!

"Then ensued a scene which beggars description. Pandemonium—all its devils armed, raged around us. A forest of spears were levelled; thirty or forty bows were drawn taut; as many barbed arrows seemed already on the wing; thick, knotty clubs waved above our heads; two hundred screaming black demons jostled with each other, and struggled for room to vent their fury, or for an opportunity to deliver one crushing blow or thrust at us.

"In the meantime, as soon as the first symptoms of this manifestation of violence had been observed, I had sprung to my feet, each hand armed with a loaded self-cocking revolver, to kill and be killed. But the apparent hopelessness of inflicting much injury upon such a large crowd restrained me, and Safeni turned to me, almost cowed to dumbness by the loud fury around us, and pleaded with me to be patient. I complied, seeing that I should get no aid from my crew; but, while bitterly blaming myself for having yielded—against my instincts—to placing myself in the power of such savages, I vowed that if I escaped this once, my own judgment should guide my actions for the future.

"I assumed a resigned air, though I still retained my revolvers. My crew also bore the first outburst of the tempest of shrieking rage which assailed them with almost sublime imperturbability. Safeni crossed his arms with the meekness of a saint. Baraka held his hands palms outward, asking with serene benignity:

"'What, my friends, ails you? Do you fear empty hands and smiling people like us? We are friends, we came as friends to buy food, two or three bananas, a few mouthfuls of grain or potatoes, or *muhogo* (cassava), and, if you will permit it, we will depart as friends.'

"Our demeanor had a great effect. The riot and noise seemed to be subsiding, when some fifty newcomers rekindled the smouldering fury. Again the forest of spears swayed on the launch, again the knotty clubs were whirled aloft, again the bows were drawn, and again the barbed arrows seemed flying. Safeni received a push which sent him tumbling, little Kirango received a blow on the head with a spear-staff, Saramba gave a cry as a club descended on his back.

"I sprang up this time to remonstrate, with the two revolvers in my left hand. I addressed myself to an elder, who seemed to be restraining the people from proceeding too far. I showed him beads, cloth, wire, and invoked the names of Mtesa, and Antari their king.

"The sight of the heaps of beads and cloth I exposed awakened, however, the more deliberate passions of selfishness and greed in each heart. An attempt at massacre, they began to argue, would certainly entail the loss of some of themselves. 'Guns might be seized and handled with terrible effect even by dying men, and who knows what those little iron things in the white man's hands are?' they seemed to be asking themselves. The elder, whatever he thought, responded with an affectation of indignation, raised his stick, and to right and left of him drove back the demoniac crew. Other prominent men now assisted this elder, whom we subsequently discovered to be Shekka, the king of Bumbireh.

"Shekka, then, having thus bestirred himself, beckoned to half a dozen men and walked away a few yards behind the mass. It was the '*shauri*,' dear to a free and independent African's heart, that was about to be held. Half the crowd followed the king and his council, while the other half remained to indulge their violent, vituperative tongues on us, and to continually menace us with either club or spear. An audacious party came round the stern of the boat and, with superlatively hideous gestures, affronted me; one of them even gave a tug at my hair; thinking it was a wig. I revenged myself by seizing his hand, and suddenly bending it back, almost dislocated it, causing him to howl with pain. His comrades swayed their lances, but I smilingly looked at them, for all idea of self-preservation had now almost fled.

"The issue had surely arrived. There had been just one brief moment of agony when I reflected how unlovely death appears in such guise as that in which it then threatened me. What would my people think as they anxiously awaited the never-returning master? What would Pocock and Barker say when they heard of the tragedy of Bumbireh? And my friends in America and Europe! Tut, it is only a brief moment of pain, and then what can the ferocious dogs do more? It is a consolation that if anything it will be short, sharp, sudden—a gasp, and then a silence—forever and forever! And after that, I was ready for the fight and for death.

"'Now, my black friends, do your worst; anything you choose; I am ready.'

"A messenger from the king and council arrives, and beckons Safeni. I said to him: 'Safeni, use your wit.'

"'Please God, master,' he replied."

The African, like all savages, is possessed by a curiosity easily aroused, and the natives followed Safeni, observing his every motion as he endeavored to make himself understood. As Mr. Stanley observes, Safeni proved himself "a born diplomat." He used all the arts of the pantomime. His face was sweet and smiling; his hands made most eloquent gestures; he exhibited all the graces and eloquence of the advocate, pleading before the jury for a client in danger for his life. In a short time he came back to his party radiant with hope, declaring it was all right, that they were safe; but that the savages insisted they should stay with them until they should hold their *shauri*, when they would sell food to the starving party. But even as he was relating this, several men came forward and suddenly grabbed all the oars. Safeni was about to resist, but Stanley called out;

"'Let them go, Safeni!'

"A loud cheer greeted the seizure of the oars. I became convinced now that this one little act would lead to others; for man is the same all over the world. Set a beggar on horseback and he will ride to the devil; give a slave an inch, and he will take an ell; if a man submit once, he must be prepared to submit again."

It was truly a desperate case, yet Stanley and his men could do nothing. The *shauri* proceeded; a messenger came demanding gifts; they were handed over without a word of protest. Noon came; and the savages, sure of their prey, withdrew to their villages for food and drink; for, as the poet asks, "Where is the man who can live without dining?" The half-starved men in the boat were visited by the women, who consoled them with the assurance of being killed very soon; if, however, they could induce Shekka to make blood-brotherhood or eat honey with one of them, peace would ensue and they would be safe.

"About 3 P. M. we heard a number of drums beaten. Safeni was told that if the natives collected again he must endeavor to induce Shekka with gifts to go through the process of blood-brotherhood.

"A long line of natives in full war costume appeared on the crest of the terrace, on which the banana grove and the village of Kajurri stood. Their faces were smeared with black and white pigments. Almost all of them bore the peculiar shields of Usongora. Their actions were such as the dullest-witted of us recognized as indicating hostilities. Even Safeni and Baraka were astounded, and their first words were:

"'Prepare, master. Truly, this is trouble.'

"'Never mind me,' I replied; 'I have been ready these three hours. Are you ready, your guns and revolvers loaded, and your ears open this time?'

"'We are,' they all firmly answered.

"'Don't be afraid; be quite cool. We will try, while they are collecting together, the women's suggestion. Go frankly and smiling, Safeni, up to Shekka, on the top of that hill, and offer him these three *fundo* of beads, and ask him to exchange blood with you.'

"Safeni proceeded readily on his errand, for there was no danger to him bodily while we were within a hundred and fifty yards, and their full number as yet unprepared. For ten minutes he conversed with them, while the drums kept beating, and numbers of men painted for war were increasing Shekka's force. Some of them entertained us by demonstrating with their spears how they fought; others whirled their clubs like tipsy Irishmen at Donnybrook fair. Their gestures were wild, their voices were shrill and fierce, they were kindling themselves into a fighting fever.

"Safeni returned. Shekka had refused the pledge of peace. The natives now mustered over three hundred. Presently fifty bold fellows came rushing down, uttering a shrill cry. Without hesitation they came straight to the boat, and hissing something to us, seized our Kiganda drum. It was such a small affair, we did not resist; still the manner in which it was taken completely undeceived us, if any small hope of peace remained. Loud applause greeted the act of gallantry.

"Then two men came down toward us, and began to drive some cows away that were grazing between us and the men on the hill. Safeni asked of one of them:

"'Why do you do that?'

"'Because we are going to begin fighting presently, and if you are men, you may begin to prepare yourselves,' he said, scornfully.

"'Thanks, my bold friend,' I muttered to myself; 'those are the truest words we have heard to-day.'

"The two men were retiring up the hill.

"'Here, Safeni,' I said, 'take these two fine red cloths in your hand; walk slowly up after them a little way, and the minute you hear my voice run back; and you, my boys, this is for life and death, mind; range yourselves on each side of the boat, lay your hands on it carelessly, but with a firm grip; and when I give the word, push it with the force of a hundred men down the hill into the water. Are you all ready, and do you think you can do it? Otherwise we might as well begin fighting where we are.'

"'Yes, *Inshallah*, master,' they cried out with one voice.

"'Go, Safeni!'

"I waited until he had walked fifty yards away, and saw that he acted precisely as I had instructed him.

"'Push, my boys! Push for your lives!'

"The crew bent their heads and strained their arms. The boat began to move, and there was a hissing, grinding noise below me. I seized my double-barreled elephant rifle and shouted: 'Safeni! Safeni! Return!'

"The natives were quick-eyed. They saw the boat moving, and with one accord they swept down the hill uttering the most fearful cries. My boat was at the water's edge.

BAFFLED SAVAGES.

" 'Shoot her into the lake, my men; never mind the water!'

"And clear of all obstructions she darted out upon the lake. Safeni stood for an instant on the water's edge, with the cloths in his hand. The foremost of a crowd of natives was about twenty yards from him. He raised his spear and balanced himself.

" 'Spring into the water, man, head first?' I cried.

"The balanced spear was about to fly, and another man was preparing his weapon for a deadly cast, when I raised my gun and the bullet ploughed through him and through the second. The bowmen halted and drew their bows. I sent two charges of duck-shot into their midst with terrible effect. The natives retreated from the beach on which the boat had lately lain.

"Having checked the natives, I assisted one of my men into the boat, and ordered him to lend a hand to the others, while I reloaded my big guns, keeping my eyes on the natives. There was a point about a hundred yards in length on the east, which sheltered the cove. Some of the natives made a rush for this, but my guns commanded the exposed position, and they were obliged to retire.

"The crew seized their rifles, but I told them to leave them alone, and to tear the bottom-boards out of the boat and use them as paddles; for there were two hippopotami advancing on us open-mouthed, and it seemed as if we were to be crushed in the water after such a narrow escape from the ferocious people ashore. I permitted one of the hippos to approach within ten yards, and, aiming between his eyes, perforated his skull with a three-ounce ball, and the second received such a wound that we were not molested by him.

"Meanwhile, the savages, baffled and furious at seeing their prey escape, had rushed, after a short consultation, to man two canoes that were drawn up on the beach at the northwest corner of the cove. Twice I dropped men as they were endeavoring to launch the boats; but they persisted, and finally launching them, pursued us vigorously. Two other canoes were seen coming down the coast from the eastern side of the island. Unable to escape, we stopped after we had got out of the cove and waited for them.

"My elephant rifle was loaded with explosive balls for this occasion. Four shots killed five men and sank two of the canoes. The two others retired to assist their friends out of the water. They attempted nothing further, but some of those on shore had managed to reach the point, and as we resumed our paddles, we heard a voice cry out:

" 'Go and die in the Nyanza!'

"And saw them shoot their arrows, which fell harmlessly a few yards behind us. We were saved!"

It was five o'clock in the evening; they had had no food all day, and had only four bananas in the boat for twelve hungry men. The weak boards which they had for paddles did not answer the purpose very well, and in the dead calm which succeeded a gentle breeze, they were able to make only three-quarters of a mile an hour. A gale came up, and too weak to paddle any more they gave themselves up to the fury of the winds. It sank at last, and ordering that one of the thwarts should be chopped up, Stanley made coffee with which to refresh his half-starved companions.

They had had but little food before leaving Alice Island, on April 27; and this coffee, with the four bananas, was all that passed their lips until the afternoon of the 30th. They landed, then, on an uninhabited island; the leader shot a brace of large fat ducks; two of the men found some bananas, and two others found some luscious berries.

Continuing their voyage, they landed at the cove of Wiru May 4, and bought some food of the natives. Two days later, after a storm that brought to mind the parting words of the natives of Bumbireh, they reached Kagehyi, and were heartily welcomed by the others. There was but one white man among the shore party, and Stanley inquired where Frederick Barker was, and why he did not come to meet them.

"Because," answered Frank Pocock, his face clouding with the recollection of loss, "he died twelve days ago, and he lies there."

As he spoke, he pointed to a low mound of earth by the lake. Thus two of the four white men who had set out from Zanzibar had died on the way; and the journey was not half done.

It was Stanley's intention to return to Uganda with his full party, but the opposition of a chief whose territories lay between Kagehyi and Mtesa's country made it impossible to make the journey by land, as he wished to do. He therefore decided to make it by water, as before; but had much difficulty in obtaining canoes for the purpose. At last, after a personal visit to Lukongeh, the chief of Ukerewe, he succeeded in getting twenty-three. These were very old, and he at once set his men to work to repair them, while he began negotiations for provisions. The vessels were for the transportation of one hundred and fifty men, women and children; twelve thousand pounds of grain, five hundred pounds of rice, a hundred loads of beads, cloth and wire, and thirty cases of ammunition. Most of the last-named article was on the Lady Alice. The flotilla sailed at 9 A. M. on June 20; but before they reached the Miandereh Islands that night, five canoes had sunk, with five guns, one case of ammunition, and twelve hundred pounds of grain. Fortunately, all the people were saved; but it was only by the most strenuous efforts on the part of Stanley and his men. It is in connection with their brave behavior this night that we first hear of the two brothers, Uledi and Shumari, whose names were afterward to be more prominent in the story. The canoes were thoroughly inspected the next day, and the work of repairing them was not shirked as it had been before starting from Kagehyi.

Leaving a garrison of forty-four men at Refuge Island, which they reached June 24, Stanley returned to Kagehyi for the last time; and rejoined the other party July 11. Leaving a garrison at Miandereh again (for his canoes were not numerous enough to transport the whole party at once) he went on his way toward Uganda.

He must of course pass Bumbireh on his way thither; and it was necessary to give the chief of that island a lesson. The king of Iroba was captured; and being a neighbor of the chief of Bumbireh, was held as a hostage until his subjects had captured Shekka. Fortunately, they were about this time reinforced by a number of men whom Mtesa had dispatched to hunt up Stanley; so that the strength of the party now encamped on Mahyiga Island was four hundred and seventy men. This was the condition of affairs when messengers came from Antari, king of Ihangiro, the superior of Shekka, demanding the release of that chief. It was promised that when they should be released, Antari's people would sell food to the travelers. But this was a mere pretext by which Antari sought to gain the confidence of Stanley, preparatory to a trial of strength; and when some of the Waganda, deceived by the apparent friendliness, ventured to Bumbireh, they were attacked and eight of them badly wounded, six dying from the effects of their injuries after the arrival of the party in Uganda.

It was a question in Stanley's mind what course should be pursued. Had it been a purely military expedition there would of course have been no doubt; but for some time he hesitated about striking a blow except in direct self-defense. Finally, however, he decided that gratitude to Mtesa and his Waganda demanded that blood should atone for blood.

More than this, it was dangerous to leave such a deed unavenged; for the savage cannot understand forbearance, which to him seems cowardice; patience, which is to him evidence of effeminacy. As he could not see any way to avoid the conflict, he determined to meet them on their own island, and by one decisive stroke break this overweening savage spirit. But Stanley's own words must tell of the just punishment inflicted.

"We steered straight towards the more exposed hill-slopes. The savages, imagining that we were about to effect a landing there, hurried from their coverts, between two thousand and three thousand in number. I examined the shores carefully, to see if I could discover the canoes which had conveyed this great number of warriors from the mainland. Meanwhile we pulled slowly, to afford them time to arrange themselves.

"Arrived within a hundred yards of the land, we anchored in line, the stone anchors being dropped from midships that the broadsides might front the shore. I told Lukanjah of Ukerewe to ask the men of Bumbireh if they would make peace, whether we should be friends, or whether we should fight.

"'*Nangu, nangu, nangu!*' (No, no, no!) they answered loudly, while they flourished spears and shields.

"'Will they not do anything to save Shekka?'

"'*Nangu, nangu!* Keep Shekka; he is nobody. We have another M'kama' (king).

"'Will they do nothing to save Antari's son?' [who also was held as a hostage.]

"'*Nangu, nangu.* Antari has many sons. We will do nothing but fight. If you had not come here, we should have come to you.'

"'You will be sorry for it afterward.'

"Huh!' incredulously; we are ready; come on.'

Further parley was useless; so each man having taken aim was directed to fire into a group of fifty or thereabouts. The result was several killed and wounded. The savages, perceiving the disastrous effect of our fire on a compact body, scattered, and came bounding down to the water's edge, some of the boldest advancing until they were hip-deep in water; others, more cautious, sought the shelter of the cane-grass, whence they discharged many sheaves of arrows, all of which fell short of us.

"We then moved to within fifty yards of the shore, to fire at close quarters, and each man was permitted to exercise himself as he best could. The savages gallantly held the water-line for an hour, and slung their stones with better effect than they shot their arrows. The spirit which animated them proved what they might have done had they succeeded in effecting a landing at Mahyiga by night, but here, however, the spear, with which they generally fight, was quite useless.

"Perceiving that their spirit was abating, we drew the canoes together, and made a feint as though we were about to rush forward by hundreds with their spears on the launch. The canoes were then suddenly halted, and a volley was fired into the spearmen, which quite crushed their courage, causing them to retreat up the hill far away from the scene. Our work of chastisement was complete.

"The Waganda spearmen, two hundred and thirty strong, who had been, up to this time, only interested spectators, now clamored loudly to be permitted to land, and to complete the work of vengeance. M'Kwanga was fierce in his demands; the Wangwana seconded the Waganda, and in their hot ardor several of the canoes rushed on the shore; but as this extremity was not my object, I resisted them; and when, despite my refusal, they persisted in their attempts to land, I threatened to fire on the first man, Mgwana or Mganda, who set foot on the shore; and this threat restored order."

The way being thus cleared, they proceeded on their journey, and reached Dumo, in Uganda, a week later (August 12, 1875). Here they learned that Mtesa was making preparations for a war against the Wavuma. Before they reached Ntewi, he had already marched against Usoga. Two courses were open to Stanley; either he could attempt the journey to the Albert Nyanza unaided, or he could proceed to Mtesa's camp, and thence prosecute the journey. He decided upon the latter course, believing that the delay would be made up by the shorter route which Mtesa's help would enable him to take.

He found the emperor of Uganda and his warlike court encamped about the Ripon Falls. Mtesa received him with great cordiality, but informed him that it was not customary for strangers to proceed on their journey while the Kabaka was at war; if Stanley would but wait until he had chastised the insolent Wavuma, he should have guides to Muta Nzige. Stanley was also informed that the natives of the country lying along the route, under their chief, Kabba Rega, were at war with the whites of Kaniessa (Gondokoro), and hence that a considerable force would be required. There was nothing for it, then, but to await the end of Mtesa's war.

GREAT NAVAL BATTLE BETWEEN THE WAGANDA AND THE WAVUMA.

Mtesa attempted to end it by negotiations, but his peace party, dispatched to the Wavuma camp on Ingira Island, was massacred before his very eyes. He decided at length to give battle to the enemy daily becoming bolder and more boastful. The result was that the Wavuma were left masters of the situation. Mtesa threatened that in the next battle, the chief who behaved cowardly should be burned, while his lands should be given to the peasant who distinguished himself. Let us again quote the words of Stanley:

"The entire war-fleet of two hundred and thirty vessels rode gracefully on the calm gray waters of the channel. The line of battle, I observed, was formed by Chambarango, in command of the right flank, with fifty canoes; Sambuzi, Kukavya, Chikwata and Saruti, all sub-chiefs, were ranged with one hundred canoes under the command of Kauta, the imperial steward, to form the center; the left flank was in charge of the gallant Mkwenda, who had eighty canoes. Tori commanded a force of musketeers, and with his four howitzers was stationed on the causeway, which was by this time two hundred yards from the shore.

"In the above manner the fleet of vessels, containing some sixteen thousand men, moved to the attack upon Ingira. The center, defended by the flanks, which were to menace the rear of the Wavuma should they approach near the causeway, resolutely advanced to within thirty yards of Ingira, and poured in a most murderous fire among the slingers of the island, who, imagining that the Waganda meant to carry the island by storm, boldly stood exposed, resolved to fight. But they were unable to maintain that courageous behavior long. Mkwenda then moved up from the left, and attacked with his musketeers the Wavuma on the right, riddling their canoes, and making matters specially hot for them in that quarter.

"The Wavuma, seeing matters approaching a crisis, and not wishing to die tamely, manned their canoes, and a hundred and ninety-six dashed impetuously, as at first, from the rushes of Ingira with shrill loud yells, and the Waganda lines moved backward to the center of the channel, where they bravely and coolly maintained their position. As the center of the Uganda line parted in front of the causeway, and disclosed the hotly advancing enemy, Tori aimed the howitzers and fired at a group of about twenty canoes, completely shattering more than half of them, and re-loading one quickly, he discharged several bolts of iron three inches long among them with terrible effect. Before this cool bearing of the Waganda, the Wavuma retired to their

WAR CANOE OF THE WAVUMA ADVANCING TO BATTLE.

island again, and we saw numbers of canoes discharging their dead and wounded; and the Waganda were summoned to the Nakaranga shore to receive the congratulations of the emperor and the applause of the vast multitude. Mtesa went down to the water's edge to express his satisfaction at their behavior.

"'Go at them again,' said he, 'and show them what fighting is.'

"And the line of battle was again formed, and again the Wavuma darted from the cover of the reeds and water-cane with the swiftness of hungry sharks, beating the water into foam with their paddles, and rending the air with their fearful yells. It was one of the most exciting and animating scenes I ever beheld; but, owing to the terror of the stake with which their dread monarch had threatened them, the Waganda distinguished themselves for coolness and method, and the Wavuma, as on a former occasion, for intrepidity and desperate courage.

"A third time the Waganda were urged to the battle, and a third time the unconquerable and desperate enemy dashed upon them, to be smitten and wounded sore in a battle where they had not the least chance of returning blow for blow without danger of being swept by the cannon and muskets on the causeway.

A third battle was fought a few days after between one hundred and seventy-eight Wavuma canoes and one hundred and twenty-two Waganda; but had the Waganda possessed the spirit and dash of their enemies, they might have decided the war on this day; for the Wavuma were greatly dispirited. A fourth battle was fought the next day by two hundred and fourteen Waganda canoes and two hundred and three Wavuma canoes, after the usual delay and premonitory provocation. The Wavuma obtained the victory most signally. * * * The Waganda were disorganized and dispirited after the signal defeat they had experienced. * * * On inquiring into the cause of the disaster, I learned that Mtesa's gunpowder was almost exhausted, and that he had scarcely a round left for each musket."

Although Stanley was bound to Mtesa by past evidences of friendship, as well as by the hope of assistance in the future, he could not but feel strong admiration for the heroic Wavuma; and bent his energies "upon a solution of the problem how to injure none, but satisfy all." While he was considering this puzzling question, he was summoned to the council-chamber, where Mtesa was making ready to torture to death a Wavuma who had fallen into his hands. The emperor had but a few days before announced himself a Christian; and Stanley now warmly protested against such an un-Christian act. His arguments were disregarded for a long time; but finally, Mtesa listened to him. Stanley then promised to build a structure which should terrify the Wavuma, if Mtesa would but give him plenty of help.

The Waganda are timid about fighting on water, being unused to the unstable element; it was for this reason that Stanley had advised the building of a causeway from the mainland to the island, that they might thus be on a more equal footing with the seamen Wavuma; but the Waganda chiefs did not take kindly to the idea, and the causeway was not finished. Mtesa now gave orders that Stanley's directions should be minutely obeyed.

He selected three of the strongest built canoes, each seventy feet long and six and one-half feet wide; and had them drawn up four feet from each other. Tall trees were laid across them, and lashed firmly to the thwarts. Seven-foot poles were lashed to the thwarts of the outer canoes, and long poles, one inch in diameter, twisted in among these. When completed, it resembled an oblong stockade, which the spears of the enemy could not penetrate; and formed a floating fort, propelled by invisible rowers, and manned by more than two hundred men. This immense structure slowly advanced toward the island, while a voice from within asked the Wavuma if they were ready to submit to Mtesa now; if they went through the form of submission, he offered pardon to all; if they refused, this terrible thing would blow them into atoms. The Wavuma, terrified by the strange thing, which doubtless contained some powerful spirits, yielded to the demand; and the mysterious structure solemnly began its way back to the cove whence it had started. Thus the Wavuma, like the Trojans, were conquered by strategy when their determined valor defied open force.

Returning to the old capital at Ulagalla Oct. 29, Mtesa granted the desired guide and escort to Stanley for his visit to the Albert Nyanza. They coasted along the shores of the Victoria Nyanza as far as Dumo, where the greater part of Stanley's force had been left; and then began their overland march; carrying the Lady Alice and a canoe which had been named the "Livingstone." Their route lay directly through Unyoro, the king of which country, Kabba Rega, was then engaged in war with the white governor at Gondokoro; but the escort provided by Mtesa consisted of more than two thousand men, and Stanley's own force numbered one hundred and eighty; so that they were not attacked by the natives.

They reached the shores of the lake in January; but there was a precipice with a sheer descent of fifty feet, down which the boats must be lowered; and while they were debating about the best way to accomplish this, hostile demonstrations by the natives frightened the Waganda, who were already discontented; and the leader of that force determined to return. Stanley was advised by his captains that half of his own force would accompany the Waganda in spite of all they could do; and he was therefore compelled to return with them. With the punishment that Mtesa inflicted upon his disobedient subjects, we have nothing to do. He expressed the greatest regret to Stanley that they had not fulfilled their orders; and offered a force of a hundred thousand men for the accomplishment of the traveler's purpose, if that number should be necessary. The offer was, however, declined; and Stanley left Uganda.

Stanley next visited Rumanika, the gentle king who was subordinate to the fiery Mtesa. The dusky giant (for Rumanika was six feet six in his bare feet) received Stanley with much kindness, and praised his country, Karagwe. He claimed not only the great river, Kagera, but a more wonderful thing still, the Hot Springs of Mtagata. Under the escort of this chief, Stanley began the circumnavigation of Lake Windermere, March 8; and made several similar excursions from his camp on the Kagera.

March 11, Rumanika furnished him with an escort of thirty men and a guide for his visit to Mtagata Hot Springs, which they reached after two days' journey. These remarkable springs are six in number, the temperature varying from one hundred and seven degrees Fahrenheit to one hundred and twenty-nine and one-half degrees. A sample of the water taken to London and there analyzed, showed it to be faintly alkaline, holding sodium carbonate in solution. The natives praised the waters of the springs so highly that Stanley resolved to test them in his own person; but although he remained three days there and drank an enormous quantity of the water, he experienced no good. He intimates that the benefit received in cutaneous diseases results more from the unusual cleanliness than from any virtue in the water itself.

A great deal of information was received from Rumanika

HOT SPRINGS OF MTAGATA.

concerning the geography of the surrounding country; and his sub-chiefs added their quota. Rumanika's knowledge (not drawn from personal experience) included a race of people but two feet high, another with tails, and still another with ears so long that they touched the ground when the man stood upright, and when he lay down, formed a sleeping mat and a covering from the cold.

Having traced the extreme southern sources of the Nile, from the marshy plains and cultivated uplands where they are born, down to the mighty reservoir called the Victoria Nyanza, Stanley, on April 7, resumed his "journey in a southerly direction, and traveled five miles along a ravine, at the bottom of which murmured the infant stream Luhugati. On coming to its source we ascended a steep slope until we stood on the summit of a grassy ridge at the height of five thousand six hundred feet by aneroid. Not until we had descended a mile to the valley of Uyagoma did I recognize the importance of this ridge as the water-parting between one of the feeders of the Lake Victoria and the source of the Malagarazi, the principal affluent of Lake Tanganyika."

Descending into the basin of the Tanganyika, the expedition arrived at Serombo April 22, and here received a visit from the mighty Mirambo whose war with the Arabs was now at an end. He insisted on making blood-brotherhood with Stanley, and tried to excel the white man in the generosity of his gifts.

We need not follow them through the uneventful journey to the shore of the Tanganyika. They arrived at Ujiji May 27, 1876. Providing for the well-being of his followers during his absence, Stanley set out, June 11, with eleven men and two boy gun-bearers, to circumnavigate the lake, with the view of finding its outlet. The Lady Alice was accompanied by a canoe lent by an Arab, called the Meofu. The Arabs of Ujiji were quite convinced that these vessels would never be able to live in the Tanganyika, and predicted the most doleful things.

They arrived at the banks of the Lukuga July 16. It will be remembered that Cameron positively asserted that this river flows out of Lake Tanganyika. Stanley was unable to find any current; and decided that what had been a river, the affluent of Tanganyika, was now but a creek or inlet, above which were marshes and ooze. He explains this by supposing that the surface of Tanganyika has been steadily rising, until the lake is now above the mouth of the original river; and adduces proof that the lake had actually risen considerably since the time that he, in company with Livingstone, explored its shores. His recollections of particular points were confirmed by Arabs resident at Ujiji.

The circumnavigation of the lake was completed July 31, after an absence of fifty-one days from Ujiji. Stanley found the small-pox raging in this place, and it had carried off five of his men, who had evaded vaccination at Rosako. The fever attacked him, as it had also attacked his lieutenant, Frank Pocock, during his absence; and to add to their troubles, thirty-eight men deserted on the eve of their departure from Ujiji. Five more disappeared during the first stages of their journey, one of whom was Kalulu. Stanley determined to recover these men, for he had shortly before treated them with the greatest generosity, distributing three hundred and fifty pounds' worth of cloth among them gratuitously. Pocock and Kacheche were sent after the deserters, and captured seven, one of whom was Kalulu; these receiving merited punishment, an end was put to misconduct and faithlessness for the time.

The shores of the Luama were reached October 11; and they followed this stream for a distance of two hundred and twenty miles, to its confluence with the greater river. The Luama here was about four hundred yards wide; the Lualaba, one thousand four hundred. "A broad river, of a pale grey color, winding slowly from south and by east. * * * A secret rapture filled my soul as I gazed upon the majestic stream. The great mystery that for all these centuries Nature had kept hidden away from the world of science, was waiting to be solved. * * * Before me lay the superb river; my task was to follow it to the ocean."

At the village of Mkwanga, eight miles from the confluence of these rivers, they met with Tippu Tib, otherwise Hamed bin Mohammed, a noted Arab trader with whom Cameron had had dealings; and from whom they learned how the Englishman had failed to obtain the canoes necessary for the descent of the Lualaba. The Arab endeavored to dissuade him from the attempt; and painted the difficulties of the journey in strong colors. Stanley himself saw what they were; Livingstone the Beloved had failed to overcome them by persuasion; Cameron had failed to overcome them with his forty-five Snider rifles—an argument more generally understood by the savages. Tippu-Tib would not consent to be his escort unless Stanley would return to Nyangwe with him. What should be done? Stanley took his trusty lieutenant into council, and carefully stated all the advantages and difficulties of the various alternatives that presented themselves. Both were at heart anxious to explore the Lualaba to its mouth, but neither would say so. Under these circumstances, Frank made a proposition.

"'I say, sir, let us toss up; best two out of three to decide it.'

"'Toss away; here is a rupee.'

"'Heads for the north and the Lualaba; tails for the south and Katanga.'

"Frank stood up, his face beaming. He tossed the rupee high up. The coin dropped.

"'What is it?' I asked.

"'Tails, sir,' said Frank, with a face expressive of strong disapproval.

"'Toss again.'

"He tossed again, and tails was again announced—and six times running tails won. We then tried straws—the short straws for the south the long straws for the River Lualaba—and again we were disappointed, for Frank persisted in drawing out the short straws, and in leaving the long straws in my hands.

"'It is of no use, Frank. We'll face our destiny despite the rupee and the straws. With your help, my dear fellow, I will follow the river.'"

A contract was concluded with Tippu Tib, by which the trader agreed to accompany them sixty marches, of four hours each, when, if they found the country hostile, they should return with him to Nyangwe; if they met Portuguese or Arab traders, a portion of the expedition was to continue the journey with them, and the remainder to return with Tippu Tib. This arrangement prevented desertions, as no Arab would harbor a runaway from an expedition with which one of their own countrymen was connected.

November 5, 1876, they left Nyangwe, one hundred and forty-six men comprising the expedition proper, while Tippu-Tib mustered seven hundred. Their road lay through the dense, almost impenetrable forest; and their progress at first was necessarily slow. So slow, indeed, that the Arab trader became disgusted, and regardless of the loss of the money, which was to be forfeited if he refused to fulfill his part of the contract, announced that he intended to return. Arguments at length persuaded him to compromise, and the expedition again took up the line of march.

STANLEY AND HIS FORCE ON THE MARCH.

In a village of Uvinza, Stanley found the principal street decorated with skulls which looked to him like those of the human species. The chief and his people, however, informed him that they were soko skulls; that the sokos stole their bananas, and were because of that hunted by his people, the flesh being used for meat. Stanley purchased two of the skulls, some of which bore the marks of the hatchet which had caused death; and on his return to England submitted them to Professor Huxley. The eminent scientist unhesitatingly pronounced them human, one being a man's, the other a woman's; thus showing that the Wavinza are cannibals.

November 19, they reached a point on the Lualaba forty-one miles north of Nyangwe, in latitude three degrees thirty-five seconds south, and twenty-five degrees, forty-nine seconds east longitude. From this point, Stanley speaks of the river as the Livingstone, claiming that as the name is changed each time it receives an affluent, it is useless to attempt to follow the native designations. Here it was, while busily planning the future journey, that Stanley suddenly saw his way clear before him. They had encamped on the banks of the river, and he had been considering the means of crossing it.

"I sprang up; told the drummer to call to muster. The people responded wearily to the call. Frank and the chiefs appeared. The Arabs and their escort came also, until a dense mass of expectant faces surrounded me. I turned to them and said:

"'Arabs! Sons of Unyamwezi! Children of Zanzibar! Listen to words. We have seen the Mitamba of Uregga. We have tasted its bitterness, and groaned in spirit. We seek a road. We seek something by which we may travel. I seek a path that shall take me to the sea. I have found it.'

"'Ah! A-ah-h!' and murmurs and inquiring looks at one another.

"'Yes! *El hamd ul Illah!* I have found it. Regard this mighty river. From the beginning it has flowed on thus, as you see it flow to-day. It has flowed on in silence and darkness. Whither? To the Salt Sea, as all rivers go. By that Salt Sea, on which the great ships come and go, live my friends, and your friends, Do they not?'

"Cries of 'Yes! yes!'

"'Yet, my people, although this river is so great, so wide and deep, no man has ever penetrated the distance lying between this spot on which we stand and our white friends who live by the Salt Sea. Why? Because it was left for us to do!'

"'Ah, no! no! no!' and despairing shakes of the head.

"'Yes,' I continued, raising my voice; 'I tell you, my friends, it has been left from the beginning of time until to-day for us to do. It is our work, and no other. It is the voice of Fate! The ONE GOD has written that this year the river shall be known throughout its length! We will have no more Mitambas; we will have no more panting and groaning by the wayside; we will have no more hideous darkness; we will take to the river, and keep to the river. To-day I shall launch my boat on that stream, and it shall never leave it until I finish my work. I swear it!'

"'Now, you Wangwana! You who have followed me through Turu, and sailed around the great lakes with me; you have followed me like children following their father through Unyoro and down to Ujiji, and as far as this wild, wild land, will you leave me here? Shall I and my white brother go alone? Will you go back and tell my friends that you left me in this wild spot, and cast me adrift to die? Or will you, to whom I have been so kind, whom I love as I would love my children, will you bind me, and take me back by force? Speak, Arabs! Where are my young men, with hearts of lions? Speak, Wangwana, and show me those who dare follow me!'

"Uledi, the coxswain, leaped upward, and then sprang towards me, and kneeling grasped my knees and said:

"'Look on me, my master! I am one! I will follow you to death!'

"'And I,' Kacheche cried.

"'And I, and I, and I,' shouted the boat's crew,

"'It is well. I knew I had friends. You then who have cast your lot with me stand on one side, and let me count you.'

"There were thirty-eight. Ninety-five stood still and said nothing.

"'I have enough. Even with you, my friends, I shall reach the sea. But there is plenty of time. We have not yet made our canoes. We have not yet parted with the Arabs. We have yet a long distance to travel with Tippu Tib. We may meet with good people, from whom we may buy canoes. And by the time we part I am sure that the ninety-five men now fearing to go with us will not leave their brothers, and their master and his white brother, to go down the river without them. Meantime, I give you many thanks, and shall not forget your names.'"

While Stanley was speaking to the Arabs, endeavoring to

persuade them that cataracts and cannibals were dangers which he should overcome, a canoe had approached from the opposite bank, with two men in it. They demanded a thousand cowries for each man whom their tribe should set across the river; and being offered ten, withdrew, uttering a peculiar cry, which Stanley's interpreter declared was a war-cry. Stanley crossed the river in the Lady Alice, and entered into negotiations with the horde of savages that he found there. It was agreed, upon the demand of the natives, that ten men should go from each side to a certain island the next morning and make blood-brotherhood. Fortunately the white man was on his guard; and secretly posted a reserve of twenty men in the bushes before sending off Frank and the stipulated escort. The savages landed later, and although they behaved well at first, by the time that six canoes had discharged their human cargo they became so violent that had not Frank and his men risen with their guns ready they would bave been speared where they sat. Seeing the state of affairs, the reserve emerged from the bushes. Stanley, who was four minutes' row up the stream in the Lady Alice, bade his men bend to their oars; and the treacherous savages, seeing that their wiles had been foreseen, took to their canoes and paddled away.

Stanley then landed thirty men with axes on the other side of the river; and floating down to a point opposite the Wenya village, tossed a small bag of beads on shore, and professed himself willing to pay for the ferriage, explaining that it was useless for them to resist longer, as thirty of his men were already landed in their country, A good understanding seemed to be thus established; and the expedition was ferried over in safety.

But the natives seized the first opportunity to decamp; and when the travelers went to their village the next morning, to cement the new friendship by means of gifts, not a soul was to be found. It was the same in the neighboring villages; the alarm had spread from place to place during the night.

The force was now divided, thirty-six men, including Stanley, forming the river party, while the remainder marched by land. The river party arrived November 23, at the mouth of the Ruiki, and after waiting until the next morning, rowed up stream to look for the others. Not finding any trace of them, the boat returned to the camp, where about two-thirds of this small party had been left as a garrison. It had been attacked during the leader's absence; but although there were several sheaves of iron-headed and wooden spears, besides reed arrows,

FIGHTING THEIR WAY AROUND THE CATARACTS.

in the camp, no one of the travelers had been wounded. The land party did not arrive until the next day; and told of having been attacked, three of their number being killed. They had lost the road and were thus delayed.

The rapids of Ukassa were passed the next day; not without danger from the natives as well as from the waters; and from this point forward we find the two perils constantly besetting the adventurers. Nor was this all; such was the physical condition of the men, that "there was enough work in the stricken expedition for a dozen physicians. Every day we tossed two or three bodies into the deep waters of the Livingstone—poor creatures, what a life! wandering, ever wandering, in search of graves."

Let us follow the history of a few days more minutely than ever; to see what were the difficulties besetting them. It is December, and they have passed the island of Mpika about the middle of the month.

"While rowing down, close to the left bank, we were surprised by a cry from one of the guards of the hospital canoes. and turning round saw an arrow fixed in his chest. The next instant, looking towards the bank, we saw many men in the jungle, and several arrows flew past my head in extremely unpleasant proximity.

"We sheered off, pulling hard down stream. * * * We drew in shore, and sending out ten scouts to lie in wait in the jungle, I mustered all the healthy men, about thirty in number, and proceeded to construct a fence of brushwood. Presently a shriek of agony from another of my men rang out through the jungle, followed immediately by the sharp crack of the scouts' Sniders, which again was responded to by an infernal din of war-horns and yells, while arrows flew past us from all directions. Twenty more men were at once sent into the jungle to assist the scouts, while, with might and main, we labored to surround our intended camp with tall and dense hedges of brushwood, with sheltered nooks for riflemen. After an hour's labor, the camp was deemed sufficiently tenable, and the recall was sounded. The scouts retreated on the run, shouting as they approached:

"'Prepare! prepare! they are coming!'

"About fifty yards of ground outside of our camp had been cleared, which, upon the retreat of the scouts who had been keeping them in check, was soon filled by hundreds of savages, who pressed upon us from all sides but the river, in the full expectation that we were flying in fear. But they were mistaken, for we were at bay, and desperate in our resolve not to die without fighting. Accordingly, at such close quarters the contest became terrific. Again and again the savages hurled themselves upon our stockade, launching spear after spear with deadly force into the camp, to be each time repulsed. Sometimes the muzzles of the guns almost touched their breasts. The shrieks, cries, shouts of encouragement, the rattling volley of musketry, the booming war-horns, the yells and defiance of the combatants, the groans and screams of the women and children in the hospital camp, made together such a medley of hideous noises as can never be effaced from my memory. For two hours this desperate conflict lasted. More than once, some of the Wangwana were about to abandon the struggle and run to the canoes, but Uledi the coxswain and Frank threatened them with clubbed muskets, and with the muzzles of their rifles drove them back to the stockades. At dusk the enemy retreated from the vicinity of the clearing; but the hideous alarms produced from their ivory horns, and increased by the echoes of the dense forest, continued; and now and again a vengeful poison-laden arrow flew by with an ominous whiz to quiver in the earth at our feet, or fall harmlessly into the river behind us."

A strict watch was kept during the night; but the men in the camp were so quiet that those in the jungle thought they slept, and attacked them. In the morning, they rowed about five hundred yards down the river, and occupied a deserted village on the right bank.

"We were not long left unmolested. The savages recovered their wits, and strove desperately to dislodge us, but at each end of the village, which was about three hundred yards long, our muskets blazed incessantly. I also caused three or four sharpshooters to ascend tall trees along the river banks, which permitted them, although unseen, to overlook the tall grasses and rear of the village, and to defend us from fire. * * * The combat lasted till noon, when, mustering twenty-five men, we made a sally, and succeeded in clearing the skirts of the village for the day. * * * During the night there was a slight alarm, and now and then the tapping on the roofs and the pattering among the leaves informed us that our enemies were still about, though we did not reply to them. The next morning an assault was attempted; but the enemy retreated almost immediately into the jungle.

"About noon, a large flotilla of canoes was observed ascending the river close to the left bank, manned by such a dense mass of men that any number between five hundred and eight hundred would be within the mark. We watched them very carefully until they had ascended the river about half a mile above us, when, taking advantage of the current, they bore down towards us, blowing their war-horns, and drumming vigorously. At the same moment, as though this were a signal in concert with those on land, war-horns responded from the forest, and I had scarcely time to order every man to look out when the battle-tempest of arrows broke upon us from the woods. But the twenty men in the nests at the corners of the villages proved sufficient to resist the attack from the forest-side, Frank Pocock being in charge of one, and Sheikh Abdallah of the other, while I, with twenty men lining the bushes along the water line, defended the river side.

"This was a period when every man felt that he must either fight or resign himself to the only other alternative, that of being heaved a headless corpse into the river. * * * Therefore, though the notes of the war-horns were dreadful, our foes pertinacious and numerous, and evidently accustomed to victory, I failed to observe one man among my people then fighting who did not seem desirous to excel even Uledi the coxswain.

"The battle had continued half an hour with a desperate energy, only qualified by our desperate state. Ammunition we possessed in abundance, and we made use of it with deadly effect, yet what might have become of us is doubtful, had not the advanced guard of Tippu Tib and our land division arrived at this critical juncture, causing dismay to the savages in the forest, who announced the reinforcement by horns to the savages in the canoes, many of whom were making strenuous efforts to effect a landing. The river savages, upon hearing these signals, withdrew, but as they were paddling away they proclaimed their intention of preventing all escape, either up river or down river, and expressed their contempt for us by throwing water towards us with their paddles. We saw the canoes mysteriously disappear behind an island, situated about sixteen hundred yards off and opposite to our camp."

That night, Stanley and Pocock, with crews of picked men, made their way, with muffled oars, to the island, and captured thirty-eight of the enemy's canoes. This enabled them to make their own terms with the savages, who were glad enough to make blood-brotherhood with Safeni for the return of fifteen of their vessels. Stanley had lost four men killed in the contest and thirteen wounded.

CUTTING OUR WAY THROUGH THE FOREST.

Stanley now determined to dispense with his Arab escort; and since a sufficient number of canoes had been procured, to take to the river in good earnest. Food must be procured and prepared for at least twenty days; the canoes must be thoroughly overhauled, and lashed in couples, to prevent their capsizing. The vessels were named by the Zanzibaris after those which visited their native place; except half a dozen, which were christened by the two white men.

Christmas day was passed pleasantly and happily. Three days later the final farewells were spoken; the Arabs returned toward the starting-point, and the expedition sailed down the river, toward the Unknown.

For a week they journeyed through a country where the war-cry, frequently heard, was "Meat!" but fortunately they were not seriously molested, as their camp was always well guarded at night; and the fame of their prowess had evidently preceded them. On January 4, 1877, they came within hearing of the first cataract of Stanley Falls. But louder yet sounded the piercing yells of the savage Mwana Ntaba from both sides of the great river. This tribe had attacked them the previous afternoon, but had been repulsed, a huge canoe of theirs being captured by the Lady Alice. Theirs was a terrible alternative; either they must face the cannibals, collected in they knew not what numbers, or they must dare the cataracts. Possibly it was only a choice between deaths, by knives or by drowning; the latter was certain, if they chose the water route; the former left room for hope, if they chose the land route. They therefore decided to fight their way around the cataracts.

"There was only one way to resolve the problem, and that was to meet the Bakumu and dare their worst, and then to drag the canoes through the dense forest on the left bank. Accordingly, we prepared for what we felt assured would be a stubborn contest. At early dawn of the 10th of January, with quick throbbing pulses, we stole up the river for about a mile, and then with desperate haste dashed across to the shore [from the island where they had been encamped] where we became immediately engaged. We floated down to the bend just above the cataract, and there secured our boats and canoes out of the influence of the stream. Leaving Frank with eight men and sixty axes to form a stockade, I led thirty-six men in a line through the bushes, and drove the united Baswa and Bakumu backward to their villages, the first of which were situated a mile from the river. Here a most determined stand was made by them, for they had piled up heaps of brushwood, and cut down great trees to form defenses, leaving only a few men in front. We crept through the jungle on the south side and succeeded in forcing an entrance and driving them out. We had thus won peace for this day, and retreated to our camp. We then divided the expedition into two parties, or relays, one to work by night, the other by day, after which I took a picked body of pioneers with axes and guns and cut a narrow path three miles in length, blazing the trees as a guide, and forming rude camps at intervals of half a mile. * * *

"We were not further disturbed during this day. In the evening Frank began his work with fifty axemen, and ten men as scouts, deployed in the bushes in front of the working party. Before dawn we were all awakened, and making a rush with the canoes, succeeded in safely reaching our first camp by 9 A. M., with all canoes and baggage. During the passage of the rear-guard the Bakumu made their presence known to us by a startling and sudden outburst of cries; but the scouts immediately replied to them with their rifles, and maintained their position until they were supported by the other armed men, who were now led forward as on the day before. We chased the savages two miles inland, to other villages which we had not hitherto seen; and these also we compelled them to abandon."

Thus the work of passing the cataracts went on, night and day, and after seventy-eight hours' immense exertions, the canoes were launched once more. But their difficulties were not yet at an end. Three cataracts had been passed in safety; how many remained below? But perhaps an extract from Stanley's journal will give a more vivid picture of the occurrences the day after the third cataract was safely passed than any other words could do:

"January 14.—As soon as we reached the river we began to float the canoes down to a two-mile stretch of rapids to a camp opposite the south end of Ntunduru Island. Six canoes were taken down safely by the gallant boat's crew. The seventh canoe was manned by Muscati, Uledi Muscati, and Zaidi, a chief. Muscati, the steersman, lost his presence of mind, and soon upset his canoe in a piece of bad water. Muscati and his friend Uledi swam down the furious stream to Ntunduru Island, whence they were saved by the eighth canoe, manned by stout-hearted Manwa Sera and Uledi, the coxswain of the Lady Alice; but poor Zaidi, the chief, paralyzed by the roar of the stream, unfortunately thought his safety was assured by clinging to his canoe, which was soon swept past our new camp, in full view of those who had been deputed with Frank to form it, to what seemed inevitable death. But a kindly Providence, which he has himself gratefully acknowleged, saved him even on the brink of eternity. The great fall at the north end of Ntunduru Island happens to be disparted by a single pointed rock, and on this the canoe was driven, and, borne down by the weight of the waters, was soon split in two, one side of which got jammed below, the other tilted upward. To this the almost drowned man clung, while perched on the rocky point, with his ankles washed by the stream. To his left, as he faced up stream, there was a stretch of fifty yards of falling water; to his right were nearly fifty yards of leaping brown waves, while close behind him the water fell down sheer to six or eight feet, through a gap ten yards wide, between the rocky point on which he was perched and a rocky islet three hundred yards long.

"When called to the scene by his weeping friends from my labors up river, I could scarcely believe my eyes, or realize the strange chance which placed him there; and certainly a more critical position than the poor fellow was in cannot be imagined. * * * The solitary man on that narrow pointed rock was apparently calmer than any of us; though we could approach within fifty yards, he could not hear a word we said; he could see us, and feel assured that we sympathized with him in his terrible position.

"We then, after collecting our faculties, began to prepare means to save him. After sending men to collect rattans, we formed a cable, by which we attempted to lower a small canoe, but the instant it seemed to reach him the force of the current hurrying to the fall was so great that the cable snapped like packthread, and the canoe swept by him like an arrow, and was engulfed, shattered, split, and pounded into fragments. Then we endeavored to toss toward him poles tied with creepers, but the vagaries of the current and its convulsive heaving made it impossible to reach him with them, while the man dared not move a hand, but sat silent, watching our futile efforts, while the conviction gradually settled on our minds that his doom, though protracted, was certain.

"Then, after anxious deliberation with myself, I called for another canoe, and lashed to the bow of it a cable consisting of three one-inch rattans twisted together and strengthened by all the tent ropes. A similar cable was lashed to the side, and a third was fastened to the stern, each of these cables being ninety yards in length. A shorter cable, thirty yards in length,

RESCUE OF ZAIDI BY ULEDI.

was lashed to the stern of the canoe, which was to be guided within reach of him by a man in the canoe.

"Two volunteers were called for. No one would step forward. I offered rewards. Still no one would respond. But when I began to speak to them, asking them how they would like to be in such a position without a single friend offering to assist in saving them, Uledi the coxswain came forward and said:

"'Enough, master, I will go. *Mambu Kwa Mungu'*—My fate is in the hands of God.

And immediately he began preparing himself by binding his loin-cloth firmly about his waist. Then Marzouk, a boat-boy, said:

"'Since Uledi goes, I will go too.'

"Other boat-boys, young Shumari and Aaywa, offered their services, but I checked them, and said:

"'You surely are not tired of me, are you, that you all wish to die? If all my brave boat-boys are lost, what shall we do?'"

Uledi and his friend Marzouk stepped into the canoe with the air of gladiators, and we applauded them heartily, but enjoined on them to be careful. Then I turned to the crowd on the shore who were manning the cables, and bade them beware of the least carelessness, as the lives of the three young men depended on their attention to the orders that would be given.

"The two young volunteers were requested to paddle across the river, so that the stern might be guided by those on shore. The bow and side cables were slackened until the canoe was within twenty yards of the roaring falls, and Uledi endeavored to guide the cable to Zaidi, but the convulsive heaving of the river swept the canoe constantly to one side, where it hovered over the steep slope and brown waves of the left branch, from the swirl of which we were compelled to draw it. Five times the attempt was made, but at last, the sixth time, encouraged by the safety of the cables, we lowered the canoe until it was within ten yards of Zaidi, and Uledi lifted the short cable and threw it over to him and struck his arm. He had just time to grasp it before he was carried over into the chasm below. For thirty seconds we saw nothing of him, and thought him lost, when his head rose above the edge of the falling waters. Instantly the word was given to haul away, but at the first pull the bow and side cables parted, and the canoe began to glide down the left branch with my two boat-boys on board! The stern cable next parted, and, horrified at the result, we stood muttering: '*La il Allah, il Allah,*' watching the canoe severed from us drifting to certain destruction, when we suddenly observed it halted. Zaidi, in the channel clinging to his cable was acting as a kedge-anchor, which swept the canoe against the rocky islet. Uledi and Marzouk sprang out of the canoe, and leaning over assisted Zaidi out of the falls, and the three, working with desperate energy, succeeded in securing the canoe on the islet.

"But though we hurrahed and were exceedingly rejoiced, their position was still but a short reprieve from death. There were fifty yards of wild waves, and a resistless rush of water, between them and safety, and to the right of them was a fall three hundred yards in width, and below was a mile of falls and rapids, and great whirlpools, and waves rising like little hills in in the middle of the terrible stream, and below these were the fell cannibals of Wane-Mukwa and Asama.

"How to reach the island was a question which now perplexed me. We tied a stone to about a hundred yards of whipcord, and after the twentieth attempt they managed to catch it. To the end of the whipcord they tied the tent rope which had parted before, and drawing it to our side we tied the stout rattan creeper, which they drew across taut and fastened to a rock, by which we thought we had begun to bridge the stream. But night drawing nigh, we said to them that we would defer further experiment till morning.

"Meantime the ninth canoe, whose steersman was a supernumerary of the boat, had likewise got upset, and he out of six men was drowned, to our regret, but the canoe was saved. All other vessels were brought down safely, but so long as my poor faithful Uledi and his friends are on the islet, and still in the arms of death, the night finds us gloomy, sorrowing, and anxious.

"January 15.—My first duty this morning was to send greetings to the three brave lads on the islet, and to assure them that they should be saved before they were many hours older. Thirty men with guns were sent to protect thirty other men searching for rattans in the forest, and by nine o'clock we we possessed sixty strong canes, besides other long climbers, and as fast as we were able to twist them together they were drawn across by Uledi and his friends. Besides, we sent light cables to be lashed round the waist of each man, after which we felt trebly assured that all accidents were guarded against. Then hailing them I motioned to Uledi to begin, while ten men seized the cable, one end of which he had fastened around his waist. Uledi was seen to lift up his hands to heaven, and waving his hands to us as he leaped into the wild flood, seizing the bridge cable as he fell into the depths. Soon he rose, hauling himself hand over hand, the waves brushing his face, and sometimes rising over his head, until it seemed as if he scarcely would be able to breathe; but by jerking his body occasionally upward with a desperate effort, he so managed to survive the waves and to approach us, where a dozen willing hands were stretched out to snatch the half-smothered man. Zaidi next followed, but after the tremendous proofs he had given of his courage and tenacious hold we did not much fear for his safety, and he also landed, to be warmly congratulated for his double escape from death. Marzouk, the youngest was the last, and we held our breath while the gallant boy was struggling out of the fierce grasp of death. While yet midway the pressure of water was so great that he lost his hold of two cables, at which the men screamed in terror lest he should relax his hold altogether from despair; but I shouted harshly to him:

"'Pull away, you fool. Be a man.'

"At which with three hauls he approached within reach of our willing hands, to be embraced and applauded by all. The cheers we gave were so loud and hearty that the cannibal Wane-Mukwa must have known, despite the roar of the waters, that we had passed through a great and thrilling scene."

We need not follow them through their almost daily encounters with the hostile natives, many of whom were cannibals; some of them were driven off, others were glad to make friends with the white men and their followers. They arrived at the mouth of the Aruwimi, February 1. At this point in the river, they had seen many canoes. Stanley continues:

"We heard shouts of defiance or threats, we knew not which—we had become indifferent to the incessant noise and continued fury. * * * As soon as we have fairly entered the waters [of the Aruwimi] we see a great concourse of canoes hovering about some islets which stud the middle of the stream. The canoe-men, standing up, give a loud shout as they discern us, and blow their horns louder than ever. We pull briskly on to gain the right bank, and come in view of the right branch of the affluent, when, looking up stream, we see a sight that sends the blood tingling through every nerve and fiber of the body, arouses not only our lively interest, but also our most lively apprehensions—a flotilla of gigantic canoes bearing down upon us, which both in size and numbers eclipse anything encountered hitherto! Instead of aiming for the right bank, we form in line, and keep straight down the river, the boat taking position behind. Yet after a moment's reflection, as I note the numbers of the savages, and the daring manner of the pursuit, and the apparent desire of our canoes to abandon the steady compact line, I give the order to drop anchor. Four of our canoes affect not to listen, until I chase them, and threaten them with my guns. This compelled them to return to the line, which is formed of eleven double canoes, anchored ten yards apart. The boat moves up to the front, and takes position fifty yards above them. The shields are next lifted by the non-combatants, men, women, and children in the bows, and along the outer lines, as well as astern, and from behind these the muskets and rifles are aimed.

"We have sufficient time to take a view of the mighty force bearing down on us, and to count the number of the war-vessels which have been collected from the Livingstone and its great affluent. There are fifty-four of them! A monster canoe leads the way, with two rows of upstanding paddles, forty men on a side, their bodies bending and swaying in unison as with a swelling barbarous chorus they drive her down toward us. In the bow, standing on what appears to be a platform, are ten prime young warriors, their heads gay with feathers of the parrot crimson and gray; at the stern, eight men with long paddles whose tops are decorated with ivory balls, guide the monster vessel; and dancing up and down from stem to stern are eight men who appear to be chiefs. All the paddles are headed with ivory balls, every head bears a feather crown, every arm shows gleaming white armlets. From the bow of the canoe streams a thick fringe of the long white fiber of the Hyphene palm. The crashing sound of large drums, a hundred blasts from ivory horns, and a thrilling chant from two thousand human throats, do not tend to soothe our nerves or to increase our confidence. However, it is neck or nothing. We have no time to pray, or to take sentimental looks at the savage world, or even to breathe a sad farewell to it. So many other things have to be done speedily and well.

"As the foremost canoe comes rushing down, and the consorts on either side beating the water into foam, and raising their jets of water with their sharp prows, I turn to take a last look at our people, aud say to them:

"'Boys, be firm as iron; wait until you see the first spear, and then take aim. Don't fire all at once, keep aiming until you are sure of your man. Don't think of running away, for only your guns can save you.'

"Frank is with the Ocean on the right flank, and has a choice crew, and a good bulwark of black wooden shields. Manwa Sera has the London Town—which he has taken charge of instead of the Glasgow—on the left flank, the sides of the canoe bristling with guns, in the hands of tolerably steady men.

"The monster canoe aims straight for my boat, as though it would run us down; but when within fifty yards swerves aside, and when nearly opposite, the warriors above the manned prow let fly their spears, and on either side there is a noise of rushing bodies. But every sound is soon lost in the ripping and crackling of musketry. For five minutes we are so absorbed in firing that we can take note of nothing else; but at the end of that time we are made aware that the enemy is re-forming about two hundred yards above us.

"Our blood is now up. It is a murderous world, and we feel for the first time that we hate the filthy, vulturous ghouls that inhabit it. We therefore lift our anchors, and pursue them up stream along the right bank, until rounding a point we see their villages. We make straight for the banks, and continue the fight in the village streets with those who have landed, hunt them out into the woods, and there only sound the retreat, having returned the daring cannibals the compliment of a visit."

Still floating down the river, they came to the country of the Bangala February 14. Stanley had some hopes of conciliating this tribe by means of gifts, as they were somewhat accustomed to the visits of the traders; for the travelers were now indeed approaching the portion of the river which was known to the merchants. Let us see how these efforts to make friends succeeded:

"We had left Observation Island about half a mile behind us when the prows of many canoes were seen to emerge out of the creek. I stood up and edged toward them, holding a long piece of red cloth in one hand and a coil of brass wire in another. We rested on our oars, and the men quietly placed their paddles in the canoe, and sat up, watchful, and ready for contingencies. As we floated down, numbers of canoes advanced.

"I hailed the natives, who were the most brilliantly decorated of any that I had seen. * * * The natives returned no answer to my hail; still I persisted. I observed three or four canoes approaching Frank's vessel with a most suspicious air about them, and several of their canoes menacing him, at

FIGHT AT THE CONFLUENCE OF THE ARUWIMI AND CONGO RIVERS.

which Frank stood up and menaced them with his weapon. I thought the act premature, and ordered him to sit down and look away from them. I again raised the crimson cloth and wire, and by pantomime offered to give it to those in front, whom I was previously addressing; but almost immediately those natives who had threatened Frank fired into my boat, wounding three of my young crew, and two more natives fired into Frank's canoe, wounding two. The missiles fired into us were jagged pieces of iron and copper precisely similar to those which the Ashantees employed. After this murderous outrage there was no effort made to secure peace. The shields were lifted, and proved capital defenses against the hail of slugs. Boats, shields and canoes were pitted, but only a few shields were perforated.

"The conflict began in earnest, and lasted so long that ammunition had to be redistributed. We perceived that, as the conflict continued, every village sent out its quota. * * * At three o'clock, I counted sixty-three canoes opposed to us. * * * And, allowing five guns on an average to each of the sixty-three canoes, there were three hundred and fifteen muskets opposed to our forty-four. Their mistake was in supposing their slugs to have the same penetrative power and long range as our missiles had. * * * After the departure of the wounded chief to the shore, the firing became desultory, and at 5:30 P. M. our antagonists retired, leaving us to attend to our wounded, and to give three hearty cheers at our success. This was our thirty-first fight on the terrible river—the last but one—and certainly the most determined conflict that we had endured."

The thirty-second fight took place March 9, a band of savages attacking them just as they were preparing breakfast; fourteen men were wounded before the savages were repulsed, but none were killed.

March 11, they arrived at a widening of the river into a lake-like expanse, which the leader, at the suggestion of his lieutenant, named Stanley Pool. Although their struggles with the natives were now at an end, having reached a point where they were more accessible to trade, the travelers found that they were by no means safe from dangers by river. Just below that expansion of the stream which was thus christened, are the cataracts now known as Livingstone Falls; and here new trials awaited them.

Passing several bad pieces of river, they had reached a point just below the Cauldron, and Stanley was superintending ar-

BATTLE WITH FLEET OF WAR CANOES.

rangements for a camp on the hard white sand of the river-bank. Glancing up, to his horror he saw the Crocodile, one of the canoes, in mid-river, far below the point which they had rounded, gliding with the speed of an arrow toward the falls over the treacherous calm water. Human strength availed nothing; he could but watch the vessel as she darted over the fall, bearing with her his boy Kalulu and four others. They saw it whirled round three or four times, then plunged down into the depths; out of which the stern presently emerged pointed upward; and then they knew that Kalulu and his canoe-mates were no more.

Death of Kalulu.

A second canoe darted by the horrified spectators, but almost by a miracle, shot over the falls, and was brought to land below, the two men in it escaping harm. A third canoe darted past them, having but one man in it; but he was less fortunate than the others, and was whirled down to instant death.

In remembrance of the victim who had been most intimately connected with the leader, his body-servant Kalulu, the cataract was named Kalulu Falls. But Stanley himself was not to escape danger from the violence of the river. He had devised

SHOOTING THE RAPIDS OF THE CONGO.

a means of descending the river in safety even in the midst of rapids, by means of cables of cane; but the impediments were greater at this point than they had ever been before, and by a careless slacking of the stern cable, the current swept the boat from the hands of that portion of the crew whose duty it was to lower her cautiously down the fall, to the narrow line of ebb-flood below the rocky projection. It was useless to direct the men; for the human voice was drowned in the roar of the mad waters; oars were only useful to assist the helm, for they were flying with terrific speed past the series of boulders which strangled the river.

"After two miles we were abreast of the bay or indentation at which we had hoped to camp, but the strong river mocked our efforts to gain it. The flood was resolved we should taste the bitterness of death. A sudden rumbling noise, like the deadened sound of an earthquake, caused us to look below, and we saw the river heaved bodily upward, as though a volcano was about to belch around us. Up to the summit of this watery mound we were impelled; and then divining what was about to take place, I shouted out:

"'Pull, men, for your lives!'

"A few frantic strokes drove us to the lower side of the mound, and before it had finished subsiding, and had begun its usual fatal circling, we were precipitated over a small fall, and sweeping down toward the inlet into which the Nkenke cataract tumbled, below the lowest line of the Lady Alice rapids. Once or twice we were flung scornfully aside, and spun around contemptuously, as though we were too insignificant to be wrecked; then availing ourselves of a calm moment, we resumed our oars, and soon entering the ebb-tide, rowed up river and reached the sandy beach at the junction of the Nkenke with the Livingstone."

June 3, Stanley left the camp at Mowa to proceed to Zinga, in order to establish a camp at the latter place; the boats were then to be transported overland, since the river would not allow of a voyage between these two points. Frank Pocock was left behind, for the time, until the leader should send men back with a hammock to carry him forward, for he was suffering so much with ulcers on both feet that he was quite lame. The shoes of both had given out, though Stanley managed to keep his, tattered and slit as they were, upon his feet; and the slightest wound from the roughness of the road is liable in that climate to be poisoned by the bite of the insects. But Pocock was impatient, and insisted upon being taken in a

DEATH OF FRANK POCOCK.

canoe which Uledi had been ordered to proceed with. In vain the faithful servitor argued that it was not safe for them to go by river; the young Englishman, a waterman by training, laughed at his fears, and declared it was but cowardice which made him and his comrades hesitate. The boatmen were at last goaded by these taunts to undertake that which their better judgment told them was simply fool-hardy.

"In a few seconds they had entered the river; and in obedience to Frank, Uledi steered his craft for the left side of the river. But it soon became clear that they could not reach it. There was a greasy slipperiness about the water that was delusive, and it was irresistibly bearing them broadside over the falls; and observing this, Uledi turned the prow, and boldly bore down for the center. Roused from his seat by the increasing thunder of the fearful waters, Frank rose to his feet, and looked over the heads of those in front, and now the full danger of his situation burst upon him. But too late! They had reached the fall, and plunged headlong amid the waves and spray. The angry waters rose, and leaped into their vessel, spun them round as though on a pivot, and so down over the curling, dancing, leaping crests they were borne, to the whirlpools that yawned below. Ah! then came the moment of anguish, regret, and terror!

"'Hold on to the canoe, my men; seize a rope, each one,' said he, while tearing his flannel shirt away. Before he could prepare himself, the canoe was drawn down into the abyss, and the whirling, flying waters closed over all. When the vacuum was filled, a great body of water was belched upward, and the canoe was disgorged into the bright sunlight, with several gasping men clinging to it. When they had drifted a little distance away from the scene, and had collected their faculties, they found that there were only eight of them alive; and alas for us who were left to bewail his sudden doom, there was no white face among them. But presently, close to them, another commotion, another heaving and belching of waters, and out of them the insensible form of the 'little master' appeared, and they heard a loud moan from him. Then Uledi, forgetting his late escape from the whirling pit, flung out his arms and struck gallantly toward him, but another pool sucked them both in, and the waves closed over him before he could reach him; and for the second time the brave coxswain emerged, faint and weary—but Frank Pocock was seen no more."

This was not the last of Stanley's troubles; many of his men, seeing no apparent hope of reaching smoother waters or a less difficult road, declared that they would go no further; and more than thirty of them actually set out on their journey back. They were, however, persuaded to return; not only by those who remained faithful to him, but by the determination of the natives to help none of those who had deserted their white master.

He had thought it slow traveling when, from the 16th of March to the 21st of April inclusive, a period of thirty-seven days, the expedition had made but thirty-four miles' progress; but it required thirty days to transport the expedition from Mowa to Zinga, a distance of three miles; and four men had been drowned during that time.

Late in July they reached the Yellala. Here the boats were abandoned, even the Lady Alice being left to bleach and rot on the shores of the mighty river; and everything not absolutely necessary being given to the men to buy food, the worn and weary and sadly diminished expedition set out on the way to the coast, five or six days off.

They were literally starving men, for the food which they were able to obtain from the natives was small in quantity and poor in quality. Nearly forty of them were sick, with dysentery, ulcers, or scurvy; they had no fear of death left, and no hope of life; they dragged themselves wearily onward, not knowing who would be the next to fall, only sure that none of them would again reach their home.

And what of the leader? He had shared all their trials; he was hungry and weary and footsore and heartsore as they were; he had seen the last companion of his own race swept away by the remorseless Congo, it was on him that the responsibility of the whole expedition rested; but the indomitable spirit which was lacking in the "untutored mind" of the black men bore him up and gave him strength to utter words of encouragement to them.

They arrived at the village of Nsanda August 4; the chief seemed kindly and pleasant. He informed the new-comer that he had frequently been to Boma, that he carried ground-nuts there and exchanged them for rum. Suddenly Stanley asked him if he would carry a letter to Boma, and allow three men of the expedition to accompany him. He promised to send two of his young men, and Stanley wrote his letter—an appeal "To any Gentleman who speaks English at Embomma" for such help as was needed—food for immediate use, and cloth with which to purchase further supplies. Uledi, Kacheche, and two others, one of whom was a pupil of the Universities' Mission at Zanzibar, and was to act as interpreter, volunteered for the journey; and two guides were furnished by the chief.

The expedition marched on more slowly, finding it impossible to procure food where they were; "Wait for the market-days," they were told. Two days later, while they were encamped near Banza Mbuko, and Stanley was thoroughly sick at heart because of the distress of his starving people, the messengers returned, bringing with them rice, sweet potatoes and fish in generous quantities for all hands, and rum and tobacco in smaller quantities, to be dealt out by the master; with such luxuries as wheaten bread, butter, tea, coffee loaf-sugar, jam, sardines, salmon, plum-pudding, ale, sherry, port and champagne for the white man who had left all these behind him three years before.

Messengers were dispatched bearing the hearty thanks of the now well-fed men, and then the main body again took up the line of march. August 9, 1877, they prepared to greet the "van of civilization," the 999th day after their departure from Zanzibar. Of the welcome which there awaited him at the hands of those who had so promptly and generously responded to his appeal, we need not speak; our story draws to a close as the gaunt and way-worn men descend the slope toward the white town of Boma, and start with surprise as they see a steamer anchored in the broad brown river.

Here they remained two days; and then proceeded down the river on this steamer to Kabinda. The sickness of many members of the expedition detained Stanley here for some time, as he was anxious to see all his men off to Zanzibar before sailing for Europe: but at last he was free to return, and though he chose to accompany the members of the expedition as far as the Cape of Good Hope on their return journey, he was still eagerly looking forward to the home-coming. Yet, even at this time, he was not unmindful of the feelings of his followers; he saw that they were sorrowful, and guessed the reason; they acknowledged that it was so, that their hearts were heavy because he was about to leave them while they were still far from their homes; and he resolved to accompany them on the voyage from Cape Town to Zanzibar. November 26, they arrived at the end of their return journey; and December 13, having paid off his men and also what was due to the surviving relatives of those who had not returned, Stanley embarked for England. A journey through the Dark Continent, was, for the first time in the history of the world, an accomplished fact.